FIELDING'S

BERMUDA AND THE BAHAMAS

1992

FIELDING'S ALPINE EUROPE 1992
FIELDING'S AUSTRALIA 1992
FIELDING'S BENELUX 1992
FIELDING'S BERMUDA AND THE BAHAMAS 1992
FIELDING'S BRITAIN 1992
FIELDING'S BUDGET EUROPE 1992
FIELDING'S CARIBBEAN 1992
FIELDING'S EUROPE 1992
FIELDING'S HAWAII 1992
FIELDING'S ITALY 1992
FIELDING'S MEXICO 1992
FIELDING'S PEOPLE'S REPUBLIC OF CHINA 1992
FIELDING'S SCANDINAVIA 1992
FIELDING'S SELECTIVE SHOPPING GUIDE TO EUROPE 1992
FIELDING'S SPAIN AND PORTUGAL 1992

FIELDING'S ALASKA AND THE YUKON
FIELDING'S BUDGET ASIA Southeast Asia and the Far East
FIELDING'S CALIFORNIA
FIELDING'S FAMILY VACATIONS USA
FIELDING'S FAR EAST 2nd revised edition
FIELDING'S HAVENS AND HIDEAWAYS USA
FIELDING'S LEWIS AND CLARK TRAIL
FIELDING'S LITERARY AFRICA
FIELDING'S TRAVELER'S MEDICAL COMPANION
FIELDING'S WORLDWIDE CRUISES 5th revised edition

FIELDING'S
BERMUDA AND THE BAHAMAS
1992

BY
RACHEL JACKSON CHRISTMAS
AND
WALTER CHRISTMAS

FIELDING TRAVEL BOOKS
c/o WILLIAM MORROW & COMPANY, INC.
1350 Avenue of the Americas, New York, N.Y. 10019

Recognizing the importance of what has been written, it is the policy of William Morrow
and Company, Inc., and its imprints and affiliates to print the books we publish on acid-
free paper, and we exert our best efforts to that end.

ISSN: 0739-0769

ISBN: 0-688-08954-2

Printed in the United States of America

Ninth Edition
1 2 3 4 5 6 7 8 9 10

Text design by Marsha Cohen/Parallelogram

ABOUT THE AUTHORS

Walter Christmas has served as a corporate public relations director and as a public relations consultant. As advisor to the Ghana Information and Trade Center, he helped develop investment opportunities and tourism for that nation. His intimate knowledge of Bermuda and the Bahamas was gained from innumerable business and vacation trips.

Now a free-lance writer, **Rachel Jackson Christmas** has worked as an editor at a major New York publisher. Her articles on travel and other subjects have appeared in periodicals including *The New York Times, The Washington Post, Travel & Leisure, Ms., Essence,* and *Newsweek.* The author of *Fielding's Hawaii,* she is well acquainted with Spain, Mexico, and the Caribbean, in addition to Bermuda, The Bahamas, and Pacific islands.

The Christmases, father and daughter, live in New York City.

CONTENTS

LIST OF MAPS

WHAT'S INSIDE

Sights

Throughout this book, you'll find "Attractions at a Glance" lists followed by descriptions of each area and its sights. The attractions we consider extra special are marked with an asterisk (*).

Hotel Ratings

We have used a star-rating system to give you more information about hotels. These ratings are based on our own opinions as well as those of guests and residents of the islands.

☆ hollow stars indicate comfort, variety, and quality of facilities

★ in addition to all of the above, filled stars indicate charm, atmosphere, impressive decor, and/or exceptional service

★★★★★ Top of the line
★★★★ Excellent
★★★ Very good
★★ Good
★ Plain or modest

No Stars Guest houses or housekeeping units; low-budget hotels that have limited facilities and/or services; or accommodations undergoing major renovations or other changes at press time.

Hotel Quick-Reference Charts include basic information about the accommodations we describe and highly recommend as well as about other accommodations.

Hotel Prices

Unless otherwise indicated, the daily EP (no meals) rates of standard double rooms in season are categorized as follows:

BERMUDA

Expensive: More than $175
Moderate: $100–$175
Inexpensive: Less than $100

BAHAMAS

Expensive: More than $150
Moderate: $85 to $150
Inexpensive: Below $85

Restaurant Prices

The following prices are based on the approximate cost, per person, of a full dinner. Lunch and breakfast will be about 15% to 25% less.

Expensive: More than $50
Moderate: $30 to $50
Inexpensive: Less than $30

Updates

During our frequent trips to Bermuda and The Bahamas, we gather the most accurate and up-to-date information possible. However, hotels, restaurants and their menus, sights, airlines, and cruise line schedules do change during the course of the year. We welcome any comments or suggestions about things that may have changed since our most recent visit or about the guide in general. Write to us c/o Fielding Travel Books, William Morrow & Co., Inc., 1350 Avenue of the Americas, New York, NY 10019.

Note that all prices quoted should be considered approximate.

ACKNOWLEDGMENTS

Special thanks go to the staffs of the Bermuda Department of Tourism, and the Bahamas Ministry of Tourism.

The assistance and knowledge of the following people made an invaluable contribution to the book: Pamela H. Wissing, Charles Webbe, Randy and Linda Horton, Eileen Fielder, Erma Grant-Smith, and Nelson and Brenda Reynolds.

We will always remember the encouragement, support, and sense of humor of the late Eunice Riedel. We are grateful to have had the opportunity to work with her.

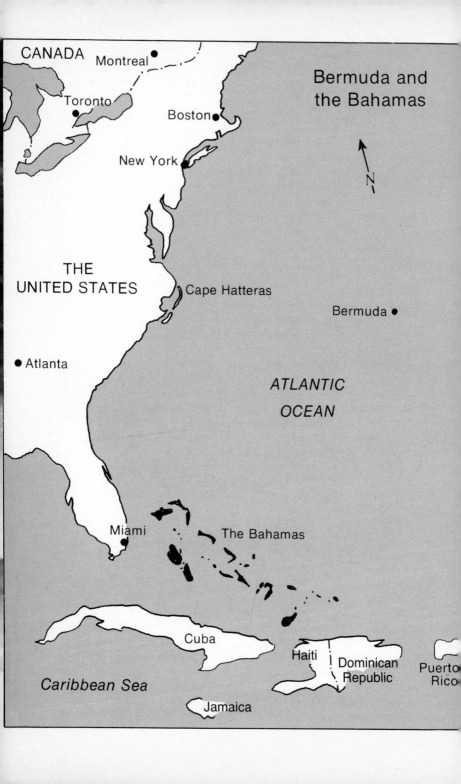

CHOOSING YOUR ATLANTIC ISLE

The tiny island of Bermuda lies isolated in the Atlantic, some 570 miles southeast of Cape Hatteras, North Carolina, the nearest land. Farther south and closer to the Caribbean, The Bahamas is 40 miles off the tip of Florida. Bermuda and The Bahamas have similarities, but it is their special differences that will determine which one you choose for your visit.

Contrary to popular belief, neither country is in the Caribbean. However, they both ally themselves with the Caribbean tourist association because of their proximity and common interests. Bermuda—the oldest existing British self-governing colony—is some 700 miles from New York, more than 800 from Halifax, Nova Scotia, and over 900 from Nassau, the capital of The Bahamas. Actually a string of islands connected by bridges and causeways, Bermuda gives the illusion of being one long strip of land. Almost 21 square miles, it is about the size of Manhattan. It is so narrow that no matter where you are, the unbelievably blue-green sea is never more than a mile away and is rarely out of sight.

On the other hand, The Bahamas—independent from Britain since 1973—is an archipelago of more than 700 islands and islets (or cays, pronounced "keys"), stretching out into the Atlantic for about 400 miles. Only about two dozen islands are inhabited, and some landfalls are no larger than boulders. Beginning off the coast of Florida, the Bahamas almost reaches Hispaniola, the Caribbean island shared by Haiti and the Dominican Republic.

Island Highlights

Bermuda, sparkling clean, with its pastel, white-roofed houses, exudes order. Yachts, cruise ships, and other seacraft anchor in the marinas of the town of St. George's, the city of Hamilton, and Dockyard, against postcard backgrounds. Bermuda's extensive south shore is bordered by some of the world's finest beaches. In addition to comfortable living, the island offers enough sports and sightseeing attractions to satisfy even the most energetic vacationer.

Among the wide variety of sports facilities, the island boasts many first-rate golf courses. Groups of North American businessmen often fly down just for a weekend on the green. Other attractions include underground grottos, the Botanical Gardens, an indoor-outdoor maritime museum, and house and garden tours. There are also 17th-century forts, the oldest Anglican church in the Western hemisphere, and a historic lighthouse from which nearly all of Bermuda is visible.

The Bahamas has the mellowed colonial charm of old Nassau contrasted with the young, modern city of Freeport, and the quiet natural beauty of the Family Islands. In Nassau, you'll see flower-bedecked villas whose walls are overgrown with lush tropical foliage. Notorious, busy Bay Street, lined with stores, boutiques, and restaurants, is the city's main thoroughfare. Cruise ships dock near bustling Rawson Square, where taxis and horse-drawn carriages await passengers. Historic sights, such as Government House and the gardens of the 19th-century Royal Victoria Hotel, are within walking distance of the square. A short jitney ride or a stroll from downtown Nassau takes you to the bridge to Paradise Island, the home of some of the more glittery hotels.

Freeport, developed in the '60s, has broad, palm-lined avenues and high-rise, balconied hotels and condominiums. It was designed to attract visitors as well as to become the center of industrial development. Here you can find everything from casinos and gourmet restaurants to the International Bazaar, Port Lucaya waterfront esplanade, and exciting night club revues.

Sparsely settled and as windswept as a Winslow Homer watercolor are the Family Islands, formerly called the Out Islands. They present a less hectic way of life than Nassau or Freeport and attract the dedicated fisherman as well as the devoted yachtsman. On many of these islands, chickens, goats, and sheep roam through yards and across winding dirt roads. Sun worshipers can find stretches of deserted, palm-shaded, pink-sand beaches where they can spend the day undisturbed. Divers can explore undersea wrecks (including a train) as well as caves and the wonders of subtropical marine life. There are also New England–like villages set against the sea and tropical foliage.

The atmosphere of the Family Islands encourages living close to nature without the formalities of attention to dress and rigid schedules. However, it is also possible to find out-island resorts where guests dress for dinner, or meet for cocktails on elegant terraces as the sun settles beyond the sea.

Although many people consider the weather in both countries ideal at any time of year, Bermuda's most popular season is spring and summer and The Bahamas' is winter. The Bahamas is somewhat warmer than Bermuda in the winter. Bathed by the Gulf Stream, Bermuda is subtropical, with daytime temperatures from May to November in the mid-80s (Fahrenheit) and evening temperatures in the 70s. During the remainder of the year, the daytime temperature is in the 60s and 70s.

The Tropic of Cancer cuts through The Bahamas, bringing the warmest weather to the southernmost islands and cooler, Gulf Stream temperatures to the northern islands, which include Nassau and Freeport. During the winter and spring, temperatures are in the 70s, and during the summer and fall, in the 80s.

Hurricanes, which often hit the Caribbean area soon after August, seldom strike The Bahamas or Bermuda. When storms do occur, bringing dramatic cloud formations and churning waters, they are generally over quickly, followed by sun and blue skies.

During the high seasons in Bermuda and The Bahamas, accommodations are filled and the islands bustle with visitors. Accordingly, rates are higher and attractions more crowded. While off-season rates are appreciably lower, many travelers save money during the rest of the year as well by using guest houses and other small accommodations. Especially in The Bahamas' less developed Family Islands, the locally operated hotels and guest houses are much less expensive than larger hotels. Some have no more than three or four rooms. In Bermuda there is an abundance of well-maintained housekeeping apartments, most of them close to beaches, and with their own pools. If you choose housekeeping facilities, however, note that grocery prices are high since most food is imported, so you may want to bring some canned goods from home. Another way to save money is to eat at the small restaurants specializing in homestyle cuisine.

In Bermuda and in Nassau and Freeport, there is a variety of restaurants, including Italian, French, and Chinese, as well as those specializing in local cuisine. Particularly on the Family Islands, menus revolve around treats from the sea, but dishes for landlubbers are also available. Depending on where you go, you can have a steak or lobster dinner or, if feeling adventurous, sample such delicacies as cracked conch or shark hash on toast.

The Human Factor

For nearly four centuries, the cultures of Indians, Europeans, Africans, Americans, and West Indians have been melding to form the colorful ways of life unique to Bermuda and The Bahamas. While you can have afternoon tea in Bermuda and climb the Queen's Staircase in The Bahamas, you can also enjoy the influences of the African and Indian ancestors of islanders. At Christmastime, for instance, when the streets fill with the music of masked dancers dressed in bright, elaborate costumes, you can witness a 300-year-old tradition with roots in Africa. Called gombey in Bermuda, this music and dance is known as goombay in The Bahamas, and is found in various forms in a number of West Indian countries.

Getting Acquainted

Whether you are on your honeymoon, addicted to beaches, or just looking for a change of pace, you will do yourself an injustice if you do not make an effort to get to know local people and learn something about the way they live.

As you travel around the islands, you will find that people are very friendly and helpful. However, as is too often the case in countries that rely heavily on tourism, some islanders have felt slighted or taken for granted by visitors. Many Bermudians and Bahamians have expressed resentment of visitors who act as if local people exist solely to accommodate tourists. But if you treat people as you would like to be treated, talk to clerks and cab drivers, and visit beaches, restaurants, and night spots frequented by locals, your stay will be enhanced tremendously.

In both Bermuda and The Bahamas meeting residents can be simple. Locals often strike up conversations with visitors in pubs, night clubs, or at the beach. In Nassau, Freeport, and Eleuthera, you can take part in the celebrated free ''People-to-People'' program where, for example, you can spend an evening at the theater with a Bahamian couple, be a guest at their home for a meal, or have tea at Government House.

For fast-moving Americans, Bermuda may more closely resemble home in regard to pace and service. At many restaurants and resorts in The Bahamas, life is slower, more relaxed, and service more casual. Visitors to either country will suffer no discomfort if they adapt to the flow and ambience of their surroundings.

No matter what you do or where you go in Bermuda or The Bahamas—whether you choose Bermuda's spectacular south shore or its busy capital, whether you crave the fast pace of Nassau or the seclusion of a Bahamian cay—you're in for a memorable visit.

BERMUDA

WHY BERMUDA?

Bermuda welcomes visitors wholeheartedly, with friendly greetings, long stretches of beach, and a host of sports and sights. If the first things you notice about this tiny island aren't its beauty and cleanliness, it will only be because you're stunned by the turquoise hues of the surrounding waters. Bermudians are proud of the island's trim appearance. Even the wildest of the colorful vegetation seems to have had a gardener's touch. You won't find any casinos, and there are only a few fast-food restaurants. The only street vendors you might come across are the few selling fish or fruits and vegetables.

Small white-roofed homes dot the low hills. Waterside and inland roads pass patchwork farms with plots of sweet potatoes, broccoli, bananas, and onions. Pink and blue public buses, which always seem to be on schedule, peacefully coexist with mopeds and the new-looking compact cars. Ferries and cruise ships glide in and out of the harbors and some beaches even have pink sand.

The oldest existing British self-governing colony, Bermuda is anchored in the Atlantic (not the Caribbean), nearly 600 miles from Cape Hatteras, North Carolina, the closest land. Considered one island, it is really almost 150 islands, only about 20 of which are inhabited. The seven largest are connected by bridges and causeways, creating a 21-square-mile fish-hook-shaped strip about the size of Manhattan. At its widest point, Bermuda is barely two miles across.

Any time of year is a good time to visit this subtropical island tempered by the Gulf Stream. During the summer season, from May to mid-November, temperatures average 80°F (26.7°C). The rest of the year, temperatures range from the 60s to the 70s. Rainfall is evenly

Bermuda

ATLANTIC OCEAN

Long Bay

Mangrove
Bay

Somerset Village

Cobbler's I.

Spanish Pt.

PEMBROKE

SOMERSET RD.

Great Sound

Ferry

PITTS BAY RD.

Hamilto

SANDY'S

Ferry

Ely's
Harbour

Hamilton Harbour

Ferry

PAC

U.S. Naval Air
Station Annex

HARBOUR RD.

MIDDLE RD.

Little Sound

WARWICK

SOUTH SHORE RD.

Elbow B

MIDDLE ROAD

SOUTHAMPTON

Warwick Long Bay

Horseshoe Bay

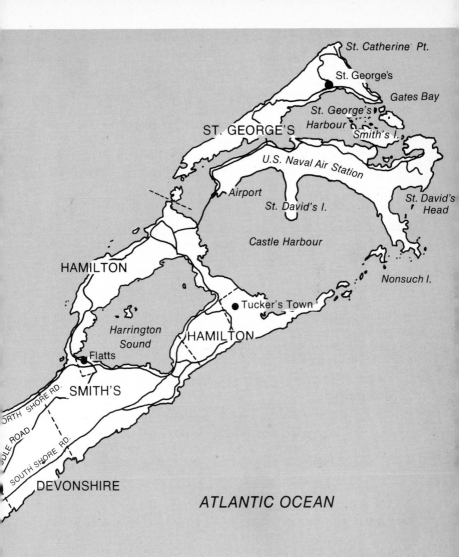

St. Catherine Pt.

St. George's

Gates Bay

St. George's
Harbour

Smith's I.

ST. GEORGE'S

U.S. Naval Air Station

St. David's
Head

Airport

St. David's I.

Nonsuch I.

Castle Harbour

HAMILTON

Tucker's Town

Harrington
Sound

HAMILTON

Flatts

SMITH'S

NORTH SHORE RD.

MIDDLE ROAD

SOUTH SHORE RD.

DEVONSHIRE

ATLANTIC OCEAN

N

spread throughout the year, so there is no rainy season, and hurricanes are virtually unheard of.

A trip to Bermuda can mean getting to know Bermudians, who are the most important reason the island is the way it is. Visitors and locals use the same buses, eat in the same restaurants, shop in the same stores, and swim at the same beaches, the best of which are public. While walking or riding a moped, if you pause at an intersection and appear even mildly confused, someone will be sure to ask, "Lost? Need help?"

Sports

Bermuda's south shore has some of the most beautiful beaches in the world. Scuba divers, snorkelers, and those who like fishing will want to explore the reefs surrounding the top of the extinct volcano that is the island's foundation. Horseback riding is popular both along the coast and through wooded trails. There is more golf per acre here than in any other country—you could play on a different course each day of the week and still have two to go. In addition to renting boats with or without skippers, taking sailing lessons, kayaking, and chartering yachts, you can waterski or learn to windsurf or parasail. Tennis buffs have 100 courts to choose from.

Sightseeing

Exercising is only the beginning of what there is to do in Bermuda. Among other attractions, you can visit an aquarium and zoo, 17th-century churches and houses, historic forts; relax in public gardens and parks; wander through nature reserves; and explore underground caves and a replica of a ship built by the early settlers. In the spring, the agricultural exhibition at the Botanical Gardens celebrates the island's farmers. Many of them are Portuguese immigrants or descendants of those who came from the Azores to fill agricultural jobs in the 1850s.

Bermuda's natural beauty is one of the most pleasing sights of all, from the roads decorated with hibiscus, bougainvillea, oleander, and morning glory to the rosy beaches with striking rock formations. Bermudians often dare visitors to find two leaves that are alike on the brown and burgundy "match-me-if-you-can" shrubs that are all over the island. Wispy casuarina trees that lean with the breeze are also everywhere. Since the climate is subtropical, the island has few indigenous palms. If you are visiting in the spring, amid the profusion of greenery, Easter lilies, and other flowers, you may notice trees with rust-colored autumnal leaves. These are Fiddlewoods, which got a bit confused after being uprooted from their Australian home to be grown for fuel in Bermuda. Here their leaves turn burnt orange and drop off in the spring instead of the fall, but by July they are green again. Amid Bermuda's winter greenery, poincianas stand naked. In spring, they burst into bloom. Also look out for graceful white longtails (Bermuda's national bird), which migrate to the island with the onset of spring.

If your itinerary includes more than basking in the sun, one of the first things you should do is get a *Handy Reference Map,* available at hotels or offices of the Visitors' Service Bureau. *The Bermuda Railway Trail Guide* will help joggers, walkers, and cyclists choose scenic routes.

There are no cars for rent here, and it's just as well, because the other modes of transportation are more fun. Among visitors and many Bermudians, the most popular way of getting from one place to another is by moped, which you can rent by the day or the week. Pedal bikes are also available for rent. As in Britain, driving is on the left. The island's public buses will take you almost anywhere, and you ride with Bermudians going about their daily business. Many visitors enjoy seeing the sights from horse-drawn carriages. Through most hotels or the Visitors' Service Bureau, you can arrange to take bus tours. Look for taxis with blue flags on their hoods, because the drivers are qualified tour guides who will show you the island for about $20 an hour for up to four passengers or $30 for five or six people.

At night you can dance at clubs and discotheques, listen to calypso, reggae, classical, or rock music, or see a local play or revue.

The Bermudians

In culture and appearance, Bermuda bears less resemblance to its Caribbean neighbors than The Bahamas does. At first glance, this colony of nearly 60,000 people may seem like a small, warm version of its mother country. Hotels and restaurants serve afternoon tea; people play darts in pubs over English ale; barristers wear powdered wigs; and cricket and football (soccer) are national pastimes. Bermuda shorts, still worn by males from waiter to policeman, were introduced by the British military at the turn of the century.

However, on closer look the island proves to be a colorful combination of a variety of other cultures as well. The often more subtle influences of the non-British heritage can be seen in the gombey, calypso, and reggae music, with roots in Africa and the West Indies; the popularity of St. Paul's African Methodist Episcopal Church; the hoppin' john (black-eyed peas and rice) also eaten by African-Americans and people from the Caribbean; the Portuguese red bean soup common on restaurant menus; and streets like Silk Alley and Barber's Alley, named in honor of slaves and freed blacks. More than 60% of the population is comprised of descendants of enslaved people, most of whom were brought not directly from Africa, but from America and the West Indies. The rest of the residents are of European background, including, most recently, Portuguese immigrants from the Azores. A small portion of the population is made up of descendants of Native Americans brought to Bermuda as indentured servants. As you chat with taxi drivers, clerks, waiters, and other residents, you'll discover that the vast majority of Bermudians are very well educated.

If you listen closely, you'll notice that Bermudians, like Bahamians, often pronounce their "w"s as "v"s—and "wice wersa." "Vhat you know?" is a common greeting and you may be asked if you are enjoying your "wacation." This pronunciation is thought to have come from 18th- and 19th-century England and America. Sometimes *w*s end up sounding like a cross between an *r* and a *w,* so that "Wendy" becomes "Rendy." Like the British, Bermudians often punctuate their sentences with "mate." They would say that this is "different to" (not "different from") the way Bahamians, who sprinkle many conversations with "mahn," speak. To find out more about Bermudian lingo, flip through a booklet called *Bermewjan Verds,* at a local library.

For an inside look at Bermudian life, take part in the Open Houses and Gardens tours conducted each spring. Hosts will point out traditional architectural characteristics and give you significant historical information. The pastel-colored, white-roofed houses throughout the island are identified by names, not numbers. "Wreck Hill House," "Pumpkin Patch", and even "Bacardi on the Rocks" are just a few. Buildings are constructed of limestone, coral, cement blocks, and Bermuda cedar. The stair-step roofs catch rainwater, which is stored in underground tanks. Next to some of the older homes, you will see miniature houses with pyramid-shaped roofs topped with balls. These are butteries, or cooling houses, the ancestors of refrigerators. The architecture of other buildings ranges from the simplicity of whitewashed St. Peter's Church to the Florentine detail of the Cabinet Building.

Making Merry

Traditions, whether solemn or filled with happy abandon, live long in Bermuda. Gombey dancers bounce through the streets on New Year's Day, Good Friday, Easter, Labour Day, Boxing Day (December 26), and during Heritage Month (May) and off season (mid-November through March). Called goombay in The Bahamas, this type of music and dance began during slavery. "Gombey" is a Bantu word meaning both rhythm and goatskin drum. The dancers' acrobatic leaps, turns, and high kicks are West African in origin. The colorful, elaborate fringed costumes are decorated with tassels, ribbons, beads, and bits of mirrors, and the feathered headdresses are sometimes four feet high. Wearing masks of distorted faces is said to have begun in order to hide the identities of the dancers. This was because the dances often represented antislavery protests. The American Indian influence was more apparent at the time when folk dramas were common, and dancers carried tomahawks and bows and arrows. Now called the captain, the "leading Indian" would go ahead of the group to chalk Indian symbols in front of homes that were receptive to the dancers. Today, crowds still follow the dancers and fall into the rhythm as they make their way around the island.

On Good Friday, gombey dancers head for Horseshoe Bay beach. This is where the most popular of the island's many kite day festivals is held. The frame of the traditional kite flown on Good Friday forms a cross, representing the one used to crucify Christ. This kite is shaped like a long, narrow diamond. Christ's rise into heaven on Easter was once symbolized by the kite's climb into the sky. The sizes and shapes of kites have become increasingly whimsical and diverse over the years and much of the religious significance is history. Nowadays, fluttering overhead will be every kind of kite from the hexagonal tissue-paper variety (considered *real* kites by purists) to the nylon ones shaped like fish, birds, sting rays, and bats. Some are a mere two or three feet wide while others span 15 feet. The sound you'll hear does not come from some strange bird, but from "hummers"—streamers that make a loud noise as the kites dip and swirl in the wind.

It has been said that more Bermudians living abroad return home for Cup Match than for Christmas. The two days in late July or early August during which these championship cricket games between St. George's and Somerset take place are public holidays. The annual event began at the turn of the century to commemorate both Sir George Somers (who stumbled upon Bermuda in 1609) and the abolition of slavery. Picture the World Series in the middle of a Caribbean carnival, and you'll have an idea of what the festivities are like. To enjoy Cup Match, you need not know a thing about cricket. Simply be prepared for serious socializing. At food stalls, the aromas of mussel pie, fish chowder, peas and rice, and other local favorites all vie for your attention. Reggae and calypso will have you moving to the beat. If you're ready to win some and lose some, take a chance with the board game called Crown and Anchor (also known as "the Stock Market"). Only during cricket championships is gambling legal in Bermuda.

Wining and Dining

Not only can you take part in traditions in Bermuda, but you can also taste them. Hot cross buns are served on Easter Sunday. Some people consider codfish with potatoes and bananas the trademark of a truly Bermudian breakfast. And cassava pie finds its way onto many a table at Christmas (the early English settlers began preparing this cassava-root crust stuffed with poultry, pork, and eggs). Bermudian specialties you can try during the rest of the year include Bermuda lobster (similar to crayfish), mussel pie, conch (pronounced "conk") fritters or stew, shark hash on toast, turtle steak, pumpkin, fish chowder spiced with black rum and sherry peppers, and Portuguese red bean soup. Wash it all down with ginger beer. Popular mixed drinks are rum swizzles (fruity concoctions that sneak up on you) and Dark and Stormies (made with black rum and ginger beer).

The Parishes

Bermuda's nine parishes—Sandys, Southampton, Warwick, Paget, Pembroke, Devonshire, Smith's, Hamilton, and St. George's—were originally eight districts called tribes, with St. George's being common land. The many tribe roads, the narrow rustic lanes that cross the island from north to south, are remnants of the past. Note that the old town of St. George's, the original capital, is in St. George's Parish, but the present capital, Hamilton, is in Pembroke Parish (not Hamilton Parish).

The 17th-century town of St. George's, which has changed little since it was founded in 1612, provides an exciting contrast to the more modern, bustling city of Hamilton. Each parish has a personality all its own. No matter where you decide to stay, the rest of Bermuda is only a quick ride away. Accommodations throughout the island range from self-contained resorts to small guest houses. You can even rent a room, including breakfast, in a private home. (Arrangements for this are made before arrival by contacting the Visitors' Service Bureau, Front Street, Hamilton.) Many visitors save money by staying in housekeeping apartments. Most accommodations have pools, and all are either on a beach or close by.

The Early Days

It is difficult to imagine that Bermuda was once known as the "Isles of Devils" and avoided with a passion by sailors. But long before the first settlers arrived, this remote, uninhabited cluster of islands surrounded by dangerous reefs meant disaster for ships. The mistakes of navigators can be seen in the wrecks of Spanish galleons and British vessels that have been eroding on the ocean floor for centuries. Even Shakespeare, in *The Tempest,* wrote about "the still vex't Bermoothes."

A Spanish voyager, Juan de Bermudez, is the first person on record to have come upon what is now Bermuda, where his ship was wrecked in 1503. But Spain, more concerned with seeking gold, did not claim the islands. The reefs, rocks, and inlets permitted pirates to lure trade ships and exploring vessels to wreckage. For a long period, this was the center of pirate activity.

When a later Spanish galleon struck rocks near these islands, Captain Diego Ramirez sent a small boat ashore in search of fresh water. Birds chattering in the dark of night sounded like creatures saying *"Diselo, diselo,"* Spanish for "Tell 'em, tell 'em." The frightened crew remembered tales of these devil-inhabited islands and thought that the "voices" meant that the devil was trying to tell them something. They were convinced of this when they suddenly found the boat's rudder broken. The captain ordered Venturilla, the first known black man to reach Bermuda, to go ashore to cut a piece of wood for a new rudder. Once ashore and descended upon by flapping birds, Venturilla called out for help. When his rescuers reached him, they soon discovered that the creatures were not only birds, but also good to eat.

In 1609, the *Sea Venture,* the flagship of a fleet on its way to the Jamestown Colony from England, ran aground at what is now St. Catherine's Point in St. George's. Sir George Somers, the admiral, and Sir Thomas Gates, the lieutenant governor of Virginia, came safely ashore along with nearly 150 other men, women, and children. Here, Admiral Somers and the crew built two ships from the wreckage of their vessel. The larger of the two was christened the *Deliverance* and the voyage continued to Jamestown, where all but one of the other ships had landed.

Gates and Somers found the colony in bad shape, with many people starving. Almost a year after the wreck of the *Sea Venture,* Somers returned to Bermuda to get fish, fowl, and hogs to take back to Virginia. But Somers died before leaving Bermuda this time. His heart was buried near the garden he had planted when he was first on the island and his body was taken back to England.

Two years later another group of settlers arrived from England and in 1620 British colonial government was formally installed through the chartered company. A governor was appointed and the colony was ruled from overseas. After 1684 the colony became self-governing and is now the oldest self-governing British colony in existence. Founded in 1612, St. George's remained Bermuda's capital until 1815, when the seat of government was moved to the more centrally located city of Hamilton in Pembroke Parish. In 1834 slavery was abolished.

Government

Bermuda's government is made up of a governor appointed by the Queen; the Cabinet headed by the premier, an elected official; the Senate, or upper House of Parliament; and the House of Assembly, or lower House. All members of the Cabinet are appointed by the premier. The House, an elected body, is comprised of 40 members of parliament. The 11-member Senate is responsible for approving bills passed by the House. English law, apparent in the traditional wigs and robes of the justices, guides the Supreme Court, headed by a Chief Justice. An Appeals Court and two lower courts are also part of the judicial system.

Economy

According to 1988 World Bank figures, Bermuda enjoys the highest standard of living in the world, with a per capita income of $20,420. There is no personal income tax, no national debt, and virtually no unemployment. Unfortunately, prices are also high. Many Bermudians hold two or even three jobs. A simple two-bedroom cottage would cost more than $300,000. Before the economy settled comfortably into tourism, at various times whaling, shipbuilding, privateering, and farming thrived. At the end of the 19th century, farming flourished, especially where the Bermuda onion was concerned. Onions were exported to New York in great numbers, and Bermudians acquired the nickname "Onions." When U.S. farmers learned how to simulate Bermuda's farming conditions, the island's export onion market collapsed.

With the steamship at the turn of the century came the healthy development of tourism, which now accounts for the largest portion of the economy. The Princess Hotel, one of the island's first, was named in honor of Princess Louise, the daughter of Queen Victoria. According to one story, when the Princess was out on one of her frequent walks during a visit to Bermuda, she stopped at a cottage to ask for a drink of water. The woman of the house said she was too busy to get it because she was ironing a blouse for her trip to St. George to see the Princess. The Princess offered to iron the blouse while the woman went to get the water. After drinking it and telling her host who she was, Princess Louise finished ironing the blouse.

THINGS TO KNOW

COSTS ● Although the cost of living in Bermuda is high, you will certainly get your money's worth. Accommodations range from resort hotels to rooms in private homes. In between there are small hotels, guest houses, cottage colonies, and housekeeping apartments. Many large hotels and cottage colonies have MAP rates (where the price of the room includes breakfast and dinner). Some hotels offer a choice of MAP, BP (full breakfast), or EP (room only). During the high season (summer), cottage colonies tend to require MAP, and some also require a minimum number of nights' stay. Most of the smaller hotels offer MAP,

BP, and EP. Most guest houses offer EP, BP, and CP (light breakfast).

In high season, from March through November, double rooms in large hotels begin at about $180 a night EP. Small hotel rates begin around $130 EP. Double rooms in guest houses start at about $60. A housekeeping apartment for two in season would be about $70 and up per night EP. A room in a private home, including breakfast and a shared bath, is about $50. During the rest of the year, when temperatures are cooler, prices are considerably lower. A service charge of about 10% will be added to the cost of your room to cover room and board tips. Some hotels add an energy surcharge. All room rates are subject to a 6% government tax. *Note that many accommodations do not accept credit cards.*

In conjunction with hotels, some airlines offer money-saving packages throughout the year. Some hotels gear packages to visitors with special interests, such as tennis players, golfers, honeymooners, and families.

Riding convenient public buses or renting mopeds by the week instead of the day will also save you money. The best shopping buys are in European imports, such as china and woolens. Film is expensive, so it is best to take enough for the whole trip. There are several photo processing shops in Hamilton that will develop your film the same day or within 24 hours. Liquor prices tend to be somewhat lower than in most areas of the U.S.

Golf course and tennis court fees are reasonable, and most beaches are public. Some restaurants featuring Bermudian cuisine, particularly those emphasizing homestyle cooking, are less expensive than other restaurants.

TRAVELING WITH CHILDREN • Airlines offer discounts for children, from 10% to 75%, depending on the age of the child. Those under age two fly free.

Some accommodations have age restrictions on accepting children. Consult the **Hotel Quick-Reference Charts** or your travel agent for information about specific accommodations. Many of the larger hotels have special facilities for children, such as cribs and high chairs, as well as babysitters. They also have reduced rates for children, and offer family packages. Some allow children to share adults' rooms at no additional cost. During the summer, the Grotto Bay Beach Hotel hosts a "day camp" for children of guests. Supervised summer children's programs are also run by Elbow Beach, Marriott's Castle Harbour, and the Southampton Princess among others.

There are golf and tennis tournaments for vacationers under age 18. Contact the Bermuda Golf Association, P.O. Box HM 433, Hamilton, HM BX Bermuda, or the Bermuda Lawn Tennis Association, P.O. Box HM 341, Hamilton, HM BX Bermuda.

Lee Bow Riding Centre caters to horseback riders who are age 18 and under.

The legal drinking age is 18.

TRAVEL FOR THE DISABLED • Although facilities for the disabled are not extensive in Bermuda, some accommodations, including several of the larger hotels and cruise ships, are well equipped for those confined to wheelchairs. Senior citizens and disabled people who will need special assistance should contact, in advance, the accommodation where they plan to stay. For more information, get a free copy of *The Access Guide to Bermuda for the Handicapped Traveller* from a Department of Tourism office or contact the Society for the Advancement of Travel for the Handicapped, P.O. Box HM 449, Hamilton, HM BX Bermuda.

SPECIAL SERVICES • Don't worry about falling off your diet: For up-to-date information about **Weight Watchers** meetings in Bermuda, call (212) 896–9800.

You can get information about **Alcoholics Anonymous** meetings by contacting Bermuda Intergroup, P.O. Box WK 178, Warwick, WK BX Bermuda; Tel: (809) 295–1537.

WHEN TO GO • **Weather** • The warmest season is from May through October, the official beach season. The rest of the year—when the weather can vary daily from pleasantly cool to pleasantly warm—is perfect for tennis, golf, and occasional outdoor swimming. (Some hotels and guest houses close for a few weeks in November, December, and January.) Bermuda has no rainy season and rainfall is usually brief.

Average Daily Temperatures

	Fahrenheit	Centigrade
January	68°	20°
February	67°	19°
March	68°	20°
April	71°	22°
May	75°	23°
June	80°	27°
July	85°	29°
August	86°	30°
September	84°	29°
October	79°	26°
November	74°	23°
December	70°	21°

Holidays and Special Events • The off season, when the Department of Tourism sponsors many activities to attract visitors during the cooler weather, lasts from about mid-November through March. Among other activities, you can watch football (soccer) or rugby matches, go on a walking tour of the old town of St. George's, or see kilted bagpipers, drummers, and dancers perform the Skirling Ceremony at Fort Hamilton. The annual Bermuda Festival of the Performing Arts takes place in January and February. Performances, held at the City Hall Theatre in Hamilton or the Empire Room at the Southampton Princess, feature opera, ballet, chamber music, jazz, and drama. For further information, the fax number is (809) 292–5779.

Boxing Day (December 26), New Year's Day, and other holidays signal the appearance of gombey dancers beating goatskin drums. Note that during the off season, some hotels may have fewer daily activities and less frequent nightly entertainment.

During Bermuda College Weeks, in March and April, scores of moped-riding visiting students take part in weekly activities in their honor. Once a month, from April through October, except August, the Bermuda Regiment performs the Beating Retreat Ceremony on Front Street in the city of Hamilton, in St. George's, and at the Dockyard.

In St. George's Harbour on alternate Sunday afternoons beginning in May, Bermuda dinghies, those small boats with enormous sails, are out in full force at Ferry Reach. Check at your hotel or in the newspaper for the powerboat races taking place here on summer weekends.

Each year on Good Friday, the skies are ablaze with hundreds of boldly colored kites during the Bermuda Kite Festival. To join the fun, just buy a kite or bring your own. In the Peppercorn Ceremony in April, the governor collects the annual rent of one peppercorn for the use of the Old State House in St. George's. Everybody looks forward to the festivities during Cup Match each July or August, when cricket teams from the west and the east ends of the island battle each other for the championship.

Another good way to mingle with Bermudians is to attend the Woman '91 Exhibition in March. Geared to both sexes, activities include musical and dance performances, photographic exhibitions, aerobics classes and a 5-km race, cooking demonstrations, lessons on gardening techniques, fashion shows, and speakers on local and international cultural and political issues.

The following list of these and other events will help you decide when to visit. (Also see Making Merry, p. 10):

Special off-season events	through March 31
Bermuda Festival of the Performing Arts	mid-January–February
Bermuda International Marathon and 10 Kilometre Race	January

Regional Bridge Tournament	January–February
Bermuda Valentine's Mixed Golf Foursomes	February
Annual Bermuda Invitational Rendezvous Bowling Tournament	February
Annual Street Festival	February
Annual Bermuda Square and Round Dance Convention	February
National Trust Week (includes Children's Day at Spittal Pond)	mid-February
Annual Sandys Rotary Club Invitational Golf Classic	mid-February
International Championship Dog Show	March
Harvard Hasty Pudding Show	March
Bermuda College Weeks	mid-March to mid-April
Open Houses and Gardens Tours	April and May
Beat Retreat Ceremony	April through October (except August) and periodically at other times
Invitational International Race Week	April and May
Palm Sunday Walk	March
Bermuda Kite Festival	Good Friday
Peppercorn Ceremony	April
Agricultural Exhibition	April
Bermuda Game Fishing Tournament	Year round
Bermuda Heritage Month	May
Bermuda Day	May 24
Queen's Birthday Parade	June 18
Bermuda Fitted Dinghy Races	June–October
Bermuda Ocean Yacht Race (Newport, RI, to Bermuda)	June (even years)
Blue Water Cruising Race	June (odd years)
Multi-Hull Ocean Yacht Race	June (odd years)
Cup Match (cricket) and Somers Day	July 30 and 31
Bermuda Civic Ballet	August
Bermuda International Triathlon*	September or October

*For current information contact Bermuda International Sports Marketing, Ltd., 30 Rockefeller Plaza, New York, NY 10112, (212) 333–7600.

Convening of Parliament   November
Remembrance Day Parade   November
Special off-season events   November 15–March 31
Bermuda Goodwill Golf   December
  Tournament
Boxing Day   December 26

Other holidays are New Year's Day, Good Friday, Christmas, and Labour Day.

GETTING THERE BY AIR

From USA	*Via*
New York, Raleigh-Durham	American Airlines
Newark	Continental
Boston, Atlanta	Delta Airlines
Boston	Northwest
New York	Pan Am
Washington, DC	United
Baltimore; Philadelphia; New York	US Air
Tampa, San Juan	British Airways
From CANADA	
Toronto	Air Canada
From UK	
London	British Airways
From OTHER COUNTRIES	
Caribbean, South America	British Airways

    Flight time from New York is about 2 hours; from Toronto, about 2½. Transportation by taxi from the airport to your accommodation will range from about $13 if you're staying in St. George's (where the airport is located) to about $33–38 if you're staying in Sandys, at the far end of the island. Airport limousines (shuttle buses) are less expensive (from about $4–16 per person each way).

GETTING THERE BY SEA • During the summer, a cruise is a pleasant way to reach Bermuda. Although time spent on the island may be brief, passengers can take full advantage of shipboard pampering, relaxation, and fun. Several lines, departing from New York and Florida, offer 3–7 day cruises to Bermuda with stops for sightseeing and shopping. On board are indoor and outdoor swimming pools, sun bathing decks, exercise rooms, endless dining, and many forms of entertainment. Some ships even present Las Vegas–style shows. The Royal Viking Line features jazz cruises. Since there is no legal gambling in

Bermuda, the ships' famed casinos are a real attraction for some travelers when not in port.

While some ships carry several hundred passengers, others have space for more than 1000. Accommodations range from modest to luxurious, with well-appointed rooms and suites. Some lines offer attractive package deals that include air or land transport to the departure point. Others permit children to share staterooms with parents without additional charge. Extras generally include bar service, shore excursions, and on board tipping.

From time to time, the Respiratory Health Association and the Norwalk Hospital Better Breathing Club run an 8-day cruise to Hamilton and St. George's for sufferers from diseases such as asthma and emphysema. A physician's referral is needed and sufferers are encouraged to travel with a friend or relative. Pulmonary physicians and nurses are aboard to administer medications, conduct group discussions, and hold breathing and mild physical exercise sessions. For current information on cruises, call the Respiratory Health Association in Paramus, NJ, at (201) 843–4111.

Most ships dock at Hamilton, the capital. Quieter St. George's, the old capital, and the Dockyard are ports for some. These brilliant, sun-drenched ships gleaming at the foot of Hamilton's Front Street or anchored out in St. George's harbor or at Dockyard (Somerset) make a thrilling sight.

Because cruise schedules change frequently from year to year and season to season, check with the cruise line or a travel agent for current sailing times, number of days, and the particular ships making the trips you want. Following are lines that currently provide cruises to Bermuda during the summer:

Cruise Line	Destination	No. Passengers	Facilities	From
Celebrity Cruises 900 Third Avenue New York, NY 10022 (212) 750–0044, (800) 223–0848				
Horizon	St. George's Hamilton	1200	OP, C	New York
Meridian	Somerset	1100	OP, C	Ft. Lauderdale
Commodore Cruise Line 800 Douglas Road Coral Gables, FL 33134 (305) 529–3000 (800) 237–5361				
Enchanted Isle	Hamilton	713	C, OP, S	New York

Cruise Line	Destination	No. Passengers	Facilities	From
Cunard Line 555 Fifth Avenue New York, NY 10017 (212) 661–7777, (800) 221–4770				
Sagafjord	St. George's Hamilton	589	OP, IP, C	Ft. Lauderdale
Holland America Line 300 Elliott Avenue West Seattle, WA 98119 (206) 281–3535				
Westerdam	Hamilton	1476	2 OP, C, S	New York
Royal Caribbean Cruise Line 1050 Caribbean Way Miami, FL 33132 (305) 379–2601, (800) 327–6700				
Nordic Prince	Hamilton	1038	OP, C	New York
Royal Viking Line 2 Alhambra Plaza Coral Gables, FL 33134 (305) 447–9660				
Royal Viking Star	Hamilton St. George's	710	2 OP, C	New York

Key
IP Indoor Pool
OP Outdoor Pool
C Casino
S Spa or exercise facilities

ENTRY AND DEPARTURE REQUIREMENTS • Travel Documents

• All visitors must have a return or onward ticket upon arrival in Bermuda. They must also have identification that will permit them to return home or visit another country. Acceptable documents for American travelers are a passport, an original birth certificate, a U.S. naturalization certificate, or a U.S. alien registration card. Canadian citizens must have *one* of the following items: a passport, an original birth certificate, or a certification of citizenship.

Smallpox vaccination certificates are required only from visitors who, within the preceding 14 days, have been in a country that is infected.

Departure Tax • A $15 tax will be collected from each adult passenger at Bermuda Airport upon departure. Children under age 12 pay $5, and those under age 2 are exempt. Cruise ship passengers pay $60 (usually), included in the price of each ticket.

Length of Stay • All visitors may remain in Bermuda for up to three weeks from arrival. You can obtain permission to stay longer through immigration officials at the Bermuda Airport upon arrival. To stay indefinitely, you must apply in advance to the Chief Immigration Officer, Ministry of Home Affairs, P.O. Box HM 1364, Hamilton HM FX, Bermuda.

Pets • Small well-behaved dogs and other pets are permitted at some hotels and guest houses. Permission must be obtained in advance. You will also need to obtain a permit in advance from the Department of Agriculture, P.O. Box HM 834, Hamilton HM CX, Bermuda. While airlines can carry pets as cargo or excess baggage, animals are not allowed on cruise ships. Refer to the **Hotel Quick Reference Charts** to see which hotels accept pets.

Customs • Entry—Clothing and articles for personal use, such as sports equipment and cameras, may be taken in duty free. Also duty free are 50 cigars, 200 cigarettes, 1 pound (.454 kgs) tobacco; 1 quart (1.137 litres) hard liquor; 1 quart (1.137 litres) wine; and 20 pounds of meat. Other foodstuffs may be dutiable at 5% to 20% of their value. All imports may be inspected upon arrival. Visitors may claim a $25 duty-free gift allowance.

Departure—The merchandise visitors can take back duty free is as follows. U.S. Citizens: $400 after 48 hours and every 30 days. Canadians: $100 after 48 hours and once every three calendar months, or $300 after seven days once every calendar year. U.K. citizens: £28.

To take plants out, you must have prior permission from your own country. You should also check your state or country's liquor and tobacco laws before going to Bermuda.

U.S. Customs preclearance is available in Bermuda for all scheduled flights. All passengers going to the U.S. are required to fill out written declaration forms before clearing U.S. Customs in Bermuda. All Bermudian hotels, travel agencies, and airline offices provide these forms.

The duty you pay on items beyond your duty-free allowance is reasonable.

Drugs and Firearms • Importation of, possession of, or dealing with illegal drugs (including marijuana) is an offense punishable with fines up to $5,000 or three years in prison, or both. Customs inspectors may conduct body searches at their discretion.

No firearm, part of a firearm, or ammunition may be taken into Bermuda without a license granted by the Commissioner of Police. Permits will only be granted to rifle club members attending sports meetings in Bermuda.

Spearguns and similar dangerous weapons are considered firearms. Antique weapons, at least 100 years old, may be imported if the visitor can prove that they are antique. Imprisonment or heavy fines may be the consequences of importing firearms or ammunition without a license.

BEING THERE • **Language** • The language of Bermuda is English, accented with British, American, and to a lesser degree, West Indian influences. Bermudians, like Bahamians, are known for interchanging "v"'s with "w"'s so that "Where were you?" is pronounced "Vhere vere you?" This is thought to date back to 18th-century England and America.

Spending Money • The Bermudian dollar (BD$) is equal to the U.S. dollar. U.S. currency is widely accepted at hotels, restaurants, and stores. You will often get a combination of U.S. and Bermudian bills and coins in your change. U.S. travelers checks are accepted everywhere. You can use credit cards in almost all restaurants and stores, as well as some hotels. Exchange rates for Canadian, U.K., and other currency are subject to daily fluctuations. An **American Express** office is on Bermudiana Road, near Front Street. **Visa** cardholders can obtain cash advances (in Bermudian currency) at Bank of Bermuda automatic teller machines throughout the island.

Tipping—a 10% to 15% gratuity covering room, board (if board is included in the price of the room), and porter service will be added to most accommodation bills. When tips are not included, the accepted amount for restaurants and other services is 15%.

Business Hours • Stores and offices are open from 9 a.m. to 5 p.m., except in Hamilton from May through Labour Day, when many shops remain open until 9 p.m. on Wednesdays, and during December, when most don't close until 9 p.m. Some of the smaller shops, such as those in hotels, close for lunch. Banks are open from 9:30 a.m. to 3:00 p.m. Monday through Friday and reopen on Fridays from 4:30 to 5:30 p.m.

Dress • Women are asked not to wear short shorts, bathing suits, bikini tops, or curlers in the street or in dining rooms, cocktail lounges, or lobbies of hotels. Men are requested to wear shirts when not on the beach or by the pool. Bare feet and short shorts are only acceptable in swim areas. Conservative sportswear is acceptable everywhere. The larger hotels have more formal dress codes than guest houses or small hotels. Dress requirements are more formal in the summer season (from Mar. through Nov.) than at other times of the year. In season, men are requested to wear jackets and ties at night. During the winter season, fall clothes will be necessary, including a lightweight coat or jacket.

Getting Around • Be sure to get a *Handy Reference Map* and public transport schedule from your hotel or a Visitors' Service Bureau office. There are no cars for rent in Bermuda, but transportation is efficient and enjoyable. Taxis or shuttle buses will take you to and from the airport. The old railroad right-of-way that runs through the island is a popular route for joggers and cyclists (see *The Bermuda Railway Trail Guide*). With the onset of cars in the late '40s, Bermuda's train was sold to British Guiana (now Guyana).

By Cycle: Motor-assisted cycles, mopeds or scooters, are the most popular form of transportation. They can be rented (along with pedal bikes) at hotels and at less expensive independent cycle shops around the island. Mopeds begin at about $20 a day (or less if rented for several days). Double seaters cost about $35 a day. No driver's license is required, but moped drivers must be at least 16 years old. (You may need to leave a driver's license or a credit card as a deposit.) At all times, drivers are required by law to wear the helmets given when the moped is rented. Gas stations are open from 7 a.m. to 7 p.m., Mon. through Sat., with limited hours on Sun. and holidays. If you've never ridden before, don't worry. You'll have as much time as you need to practice in an open area before hitting the road. *Driving is on the left-hand side of the road, and the speed limit is 35 kilometers (20 miles) per hour.*

By Bus: Bermuda's pink buses are another convenient, inexpensive way to get around. At hotels and Visitors' Service Bureau offices, you can pick up the public transport schedule, which includes ferries. Bus fares range from $1.25 to $2.50 for adults, depending on the distance, and exact change in coins is required. Children aged 3–13 pay 55¢ and those under 3 ride free. At the Washington Street Terminal in the city of Hamilton, you can buy money-saving books of tickets. Bus stops are marked by green-and-white-striped poles.

The current Public Transport bus and ferry schedule, which can be obtained at the Central Bus Terminal in Hamilton, recommends a do-it-yourself sightseeing bus and ferry tour of Bermuda for $10.75.

By Taxi: All taxis are metered in Bermuda. From the airport to Sandys, the parish farthest away, the ride should cost from about $33–$38. To the city of Hamilton, in the middle of the island, it should be about $20. To St. George's, the parish where Bermuda's airport—the Civil Air Terminal—is located, the fare will be about $13; and to nearby Hamilton Parish, about $8 to $11.

Most of the island's cabs are compact, carrying a maximum of four passengers. The meter begins at $2.60. The first mile is $4. Each additional mile is $1.60. Each piece of luggage carried in the trunk or on the roof will add 25¢ to your tab. Between 10 a.m. and 6 p.m. and on Sundays and public holidays, you'll pay a 25% (one to four people) or a 50% (five or six people) surcharge. Bermuda has a handful of six-seater London taxis and small vans. At night, be prepared to wait a while for a taxi, even when you call one.

For about $20 an hour (for up to four people) or $30 (for five or six passengers), taxis with blue flags on their hoods give sightseeing tours. The flag indicates that the driver is a qualified tour guide. Whenever you are riding the blue-flagged taxis to and from hotels and restaurants, take the opportunity to ask the driver questions about the sights you're passing.

By Ferry: Ferries take scenic routes through Hamilton Harbour and Great Sound, stopping at the city of Hamilton, and Paget, Warwick, and Sandys parishes. The fare from Hamilton to Paget and Warwick is $1, and $2 from Hamilton to Sandys (often called Somerset by Bermudians). On the ferries between Somerset and Hamilton, if you arrive early enough and there is room, you can take your moped along for $2 extra. Pedal bikes ride for free. All cyclists must disembark at the first stop. You can pick up public transport schedules at hotels and Visitors' Service Bureau offices. (Also see By Bus.)

By Horse-Drawn Carriage: Particularly in the summer season (from March through Nov.) you will see horse-drawn carriages on Front Street in Hamilton. Some hotels will make arrangements for their guests. Depending on whether you'd rather be pulled by one or two horses, the cost is about $15 or $20 for the first half-hour and $10 or $15 for each additional half-hour.

Time ● Bermuda is one hour later than Eastern Standard Time. As in the United States, Daylight Saving Time is in effect beginning in April and ending in October.

Mail ● International postal service from Bermuda is efficient and airmail leaves and arrives daily. A 24-hour cable service is available, with night letter and full rates as well as several express mail services.

Telephones ● When making calls from most public phones, be sure to have your coins ready to be dropped in as soon as (and only after) you've dialed and someone has answered.

Electricity ● Electricity is 110 volts, 60 cycles A.C., so North American appliances can be used. Those from most other regions will need adapters.

Medical Concerns ● Tap water in Bermuda is filtered and therefore perfectly safe to drink. Hotels and guest houses will arrange visits to doctors and dentists, if necessary. All dentists and physicians are private and fees are comparable to those in the U.S. King Edward VII Hospital is Bermuda's general hospital and it has 24-hour emergency facilities. Blue Cross/Blue Shield is accepted.

Publications ● *The Royal Gazette* is Bermuda's daily paper. *The Mid-Ocean News* and the *Bermuda Sun* are weekend papers published on Fridays. *Bermuda Times* is a monthly paper. Many people also enjoy flipping through *Bermuda Business,* a slick monthly glossy magazine.

Visitor Information ● The Bermuda Department of Tourism is located at Global House, 43 Church Street in Hamilton. The mailing address is P.O. Box HM 465, Hamilton, HM BX Bermuda. It produces helpful free brochures, such as the *Handy Reference Map,* the *Sportsman's Guide,* the *Golfer's Guide,* the *Honeymooners' Guide,* and *Bermuda Shoppers' Guide. This Week in Bermuda* and *Preview of Bermuda* are other free brochures that you can pick up at hotels or stores. The Department of Tourism also has offices in the following locations:

New York
310 Madison Avenue
New York, NY 10017
USA (800) 223-6106 or
(212) 818-9800

Boston
44 School Street, Suite 1010
Boston, MA 02108
USA (617) 742-0405

Atlanta
235 Peachtree Street, N.E.
Atlanta, GA 30303
USA (404) 524-1541

Chicago
150 N. Wacker Drive
Chicago, IL 60606
USA (312) 782-5486

Toronto
1200 Bay Street
Toronto, Ontario
Canada M5R 2A5
(800) 387-1304

Los Angeles
John A. Tetley, Inc.
Suite 601, 3075 Wilshire Blvd.
Los Angeles, CA 90010
(213) 388-1151

The Visitors' Service Bureau is located at the Ferry Dock in Hamilton, and has offices in Bermuda Airport, King's Square in St. George's, and Sandys Parish. The larger hotels have social desks where sightseeing trips and tours are arranged.

Bookstores have many books by international authors as well as by Bermudians about all aspects of the country's life.

Tune into radio station VSB 1160 for tips on island activities and special events, general information about Bermuda, and local music.

WHAT TO SEE AND DO

ATTRACTIONS AT A GLANCE

BNT—A Bermuda National Trust property

	Parish	*Page*
Art Galleries		
Bermuda Arts Centre at Dockyard	Sandys	33
Bridge House	Town of St. George's	63
Bermuda Society of Arts	City of Hamilton, Pembroke	45
Other Galleries	Various locations	76
Churches		
*The Cathedral of the Most Holy Trinity (Bermuda Cathedral)	City of Hamilton, Pembroke	44
Cobbs Hill Wesleyan Methodist Church	Warwick	37
Old Devonshire Church	Devonshire	49
The Old Rectory (BNT)	Town of St. George's	62
St. James's Church	Sandys	34
*St. Peter's Church	Town of St. George's	62
St. Theresa's Cathedral	City of Hamilton, Pembroke	45
The Unfinished Church	St. George's	62
Forts		
*Fort Hamilton	Pembroke	47
*Fort St. Catherine	St. George's	64
Scaur Hill Fort	Sandys	34
Gates Fort	St. George's	64
Gardens, Parks, and Nature Reserves		
*Admiralty House Park	Pembroke	47
*Botanical Gardens	Paget	39

Edmund Gibbons Nature Reserve	Devonshire	49
Gilbert Nature Reserve (BNT)	Sandys	34
Gladys Morrel Nature Reserve (BNT)	Sandys	33
North Nature Reserve (BNT)	Smith's	52
Paget Marsh (BNT)	Paget	39
*Palm Grove Gardens	Devonshire	49
*Par-La-Ville Gardens	City of Hamilton, Pembroke	47
Scaur Lodge Property (BNT)	Sandys	34
Somers Gardens	Town of St. George's	63
Spittal Pond (BNT)	Smith's	51
Victoria Park	City of Hamilton, Pembroke	45

Government Buildings

City Hall	City of Hamilton, Pembroke	45
Old State House	Town of St. George's	63
*Sessions House	City of Hamilton, Pembroke	44
*The Cabinet Building	City of Hamilton, Pembroke	42
Town Hall	Town of St. George's	60

Historical Sights

"Attack on Washington" Audio-visual Show	Sandys	33
The Bank of Bermuda Ltd. Coin Collection	City of Hamilton, Pembroke	42
"Bermuda Journey" Audio-Visual Show	St. George's	60
Black Watch Pass and Well	Pembroke	47
Carter House	St. George's	65
*Deliverance II	Town of St. George's	60
Devonshire Dock	Devonshire	48
Featherbed Alley Print Shop	Town of St. George's	62
*Gibbs Hill Lighthouse	Southampton	36
*King's Square	Town of St. George's	58
Old State House	Town of St. George's	63
Palmetto House	Devonshire	49
Perot Post Office	City of Hamilton, Pembroke	46
Somerset Bridge	Sandys	35
Spanish Rock	Smith's	52
Springfield Mansion (BNT)	Sandys	33

*Tucker House (BNT)	Town of St. George's	60
*Verdmont House (BNT)	Smith's	51
Tom Moore's Tavern/Walsingham	Hamilton Parish	55

Libraries

The Bermuda Library	City of Hamilton, Pembroke	45
St. George's Library (BNT)	Town of St. George's	61
Springfield Library (BNT)	Sandys	33

Local Industries

The Bermuda Perfumery and Gardens	Hamilton Parish	54
Craft Market at Dockyard	Sandys	32

Museums and Animals

*Bermuda Aquarium, Museum, and Zoo	Hamilton Parish	54
Bermuda Biological Station	St. George's	64
Bermuda Historical Society Museum	City of Hamilton, Pembroke	46
*The Carriage Museum	Town of St. George's	61
The Confederate Museum (BNT)	Town of St. George's	58
*The Maritime Museum	Sandys	32
St. George's Historical Society Museum	Town of St. George's	63

Natural Wonders/Attractions

Cathedral Rocks	Sandys	35
*Crystal Caves	Hamilton Parish	55
Devil's Hole	Smith's	52
Amber Caves of Leamington	Hamilton Parish	55
Natural Arches	St. George's	64
Sea Gardens	Sandys	33

THE PARISHES AND THEIR SIGHTS FROM WEST TO EAST

SANDYS

Pronounced "Sands" or simply referred to as Somerset by Bermudians, Sandys is comprised of Ireland Islands north and south, Boaz, Watford, and Somerset islands, and the northeastern tip of the main island. Throughout their history, the people of this parish have stood out from those of the rest of the island, particularly where political opinion is concerned. For instance, while most of Bermuda aided the South during the American Civil War, many people of Sandys supported the North's Union Army. In an ongoing present-day battle between the east and the west, Sandys' cricket team fights it out with the team from St. George's every July or August during festive Cup Match.

To get here, you can cross the world's smallest drawbridge. Once in Bermuda's westernmost parish, you can visit two nature reserves, an 18th-century parish church, an old plantation with a mansion and slave quarters, a 19th-century fort and a maritime museum. There are two harbors, one with a striking natural coral formation. But one of the most pleasant ways to spend time in Sandys is to stroll or ride through the rural village of Somerset, in the center of the parish.

The 45-minute ferry ride from Hamilton to the Watford Bridge dock is a particularly relaxing and scenic way to reach the village, which is not far from the dock. Late in the afternoon, children often congregate at the docks in Sandys to dive off the pier or fish. Walking to Somerset, you'll pass a military cemetery and a monument in memory of Bermudians who died of pneumonia in April 1916. In Somerset you can wander along narrow roads bordered by fragrant wild hedges, and admire peaceful bays and pretty houses with well-kept grounds. Some of the stores are branches of those in Hamilton, such as the Irish Linen Shop. For rest and refreshment, you have a choice of several restaurants and pubs, including The Loyalty Inn and Somerset Country Squire. From the center of the village, a ten-minute walk west along Somerset Road will take you to Springfield and the Gilbert Nature Reserve, an old plantation with part of the mansion now used as a library. Along the way, you'll come to Dean's Bakery & Deli, which serves delicious cassava pie, and Simmons Ice Cream Factory and Variety Store, which scoops up exceptional rum raisin ice cream.

Bordering one side of the village is Mangrove Bay, named for the tangled trees that line the shore. The beach closest to the center of the village is small, shady, and filled with the sounds of traffic from nearby Mangrove Bay Road. It is, therefore, not nearly as nice as other beaches in the parish or in the rest of Bermuda, but it affords a picturesque view of the cove, speckled with small boats. At Mangrove Bay Wharf, northeast along Mangrove Bay Road, arrange sailing or fishing expeditions or take sightseeing boats out to the reefs to swim or snorkle. Northwest of the wharf is Cambridge Beaches, Bermuda's oldest cottage colony. Long Bay, southwest of the cottage colony, is where you will find the parish's most beautiful beaches. Off Daniel's Head, at the southwest end of Long Bay, is Sea Gardens, the underwater spectacle of marine life on and around a sunken vessel.

The economy of the area north of Somerset Village once thrived on shipbuilding. Then life here seemed to fall into a deep sleep. For more than a decade the Maritime Museum, in the former Royal Naval Dockyard, was the only reason visitors ventured to Bermuda's remote northwesternmost tip. After years of speculation, the Dockyard area has undergone extensive redevelopment. With a major cruise port (the island's third), the new Marina Real del Oeste, an arts center, a crafts market, and new restaurants and shops, this region may eventually be almost as appealing to activity-oriented tourists as Hamilton and St. George's have always been. Now visitors may even tour the vicinity underwater—in a submarine—during the summer. To truly enjoy the tranquility and isolation of Bermuda's West End, avoid the area on days when the cruise ship is anchored offshore. Of the many ways to reach Dockyard—including public bus, cycle, and taxi—we find the ferry the most relaxing. If you're staying in Sandys, you can get around in the vans run by **Sandys Taxi** from Somerset to Dockyard. Along with Bermudians, you'll drive through residential neighborhoods with narrow lanes set off by flowering gardens.

South of Somerset Village, on the western side of the island are the attractive parish church of St. James's (next to the Visitors' Service Bureau) and busy Ely's Harbour, which once protected smugglers and traders alike from storms at sea. Wreck Hill and Scaur Lodge Property overlook the harbor, where you can see Cathedral Rocks, an unusual coral formation not far south of the village. On the eastern side of the island, visit the Gladys Morrell Nature Reserve, near Cavello Bay. Then stop for a picnic at Scaur Hill Fort, which sits above Great Sound. Somerset Bridge, which joins Somerset Island to the main island, is so small that you may not notice it if you aren't paying attention when you cross it. Once past the U.S. Naval Air Station Annex, on the peninsula between Great Sound and Little Sound, you will be in Southampton.

Throughout Bermuda, the clearly marked old railway right-of-way is a serene path for jogging or walking. However, if you want to ride a moped or a bicycle along the trail, Sandys and Southampton are the places to do it, since there are no steps or other obstructions. This is also the most scenic part of the trail, which periodically joins the main road. You'll zip by high stone walls, under bridges, past a farm, between trees whose branches almost meet overhead. Views of the ocean, Gibbs Hill Lighthouse, and perhaps a cruise ship add to the beauty of the route.

***The Maritime Museum** • *at the tip of North Ireland Island; tel: 234–1418* • The Maritime Museum is a tribute to the island's 300-year nautical history. It is housed in the former Royal Naval Dockyard, once the British Empire's largest drydock. Slaves, free blacks, and convicts brought from England built the dockyard in the mid-19th century. Many of these workers died during an outbreak of yellow fever. Especially if you approach by ferry, the clock towers are an impressive sight. In sharp contrast to most of the buildings in Bermuda, which are painted pastels, the buildings at Dockyard are the natural beige of limestone.

The public has enjoyed the museum's indoor and outdoor exhibits since the 1975 opening ceremony attended by Queen Elizabeth. Within the buildings that once stored munitions and served as workshops, exhibits tell you about pearl diving, boat building, and whaling. Also on display are memorabilia such as the famous Tucker Treasure, maritime maps, and sailing craft (including the 17-foot skiff in which two young Bermudians sailed some 700 miles to New York in 1935). A mounted copy of a June 19, 1937, *New York Herald Tribune* article announces, "24 Passengers Fly in Clipper to Bermuda" and an advertisement boasts, "Bermuda in Five Hours" from New York. Nearby, the menu from the "Pan American Airways flying boat" is posted. The past few decades may have shaved several hours off air time, but the filet mignon and strawberry sundae served on the inaugural flight sound a whole lot more appetizing than today's standard airborne meals. In the "Keep Yard" you will be watched over by the statue of Neptune, once the figurehead on the HMS *Irresistible,* an old British battleship.

The mansion on a hill overlooking the dockyard is the Commissioner's House, dating from the early 19th century and thought to be the most expensive home ever built on a military base. This lavish example of period architecture is closed to the public for restoration. A 1992 grand opening is scheduled to coincide with the 500th anniversary of Columbus's landing. *Museum open daily, 10 a.m.–5 p.m. Closed*

Christmas Day. Admission: adults—$5; children under age 12 and senior citizens—$1.

Craft Market • *Building 28, Dockyard, Ireland Island; tel: 234–3208* • Browse through crafts including pottery, paintings on cedar, dolls, and highly detailed miniature furniture. *Open daily from 11 a.m. to 4 p.m. No admission fee.*

"The Attack on Washington" • *Neptune Cinema, Dockyard, Ireland Island; tel: 238–0432 or 234–1709* • Whether or not you've always wondered exactly how Bermuda fit into the War of 1812, this dramatic audio-visual presentation is worth a stop. With flashing lights and the sound of gun blasts, the show wraps viewers in the confrontation between the American settlers and the British, who sailed to Washington from Bermuda's Royal Naval Dockyard. The 100-seat theater adjacent to the Craft Market is located in the Cooperage, where barrels were once made. *Admission: $4 for adults, $2 for children. Daily shows every half hour from 10 a.m. to 4 p.m.*

Bermuda Arts Centre • *Dockyard, Ireland Island, Sandys; tel: 234–4280* • The striking exhibits of paintings and the displays of hand-made jewelry change periodically. *Open from 10 a.m. to 4:30 p.m,. Tuesday–Friday and 10 a.m. to 5 p.m. on Saturday and Sunday. Closed on Christmas Day and all of January. Admission: $1.50 adults; children under 12, students, and senior citizens, 75¢.*

Gladys Morrel Nature Reserve • *off East Shore Road, near Cavello Bay* • In memory of the woman who once owned the land, these two acres of open space were given to the Bermuda National Trust in 1973 by the Sandys Chapter of the Daughters of the Empire. *Open daily. Free admission.*

Sea Gardens • *off Daniel's Head; visits may be arranged through glass-bottom boat, scuba diving, or snorkeling tours (most Sea Gardens tours require reservations)* • Located not in Bermuda, but beneath its turquoise waters, Sea Gardens offers a clear view of the *Vixen,* a coral covered wreck. The vessel, a World War I British gun-boat, was purposely sunk to block the channel. Whether you choose to visit the site by glass bottom boat or on a snorkeling or scuba diving tour, you will see a colorful variety of coral that has found a home on the ship's hull. If you approach the gardens by boat, you'll be greeted by large swarms of angelfish, gray snapper, and chub, which have become accustomed to the dog food fed them by friendly skippers.

Springfield Library/Springfield Mansion • *Middle Road, off Somerset Road, Somerset Village; tel: 234–1980* • The nicest rooms in this well-preserved 17th-century plantation home are now the Somerset branch of the Bermuda Library. Beginning with the old arched Bermuda gateway, the mansion and its surroundings are fascinating from an architectural and historical standpoint. The outbuildings include slave quarters, the original kitchen, and a buttery—a tall shed for refrigeration, built over a stream. *Mansion open Mon., Wed., and Sat. 9 a.m.– 5 p.m.; closed from 1–2 p.m. and all holidays. Grounds open daily. Free admission.*

Gilbert Nature Reserve • *Middle Road, off Somerset Road, Somerset Village* • Adjoining the Springfield Library, Gilbert Nature Reserve was once part of the mansion's land. It was named after the family who owned the property from 1700 until 1973, when it was acquired by the Bermuda National Trust and the Bermuda Audubon Society. The reserve is comprised of five acres of unspoiled woodland, open space, and planting land. *Open daily. Free admission.*

St. James's Church • *between Church Valley Road and Somerset Road, near Church Bay* • Massive iron gates and a long road lead to this Anglican parish church, with its glistening needlelike spire and polished cedar doors. While the present structure was built in 1789 to replace a church destroyed by a hurricane, no one is certain when the original church was built. Aisles were added to the new church early in the 19th century; when its spire was struck by lightning 100 years later, the present spire was designed by a local architect. The bright crypts and tombstones that line the long entryway seem surprisingly cheerful. *Open daily, from 10 a.m.–5 p.m.*

Scaur Hill Fort • *Somerset Road, near Somerset Bridge; tel: 234– 0908* • On a hill above the coast of the Great Sound, this fort was built under orders from the Duke of Wellington in 1834. You can see the old bunkers, dry moats, and battlements built into the hilltop, and even search for the tunnel that leads to the ocean. Not only does the fort's location afford a view of Ely's Harbour on the other side of Somerset Island, but you can also see the rest of Bermuda (except St. David's, in the easternmost parish of St. George's). Before using the telescope to explore the islands, enjoy lunch at one of the picnic tables on the well-manicured lawns within the walks. When facing the sound, on the north side of the fort, you can see the London Milestone, a rock with "London 3076 Miles," carved into one side and "27th Regiment, R.E., 1906," inscribed on the other. On Thursdays, during Rendezvous Time (mid-November through March), join in a treasure hunt. *Open daily, 9 a.m.–4:30 p.m. Free admission.*

Scaur Lodge Property • This is a picturesque lookout point near the fort but on the other side of Somerset Island, above Ely's Harbour.

It also overlooks Scaur Bay and the unusual formation called Cathedral Rocks.

Cathedral Rocks • *near Somerset Bridge* • These medieval arches and pillars are actually a natural coral formation that has been so battered by the sea that it now resembles Gothic architecture. The pink sand and small pools filled with colorful sea creatures make a visit to this spot even more worthwhile. Cathedral Rocks can be reached for picnicking or exploring by a path ¼-mile west of Somerset Bridge.

Somerset Bridge • *between the main island and Somerset Island, east of Cathedral Rocks* • This 17th-century bridge's claim to fame is that it is the smallest drawbridge in the world. The hand-operated draw is only 22 inches wide, just enough space to allow the mast of a sailboat to pass through. The shores connected by the bridge are alive with color from April to August when red, yellow, pink, and white oleanders are in full bloom.

SOUTHAMPTON

Southampton, a narrow strip of land bordered by some of the island's most spectacular beaches, stretches from the U.S. Naval Air Station Annex to Riddell's Bay. Its verdant open spaces and long sandy beaches divided by boulders and secluded coves may seem to be nature at its best. While walking, riding, or jogging along South Shore Road, you will have a wonderful view of the Atlantic shoreline below. The foaming breakers, not too far out to sea, let you know where reefs lie hidden under the blue-green waters. The public beach at Horseshoe Bay is one of Bermuda's most popular, among locals as well as visitors. South shore beaches tend to have larger waves than elsewhere on the island, and many people prefer them to those with calmer waters.

From the top of Gibbs Hill Lighthouse, the panoramic view takes in almost all of Bermuda. If the climb is not enough exercise, you can play 18 holes of golf on a championship course, the public, government-owned Port Royal Golf Course at the western end of the parish.

When Richard Norwood divided the island in the original 1616 survey, this part of Southampton was considered "overplus" land and was seized by the governor, Daniel Tucker, for his personal use. Although Governor Tucker was forced to give up most of the land when the Bermuda Company shareholders objected, members of the prominent Tucker family continued to live in this area for generations.

The cove near Southampton's border with Sandys is called George's

Bay, after one of the governor's descendants. The land on which the U.S. Naval Air Station Annex is located was formerly known as Tucker's Island. One of the most famous (or infamous) members of this family is Colonel Henry Tucker, who helped steal Bermudian gunpowder for the American colonists during the Revolutionary War. To learn more about the Tuckers and their contributions to Bermudian (and American) history, visit Tucker House in the town of St. George.

Waterlot Inn, run by the Southampton Princess, is one of Southampton's many good restaurants. At Henry VIII Restaurant & Pub, waiters are dressed as if they just stepped out of the 16th century. At Tio Pepe (near the Horseshoe Bay beach entrance) the choices range from pizza to crab legs.

*Gibbs Hill Lighthouse ● *off St. Anne's Road; tel: 238–0524* ● Before this lighthouse began operating in 1846, many ships were wrecked off the western end of Bermuda on coral reefs extending more than a dozen miles out to sea. One of the few lighthouses in the world made entirely of cast iron, it was constructed in England and shipped in sections to Bermuda where it stands 362 feet above the ocean. Once wound by hand every half hour, the machinery now runs on electricity and is fully automatic. Gone are the days when whale oil and paraffin were used to light the beacons. The beam from the 1500-watt bulb can be seen by ships for 40 miles, and by planes flying at altitudes of 10,000 feet, 120 miles away. Inside, a display of historical artifacts and documents traces the past of both this lighthouse and St. David's, the one in St. George's.

The view after the 185-step climb to the top of Gibbs Hill Lighthouse is well worth the exercise. From the small circular balcony, you can see almost every major landmark in Bermuda. You will certainly enjoy gazing down at the many-hued blue-green waters that blend into the deep-blue of the expansive Atlantic and surround the curving strip of land dotted with white-roofed houses. In the spring, visitors may even spot migrating whales out past the south shore reefs. *Open daily, 9 a.m.–4:30 p.m. Admission: $2; free for children under age 3.*

WARWICK

If you decide to stay in Warwick, you may find yourself quickly feeling at home. This parish offers a wide selection of housekeeping apartments in residential neighborhoods. There is also a cottage colony, as well as a few hotels and guest houses. Most accommodations have pools, and all are within walking distance of beautiful south shore beaches.

Warwick Long Bay has the longest, straightest, continuous stretch of beach in Bermuda and is known for its pale-pink sand. The beaches in the Longtail Cliffs area are also noted for the sand that is tinted by bits of shells and coral. Like Bermudians, some visitors have discovered that Jobson Cove, with its small secluded beach, is perfect for midnight skinny-dipping. The rugged cliffs overlooking the shoreline add a dramatic touch to a view of the southern coast. Toward the center of the parish is Warwick Pond, one of Bermuda's few inland bodies of water and a home for wild birds. As you wander along roads lined with flowers and thick shrubs, you will notice the contrast between newer, simple houses and larger, more elegant homes, some dating back more than 100 years.

Several Bermuda "firsts" are in this parish, which encompasses the area between Riddell's Bay Golf and Country Club and Stonehole Bay to the west, and Cobbs Hill Road to the east. From Harbour Road, along Warwick's northern shore, you will see Darrell Island to the west, a narrow strip of land with a building in the middle. Bermuda's first airport was once on this island and, during the 1930s, seaplanes bringing passengers from New York landed here. The hangars were used as movie studios during the 1950s before being demolished.

Constructed in 1922, the golf course at Riddell's Bay is the island's oldest. It is private, like Warwick's other course at the Belmont Hotel, so in order to play at either, you will need reservations or the introduction of a member. Some hotels make arrangements for their guests.

Near Longford and Ord roads, across from the Belmont Hotel and Golf Club, Christ Church is the oldest Presbyterian church (1719) in any British colony or dominion. On Morgan Road, just east of the Belmont Hotel, is Warwick Academy, the island's first school, which has been in continuous operation since 1662. Dr. Francis Patton, its best-known alumnus, was Princeton University's president from 1888 to 1913. On Cobbs Hill Road, near Paget, is Cobbs Hill Wesleyan Methodist Church, the one-room chapel planned and built in 1827 by and for slaves and free blacks who had no place to worship. For delicious wheat bread and other goodies, stop by Godfrey's Bakery.

An especially enjoyable way to get to know the area is to do it on horseback. At Spicelands Riding Centre you can take lessons or rides through wooded trails leading to grassy open spaces and sandy paths by the shore. A home-cooked breakfast is served after the 7 a.m. ride along a deserted beach.

Cobbs Hill Wesleyan Methodist Church • *Cobbs Hill Road* • In the early 19th century, when they were denied places of worship, male and female free blacks and slaves (who were permitted to work only at night during their time off) spent two years building this one-room church.

Edward Fraser, a slave brought from Barbados, was responsible not only for rallying fellow blacks, but also for securing the land and supplies. One of the few slaves who had been allowed to be educated, Fraser dedicated his life to helping other black people. He became a Methodist minister, and shortly after the church was completed in 1827, he was freed. He went to England to advocate the rights of black people, and then served as a missionary in the West Indies. Many of the people who attend the church today are descendants of those who helped build it.

PAGET

Although one of the most populous parishes and with few open spaces, Paget is among the island's most attractive areas. Its north shore faces the city of Hamilton, just across Hamilton Harbour. From three landings on the harbor—Salt Kettle, Hodsdon's, and Lower—ferries go to the city and to Sandys and Warwick parishes. If you're in a car or on a moped at the last roundabout before Hamilton, you might see Johnnie Barnes, dubbed the Unofficial Greeter of Bermuda. A retired bus driver, this charming, distinguished man stands here nearly every morning, rain or shine, and waves to passing drivers. Cobbs Hill Road to the west divides Warwick from Paget, which ends just before Berry Hill Road meets Tee Street to the east. The beaches along Paget's stunning south shore are some of Bermuda's most popular.

This parish has the widest variety of all kinds of accommodations, in beautiful locations. Coral Beach and Tennis Club, Horizons and Cottages, and the Elbow Beach Hotel are in one of the most pleasant parts of the south shore. During springtime college weeks, when the island is full of vacationing students from the States, the Elbow Beach Hotel is the center of activities. On the northern shore, smaller hotels and guest houses such as Glencoe Harbour Club and Salt Kettle House have great views of the lively harbor.

In the center of the parish, Paget Marsh is the 18-acre home of some of Bermuda's endangered trees and plants. You can see and smell more lush foliage at the 36-acre Botanical Gardens, one of the favorite stops of visitors to the island. April's grand Agricultural Exhibition, with everything from live pigs and chickens to intricate butter sculpture, is only one of the many events that take place at the gardens during the year.

Winding roads through Paget's rolling hills afford views of luxurious country houses and estates, as well as other parts of the island. Some of the homes are often part of the spring Open Houses and Gardens Tour, such as Inwood, off Middle Road, in the Rural Hill area. It was built in 1650 and expanded in 1700 to form the shape of a cross. This kind of architecture—thought to ward off evil spirits—is typical of the 18th century. Inside are 12 powder rooms, where both men and women once powdered their wigs. On Harbour Road, not far from Hamilton, is Waterville, an early 18th-century home that now houses the office of the Bermuda National Trust, with local and exotic trees in its garden.

A fine example of Bermuda Georgian architecture is Clermont, built in 1800, on Harbour Road near the Lower Ferry Landing. If the island's first tennis court had not been built on the grounds in 1873, people in the United States might not be playing tennis today. It was because of this court that Mary Outerbridge introduced tennis to the United States; she brought equipment and a book of rules to the Staten Island Cricket Club in 1874.

At the junction of Cobbs Hill and Middle Roads is Fourways Inn, one of Bermuda's most elegant and expensive restaurants, in a former home built in the 1720s. This Georgian-style structure of coral and Bermuda cedar is a delicious place to spend an evening. On the grounds is the island's newest cottage colony, also called Fourways.

Paget Marsh • *Middle Road* • This is the only area in Bermuda where a forest still exists much as it was when settlers first arrived. A mangrove swamp as well as some of the island's most attractive cedar and palmetto trees can be found on these 26 acres, along with other endangered trees and plants. The marsh is owned by the Bermuda National Trust and the Audubon Society. *Free admission. Arrangements to visit must be made by contacting the office of the Bermuda National Trust (tel: 2–6483).*

*Botanical Gardens • *Point Finger Road; tel: 236–4201* • Like an outdoor-living museum, this 36-acre expanse shows off Bermuda's exotic natural beauty. The 15 permanent attractions include the Woodlands, a miniature forest with twisting paths and plants of unusual shapes; the Exotic Plant House, filled with delicate rare specimens; and the Hibiscus Garden, where you can see many of the 150 known varieties of the flower that is native to China. Extra special is the Garden for the Blind, where even the sighted can enjoy the fragrances of lemon mint, spice trees, lavender, and oregano, to name just a few. Don't miss the aviary, which even contains squirrel monkeys in addition to several species of tropical birds. Seasonal displays include a grand agricultural exhibition in April (complete with chickens, pigs, cows, and handicrafts); dog shows in Feb., May, and Nov.; and periodic horse and bird shows. When there are no government functions scheduled, you can visit Camden House, the official residence of Bermuda's premier, on Tues. and Fri. (Nov.–Mar.) and Tues. and Wed. (the rest of the year), from noon to 2 p.m. You may ride onto the grounds in a car or on a cycle, but you must stay on the asphalt paths and must not exceed the 10 mph speed limit. *Open daily, sunrise to sunset. Guided tours leave from restaurant parking lot, Tue., Wed., and Fri. at 10:30 a.m. Free admission.*

PEMBROKE

Hamilton, the capital of Bermuda and the island's only city, is the highlight of Pembroke, a peninsula bordered by the Atlantic, the Great Sound, and Hamilton Harbour. The waterfront capital (referred to as "Town" by Bermudians) faces the bustling harbor where large cruise ships, ferries, and other craft are either docked or gliding in and out. Founded in 1790, Hamilton became the capital in 1815 when its central location was thought to be more convenient than that of the original capital, St. George's, at the extreme eastern end of the island.

The Department of Tourism, which dispenses *Handy Reference Maps,* is located in Global House on Church Street. Most of the city's many attractions are within easy walking distance of each other. Whether you take it all in from the ferry, by moped, or on foot, Front Street, full of shops and activity, is a delight. With horns blasting and colorful flags waving, cruise liners pull into the harbor on Monday mornings, remaining until they depart three days later. If you come to Hamilton by ferry, you will disembark at the western end of Front Street, by the Visitors' Service Bureau and the Bank of Bermuda, where an old coin collection is on display. The Royal Bermuda Yacht Club is behind the bank, between the U.S. Navy Shore Patrol Station and Albouy's Point, which overlooks the harbor. The yacht club sponsors the world famous Newport to Bermuda yacht race, which takes place on even-numbered years.

At this end of Front Street, a policeman directs traffic from a "birdcage." Further along there are many stores, several airline offices (Pan Am, Continental, U.S. Air, Delta, British Airways, American, Air Canada), and restaurants with balconies overlooking the harbor. Considered one of the island's most dignified public buildings, the Cabinet Building, formerly the Colonial Secretariat, takes up a block between Parliament and Court Streets.

Turning up Court Street, you'll come to Sessions House, where you can watch parliamentary debates. Churches in the area are Wesleyan Methodist Church, St. Andrew's Presbyterian, and St. Paul's A.M.E. This African Methodist Episcopal Church is one of Bermuda's leading black churches, and has its roots in the American abolition movement. You'll see the impressive Masjid Muhammad mosque on Cedar Avenue. On Dundonald Street East is an attractive building that was once the New Testament Church of God, and before that, the Colonial Opera House. Inspired by 16th-century Roman architecture, its design was taken from the plans of a black carpenter and mason who had never been off the island. The carpenter's love of Romanesque architecture had come from books. Built at the turn of the century, the building was restored after being badly hit by the hurricane of 1926. On Church Street you can see the island's most grandiose church, the Cathedral of the Most Holy Trinity, more commonly known as Bermuda Cathedral.

Further west on Church Street is the sparkling-white City Hall, which houses a theater and art gallery. This modern building was modeled after Stockholm's city hall. The Hamilton Bus Terminal, Victoria Park, and St. Theresa's Roman Catholic Cathedral are in this area.

A turn onto Queen Street, going back toward Front Street, will take you past the Bermuda Library, the Historical Society Museum, Perot Post Office—where the island's first postmaster made Bermuda's first stamps by hand—and pleasant Par-La-Ville Gardens.

Reid Street, parallel to Front, is Hamilton's second busiest shopping street. In several byways, you'll find a variety of small stores tucked between buildings. Going east, you will pass Washington Mall on your left and Walker Arcade on your right, both on the blocks between Queen and Burnaby Streets. Then, between Burnaby and Parliament Streets, you will come to Chancery Lane on your right, one of the island's nicest hidden attractions, even for nonshoppers. Fagan's Alley, with more small shops, runs from East Reid to Front in the block between Court and King Streets. If you're in the market for art, stop by Crisson and Hind Art Gallery, on the second floor of the Crisson Building on Front Street; The Gallery, in the Emporium Building on Front Street; or the Windjammer, at the corner of Reid and King streets. Bermuda National Gallery is scheduled to be housed in City Hall. The Masterworks Collection, on Front Street, includes the works of well-known and lesser-known international artists who have passed through Bermuda over the years, finding creative inspiration in the island's beauty.

On the eastern outskirts of Hamilton, along the harbor, is the Princess Hotel. It was named in honor of Queen Victoria's daughter, Princess Louise, who visited the island in 1883.

The headquarters of Bacardi Rum, off Pitts Bay Road, has become a favorite spot among Bermudians for taking wedding pictures. Many brides and grooms have stood in front of the waterfall and elaborate fountains with the bright glass and stone building in the background.

For a tasty, casual, homestyle meal (try the fried wahoo, pumpkin, blackeyed peas and rice), stop at the Green Lantern on Serpentine Road between Pitts Bay Road and Rosemont Avenue. Thick shrubbery along the southern part of Pitts Bay Road hides some posh private estates.

From the park at Spanish Point, at the eastern edge of Pembroke, you can look across the Great Sound to the Royal Naval Dockyard (where the Maritime Museum is located), Somerset Village, and the rest of Sandys Parish. After an early Spanish treasure galleon was caught on reefs here, the captain set up a large cross bearing directions to point future visitors toward drinking water. English settlers later mistook the instructions for directions to buried treasure. This spot has been known as Spanish Point ever since. Cobbler's Island is just off the coast. It was here that executed slaves were put on display as a lesson to other black people. Admiralty House Park, a relaxing hideaway, is nearby.

Just north of Hamilton, you can visit the Government Tennis Stadium and play at the club or watch local matches. Also in this area are Black Watch Pass and Well, Pembroke's parish church (St. John's), and Government House, the official residence of the Governor.

East of the city, you can stop at Fort Hamilton for a picnic overlooking the city and harbor.

THE CITY OF HAMILTON

The Bank of Bermuda Ltd. Coin Collection • *mezzanine of the Bank of Bermuda, Front Street, near Par-La-Ville Road; tel: 295–4000* • On display are samples of 17th-century "hog money," the first coins minted for Bermuda and the earliest British colonial currency. The coins bear a picture of the *Sea Venture* on one side and a hog on the other, to commemorate the ship of the early settlers and the wild pigs they found roaming the uninhabited island. You can also see every kind of British coin minted from the beginning of the 17th century to the present, as well as Spanish coins used in colonial Bermuda, and the gold piece from 1666 stamped with an elephant in honor of the African mine where the gold was found. *Exhibition open Mon. through Fri., 9:30 a.m.–3 p.m. Free admission.*

*The Cabinet Building • *Front Street between Parliament and Court Streets; tel: 292–5501* • This Hamilton landmark housing government offices was formerly known as the Colonial Secretariat. Completed in 1836, it is considered by many to be the island's most dignified public building. Along with the landscaped grounds, it occupies the entire block bordered by Front, Parliament, Reid, and Court Streets. Visitors are welcome to the upstairs Council Chamber where the Senate—Bermuda's upper house—meets every Wednesday at 10 a.m., except during the summer. Each November the Convening of Parliament

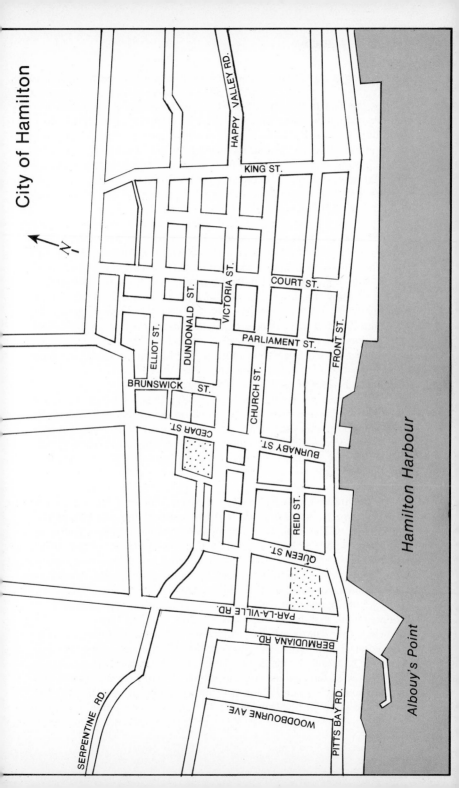

takes place in the Chamber, and the governor gives a speech in front of a carved oak "throne" made in 1642. Similar to Britain's House of Lords, the Senate is considerably less powerful than the House of Assembly, which meets in Sessions House in the block behind the Cabinet Building. Bermuda's soldiers are honored by the Cenotaph Memorial in front of the building. Several members of royalty have visited this site, including the Prince of Wales who laid the cornerstone of the memorial in 1920 (and went on to become Edward VIII, later abdicating to marry Wallis Simpson). *Open Mon. through Fri., 9 a.m.–5 p.m. Closed holidays. Free admission.*

***Sessions House** • *Parliament Street, between Reid and Church streets; 292–7408* • At Sessions House you can observe Bermuda's governing body in action. This country's parliament is the third oldest in the world, preceded by England's and Iceland's. On the second floor of the building, the lower chamber of Parliament and the House of Assembly meet (at 10 a.m. on Fri., except during the summer, and Christmas and Easter weeks). You are welcome to follow lively debates from the visitors' section of the House of Assembly. The cedarwood of the gavel used by the Speaker is more than 350 years old, and the mace carried by the Sergeant-at-Arms dates back to 1921 and is a replica of the James I Mace in the Tower of London.

When Sessions House was built in 1817, it was far less ornate than the present structure. The Jubilee Clock on the outside, along with the Florentine terra-cotta colonnade and towers, were added to commemorate Queen Victoria's Golden Jubilee in 1887. *Open Mon. through Fri., 9 a.m.–5 p.m. Visitors are asked not to appear in jeans, shorts, or beachwear.*

***Bermuda Cathedral** • *Church Street, between Parliament and Burnaby streets; tel: 292–4033* • This imposing Anglican cathedral in the middle of Hamilton is an impressive example of classic Gothic architecture with a special Bermudian flair. Built largely of two of the island's few natural resources, it was constructed of limestone, and its pews were carved from cedar. Crests of shells, palm fronds, cedar shavings, and beans hang on the wall to the left of the main altar. The intricate needlepoint kneeler-cushions were all made by members of the congregation, and the stained-glass Window of Angels was designed by a local artist. The pulpit and lectern are copies of those in St. Giles Cathedral in Edinburgh, and are considered distinctive examples of ecclesiastic sculpture. In addition to the handicrafts of the Children's Chapel in the back of the church, you can see the Warrior Chapel, which honors the country's soldiers, and two throne-chairs for special occasions. Dedicated in 1894, this cathedral is the center of the Church of England in Bermuda. It stands on the site where the original church was destroyed by arson in 1884. *Open daily from 8 a.m.–7 p.m.*

City Hall/Society of Arts • *Church Street, between Wesley Street (an extension of Queen Street) and Washington Street; tel: 292–3824* • If you want to know which way the wind is blowing, look up at the wind clock and the huge weather vane (in the shape of the *Sea Venture*) that adorn the tower of City Hall. Designed by a local architect, the building was completed in 1960 and is surrounded by a small park. City Hall is more than just the headquarters of Hamilton's municipal government. It has a theater where you can attend dramatic productions, films, and concerts (although the acoustics could be better for music) as well as an art gallery where photographs and other artwork are on display. Periodically during the off season (mid-Nov. through March), works of up-and-coming Bermudian artists are exhibited on the grounds outside. City Hall contains a time capsule that is slated to be opened in the year 2019, the colony's 500th anniversary. *City Hall open Mon. through Fri., 9 a.m.–5 p.m. Art Gallery open Mon. through Sat., 10 a.m.–4 p.m., April through November; limited hours on Saturdays December through March. Closed holidays. Free admission.*

Victoria Park • *Victoria Street and Cedar Avenue (an extension of Burnaby Street)* • In the center of Hamilton, this attractive park exemplifies the orderly beauty of the island. A favorite lunchtime spot among Bermudians as well as visitors, it has decorative shrubbery, a sunken garden, well-manicured lawns, and a gazebo where you can attend concerts during the summer.

St. Theresa's Cathedral • *corner of Cedar Avenue and Laffan Street, one block north of Victoria Park; tel: 292–0607* • The architecture and colorful walls of St. Theresa's set it apart from the more common Romanesque and Gothic styles of Roman Catholic cathedrals. Built in 1927, this church is where you can see the gold and silver chalice that Pope Paul VI gave to the Roman Catholic diocese during his visit to Bermuda in 1968. *Open daily, 8 a.m.–5 p.m.*

The Bermuda Library • *Queen Street, near Par-La-Ville Gardens, next to Perot Post Office; tel: 295–2905* • Since 1916 the Bermuda Library has been located next door to Perot Post Office, in the main house of the estate where the city's first postmaster lived with his family. Although in the early days most of the books were of a historical and scientific nature, today there is a wide selection of popular works. There is also a collection of all magazines and newspapers published in Bermuda from as far back as 1787 to the present. In the late 18th century, papers such as the *Royal Gazette* ran advertisements inviting young men looking for adventure to become privateers. The Historical Society Museum is on the first floor of this two-story former home. The large rubber tree between the library and Par-La-Ville Gardens was planted by Perot in 1847. Its branches now reach across the street. *Open Mon. through Thurs., 9:30 a.m.–6 p.m.; Fri. and Sat., until 5 p.m. Closed all holidays.*

Bermuda Historical Society Museum • *Queen Street, near Perot Post Office and Par-La-Ville Gardens; tel: 295–2487* • Don't let the small size fool you. The Historical Society Museum, on the ground floor of the old Perot mansion where the Bermuda Library is located, is full of treasures that will take you back in time. You will see antique silver, china, clothing, and Bermuda cedar furniture, as well as early coins and the sea chest that belonged to Sir George Somers, whose shipwrecked crew colonized the island. In addition to portraits of Sir George and Lady Somers that are hundreds of years old, there is a map of Bermuda thought to have been drawn by Sir George in 1610, and another map drawn several years later by Richard Norwood, who first surveyed Bermuda and divided it into the tribes that are now called parishes. On display as well are models of the three ships—*Sea Venture, Patience,* and *Deliverance*—that played such important roles in Bermuda's history. You can also see a copy of the letter written by George Washington in 1775 asking for gunpowder during the Revolutionary War. (Although loyal to Britain, Bermuda traded the gunpowder for food.) *Open Mon., Tues., Fri., and Sat., 9:30 a.m.–4:30 p.m. Closed 12:30 to 2 for lunch and on all holidays. Free admission, but donations are appreciated.*

Perot Post Office • *Queen Street, facing intersection with Reid Street (just north of the ferry landing and policeman's "birdcage" on Front Street); tel: 295–0880* • Bermuda's first postage stamp was printed by William Bennett Perot, Hamilton's first postmaster, who served for almost half a century. The building that bears his name was his home and the place where townspeople bought their stamps, all handmade and signed by Perot. Although he became the postmaster in 1816, it was not until 1848 that he began printing stamps. He had grown tired of finding that people who came while he was out often neglected to leave enough change with the letters they dropped off. Only 11 of the stamps that solved the problem are known to exist today. Some are part of a collection owned by Queen Elizabeth II. In 1986, a penny stamp made by Perot in 1861 was sold in a New York auction for $92,000.

The small whitewashed building that still serves as a post office was built in 1814, and stands in front of the peaceful Par-La-Ville Gardens once cared for by Perot himself. Next door, in the main house on what was called the Par-La-Ville estate, are the Bermuda Library, the Historical Society Museum, and the Bermuda Archives. *Open Mon. through Fri., 9 a.m.–5 p.m. Closed holidays.*

   ***Par-La-Ville Gardens** • *between Queen Street and Par-La-Ville Road* • This pleasant public park has changed little since the mid-19th century when it was designed and cared for by William Bennett Perot, the city's first postmaster. You can have a quiet picnic lunch in the shade of a palm or golden shower tree surrounded by the colorful flower beds that line the winding paths. The huge rubber tree that was planted by Postmaster Perot in 1847 is said to have disappointed Mark Twain because hot water bottles and rubber boots did not hang from its branches.

OUTSKIRTS OF THE CITY

   ***Admiralty House Park** • *near junction of North Shore and Cox Hill Roads* • The two small, secluded beaches here have nice views of a cove bordered by rugged cliffs. The spacious park, with lush, varied foliage, makes a trip here especially worthwhile. At the entrance are maps that outline a fitness program you can participate in while walking along the park's trail.

   Black Watch Pass and Well • *intersection of Black Watch Pass and North Shore Road* • Before 1934 horses and wagons traveling between Hamilton and the north shore had to struggle over a steep hill. Now you can reach North Shore Road from the city on level ground and in no time at all by cycle or car. Driving north, you will pass through what appears to be a natural tunnel. Actually, this glistening solid archway was created by the famous Scottish regiment, the Black Watch, who cut 85,000 cubic yards of rock from the side of a cliff. During the drought of 1849, they also built a well at the northern end of the passage for the poor and their cattle. The well is still in use.

   ***Fort Hamilton** • *Happy Valley Road, approach from Victoria and King Streets* • Like Fort Scaur in Sandys Parish, this fort was built as part of the defense plan of the Duke of Wellington (famous for his role in Napoleon's defeat at Waterloo). Along with several others built here during this period, Fort Hamilton was outdated by the time it was finished (in 1889), and was never used to defend the island. It was restored in 1963, after having been closed for many years because of unsafe conditions. Now the well-cared-for grounds offer an exciting perch from which to gaze down on the city of Hamilton and its busy harbor. The dry moat has been transformed into a colorful, thriving garden, and the cannons, battlements, and twisting underground tunnels are a lesson in

Victorian history. On the upper level, you can relax on one of the benches on the grassy slope. You can also visit the tea shop for lunch or a light snack. On Mondays at noon during the off season (mid-Nov. through March), the fort is alive with the sounds of a skirling ceremony, the official playing of bagpipes accompanied by Highland dancers and drummers. *Open daily, except Sat., 9:30 a.m.–5 p.m. Free admission.*

DEVONSHIRE

Devonshire is the place to go for peace and quiet. Bordered by Paget, Pembroke, and Smith's, it is one of the more tranquil parishes. It has no restaurants or hotels, only a cottage colony and a handful of guest houses and housekeeping units. Its colorful houses are scattered throughout the green hilly countryside. The gardens, 19-acre arboretum, marshes, and nature reserve as well as the historic church are popular sights. If you are staying in a housekeeping apartment, you can buy fresh fish at Devonshire Dock, on the northern shore near Pembroke. The parish also has a public 9-hole golf course at the Ocean View Golf and Country Club.

Not far from 18th-century Old Devonshire Church on Middle Road is Devonshire Marsh, called a "brackish pond" by Bermudians. In this parish that has so much water it was once called Brackish Pond itself, a distillation plant and underground wells supply much of the freshwater for the whole island. Off South Shore Road is more marshland at Edmund Gibbons Nature Reserve, the home of various species of birds and rare plants.

The cottage colony, Ariel Sands Beach Club, is on the south shore, a short distance from Palm Grove Garden, a private garden open to the public. Walk through the Chinese Moongate for good luck, then visit the garden behind a striking old home facing South Shore Road.

Children can go horseback riding at Lee Bow Riding Centre, which caters to those aged 18 and under.

A painless way to learn about Bermuda's cultural roots is to visit Devonshire's nightclub, the Clay House Inn, on North Shore Road. Its popular show features Afro-Caribbean music and dance, including limbo and a steel band. Music ranges from lively calypso to jazz and spirited renditions of selections from Handel's *Messiah*. Popular international entertainers also appear here on occasion.

Devonshire Dock • *North Shore Road, just east of Dock Hill Road, near the border with Pembroke Parish* • In the afternoon as fishermen return from the sea, this is the perfect place to buy dinner if you are staying in a housekeeping apartment or renting a private home. If catching your own is more your style, you can buy fresh bait from the fishermen if you arrive by 10 a.m. During the War of 1812, this was the romantic spot where British soldiers and local women danced to fiddles every day. Standing at the beginning of the dock and looking out at the ocean, you will see the same view that is captured in a painting that hangs in Verdmont, the lovely old mansion you can visit in nearby Smith's Parish.

Old Devonshire Church • *Middle Road, 2 miles east of the city of Hamilton; tel: 292–1348* • From the outside, this church looks like an old Bermudian cottage. It is so small that it resembles a rectory, and the new Devonshire Church beside it is often mistaken for it by visitors. Old Devonshire Church was built of limestone and cedar in 1716 on the site of a church constructed in 1623. The huge bolts and ships' timbers inside are examples of the contributions of Bermudian shipbuilders. Because of extensive fire damage caused by an Easter Sunday explosion in 1970, what you will see for the most part is a faithful reconstruction of the early 18th-century church. Fortunately, however, a number of important relics survived the blaze, including the oldest piece of church silver in Bermuda, a beaker dating back to 1590; and the oldest chancel screen on the island. Look for the Slaves' Gallery, built by slaves themselves. Each year, on the Sunday before Christmas, you can attend a candlelight carol service here. *Open daily, 9 a.m.–5 p.m.*

*Palm Grove Gardens • *South Road, just west of Devonshire Bay Road, near Brighton Hill Road* • These lush gardens are behind a traditional old mansion that faces South Road. Even the servants' quarters of this private estate are beautiful. In addition to caged tropical birds, there is a grass map of Bermuda growing in a pond and a wishing well. Honeymooners often walk through the Chinese moongate and make a wish. *Open Mon. through Fri., 9 a.m.–5 p.m. Closed holidays.*

Palmetto House • *North Shore Rd.; tel: 295–9941* • This 18th-century mansion, in the shape of a cross, has three rooms on view, furnished with fine examples of Bermudian furniture and decor. *Open Thurs. from 10 a.m. to 5 p.m. with no admission fee.*

Edmund Gibbons Nature Reserve • *South Road, west of the junction with Collector's Hill* • This marshland is the home of a variety of birds and rare species of flora native to Bermuda. The reserve was given to the Bermuda National Trust by the heirs of Edmund Gibbons, the man who preserved the land. Visitors are asked not to enter the marshy area. *Open daily. Free admission.*

SMITH'S

In Smith's, history buffs can be transported to the 17th century for a glimpse of the wealthy at home. Would-be fishermen can "catch" sharks while bird watchers wander through two nature reserves. Mystery lovers can try to figure out the origin of 400-year-old initials carved into a rock.

Along with its northern and southern oceanfronts, Smith's has a third shore on Harrington Sound, which is really a 6-mile salt water lake. If you want to stay at a housekeeping apartment, you have a few to choose from here, but there is only one hotel and one cottage colony.

Near the western border of the parish is Collector's Hill, named in honor of the tax collector who lived on it. This hill is where you will find the 17th-century mansion called Verdmont, Bermuda's most beautifully preserved old home. The Oriental Room and the nursery with its antique toys are two rooms you should not miss. This house, which is now a museum, gives the full flavor of how well-to-do Bermudians lived hundreds of years ago.

Located in the northern part of Smith's, Flatts Village, with pretty houses and tall palms, has quieted down considerably since the 17th and 18th centuries. In its heyday, the village was popular with smugglers. They would unload their ships here at night, unbeknownst to customs officials, who were in St. George's.

St. Mark's Road, which connects Verdmont and South Shore Roads, meanders over and around hills with farms, spacious estates, and great views of the south shore. On South Shore Road, just east of its intersection with St. Mark's Road, is St. Mark's Church. If you experience deja vu, you have probably been to Devonshire. St. Mark's, Smith's Parish church, is almost an exact replica of Old Devonshire Church. Spittal Pond is comprised of 60 acres near the southern shore. You may stumble onto a seafront cave here called Jeffrey's Hole, named after the runaway slave who once hid in it. The cave's opening is at the top of a cliff.

Between Spittal Pond and the shore, you will come upon Spanish Rock. For centuries, historians have been arguing whether the initials carved in the rock in 1543 are those of an early Spanish explorer or one from Portugal.

Farther east, right after Harrington Sound Road meets Knapton Hill Road, is Devil's Hole. Once a cave, it is now a deep pool where you can fish—with baited but hookless lines. You won't really catch anything—just a nibble before the fish swims away.

On the opposite shore (south shore) is John Smith's Bay. Just before the eastern border of Smith's is North Nature Reserve, at the western edge of Mangrove Lake. Here you will see a variety of animal and plant life, such as mangrove trees growing in a salty pond.

Verdmont House • *Verdmont Road, at top of Collector's Hill; tel: 236–7369* • This 17th-century mansion, where candelight concerts are held several times a year, is considered the most important of the Bermuda National Trust historic houses. It contains a wealth of Bermudian and English antique furniture and artifacts. Some historians believe it was built in 1662 by the three-time Bermuda governor, William Sayle, who founded Eleuthera in The Bahamas and colonized part of South Carolina. Others think that the land on which the house was to be built was bought by John Dickinson—with Arabian gold from pirateering—toward the end of the 17th century. At any rate, the house has been standing for more than three centuries, and although much of its furniture has been acquired by the Trust over the years, the mansion itself has changed little. Its last occupant was an eccentric woman who lived there for 75 years, until 1953, but never installed plumbing or electricity.

Notice the unusual double roof, the only one in Bermuda. Double chimneys at each end of the house enable all rooms to have fireplaces. The small crannies between the spacious fireplaces are called powder rooms because they were where people went to powder their wigs. The cedar staircase, held together by wooden pegs, is thought to be one of the best-made on the island. The walls of the house are decorated with oil portraits by John Green, a Bermudian official who owned the mansion during the late 18th century. You can see his smiling miniature self-portrait in the dining room on the ground floor. From the dining room doorway, the kitchen and slave quarters can be seen in separate buildings. They have been remodeled to serve as a residence for the curator.

In a chest at the foot of the 18th-century daybed in one of the upstairs rooms, you'll find a collection of antique clothing. Handpainted china is displayed in another room. The nursery, with its old toys, dolls, books, and cedar cradle, is a special treat. For a stunning view of the ocean, stand on the pleasant little second-floor balcony. You may also be able to see cattle grazing in the distance. *Open Mon. through Sat., 10 a.m.–5 p.m. Closed for lunch. Admission: $3; under age 12: 75¢.*

Spittal Pond • *South Road (just north of Spanish Rock)* • Encompassing almost 60 acres, this is considered the most impressive of the Bermuda National Trust's open spaces. It is the island's largest wildlife sanctuary, and from November to May about 25 species of waterfowl drop by for visits. Keep an eye out for the pretty bright orange and black crabs that scutter in and out of holes. *Free admission. Visitors are asked to remain on the pathways.*

Spanish Rock ● *off South Road, south of Spittal Pond, about 1½ miles east of Collector's Hill Road* ● On a high bluff overlooking the ocean sits a rock that caused a controversy for centuries. (Ask a Bermudian to show you the location.) Actually, it is the initials of the inscription on the rock that left historians and scholars arguing. While the cross and date (1543) were clear when the inscription was discovered by early settlers, the letters were illegible, having been badly eroded by the elements. For years the carving—which could be FK, JR, or RP—was thought by some to have been done by a 16th-century Spanish explorer. But many experts now believe that it must have been the work of one of the 32 Portuguese sailors who survived a shipwreck in 1543 on their way home from Santo Domingo in the Caribbean. The letters could be RP, for "Rex Portugaliae" and the cross, a badge of the Portuguese Order of Christ. After an unsuccessful attempt to protect the carving from further erosion, a bronze casting of it was put in its place.

Devil's Hole ● *Harrington Sound Road; tel: 293–2072* ● Since 1830, visitors have been coming to this collapsed cave where underground passages from the sea have created a deep pool. Soon after the owner began showing it that year, its popularity convinced him to start charging admission. Fish were stored here by the first colonists, who called it "Devil's Hole" because they thought the breeze rushing through it sounded like the devil's voice. It has been used as a natural aquarium since 1847, and now has about 400 fish, such as sharks and giant groupers, as well as moray eels and massive green turtles. You can feel the tug of one of these creatures at the end of one of the baited but hookless lines provided. Because this is a fish preserve, you cannot take any of the inhabitants home. *Open daily 10 a.m.–5 p.m. (January through February open Mon. through Fri. 1–5 p.m.; Sat., Sun., and holidays 10 a.m.–5 p.m.) Closed Christmas Day, Good Friday. Admission: Adults—$3.50; children between age 6 and 12, $2; age 5 and under, 50¢.*

North Nature Reserve ● *at the western end of Mangrove Lake (across the road from Pink Beach Club and Cottages)* ● This Bermuda National Trust property is an unusual area where mangrove trees grow in a brackish (salty) pond. The pond attracts several species of birds, and is filled with water fauna and flora of special interest to scientists.

HAMILTON PARISH

There is a lot to keep you busy in Hamilton, including the popular Aquarium. Bordering most of Harrington Sound, this sprawling parish also has both northern and southern coasts on the Atlantic. Not only does Hamilton offer many attractions and a great deal of pastoral beauty above ground, but visitors can also enjoy the island's subterranean wonders.

The eastern part of the parish, along Castle Harbour, has many underground caves, several of which are open to the public. Most are known only to Bermudians, who will tell the adventurous how to slither up and down ropes and avoid poison ivy when entering. Crystal Caves and Amber Caves of Leamington are two that are perfectly safe and are entered by stairs or ramps. At both, guides will show you clear lakes surrounded by huge, unspoiled stalagmites and stalactites, about 100 feet below the ground. At the Grotto Bay Beach and Tennis Club, one has been used as a discotheque called Prospero's. The beautifully kept hotel grounds are thriving with a variety of trees and smaller plants, and the view of the water is striking. Another grotto on the hotel's property, is Cathedral Cave, which you must crawl around in and can only see with the permission of the management. Unless you are a grotto aficionado, a visit to Crystal Caves, the most spectacular of public caves, should suffice.

To commune with monkeys, giant turtles, birds, and more than 70 species of sea animals, visit the Bermuda Aquarium, Museum, and Zoo, on Sound Road. Taking North Shore Road out of Smith's, you will come to the North Shore's longest beach, at Shelly Bay, named after one of the *Sea Venture* passengers. For 200 years, beginning in the 17th century, shipbuilding flourished in this area.

Farther along the road, near Bailey's Bay, is Crawl Hill, one of the highest points in the parish. The name comes from the word "kraal," a pen used to hold captured fish and turtles before they were sold. From here you will have an eye-catching view in all directions. When you come to the top of Cottage Hill, you will be at the highest point on the road between this parish and St. George's.

Attractive estates with lush gardens are along both Fractious Street and Wilkinson Avenue. On Blue Hole Hill, you will see the Swizzle Inn, popular with cyclists who stop for Rum Swizzles—one of the island's most requested drinks. The swizzleburgers are also hot items here, along with the soups, omelets, chili, fish and chips, salads, and sandwiches on the menu. Business cards of patrons are plastered all over the restaurant. Across the street is Bailey's Ice Cream Parlour, an old-fashioned spot where homemade ice cream and even Swizzle sherbet is served.

Be careful when you come to the junction of North Shore Road, Wilkinson Avenue, and Blue Hole Road, since it is one of Bermuda's busiest intersections. This is where the Bermuda Perfumery and Gardens is located. Visitors can buy perfume after learning and smelling how it is made.

Just south of the Grotto Bay Beach hotel are Crystal Caves and the adjacent branch of Trimingham's department store. At Walsingham Bay is Tom Moore's Tavern, now a gourmet restaurant. Unfortunately, the famed calabash tree, under which the Irish poet Tom Moore used to write at the turn of the century, fell victim to Hurricane Emily in September 1987. At the Amber Caves of Leamington you can dine at the Plantation Restaurant.

The Marriott chain has restored the fortresslike former Castle Harbour Hotel and Golf Club nearby. A new wing was built into the hillside and the 18-hole golf course designed by Robert Trent Jones has been refurbished. Stop here for another dramatic view of the harbor.

The Southern portion of Hamilton is sandwiched between Smith's and an isolated part of St. George's. Half of the Mid Ocean Golf Course is here, as well as Mangrove Lake and Trott's Pond, two flora and fauna filled brackish ponds.

*Bermuda Aquarium, Museum, and Zoo • *Sound Road; tel: 293–2727* • Adults as well as children will enjoy this exciting assortment of marine life, tropical animals, and even an authentic sunken treasure. As you move from tank to tank in the Aquarium holding a "listening wand" to your ear, you will learn all about the creatures in their natural-looking habitats and you'll even hear some of the sounds they make. There are several hundred specimens here, about 75 species, ranging from sharks and a long moray eel to tiny seahorses, sea anemones, live coral, and sponges. Walk through the Natural History Museum with exhibits of the island's unusual geological development and ecosystem. You can admire multicolored shells, thousand-year-old fossils, a huge topographical map of Bermuda, and a treasure from a wrecked pirate ship. Animals in the outdoor zoo include cockatoos, flamingos, monkeys, and alligators. The giant tortoises from the Galapagos Islands are some of the most striking animals here. *Open daily, 9 a.m.–4:30 p.m. Closed Christmas Day. Admission: Adults–$3.50; children age 7–16–50¢; children under 7–free.*

The Bermuda Perfumery and Gardens • *Bailey's Bay, intersection of North Shore Road, Wilkinson Avenue and Blue Hole Hill; tel: 293–0627* • Not only is this factory located in a house two centuries old, but is also adjoined by fragrant gardens where you can see and smell the raw materials—jasmine, oleander, frangipani, lilies. During a short guided tour, you'll learn how perfume used to be made in Bermuda (using flowers and animal fat). Then you'll have a firsthand glimpse of the modern chemical distillation process and watch the packing and bottling being done by hand. Although perfume-making in Bermuda is seasonal, ending after Easter, you can tour the factory and buy reasonably priced samples of the sweet fragrances year-round. *Open Mon. through Sat., 9 a.m.–5 p.m. (closes at 4:30 p.m. Nov. to March); Sundays, open 10 a.m.–4 p.m. Closed holidays. Free admission.*

*Crystal Caves • *Wilkinson Avenue, Bailey's Bay; tel: 293–0640* • Mark Twain wrote in 1908 that this was "the most beautiful cave in the world." In and around a clear subterranean lake are millions of stalactites (hanging from the ceiling) and stalagmites (coming up from the ground). These fantastic greenish-white formations were created by eons of dripping water, which you can still hear as the process continues. As rain filters through the ground above, it picks up lime, calcium, and iron. Drops of water deposit the minerals in the caves, forming this living stone, which grows a mere cubic inch every 100 years. This eerie wonderland, 120 feet below the ground, was discovered in 1907 when two young boys lost their ball down a hole and burrowed after it. Steps and a long ramp now give visitors access. Before the wooden pontoon bridge was built over the lake, which rises and falls with the Castle Harbour tides, visitors crossed the cavern by boat. Your guide will point out formations such as one that looks a lot like a sculptured poodle. When the lights are turned off, you will see a glowing group of stalagmites resembling Manhattan's skyline. A fossil of Bermuda's only indigenous bird, the cahow, was once found here. (Cahows raise their young in burrows in the ground and are nearly extinct.) *Daily tours, 9 a.m.–4:30 p.m., including holidays, except Christmas Day. Admission: Adults–$3; children aged 5–11–$1; children under 4–free.*

Tom Moore's Tavern (Walsingham) • *Harrington Sound Road, Walsingham's Bay (near Leamington Caves)* • Tom Moore, the Irish poet who lived in Bermuda in 1804, visited this old house so often that many think he owned it. However, local historians say that the house, built by a relative of the Earl of Warwick in 1652, was owned by the Trott family. For quite some time it was a tavern where guests could enjoy a drink or a meal. After being closed for years, it has reopened as a gourmet restaurant. The new owners have gone to great lengths to restore it faithfully. Nearby are several small pools fed by underground streams. There is also a lake, caves, and a tiny jungle.

Amber Caves of Leamington • *Harrington Sound Road, Bailey's Bay; tel: 293–0336* • Not as large or quite as spectacular as Crystal Caves, Leamington Caves were discovered in 1908 when a boy noticed a small opening on the hillside that he and his father were preparing to plough. Ten years later the caves were opened to the public. Here you can see amber-tinted stalagmites and stalactites that look remarkably like a frozen waterfall, diving fish, and the Statue of Liberty, to name a few. Upstairs, you can have a pleasant meal or a drink at the Plantation Club. *Open Mon. through Sat., 9:30 a.m.–4:30 p.m. Closed holidays and Dec. through Feb. Admission: Adults–$3; children under 12– $1.50; children under 4–free.*

ST. GEORGE'S

To understand how Bermuda got to be the way it is today, visitors can begin by absorbing the history of St. George's. In 1609, off St. Catherine's Point, at the northeastern tip of the parish, the early English settlers were shipwrecked on these uninhabited shores. Their vessel, the *Sea Venture,* was one of 7 ships headed for Virginia's Jamestown Colony when it was dashed on the reefs here. All 150 passengers were led safely ashore by the admiral, Sir George Somers, and Sir Thomas Gates. They remained long enough to build two new ships, the *Deliverance* and the *Patience,* on which they finally reached Jamestown.

Two years later, the same company sent another group of settlers on the *Plough* to this Atlantic island. In 1612 they founded a town, and called it St. George's in honor of Sir George Somers and the patron saint of England. St. George's remained Bermuda's capital until 1815 when the seat of government was moved to the city of Hamilton. After hundreds of years, the town of St. George—a striking contrast to Hamilton—is very much the way it was in the 17th century.

St. George's is the colony's most widely spread-out parish. It is comprised mainly of two large islands north of Castle Harbour that are connected to each other by a bridge, and to the mainland by a causeway. Exclusive Tucker's Town is on the southern side of the harbor. The lower of the two islands is almost completely occupied by Bermuda's Civil Air Terminal and the U.S. Naval Air Station.

On the northern island, the historic town of St. George's overlooks St. George's Harbour. A walk around the island's original capital will take you through narrow, picturesque, hilly streets with names such as Featherbed Alley, Aunt Peggy's Lane, Needle and Thread Alley, Duke of York Street, and Shinbone Alley. According to one story, Silk Alley, also known as Petticoat Lane, was named because 17th-century women slaves used to walk up and down it rustling their petticoats. Others say the street got its name after Emancipation, when freed black women proudly showed off their newly acquired silk undergarments.

King's Square is the focal point of the town. Look out for the Town Crier in 17th-century garb. Many visitors photograph each other in the stocks and pillory, replicas of those once used to punish gossips and people who cursed. Surrounding the square are the White Horse Tavern, where diners look out on the harbor; the Confederate Museum, with exhibits that tell of Bermuda's support of the South during the American Civil War; Pub on the Square Restaurant; Town Hall, headquarters of the local government and the multimedia show called "Bermuda Journey"; and the Visitors' Service Bureau, where you can get maps and other information. Across the bridge to Ordnance Island are the ducking stool and a life-size bronze statue of Sir George Somers. On this island visitors can explore the replica of the early settlers' ship, the *Deliverance*.

Just east of the square is 18th-century Tucker House, with its collection of antique Bermuda silver and furniture. This home of the prominent Tucker family was also the home of Joseph Rainey, a freed American slave who lived in Bermuda before returning to the South to become the first black member of the U.S. House of Representatives.

After a multi-million dollar restoration of 19th-century colonial buildings, the Somers Wharf area contains shops and restaurants, as well as the Carriage Museum.

On Duke of York Street, north of King's Square, is beautiful St. Peter's Church, built on the site of what is probably the oldest Anglican church in the Western hemisphere. Many visitors find that taking pictures of this simple whitewashed building is hard to resist. On the way into St. George's from Fort St. Catherine, you will pass an overgrown church ruin where dug-up bones solved a 100-year-old mystery. This church was begun in order to replace the deteriorating St. Peter's, then abandoned when St. Peter's was restored.

In 1801 a Methodist minister was fined and sent to jail for preaching the gospel to black people in front of St. George's Historical Museum on Featherbed Alley. In addition to antique furniture, documents, and paintings, the museum contains a rare Bible and an original 18th-century kitchen.

So that Sir George Somers could be in two places at once, his heart was buried where pretty Somers Gardens are located, and his body was sent back to England. Every April at nearby Old State House, Bermudians and visitors come to see the elaborate Peppercorn Ceremony, when a rent of one peppercorn is paid to the Governor.

At Fort St. Catherine, at the northeastern tip of the parish, there are dioramas of milestones in Bermudian history. This is the largest of Bermuda's forts and overlooks the reefs where the *Sea Venture* was shipwrecked.

St. David's Island is located on the northeastern end of the parish's southern island. The people of this seafaring area live in a historically isolated community. Many of them still think of the rest of Bermuda as "up de country." A portion of the population is made up of descendants of American Indians, mainly Pequot. Two popular local restaurants are worth a visit: the Black Horse Tavern and Dennis' Hideaway, both overlooking the water. Dennis' is known for Bermudian specialties including shark hash on toast, conch fritters, and fish chowder.

In the 19th century, Smith's Island to the west was the center of the colony's whaling activity. A story has it that a man from St. David's ended doubts about a whale's stomach being large enough to accommodate a human by crawling inside one himself. He found it quite roomy.

If you befriend a Bermudian with a boat, you might try to convince him or her to take you to Nonsuch Island in Castle Harbour, a sanctuary for the rare cahow bird. Across Castle Harbour is Tucker's Town, where half of the Mid Ocean Club and Golf Course is located. Tucker's Town was undeveloped until the 1920's when a steamship company bought some of the land to build the club and golf course. This area soon became a community for the wealthy and Bermuda's most exclusive neighborhood. Some Bermudians consider this area part of Hamilton Parish, although according to maps it is part of St. George's.

THE TOWN OF ST. GEORGE'S

*King's Square • *center of the Town of St. George's* • Here in the center of town you can sentence yourself to a few moments of fun in the stocks and pillory, cedar replicas of those that once stood in the square. Seventeenth-century townspeople landed themselves here by being caught gossiping, nagging, missing church, or cursing. Across the bridge on Ordnance Island, you'll see the ducking stool, another 17th-century humiliating and less-than-comfortable form of punishment. This is also where you'll find Bermuda's only statue, of Sir George Somers. King's Square, which has changed little since it was built, is on the waterfront. It is bordered by buildings including the Confederate Museum, Town Hall, and the Visitors' Service Bureau.

The Confederate Museum • *Duke of York Street; tel: 297–1423* • The Globe Hotel, now the museum, was once the headquarters of the Confederate representative in Bermuda. It was from St. George's that ships filled with armaments ran the blockade to the Southern states during the American Civil War. Bermuda's slaves had been freed in 1834, three decades before abolition in the United States; however, this did not stop most of the island from supporting the Confederacy for economic reasons. (St. George's had been ailing since the capital was moved to Hamilton in 1815.) The museum contains exhibits about the short-lived period when St. George's flourished during the war. *Open Mon.*

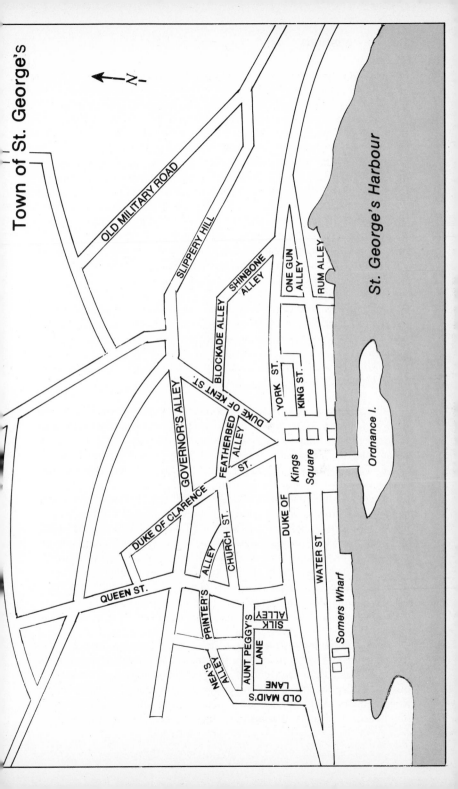

through Sat., 10 a.m.–5 p.m. Closed holidays. Admission: adults–$2.50; children under age 12–$1.00.

Town Hall • *King's Square* • Built in 1782, Town Hall is faithfully restored, with a great deal of cedar woodwork and furniture. It is still used as the headquarters of the local government. The seating arrangement of the officials reflects their positions: the mayor's chair is on the highest platform, the aldermen's chairs on a lower platform, and the councilmen's chairs on the lowest. In the 19th century, townspeople were victims of a hoax when a traveling "professor" invited them to a performance of "Ali Baba and the Forty Thieves" that he said he was staging here. As the audience waited for the show to begin, the "professor" was in another part of town stealing a safe that had been left unguarded. The angry and disappointed audience was especially pleased when he was later caught.

*Bermuda Journey • *Town Hall; tel: 297–0526* • Created by the makers of "The New York Experience" and "South Street Seaport Experience," this flashy 30-minute multi-media presentation covers Bermuda's history, culture, and heritage as well as its scenic attractions. *Open Mon. through Sat., 9 a.m. to 4 p.m. Closed holidays. Admission: $4 for adults; $2 for senior citizens and children under 12.*

*Deliverance II • *Ordnance Island, across the short bridge from King's Square* • After Sir George Somers and his crew were shipwrecked on the island's reefs in the *Sea Venture* in 1609, they came ashore and built Bermuda's first vessels, the *Deliverance* and the *Patience*. The *Deliverance,* the larger of the two, was made on St. George's Island from materials salvaged from the *Sea Venture* as well as from local cedar. Although the *Patience* was the ship constructed on Ordnance Island, this is where you can now climb aboard a full-scale replica of the *Deliverance.* In 1610 about 150 people sailed from Bermuda to Jamestown, their original destination, in the two new ships. An exploration of the *Deliverance* replica will give you a good idea of how crowded it must have been. Inside you can see wax figures dressed in period clothing. On display are also objects the early settlers brought from England. *Open daily, 10 a.m.–4 p.m. Admission: adults–$2.50; children under age 12–50¢.*

*Tucker House • *Water Street, just west of Queen Street; tel: 297–0545* • Built in 1711, this cottage became the home of members of the distinguished Tucker family in 1775. With relatives living in South Carolina and Virginia, the Tuckers were bitterly divided over the American Revolutionary War. Colonel Henry Tucker, the father of the owner of this house, tried to remain neutral. But after the American Continental

Congress ordered a halt to the exportation of food to any British colonies, he decided to act against his Mother Country. Without the knowledge of Bermuda's governor (a relative by marriage), Colonel Tucker led a group of prominent Bermudians to Philadelphia to offer salt in exchange for the supplies on which Bermuda was so dependent. But because what the Americans wanted was gun powder, not salt, they were turned down. Then one summer night in 1775, a large store of gun powder from St. George's was secretly loaded onto two American warboats in Tobacco Bay. The Governor was livid, of course, when he heard about the theft, and suspected the Tucker family. However, since the island was supplied with food throughout the war, there was no serious attempt to expose those involved in the crime.

Tucker House was also the home of Joseph Hayne Rainey, a former South Carolinian slave who rented the present kitchen. During the Civil War, he came to St. George's to get away from the South. While his wife became a dressmaker, he set up a barber shop in what is now the Joseph Rainey Memorial Room. When the war ended, he returned to the United States to be elected the first black member of the House of Representatives, during Reconstruction. A lane outside the kitchen door was named Barber's Alley in his honor.

The restored interior of this Bermuda National Trust property contains antique silver and furniture, a pearl wedding necklace strung on a rope made of human hair, and a 17th-century Cromwellian lantern clock, built with only one hand on its face to point to the hour. *Open Mon. through Sat., 10 a.m.–5 p.m. Closed for lunch and holidays. Admission: Adults–$2.50; children under age 12–75¢.*

*The Carriage Museum • *Water Street; tel: 297–1367* • Here on display are the elegant vehicles that Bermudians used before 1946, when the first private cars came to the island. These carriages range from a huge, high four-horse carriage to a child's two wheeler that was pulled by a pony. These predecessors of the automobile stand in stalls in much the same way as they would have been parked years ago. You can even climb into one and be transported into the past. Along with the Carriage House Restaurant and renovations of other landmarks on Somers Wharf, the museum is part of a multimillion dollar development program. *Open Mon. through Sat., 9 a.m.–5 p.m. Closed holidays. Donations accepted.*

St. George's Library • *Stuart Hall, Aunt Peggy's Lane; tel: 297–1912* • Any of this public library's cedar-beamed rooms is a relaxing place to sit and read. The library is located in a house built around 1706, and most of the furniture was made in Bermuda. *Open Mon., Wed., and Sat., 9 a.m.–5 p.m. Closed 1–2 p.m. for lunch, and all holidays.*

The Old Rectory • *Broad Alley (just north of St. Peter's Church)* • Said to have been built by a reformed pirate in 1705, this timber and stone cottage served as the rectory of the Reverend Alexander Richardson, a much-loved Irish bishop. A story has it that Rev. Richardson once preached an impassioned sermon against officials who refused to pay for a stranger's funeral. The rectory is now owned by the Bermuda National Trust. *Open Wed. and Sat., 10 a.m.–4 p.m. Closed one hour for lunch. Admission: free, but donations are welcome.*

*St. Peter's Church • *Duke of York Street (across from the Confederate Museum); tel: 297–8359* • St. Peter's stands on what is thought to be the site of the oldest Anglican church in the Western hemisphere. The first meeting of the island's Parliament took place here in 1620. In the present structure, built in 1713, you can see the original altar, first used in 1624. A silver communion service presented to the church by King William III in 1697 is still used regularly. Two bitter enemies gave the brass chandeliers hanging over the center aisle. The simple whitewashed building, with the long, wide brick staircase leading up to its rich brown cedar doors, is one of the most photographed sights in Bermuda. Look for famous names in the main graveyard, such as the American naval officer Richard Dale, who was killed in the final battle of the War of 1812; and Governor Sir Richard Sharples and his aide, Captain Hugh Sayers, who were assassinated in 1973. You can also visit the slaves' burial ground, a small area west of the main churchyard, where some of the graves bear first names only. *Open daily, 9 a.m.–5 p.m. Guide on duty, except Sun. and holidays.*

The Unfinished Church • *off Duke of Kent Street and Slippery Hill Road (on Barracks Hill)* • In 1874 this church was begun to replace the nearby deteriorating St. Peter's, the oldest church in Bermuda. When the foundations were being dug, something frightful was uncovered: the skeleton of a guard who had been murdered while on duty one summer night a hundred years earlier. He had disappeared that hot night during the American Revolution when the colony's store of gunpowder was stolen and loaded onto American ships—in exchange for food for Bermuda. But no church was ever completed above this once secret grave. Before it was finished, a means to restore St. Peter's was discovered, and the new church was left to become the verdant, picturesque ruin it is today. A local joke provides another explanation for this church's abandoned state: While it was being constructed, the minister was given a large sum of money and sent off to buy stained glass and other supplies. . . . Everyone is still waiting for him to return.

Featherbed Alley Print Shop • *Featherbed Alley, between Duke of Kent and Duke of Clarence streets; tel: 297–0009* • Located in a former home along with St. George's Historical Society Museum, the print shop contains a working 18th-century press. The printer invites visitors to help him print leaflets. *Open Mon. through Sat., 10 a.m.–4 p.m.; closed holidays. Free admission.*

St. George's Historical Society Museum • *Featherbed Alley, between Duke of Kent and Duke of Clarence Streets. (Shares the building with the print shop.); tel: 297–0423* • Built in 1725, this former home contains an original 18th-century kitchen and pantry with cooking utensils from that period hanging over the fireplace. You can also see antique furniture, china, documents, and paintings, much of which is said to have been acquired by privateers and pirates. In addition to a rare Bible printed in 1644 and a blubber cutter once used by Bermudian whalers, there are axe heads made by North American Indians, some of whom were early settlers of St. David's Island.

In 1801 John Stephenson, a Methodist missionary, was fined and imprisoned for preaching to black people in front of this building. Not giving in, he continued to preach to them from his cell window (in the basement of the building that is now the town post office). *Open Mon. through Sat., 10 a.m.–4 p.m.; closed holidays. Admission: $1; 50¢ for children under age 16. Free for children under 6.*

Somers Gardens • *Duke of York Street* • This small park, with its ornamental trees, indigenous flowers, and shrubbery, was once swampland. The memorial here honors Sir George Somers, whose shipwrecked *Sea Venture* crew helped him settle the island when they discovered it in 1609. Somers and his men finally reached their original destination, Jamestown, on the *Deliverance* and the *Patience,* but found the colonists there starving. Somers died in 1610, shortly after returning to Bermuda for food for the American colonists. While his body was taken back to England, his heart was buried where this quiet park is located. A life-size statue of him stands on Ordnance Island. *Open daily, 7:30 a.m.–4:30 p.m.*

Old State House • *Princess Street* • This limestone building, with mortar made of turtle oil and lime, was constructed in 1619, and is believed to be the first stone building in Bermuda. Parliament met here for years, until the capital was moved to Hamilton in 1815. Since then, the building has been rented by members of the Masonic Lodge, who pay the government a token one peppercorn a year in an elaborate ceremony every April. *Open Wed. from 10 a.m. to 4 p.m. Free admission.*

Bridge House • *Kings Square (diagonally across from Old State House)* • An art gallery can now be found in this 18th-century former home. The house got its name because a small bridge once stretched across a creek in front of it. (The creek has been filled in.) The building is owned by the Bermuda National Trust.

Bermuda Biological Station • *Ferry Reach, St. George's; tel: 297–1880 Ext. 211* • This oceanographic research facility, founded in 1903, conducts tours of its operations each Wednesday morning at 10 A.M. Its marine science reference library is used by scientists and students from around the world. In addition to labs, there is a simulated coral reef, microscopic marine life, and the research ship, *R/V Weatherbird*. Coffee and cookies are served to visitors as they gather.

OUTSIDE TOWN

Natural Arches • These two 35-foot-tall stone arches rise from the beach near Tucker's Town. For hundreds of thousands of years the relatively soft limestone here has been pounded by the ocean and hit by winds to create this striking natural sculpture. The arches were once caves whose walls and ceilings collapsed, weakened by centuries of powerful waves.

They are located at the end of South Road, Tucker's Town (next to the Mid Ocean Beach Club). Directions: Turn right at the bus stop near the end of South Road and follow signs to "Natural Arches" and "Castle Harbour Beach." At the end of this road, walk to the left of the building on the sandy path. Go up a slight incline for about 50 yards until you are as close as you can get to the ocean. You will see the arches below you to the right.

*Fort St. Catherine • *overlooking St. Catherine Beach; tel: 297–1920* • If you visit only one of the island's many forts, it should be this one. Not only is it the largest in Bermuda, but it also overlooks the reefs where the *Sea Venture* was shipwrecked in 1609, and the beach where the first settlers came ashore. Above and underground you can see dioramas of important moments in Bermudian history, reproductions of the British Crown Jewels, a display of guns used throughout the British Empire's history, and life-size replicas of the fort's kitchen and duty room. The walls are 8 feet thick and huge cannons point out to sea, but like many other forts in Bermuda, this one was never used to defend the island. The fort was first built of wood in the early 17th century under Richard Moore, the island's first governor. The present stone structure was built on the site in the 19th century and has been completely restored. *Open daily, 10 a.m.–4:30 p.m. Closed Christmas Day. Admission: adults–$2.50; children under age 12–free.*

Gates Fort • *intersection of Cut and Barry Roads, Gates Bay* • Like Fort St. Catherine, this restored fort is one of nine built under

Bermuda's first governor, Richard Moore. It was named in honor of Sir Thomas Gates, a survivor of the shipwrecked *Sea Venture*. Gates, who later became the governor of Jamestown, is said to have jumped from the *Sea Venture* lifeboat yelling, "This is Gates, his bay!" *Open daily, 10 a.m.–4:30 p.m. Free admission.*

Carter House • *Naval Air Station, St. David's; tel: 297–1150* • This limestone former house, dating from about 1640, is one of the oldest stone buildings in Bermuda. It was built by descendants of Christopher Carter, the only *Sea Venture* crew member who remained on the island until he died. The old Carter home is now a museum celebrating Bermudian culture and U.S. military history. *Open Wed. 11 a.m. to 4 p.m.*

TOURS AND CRUISES

You can tour Bermuda on land or by sea—above and below the water. Bus, glass-bottom boat, scuba diving, snorkeling, and walking tours run most frequently in the summer season (from March through Nov.). Some do not operate at all during the rest of the year.

Many hotels make bus, cruise, taxi, or other sightseeing arrangements for their guests. Go to the tour or social desk at your hotel, or a Visitors' Service Bureau for the most up-to-date information about prices and tours offered.

By Sea

Looking Glass Cruises • *Front and Queen Streets, next to Ferry Dock; 236–8000* • The glass bottom boat *Looking Glass* takes visitors on a two-hour tour of reefs and wrecks. The boat departs each day at 10 a.m. and 1:30 p.m. for $20 per person. In season, from Tuesday through Sunday at 6 p.m., a four-hour dinner cruise offers complimentary cocktails and music for $55 per person.

Bermuda Excursions, Ltd. • *Flagpole on Front Street in Hamilton; 295–8444* • From November through March, the glass bottom boat leaves at 10 a.m. and 1:30 p.m. and sails out into Great Sound visiting tiny islands and reefs. There is commentary as well as music. *$20 per person.*

Williams Marine, Ltd. • *Albouys Point, Hamilton; 238–0774* • These three-hour sails on the two-masted *Alibi* and *Sundancer* head toward the West End for snorkeling and bathing. Free drinks are served on board. *Mon.–Sat. at 10 a.m. and 2 p.m., $30 per person. A sunset sail, based upon demand, also available from 5:30 p.m. to 7 p.m., $20 per person.*

Haywards Snorkeling and Glass Bottom Boat Cruises • *Ferry Terminal, Hamilton; 292–8652; or 236–9894 after hours.* • The 54-foot *Explorer* makes two trips a day at 9:45 a.m. and 1:30 p.m. for snorkeling and swimming at the Northwest Barrier Reef. Complimentary drinks are provided and underwater cameras are available for rent. *$30 per person.*

Jessie James Cruises • *Albouys Point, 10:30 a.m.; Darrel's Wharf, 10:45 a.m. and Belmont Wharf at 10:50 a.m.; 236–4804 or 234–7725.* • This 5-and-a half hour sightseeing cruise to Somerset stops off for lunch at the Loyalty Inn. Time is allowed for shopping in Somerset. Guests of the Hamilton Princess can arrange to be picked up there. *$29 per adult; children 5 to 12: $16.*

By Land

Bus tours, usually several hours long, cover points of interest such as the St. George's/Harrington Sound area, where you'll have a chance to visit the 17th-century original capital, the aquarium and zoo, and underground caves. Some bus tours are open only to groups.

Taxi tours cost $20 to $30 an hour. These are usually the most fun because you visit only what you want to see.

Based at Sabrina's in Washington Mall in Hamilton, Appleby Walking tours (295–9093 or 236–3554) invites visitors to see the sights on foot. The hour-long jaunts, ranging from $4 to $12 per person, can introduce you to the tranquil former railway trail, the nature reserve surrounding Spittal Pond, the city of Hamilton, or historic St. George's, among other areas.

If you'd rather walk on your own, pick up one of the Heritage Walk brochures produced by the Bermuda National Trust. Painstakingly detailed with maps and text, these handy publications will guide you through such scenic regions as Sandys, Warwick, and St. George's. Brochures are available at the Bermuda National Trust headquarters at Waterville on the Harbour Road in Paget, open Monday to Friday, 9 a.m. to 5 p.m.; at the main library in Hamilton; and at any Visitors Service Bureau office.

During the spring, the Garden Club of Bermuda hosts weekly Open Houses and Gardens tours (about $8 per person).

SPORTS

NOTE · · · Most large hotels offer watersports equipment and instruction to their guests as well as to people staying elsewhere.

Beaches • The island's most attractive beaches are public, and the south shore, especially in Southampton and Warwick, has some of the nicest in the world. Waves tend to be bigger on the south shore than on the north. **Horseshoe Bay** in Southampton, with unobtrusive changing facilities and snack bar, is probably the most popular beach. We like the smaller second cove tucked away on the western side. Along with **John Smith's Bay** in Smith's, Horseshoe Bay now has lifeguards during the summer. Also in Southampton are isolated **Church Bay,** with many reefs and an abundance of marine life, and quiet and secluded **West Whale Bay,** a tiny cove at the bottom of a cliff. Beaches at both **Warwick Long Bay** and the **Longtail Cliffs** area are noted for their pink sand, colored by bits of coral and shells. Warwick Long Bay, where bathers dive off the boulders that jut out of the water, attracts many snorkelers. **Jobson Cove** in Warwick can be nice for skinny dipping after dark. On the private **Tucker's Town Beach,** you can see the 35-foot-tall Natural Arches. **Long Bay** in Sandys is also picturesque.

Bermuda International Marathon and Ten-Kilometer Race • In January, runners flock to the Bermuda International 10-kilometer race beginning at the National Stadium. The route offers views of oleander, hibiscus, palms, and the dark-blue-and-turquoise ocean. The next day is the International Marathon, where runners go through downtown Hamilton twice, and along the scenic north shore for 10 miles. For entry forms and more information, contact the Bermuda Track and Field Association, P.O. Box DV 397, Devonshire DV BX, Bermuda.

Boardsailing • (See Windsurfing.)

Boating • Most large hotels have watersports facilities for guests and other people. In Hamilton Parish, Blue Hole Water Sports (293–3328) at the Grotto Bay Beach Hotel, for example, has sunfish, water-bikes, powerboats, and yak boards (which are somewhere between a surfboard and a paddleboard). You can rent various kinds of sail-your-self boats from the following places: Rance's Boatyard, Paget (292–1843); Robinson's Charter Boat Marina, Somerset Bridge, Sandys (238–9408 or 234–0709); Salt Kettle Boat Rentals, Paget (236–4863 or 236–3612); and Mangrove Marina, Sandys (234–0914).

Prices for boats that you sail yourself range from about $25 to $75 for a half day, and $50 to $130 for a full day. You can also rent boats for one or two hours. Outboard motor boats without skippers cost from about $70 to $100 for a half day, and from $95 to $130 for a full day.

Sailing lessons are given at Salt Kettle Boat Rentals. In Salt Kettle you can also charter a powerboat or yacht with a licensed skipper. Yachts with licensed skippers can be chartered at Bermuda Caribbean Yacht Charter in Southampton (234–7266 or 238–8578); Somerset Bridge Cruises in Sandys (234–0235); Starlight Sailing Cruises in Pembroke (292–1834); Ocean Yacht Charters in Hamilton (295–1180), Longtail Cruises in Hamilton (236–4482), and Sail Bermuda in Hamilton (238–0774).

Prices for skippered yachts range from about $185 to $300 for 3 hours to $330 to $700 for 8 hours.

Bowling • If you want to keep that arm in shape, you can bowl on one of 16 lanes at the Bermuda Bowling Club & Warwick Lanes (236–5290), open Mon. through Fri., from 6 p.m.–midnight; Sat. and Sun., 2 p.m.–midnight. In February, the Annual Bermuda Invitation Bowling Tournament is held here. *$2.50 per game; shoes 50¢ per pair.*

Fishing • Many avid anglers consider Bermuda one of the world's greatest fishing areas, particularly for light tackle fishing. Fishing is best from May through November. The kinds of fish caught in different locations are as follows:

Deep sea—Wahoo, amberjack, almaco jack, rainbow runner, barracuda, dolphin, blue marlin, white marlin, blackfin tuna, yellowfin tuna, and skipjack tuna.

Reef—Greater amberjack (school size), almaco jack, barracuda, little tunny, Bermuda chub, gray snapper, yellowtail snapper, and assorted bottom fish.

Shore—Bonefish, pompano, gray snapper, and barracuda.

Spearfishing is not allowed within one mile of any Bermuda shore and spear guns are not permitted in the country. No lobsters at all can be taken from April 1 through the end of August.

Shore fishing equipment can be rented at Pompano Marina, Pompano Beach Club, Southampton (234–0222); Harbour Road Marina, Newstead, Paget (236–6060); Four Winds Fishing Tackle Co., also in Hamilton (292–7466); Salt Kettle Boat Rental in Paget (236–4863 or 236–3612); and Mangrove Marina in Mangrove Bay, Sandys (234–0914 or 234–0331). Charter boats can be rented for deep-sea fishing through Bermuda Sport Fishing Association Booking Office (295–2370); Bermuda Charter Fishing Boat Association Booking Office (292–6246); and St. George's Game Fishing and Cruising Association (297–1622). For general fishing information, contact Bermuda Game Fishing Association, P.O. Box HM 1306, Hamilton HM FX, Bermuda.

Golf • With 8 courses, Bermuda has more golf per acre than any other country. People tee off here year-round. Public courses are Ocean View Golf and Country Club in Devonshire (236–6758), Port Royal Golf Course in Southampton (234–0974 or 234–0972), and St. George's Golf Club in St. George's (297–8067), the island's newest. Others, including those at the Mid Ocean Club in St. George's, Riddell's Bay Golf and Country Club in Warwick, and the Belmont (Warwick), Marriott's Castle Harbour (Hamilton Parish), and Princess (Southampton) hotels, require introduction by a member or that arrangements be made through your hotel. The Mid Ocean Club in swanky Tucker's Town is considered the cream of the crop. All courses are 18 holes except the Ocean View Golf and Country Club, which is 9 holes. If you bring your own clubs, check with the airline you use, since some include them in the free baggage allowance while others charge a special rate. For information about golf tournaments, contact the Secretary, Bermuda Golf Association, P.O. Box HM, 433, Hamilton HM BX, Bermuda.

Helmet Diving • From May through November, visitors may walk on the ocean floor at a depth of 10–14 feet without getting their hair wet. Even nonswimmers and those wearing glasses can try helmet diving, which allows them close-up views of marine life without the skill required for scuba diving or snorkeling. Touching fish, coral, and other marine life is part of the fun. Once participants have descended a ladder and are in the water up to their necks, 70-pound lead helmets are placed on their heads. Air pumped in by tubes allows them to breathe during the 30 minutes they spend underwater. These guided tours, which are perfectly safe for children, are conducted by the Hartley's Underwater Wonderland in Smith's (292–4434) and Hartley's Under Sea Adventure in Somerset (234–2861). *Cost: about $33 per person.*

Horseback Riding • Spicelands Riding Centre in Warwick (238–8212 or 238–8246) conducts trail rides several times a day and offers private, semi-private, and group lessons. Beginning at 7 a.m., the early-morning 2-hour ride along a beach is followed by a home-cooked breakfast (about $38). Regular trail rides (about $25) are along wooded routes perfumed with flowers and paths with dramatic views of south-shore beaches below.

Lee Bow Riding Centre in Devonshire (236–4181) is especially for young people age 18 and under and has use of a 15-acre cross-country course. Here they can take trail rides or lessons for about $25 an hour. Junior event riders may attend equestrian workshops.

Jogging • Most people jog along the main roads, the beaches, and the railroad-right-of-way in Southampton and Sandys (see *The Bermuda Railway Trail Guide*). Every Tuesday at 6 p.m. from April through October, the Mid-Atlantic Athletic Club organizes a two-mile "fun run" starting at Camden House on Berry Hill Road in Paget.

Parasailing • Try the next best thing to flying like a bird at Para-Sailing Bermuda (238–2332) at the Southampton Princess, Blue Hole Water Sports at the Grotto Bay Hotel in Hamilton Parish (293–3328), or Skyrider BDA (234–1789) at Robinson's Marina in Somerset. The cost is about $35 for each (very brief, but exhilarating) flight.

Scuba Diving and Snorkeling • Diving lessons and trips are conducted from March through January. Snorkeling trips run from May through November. Most of the large hotels have facilities for scuba diving and snorkeling available to guests as well as to those staying elsewhere. Masks, snorkels, weight belts, air tanks, fins, and other equipment can be rented at hotels or bought in sporting goods stores. Warwick Long Bay on the south shore is an exceptionally attractive area for snorkelers. Hotel tour desks will have details of snorkeling and diving excursions. Dive operations include Nautilus Diving, Ltd. in Southampton (238–2332), Fantasea in Pembroke (295–3052), Blue Water Divers at Robinson's Marina in Somerset (234–1034, 234–1789, or 234–2922), Skin Diving Adventures in Somerset (234–1034), and Dive Bermuda at Dockyard (234–0225), which specializes in small personalized diving groups. (Also see Tours and Cruises.)

Spectator Sports • You can watch tennis matches as well as cricket (May to September), rugby (September to December), and football (soccer—October to April). Each year in late July or early August, the island takes two days off for Cup Match, the annual cricket tournament. Track and field events are held at the National Stadium in Devonshire at Parsons Road and Frog Lane. Consult *This Week in Bermuda* for the schedule during your visit.

Squash • Four squash courts are available to visitors at the Bermuda Squash Racquets Club in Devonshire (292–6881). Courts are open from 10 a.m.–4 p.m. and must be reserved.

Tennis • Tennis came to the U.S. from Bermuda, which now has about 100 courts at hotels and other locations. At many hotels, courts are free to guests. Tennis attire is preferred at all courts; at the Government Tennis Stadium, tennis whites are mandatory. The following have courts lit for evening play: Ariel Sands, Belmont Hotel, Marriott's Castle Harbour, Coral Beach & Tennis Club, Elbow Beach Hotel, Government Tennis Stadium, Grotto Bay Beach Hotel, Harmony Club, Port Royal Tennis Courts, Sonesta Beach Hotel, and the Southampton Princess. All year, there are tournaments you are welcome to watch. For details, contact the Tournament Chairperson, 18 Frith Farm Rd., Paget PG, Bermuda, (809) 236–7438.

Waterskiing • Best from May through September, waterskiing can be arranged through Bermuda Water Skiing at the Grotto Bay Beach Hotel in Hamilton Parish (March–November; 293–8333); Mangrove Marina in Somerset (234–0914); or Bermuda Waterski Centre in Somerset (mainly May through October, 234–3354).

Windsurfing • If this thrilling combination of surfing, sailing, and skiing is not available at your hotel, contact one of the following board-sailing outfits: Watlington's Windsurfing Bermuda (295–0808), the first such school in Bermuda, gives hour-, day-, and week-long lessons. Also try Mangrove Marina in Somerset (234–0914), Marriott's Aquatic Centre in Hamilton Parish (293–2543), or Blue Hole Water Sports in Hamilton Parish (293–3328). Sail On in Hamilton sells all kinds of windsurfing gear, as do Marriot's Aquatic Centre and Blue Hole Water Sports.

NIGHTLIFE

Clubs with shows, music, and dancing are found at many of the larger hotels and some of the smaller ones. **The Gazebo Lounge** at the Princess in Hamilton, for instance, presents shows for about $30 per person including two drinks and gratuities. Except on Sundays, the **Empire Room** at the Southampton Princess hosts a dinner show for $40 per person, not including drinks. Sometimes live bands or singers will entertain at restaurants. Pubs, mostly along or near Front Street in Hamilton, are usually filled with ale-drinkers, dart-players, and young folks trying to meet each other. **Ram's Head, Rum Runners,** and **Robin Hood** are three of the most popular. When there is a cover charge at a discotheque or night club, it is generally between $5 and $8. Note that during the off season (mid-November through March) some hotels and restaurants offer less frequent entertainment or none at all.

CITY OF HAMILTON

Scandal • *115 Front St.; tel: 292–4040* • If you're looking for the 40 Thieves Club, the wild disco that had the young crowd jumping for years, this is what you'll find instead. With a far more sophisticated approach, Scandal lures night owls not only with live music but also with snacks such as Beluga caviar, lobster cocktail, and smoked salmon. Wearing tuxedos, waiters serve a variety of coffees as well. The wine and champagne bar and the open-air balcony add to the upscale atmosphere. Musicians perform Monday through Thursday, followed by dancing ($15). On Fridays and Saturdays, the dance floor is hot all night and the sounds range from Top 40s to Swing ($12).

The Club • *Bermudiana Rd.; tel: 295–7799* • This popular disco is packed on weekends and often during the week as well. On Sunday nights it becomes a jazz club, filled with the sounds of the live band that also plays at the Sparrow's Nest. Admission is free if you dine at the first-floor Little Venice restaurant, Tavern on the Green in the Botanical Gardens, the New Harbourfront on Front Street, or La Trattoria on Washington Lane in Hamilton.

Oasis Club • *Front Street's Emporium Building; tel: 292–4978* • This nightclub is bright with exotic plants and unusual artwork. It's a good spot for dancing and mingling.

The Bermuda Comedy Club • *Front Street's Emporium Building; tel. 295–9857* • Whether the jokes are told in Bermudian, British, or American, the international comics who appear here keep their audiences laughing. On Fridays and Saturdays, the shows are followed by a live band. *Nightly except Sun. $15 cover charge. $20 with admission to the neighboring Oasis night club. Package available through Loquats restaurant includes dinner, Oasis, and the comedy club ($50).*

The Spinning Wheel • *Court St.; tel: 292–7799* • After partying til dawn at this triplex disco, people often have a pre-sunrise breakfast of codfish and potatoes. Truly a local hangout, The Spinning Wheel is located "back a' town," as Bermudians say. Some visitors may feel less like outsiders if they go with Bermudians.

The Swinging Door • *Court Street* • One of Bermuda's newest night spots, this club is another popular "back a' town" hangout.

Sparrow's Nest • *Reid St.; tel: 293–9161* • On Saturday nights, this club, open 'til 3 a.m., showcases Bermuda's best jazz musicians.

Casey's • *Queen Street; tel: 293–9549* • With music throbbing from the juke box, this local bar is always "packed out." Friday nights draw the largest crowd. This is the kind of place where you're likely to meet a lawyer in a suit chewing the cud with a construction worker with cement on his boots.

Place's Cafe, on Dundonald Street, and the Captain's Lounge and Triangle's Golf Club, both on Reid Street, are three other after-hours spots to try if you're looking for local color.

DEVONSHIRE

Clay House Inn • *North Shore Rd.; tel: 292–3193* • During the summer, this club caters to the cruise ship crowd. The mainly Afro-Caribbean revues feature limbo, glass-stomping, fire eating, and a steel band that also plays European classical music. On some nights, the audience is invited onto the dance floor. A major jazz club during the '50s and '60s, Clay House Inn has been graced by the likes of the late Hazel Scott and Chuck Mangione. Jazz bands and international entertainers such as Roberta Flack appear from time to time. *No show on Sundays. Cost: $23 with 2 drinks and gratuity.*

The Anchorage • *North Shore Rd.; tel: 292–5494* • Next door to the Clay House Inn, this is a *very* local after-hours hangout.

HAMILTON PARISH

Prospero's • *Grotto Bay Hotel; tel: 293–8333* • The big band music and the location—in a cave!—are definite lures. Open until 1 a.m.

SOUTHAMPTON

The Touch Club • *Southampton Princess Hotel; tel: 238–8000* • This crowd-pleasing disco plays all kinds of music, from snuggle up to shake it up.

SHOPPING

The island's three main shopping areas are the city of Hamilton, St. George's, and Somerset Village. Dockyard, tucked away at the northwestern tip of the island, has become a fourth mecca for spenders. A shopping center has opened in the old Clocktower building. Most stores are in Hamilton, Bermuda's capital, where the larger shops have main branches. Prices don't vary much from store to store, so you don't have to wear yourself out trying to save just a few more dollars.

For such a small place, this island has a surprisingly large number of sophisticated, multi-story department stores, most of which line Hamilton's Front Street in sherbert-colored old buildings. Even when patrons pack the stores searching through racks, piles, and shelves of merchandise during the frequent sales, most of these upscale shops maintain a hushed, dignified atmosphere. Of course, there is also a wide selection of T-shirt and sportswear stores and funky little boutiques, many in mini-malls or along narrow alleys between Front and Reid streets.

In Bermuda, friendly, helpful, non-pushy service is as prevalent as high quality goods. Perhaps this is because so many establishments are family-run and have been for generations. Staff members at more than a few stores have worked there for two and three decades, so they are more than happy to answer any questions. If you fail to find what you're looking for, don't be surprised if a salesperson sends you down the street to the competition.

Since there is no sales tax in Bermuda, prices are an average 25% lower than those in the U.S. Many stores keep their prices down by buying directly from the manufacturers. Each U.S. visitor is allowed to take home $400 worth of duty-free purchases. Up to $1000, you'll pay only a 10% duty. Bermuda is a GSP (Generalized System of Preferences) country. This means that goods that are at least 35% crafted in Bermuda can be brought into the U.S. completely duty free. Keep this in mind especially if you're in the market for fine jewelry, some of which is locally produced.

The best bargains are in European imports, which generally cost 25% to 50% less than in the U.S. Among such items are Italian, German, and French knitwear; Rolex, Tissot, Patek Philippe, and other watches; Norwegian enameled jewelry; Icelandic wool jackets, blankets, hats, and other knits; French perfumes; Porthault linens; and Florentine stationery. Wedgwood, Royal Copenhagen, Royal Crown Derby, and other china can cost 25% to 50% less than in North American retail outlets. Don't worry about shipping fragile items, by the way. Stores in Bermuda have a lot of experience in sending delicate merchandise overseas. Now that duty rates on imported jewelry have been reduced, prices for good gold and silver are competitive with those on most Caribbean islands. You can save as much as 40% on 18-carat gold jewelry, for instance.

Of course, not all merchandise in Bermuda is a bargain. Film, for example, tends to be considerably more expensive than in most parts of the U.S., so be sure to pack enough for your stay. For camera equipchment, try the **Camera Store** (on Queen between Reid and Church), **Stuart's On Reid St.** (near Queen), or **Photo Craftsmen** (on Reid St.), where film can be developed in 24 hours.

Crafts made of cedar are popular, such as clocks, candlesticks, lamps, and handbags with cedar handles. At the **Craft Market at Dockyard,** you'll find artisans at work on pottery, paintings on cedar and shells, stained glass, and dolls. One of the most popular displays is of highly detailed miniature wooden furniture, including canopied beds and Federal-style chests of drawers complete with delicate metal handles. However, lofty prices ($40 for a table, $100 for a bed, $150 for an armoire) probably ensure that they end up in only the most luxurious doll houses.

Bermuda's trademark black rum is a good buy, along with other liquor at "in-bond" (discounted) prices. You'll pick up your in-bond libations at the airport on your way home, since liquor sold at these prices may be consumed only outside Bermuda. Be sure to order it several days before your departure and know your flight number when making the purchase. For a delicious way to chew your rum, sink your teeth into a buttery slice of **Horton's Bermuda Black Rum Cake.** These baked treats come in two sizes, with the larger ones sold in decorative tins. Don't balk at the seemingly steep prices—a sliver of one of these rich cakes goes a long way. Horton's cakes are available at department stores and other shops throughout the island.

Once you see the Bermuda Regiment perform the rousing Beating Retreat Ceremony, you may want to pick up a record or cassette of their spirited marches and lively renditions of classics.

You'll come across a wide and colorful selection of sweaters in the larger shops, including **Archie Brown & Sons, Smith's,** and the **Scottish Wool Shop. Constables of Bermuda** has a variety of Icelandic sweaters, jackets, coats, and blankets. **Trimingham's,** probably the island's best-known department store, imports goods from the Far East, the U.K., East and West Germany, Hungary, Yugoslavia, and many other countries. In addition to having its own fine jewelry workshop and an extensive selection of cosmetics and perfumes, the store has a large men's department. This is also the place to go for foods such as gourmet coffee beans and British chutneys, jams, and biscuits. If you're in the market for a chic new bathing suit or sportswear, try **Sail On,** in Old Cellar Lane off Front Street; this store also sells windsurfing gear.

The **Irish Linen Shop** sells many different kinds of Souleiado fabric for about half of what you would pay in the U.S. Also sold by the yard, this distinctive material comes in nearly every shape and form, from dresses and quilted handbags to umbrellas. Known for their hand-embroidered linens, the shop specializes in custom-made tablecloths, bedding, and other items. Sheets and pillowcases in Queen Elizabeth's pattern are on display at the Front Street branch.

Watch the craftspeople at work at the Somerset branch of **Wilson's Fine Jewellers,** which also has a store in Hamilton. **Astwood Dickinson,** on Front Street, was the first jewelry store to produce a line of 14-carat gold "Bermuda Collection" pendants. They come in various shapes, including a spiny lobster, a cedar bough, a Bermuda onion, a longtail, and the *Deliverance.* Several other stores have followed suit with similar pendants and earrings. East African and South American jewelry is on sale at **Lote Tree Jewels** in Walker Arcade (between Front and Reid sts.). African imports and games, posters, greeting cards, dolls, books, and wall hangings with African or African-American themes can all be found at **True Reflections** (on Court St. between Church and Victoria).

For china and crystal, head to **Bluck's,** which also sells antique maps, silver, brass, and reproductions of famous paintings. If you can't make up your mind while you're on vacation, you can order merchandise by mail once you get home. **Heritage House** is jam-packed with oil and watercolor paintings, chess sets with whimsical pieces, the popular minutely detailed David Winter cottages, and scores of intriguing Bermudian and English antiques. You might stumble upon an inlaid wooden box, a brass lamp, a silver urn, bone and silver fish servers, a copper tea kettle—or even a brass propeller from a wrecked ship.

Another good shop is **Rubarb,** on Queen Street, which sells needlepoint. For men's and women's clothing you won't see on everyone else, try the **27th Century Boutique.** In Chancery Lane, one of the alleys between Front and Reid streets, **Flameworks** sells locally made blown glass. In nearby Bermuda House Lane, check out **Caribelle Batik Bermuda** for hand-painted clothing made with sea island cotton. Another quaint pathway lined with stores is Fagan's Alley. With three floors of shops selling clothes, jewelry, antique coins, and artwork, the **Emporium Building** on Front Street always buzzes with activity.

Windsor Place (on Queen Street between Reid and Church in Hamilton) is one of Bermuda's newest and most upscale malls, with its potted plants and archways. Brass railings border terra cotta–tiled staircases, fanlights top French doors, ceilings are covered with mirrors, and escalators lead up from the main floor, overlooked by balconies. Head to the **Complete Athlete** on the second floor if you're looking for some new running shoes, diving or reef-walking booties, the latest in bathing suits, T-shirts, and shorts, or an Aqua Jogger (strap it around your waist and it will keep you afloat while you exercise in the water).This mall also contains a variety of stores selling chic fashions.

In St. George's, **Bridge House Straw Market** sells bags, hats, and dolls, as well as bangles and T-shirts. **Frangipani,** also in St. George's, carries handmade dresses, sweaters, and shawls imported from Greece. **The Bermuda Railway Company,** with branches in several locations, is a fun place to shop for yuppie-type sportswear.

In Dockyard, art lovers should be sure to visit **Bermuda Arts Centre,** where exhibitions highlight the paintings and jewelry of local artists. In addition to this one, Heritage House, and the gallery in City Hall, the following are among the island's galleries: In Hamilton—**Pegasus** (across from the Princess Hotel), with the largest collection of prints in Bermuda; **Thistle Gallery** (Park Street), with exhibits by Bermudian and visiting artists; **Wells Art Gallery** (Washington Mall), the **Windjammer Gallery** (corner of Reid and King streets), with the largest collection of local art and photographs and also sells handmade jewelry; and **Crisson and Hind** (Front Street); in Paget—**Art House** (South Shore Road, near the Paraquet Restaurant); and in Smith's—**Minstrel's Gallery** (Flatts Hill), owned by Desmond Fountain, a prominent local sculptor.

DINING OUT

Bermuda's many restaurants offer visitors choices that range from a candlelit continental dinner at Once Upon a Table in Pembroke to a sampling of local specialties in the casual, eclectic surroundings of Dennis' Hideaway in St. David's. You can stop at an English pub for fish and chips or a Chinese restaurant for shrimp in Szechuan sauce. Bermuda is far from lacking in Italian restaurants, and visitors can also satisfy cravings for Spanish food. At Tio Pepe in Southampton, crab legs are on the menu along with pizza. The Bombay Cycle Club has a variety of vegetarian Indian dishes. Tivoli Gardens, a Danish restaurant, has a lavish smorgasbord. When you're in the mood to break the bank, head for Waterlot or Fourways, known as much for their excellent food as for their very steep prices. In Hamilton, several restaurants have balconies facing the harbor. Unfortunately, however, the stunning view of the water is often blocked by cruise ships in port. Visitors tend to dress up for dinner, whether or not they plan to go out on the town afterward.

For the most part, the best (and freshest) Bermudian food comes from the sea. Much of the meat (and shrimp, surprisingly) is imported. Two delicacies are Bermuda lobster (crayfish from island waters from September through March, and lobster from Maine the rest of the year) and rockfish. There are many other kinds of fish to try, including yellowtail, hind, wahoo, and grouper. The "Bermuda fish" on many menus is simply whatever local fish was caught that day.

Get to know the real Bermuda (and save money) by eating in local restaurants specializing in home-style cuisine, such as The Green Lantern in Pembroke; the Specialty Inn in Smith's; the Loyalty Inn and Woody's in Sandys; and Black Horse Tavern in St. George's.

Although most restaurants, in and outside of hotels, emphasize international cuisine, many serve at least one Bermudian specialty (see "Wining and Dining," p. 11). A 15% gratuity will be added to your bill at some restaurants. Especially during the summer season, most require reservations for dinner or Sunday brunch, and request that men wear jackets in the evening. At this time of year, you may even have to make reservations at the more expensive dining spots several days in advance. Many restaurants are closed or have limited hours on Sundays.

A group of small hotels and cottage colonies (Cambridge Beaches, Glencoe Harbour Club, Lantana Colony Club, Newstead, Pompano Beach Club, The Reefs, Horizons and Cottages, Waterloo House, and Stonington Beach) offer guests year-round dining exchange privileges. Those taking advantage of the program will treat themselves to some of Bermuda's finest dining in some of its most attractive settings, and in different parts of the island. Other hotels offering dining exchange privileges are the Princess and the Southampton Princess; and Palmetto Hotel, White Sands, and Ariel Sands. Evening diners may be discouraged by the steep cab fares between some of the hotels; however, you can save money in some cases by catching the last bus or ferry instead of taking a taxi both ways. While many visitors and Bermudians may ride mopeds at night, we don't recommend it.

Especially during the off season (mid-November through March), many restaurants take part in another dine-around program, one that is quite economical. The restaurants range from the informal, such as the Reid Street Cafe and Ye Olde Cock & Feather, to the elegance of the Margaret Rose and the New Harbourfront. The set menus are available in different price categories, depending on the restaurant, from about $18 to $30 per person (not including drinks) for each three-course meal. Ask for sample menus at your hotel. Be sure to make reservations at the participating restaurants, which are indicated by the abbreviation DA in the following descriptions.

SANDYS

EXPENSIVE

Lantana Colony Club • *Somerset Bridge; tel: 234–0141* • All of the dining areas, indoors and out, are arranged and decorated to make eating here a memorable experience. The main dining room, with its glass roof and polished cedar tables, is an especially pleasant place. Homegrown flowers and plants, paintings, and sculpture are everywhere. The extensive menu changes daily, ranging from well-presented, delicate hors d'oeuvres to entrees such as veal in an apple brandy sauce, wahoo with lemon butter, and roast duck. An array of desserts is served from the trolley. On Mondays dress is informal for the set sirloin dinner. There is dancing on Tuesdays, Thursdays, and Saturdays. Reservations are recommended. *No credit cards.*

MODERATE

The Blue Oyster • *Marina Real del Oeste Clubhouse, Dockyard; tel. 234–0943* • One of the Dockyard's newest eateries, this French bistro-style restaurant is a good choice for lunch. Look for seafood, veal chops, and rack of lamb. To dedicate themselves completely to the Blue Oyster's opening in the spring of '89, owners Wendy Madeiros, a native Bermudian, and Bill Meade, originally from Ireland, postponed their plans for marriage. After putting in their time at other restaurants (he as the maitre d' of the renowned Waterlot Inn, she as a bartender at Henry VIII and Somerset Country Squire), they decided that tending to their own creation took precedence over tying the knot. *Major credit cards.*

MODERATE–INEXPENSIVE

Somerset Country Squire • *Mangrove Bay Rd., Somerset Village; tel: 234–0105* • This tavern near the Watford Bridge ferry dock specializes in English and Bermudian fare. Featured are steak-and-kidney pie, sausages and mash, fish and chips, and Bermuda onion soup. Diners come miles for the curried mussel pie. You can eat outside on the terrace overlooking Mangrove Bay or downstairs in the dining room, where there is entertainment six nights a week. Dinner reservations are recommended. *No credit cards.* DA.

The Village Inn • *Watford Bridge, Somerset; tel: 234–2449 or 238–9401* • The emphasis here is on seafood, featuring international and local cuisine. With a nice view of the water, this is the first restaurant you'll see if you arrive at Somerset by ferry. *Major credit cards.*

Il Palio • *Main Rd., Somerset; tel: 234–1049 or 234–2323* • This casual Italian restaurant about a 10-minute walk from Somerset Village serves lunch and dinner and has take-out service. The spiral staircase from the downstairs bar leads up to the main dining room where northern and southern Italian food is served. The take-out pizza is popular with the young crowd. In addition to a variety of pasta, the menu includes veal, steak, roast duckling, and seafood. Reservations are suggested. Closed on Tues. *No credit cards.* DA.

Freeport Gardens • *Dockyard area; tel: 234–1692* • A short stroll from the Maritime Museum, this makes a good lunch stop. Try the peas and rice and the crispy wahoo, which is so nice and dry that it seems to have been deep fried without touching the oil. The codfish cakes, burgers, and macaroni and cheese are other good choices. Dinner menu items include veal cordon bleu, strip steak, and jumbo shrimp. *No credit cards.*

The Blue Foam • *Somerset Bridge Hotel; tel: 234–2892* • When the excavation was being done for this site, workers dug up a well-preserved cedar sign carved with the words "Blue Foam"—hence the name of this popular restaurant overlooking Ely's Harbour. We've sampled some of the island's best fish chowder with black rum and sherry peppers here. The grilled fish is also delicious. Other menu items include Cornish hen, sirloin steak with garlic butter, and pizza. Even when all the tables on the alfresco terrace are taken, you can still feel as if you're outdoors by sitting in the "greenhouse" section of the dining room.

INEXPENSIVE

Loyalty Inn • *Mangrove Bay, Somerset Village; tel: 234–1398* • As popular with locals as with visitors, this inn specializes in seafood, and is a 5-minute walk from the Watford Bridge ferry dock. At lunch time, eat on the patio overlooking Mangrove Bay. Menu selections include shrimp, lobster, omelets, burgers, and peas and rice. A 250-year-old Bermuda home was converted into this restaurant. *No credit cards.*

New Woody's Drive-In • *Ireland Island; 234–2082* • Near the West End Sail Boat Club, this local hangout serves excellent Bermuda fish and chicken dishes.

SOUTHAMPTON

EXPENSIVE

Henry VIII • *South Shore Rd.; tel: 238–1977 or 238–0908* • Across from the Sonesta Beach Hotel and right below Gibbs Hill Lighthouse, this friendly (sometimes noisy) Tudor pub and restaurant has a strolling minstrel (Wednesday nights). During Sunday brunch and all evenings (except Wednesdays), guests can join the singer-pianist for sing-alongs. Waiters are dressed in 16th-century costumes. Traditional English dishes include roast beef and Yorkshire pudding and roast prime sirloin. Bermuda mussel pie and seafood Newburg are also on the menu. The Royal Sunday Brunch consists of hot and cold entrees, salads, and desserts. Men are asked to wear jackets for dinner. *Major credit cards.* DA.

Newport Room • *Southampton Princess; tel: 238–8000* • For that elegant, no-holds-barred dinner out, the Newport Room is probably the place. In a room decorated to resemble a luxury yacht, all gleaming brass and polished teak, guests dine on Wedgwood china, drink from Waterford goblets, and use heavy English silver and fine linen napkins. The menu is continental with a touch of nouvelle cuisine and a bow to

Bermudian tradition. The elegantly clad staff provides discreet and excellent service. A refreshing sherbet is served between courses. Reservations are a must. *Major credit cards.*

Waterlot Inn • *Middle Rd.; tel: 238–0510* • Eleanor Roosevelt, Mark Twain, Eugene O'Neill, and James Thurber are some of the more famous patrons of this historic inn that began as a tavern at the turn of the century. It is now owned by the Princess Hotels. Dinner here could easily set you back $50 per person. (Much to the annoyance of forward-thinking patrons, women who dine with men are given menus without prices.) Diners may come to the private north shore pier by boat, and eat on an outdoor terrace. Before descending to the indoor dining room, they can have drinks by the cedar bar. A model ship enclosed in glass is above the tiled cedar fireplace. Downstairs, below sloping dark beam ceilings, you can try such entrees as Guinea chicks (spiny lobster, a house specialty) or curried chicken breast stuffed with banana and pimentos. The Caesar salad prepared at tableside comes with a wonderfully spicy dressing. Soft background music played on the baby grand by the bar floats downstairs. In addition to dinner served daily, the inn also has a good Sunday brunch. Reservations are essential and men are asked to wear jackets and ties in the evenings. *Major credit cards and Princess Hotels cards.* DA.

Whaler Inn • *East Whale Bay, off South Shore Rd.; tel: 238–0076* • This informal restaurant at the Southampton Princess beach club overlooks the south shore coast. Guests may eat in the dining room or on the outdoor terrace. Sunday brunch is popular here. After dinner, you can dance on the terrace until midnight.

MODERATE TO EXPENSIVE

The Reefs • *South Shore Rd.; tel: 238–0222* • Dinner reservations are mandatory for the main dining room in this small hotel overlooking the beach. The menu changes daily, offering dishes such as honeydew melon with Parma ham, French onion soup, coq au vin, roast leg of lamb, Dover sole, and cheese with fruit. A band plays during dinner. Try to make the weekly Saturday night buffet. With a dramatic ocean view, this bright, attractive dining room is an especially pleasant place for lunch. Midday selections include salads, hamburgers, tuna melts, and other sandwiches. Coconuts, down by the water, is the hotel's more casual restaurant. *No credit cards.*

Pompano • *Pompano Beach Rd.; tel: 234–0222* • Many visitors talk as much about Pompano's good food as they do about the friendly, efficient service. One of the elaborate dinner creations might be Bermuda fish filet stuffed with pistachios and truffle and scallop mousse, wrapped in spinach, and steamed with watercress sauce. Another night you might try beef stroganoff or seafood in a pastry shell, followed by raspberry cheese cake or Crepe Suzette. *Reservations recommended. No credit cards.*

MODERATE

Tio Pepe • *South Shore Rd.; tel: 238–1897* • This casual Italian and Spanish seafood restaurant near the entrance to Horseshoe Bay has everything from crab legs to take-out pizza. Closed on Tuesdays, Tio Pepe is a good family restaurant for lunch or dinner. *Mastercard, Visa, and Diner's Club.*

INEXPENSIVE

Port Royal Golf Club Restaurant • *off Middle Rd.* • From the bar and lounge of this large restaurant you can see both the ocean and the golf course. Only breakfast and lunch are served.

Riddell's Bay • *Middle Rd.; tel: 238–1090* • This informal road-side restaurant serves breakfast all day; also sandwiches, salads, beef and mussel pie, hamburgers, and fish cakes. Alcohol is not served.

Traditions • *Middle Rd.; 234–0514* • Popular with golfers, this casual restaurant serving homestyle breakfast, lunch, and dinner is across from the Port Royal Golf Course. Salad plates and sandwiches are on the menu as well as pork chops, fish, and collard greens. Cyclists can order from the take-out window.

WARWICK

EXPENSIVE

Miramar • *Mermaid Beach Club; tel: 236–5031* • Lunch and dinner are served in this split-level dining room at the water's edge. Specialties include mesquite-grilled meat and seafood, veal curry, baby lamb chops, filet mignon, and chateaubriand. DA.

INEXPENSIVE–MODERATE

The South Shore Cafe • *Dunscombe and South Shore rds.; tel: 238–9635* • No longer do visitors have to hope for an invitation to the home of a Bermudian to sample the traditional Sunday breakfast of cod-fish and potatoes in Warwick. Taking over from MacHerman's, which was at this location for many years (and was followed briefly by a Chinese restaurant), the South Shore Cafe now serves this hearty dish, along with pizza, curries, burgers, soups, and fish. Part of the restaurant is an ice cream parlor. *Open 7:30 a.m.–11 p.m.*

PAGET

EXPENSIVE

Fourways Inn • *Cobbs Hill and Middle rds.; tel: 236–6517* • French and Bermudian treats are specialties of this elegant and very expensive restaurant. Don't be surprised if you end up spending more than $60 per person for dinner. Fourways was built in 1727 as a private home and later became a pub. The original kitchen, with its spacious fireplace, has been converted into the Peg Leg Bar. The menu includes caviar, French goose liver pate, escargot, cold salmon soup with chives, mandarin duck with orange sauce, lamb, rockfish, and steak tartar. There is also an extensive wine cellar. The small courtyard, with a fountain, is a romantic place to dine. A pianist entertains with soft classical and popular music. On Thursdays and Sundays, try the gourmet brunch. *Major credit cards.*

The Norwood Room • *Stonington Beach Hotel; tel: 236–5416* • The elegant table settings, chandeliers, and tall fanlight windows facing the water and lush greenery make this restaurant especially appealing. By day, the room is bathed in sunlight. By night, it is filled with soothing piano music. The imaginative continental cuisine is as attractively presented as it is delicious. *Major credit cards.*

Glencoe Harbour Club • *Salt Kettle; tel: 296–5274* • A two-minute walk from the Salt Kettle ferry stop, this small hotel restaurant is not far from the city of Hamilton. You can sit inside, or outside near the lively bar and watch the activity in Hamilton Harbour. The menu includes Bermudian and international selections. *Major credit cards.*

INEXPENSIVE

Mungal's • *Middle and South Shore rds.; tel: 236–8563* • Also known as Chicken Coop, this late-night spot near the Harmony Club hotel features fried chicken, soup, and hamburgers, along with Indian specialties such as roti, curried chicken or goat with rice, dhall, and mango chutney. While Mungal's is open from 6 p.m. until 6 a.m., only light snacks are served after 2 a.m. *No credit cards.*

Paraquet • *South Shore Rd.; tel: 238–9678* • Three meals a day are served at this local restaurant specializing in home-style food. This is a perfect spot for families. No alcohol. *No credit cards.*

PEMBROKE

HAMILTON

EXPENSIVE

The New Harbourfront • *Front St.; tel: 295–4207* • On the second story of a building right across from the ferry landing, this upscale restaurant is a good choice for a special night out. Candles flicker in glistening hurricane vanes inside and on the balcony. Lanterns adorn the walls. The long mahogany-trimmed granite bar is so attractive that you may want to linger there, chatting with the bartender, before your meal. To start, try the breast of duck in pineapple sauce or seafood ravioli. The chilled cream of broccoli soup, pastas, and soft shell crabs are all good choices. The piano bar remains open until 1 a.m. After dining here, you'll be admitted at no charge to The Club, the after hours spot around the corner. Men are asked to wear jackets and ties at dinner. *Major credit cards.* DA.

Lobster Pot • *Bermudiana Rd.; tel: 292–6898* • This small informal restaurant decorated with lobster traps and fishnets is one of the city's most popular dining spots, particularly among locals. The menu consists of a wide variety of seafood dishes, as well as steak and chicken. *Major credit cards.* DA.

Romanoff • *Church St.; tel: 295–0333* • This continental restaurant, serving everything from crepes filled with sherried seafood to an assortment of coffees, stirs up visions of old Europe. The owner's award-winning specialty is Turnedos Alexandra (beef tenderloin flambeed with cognac at your table). Mirrored walls reflect red carnations and the warm burgundy decor. Save room for something from the dessert trolley. *Major credit cards.*

The Little Venice • *Bermudiana Rd.; tel: 295–3503* • This popular Italian restaurant serves such imaginative entrees as salmon trout baked with olives, tomatoes, capers, and dry sherry; veal scaloppine with artichokes; and filet mignon cooked in red wine. *Jacket and tie required for dinner. Complimentary admission to The Club, the disco upstairs. Major credit cards.* DA.

Chez Lafitte • *Reid St.* • Spicy Creole and Cajun specialties—a mouthwatering melange of West African, French, Native American, Spanish, and German cuisines—are featured at this slice of New Orleans. For starters, try catfish nuggets, gumbo, or turtle soup with Madeira. Then consider the crawfish stew, shrimp creole, or the shrimp-and crabmeat-topped redfish, with black-eyed peas or sweet potato puffs on the side. Finish up with Cajun country bread pudding or pecan pie.

MODERATE TO EXPENSIVE

Fisherman's Reef • *Burnaby St.; tel: 292–1619* • Located upstairs from the busy Hog Penny Pub, this cozy, nautical restaurant is a convenient and pleasant place for lunch or dinner in the center of Hamilton. The extensive menu includes cold appetizers such as avocado and prawns, smoked salmon, and scallops cocktail royal; hot appetizers such as seafood crepes, champagne oysters, and escargots; and entrees such as guinea chicks, sharks, pepper steak, and filet mignon. Banana fritters and peach melba are on the dessert menu. There is a choice of special coffees. *Major credit cards.* DA.

The New Queen • *Par-la-Ville Rd.* • This restaurant is run by a Chinese family that has been in Bermuda for more than seventy years. After a dramatic facelift, the New Queen is no longer a fast-food eatery. It now has a completely new menu (with much higher prices) that includes gourmet Szechuan selections. *No credit cards.*

Loquats • *Front St.; tel: 292–4507* • Live jazz, '50s tunes, and contemporary pop accompanies dinner here. At lunch time, ask to be seated on the balcony, with its long cedar bench running along the sides and front. The eclectic menu at this restaurant across from Number Six Passenger Terminal includes items such as corn and pumpkin chowder, Bahamian conch marinated in chili sauce with sherry peppers, souvlaki, baby back ribs, and grilled wahoo with honeyed mushrooms and bananas. Try the hot fudge brownie a la mode or pecan pie for dessert. *Major credit cards.* DA.

The Grill • *Windsor Place mall, Queen St.; tel: 295–4086* • Owned by Fourways Inn, one of the island's best (and most expensive) restaurants, the Grill provides a restful break from shopping in this attractive mall. Daily specials might be baked salmon in puff pastry, roast turkey, filet of beef Wellington, roast leg of lamb, or pasta. The seafood grilled with mushrooms, onions, peppers, and herb butter is quite good. If you happen along in the later afternoon, stop by for tea, which comes complete with scones slathered with cream and jam. *Open 7 a.m.–5 p.m.*

Port-O-Call • *Front St.; tel: 295–5373* • The owner of the unassuming Rendezvous has transformed that fast-food eatery into this gourmet seafood restaurant. (A few meat dishes are also on the menu.) The decor brings to mind the snazzy interior of a luxury yacht, and the staff is decked out in British naval uniforms. *Major credit cards.*

Monte Carlo • *Victoria Street (behind City Hall); tel. 295–5453* • One of the new kids on the block in Bermuda, this restaurant serves dishes that recall the Côte d'Azur. For starters a good choice might be terrine of duck with wild morels and pistachios in raspberry sauce or Provence-style mussels. Follow it up with beef tenderloin with shallots and red wine sauce or sauteed shrimp in a pink peppercorn sauce flambed in whiskey. Dinner crepes and pizza are also on the menu. *Closed Sundays. Major credit cards.*

MODERATE

Bombay Bicycle Club • *third floor of the Rego Furniture Building, Reid St.; tel: 292–0048* • The New Delhi chefs ensure that this attractive restaurant serves authentic Indian cuisine. Excellent tandoori specialties are cooked in a clay oven imported from India. Also on the menu are delicious vegetable, chicken, lamb, and seafood curries, and a selection of breads. Vegetarians can revel in an array of well-seasoned meatless dishes. Fans twirl from a panelled ceiling above glossy darkwood tables and peacock-style chairs. A buffet lunch is served Monday to Friday, from noon to 2:30 p.m., and dinner from 6:30 to 11 p.m. *Major credit cards.*

Rosa's Cantina • *Reid St.; tel: 295–1912* • The colorful decor creates a pleasant setting. Tables are draped with serapes, walls are decorated with maracas and tapestries, lanterns and papier-mache birds on rings hang from the ceiling beams. Mexican ceramics and potted plants have been strategically placed around the room and Mexican music plays in the background. However, created by chefs from San Antonio, the Tex-Mex items we sampled were generally either too greasy (such as the cheese flour crisp) or too bland (such as the shrimp fajitas). We had the best luck with the chimichangas and the burritos, washed down with frozen margaritas. *No credit cards.*

Ristorante Primavera • *Pitts Bay Rd. 295–2167* • Near the Princess and Rosedon hotels, this casual Italian restaurant prides itself in preparing each dish to order. Indeed, food comes steaming or bubbly hot to the table. Menu selections include soups, salads, a variety of fish and meat dishes, omelets, and, of course, pasta. *Major credit cards.*

Ram's Head Inn • *Reid Street Inn; tel: 295–6098* • Although this lively pub serves steak and kidney pie; chicken, shrimp, or fish and chips; shepherds pie; bangers and mash; ribs; and burgers, it is best known by the younger set as a hot hangout after dark. Every night, live bands turn the pub into a party. On Fridays and Saturdays, snacks are served from midnight until 3 a.m. On Sundays, you'll have to drink your meals here; the kitchen is closed.

The Balcony • *In A. S. Cooper, Front St., Hamilton; tel: 295–3961* • For the convenience of the department store's hungry shoppers, breakfast is served from 10 a.m., soon after A. S. Cooper opens. The continental dishes, bordering on the gourmet, are reasonably priced, with Japanese sushi a daily luncheon special. A traditional tea is served from 3 to 4:30 p.m., complete with finger sandwiches and scones.

Showbizz • *Reid and King sts.; tel: 292–0676* • With black-and-white tile floors and walls hung with entertainment posters, this attractive cafe has an extensive menu (although several items weren't available during our last visit). Good choices include the chicken wings with sweet and sour sauce, gazpacho, avocado crab salad, burgers, onion rings, fish cakes, and coconut shrimp. Open for lunch and dinner Monday to Friday. Dinner only on Saturday and Sunday. Closes 1 a.m. *Major credit cards.*

Hog Penny Pub • *Burnaby St.; tel: 292–2534* • Downstairs from Fisherman's Reef, this is another good place for lunch during a trip to the city. This British-style pub is popular with locals, and offers traditional pub fare such as steak-and-kidney pie, fish and chips, and bangers and mash. There is entertainment at night. Lunch and dinner are served daily except on Sundays, when only dinner is served. *Major credit cards.*

INEXPENSIVE TO MODERATE

M. R. Onions • *Par-la-Ville Rd. North; tel: 292–5012* • M. R. Onions serves up barbecued chicken and ribs, sandwiches, ice cream sodas, and alcoholic beverages. Children aged 10 and under choose from a special menu in the "Kidds Korner." Closed for lunch on Saturday and Sunday. *Major credit cards.* DA.

Portofino • *Bermudiana Rd.; tel: 292–2375 or 295–6090* • Behind a wrought-iron gate is Portofino, where you can dine in or take out freshly made original Italian specialties including 13 varieties of pizza. Phone at least 15 minutes ahead to place take-out orders. *No credit cards.*

La Trattoria • *Washington Lane, between Reid and Church sts.; tel: 292–7059* • This casual Italian restaurant is popular with families. If you've never had "pizza Pekinese" (made with snow peas, chicken, and sweet and sour sauce), here's the place to try it. The gelato is also good. Thursday is buffet night. Take-out service is available. After dinner here, you'll be admitted at no charge to The Club, the disco on Bermudiana Road. *Major credit cards.* DA.

Ye Olde Cock & Feather • *Front St.; tel: 295–2263* • This friendly pub is a good place to chat with Bermudians over a beer, fish and chips, or a game of darts. You can stay up late here, dancing to the live music after dinner. *Mastercard and Visa for dinner only.* DA.

Robin Hood • *Richmond Rd.; tel: 295–3314* • This former private home has the atmosphere of a country inn. A British-style pub and restaurant, Robin Hood is an unofficial expatriate's club, which also attracts a young crowd. Evenings include sing-alongs and games of darts. The upstairs wine bar and the hamburgers, in many varieties, are both popular. *No credit cards.*

Victoria Restaurant and Diner • *Victoria St., off Court St.; tel: 292–6977* • Peas and rice, fish chowder, fried fish, steak, and curried chicken are just a few of the items on the menu at this family-run restaurant adjoining the more casual diner. Codfish and potatoes, the traditional Bermudian breakfast, is served all day on Sundays at the diner. Sandwiches, fish, macaroni and cheese, peas and rice, and other homestyle selections are also available. *M, V.*

Rum Runners • *Front St.; tel: 292–4737* • Here you can sit on a balcony overlooking Front Street and the harbor while you eat lunch or dinner. Though serving mostly pub fare, the restaurant offers a more formal ambience in the Lord Halifax Dining Room. *Major credit cards.*

Prego • *Reid St.; tel: 292–1279* • Prego is high on the list of Bermuda's Italian restaurants. It offers an outstanding Vesuvio pizza as well as eggplant parmigiana and calamari. The service is quick and efficient. *Major credit cards.*

INEXPENSIVE
The Botanic Garden Tea Room • *Trimingham's; tel: 295–1183* • Take a break from shopping at this Front Street department store by stopping at this greenery-filled oasis for morning coffee, a light lunch, or afternoon tea.

The Red Carpet • *37 Reid St.* • Reservations are not necessary in this casual restaurant that serves sandwiches, cold plates and salads, along with a variety of coffees and exotic drinks. The Red Carpet is located in the old Armoury. It is closed on Sundays and on Saturdays only dinner is served. *No credit cards.*

Checkerboard Diner • *Brunswick St.; tel: 292–5582* • You can sample Bermudian specialties at this casual and homey restaurant.

The Spot • *Burnaby St. off Reid St.; tel: 292–6293* • What this restaurant lacks in atmosphere it certainly makes up for in good cooking. Try the delicious homemade soups, such as split pea, black-eyed-pea, vegetable barley, or yellow pea. Breakfast, lunch, and dinner are served. No alcohol is on the menu. *No credit cards.*

Mama Stella's • *Ex-Artillerymen's Club, Victoria St.; tel: 295–9897* • The name says it all—fish dinners, macaroni and cheese, just like Mama used to make. Of course the portions are generous, and you can just hear the cook murmuring, "This'll put some meat on those bones."

Soul Vegetarian Restaurant • *Reid St.; tel: 292–2897* • Run by Black Hebrews, this cafe serves lentil burgers, fried tofu sandwiches, grilled soy cheese on whole wheat toast, tofu salad, protein rolls, and a variety of soups.

The Table Spoon • *Emporium Building, Front St.; tel: 295–5203* • In a glitzy mall, this small, bright cafe is a good place to stop for breakfast, lunch, or afternoon tea. The homestyle pastries are the main attraction, especially the cinnamon-laced Bermuda apple cake, baked by the Bermudian mother-in-law of the Austrian owner. While cassava pie is usually reserved for Christmas, Easter, Cup Match, and other special occasions, it is served here year-round. Made with grated cassava root, eggs, butter, milk, and chicken, pork, or beef, this rich dish is slightly sweet. Another local favorite found here is the Sunday codfish breakfast (in a sauce of tomatoes, onions, and peppers with avocados, bananas, and boiled potatoes on the side). Lunch is kicked off with soups such as mushroom or chicken noodle, followed by salads or crabmeat, roast beef, pastrami, or other sandwiches. *Open 7 a.m.–5 p.m.*

Mac Williams • *Front St.* • Three meals a day are served at this pleasant restaurant near Waterloo House. For lunch, try the sandwiches, codfish cakes, pasta salad, peas and rice, or crabmeat on an English muffin with melted cheese. For dinner, chicken, veggie burgers, and lasagne are good choices.

The Reid Street Cafe • *Williams House, Reid St.,; tel: 292–4704* • Near many of Hamilton's stores, this cafe makes a good stop for weary shoppers. Dinner is served on Thursday, Friday, and Saturday nights only. DA.

Angle Street Deli • *Angle and Court sts.; tel: 292–5246* • You'll get generous portions of ribs, sausage and beans, meat loaf, and other hearty selections at this Mom and Pop–style deli. Bermudians know that this is one of the best places to find good home-baked desserts, such as apple or peach cobbler.

Country Life • *The Recorder Bldg., Court St. between Victoria and Church sts.; 292–1478* • Run by Seventh Day Adventists, this eatery serves imaginative vegetarian fare, such as whole wheat potato and vegetable pie, and pasta or tofu dishes. The atmosphere is very friendly, with patrons at different tables holding lively conversations. Stop by for lunch, Monday to Friday, 11:30 a.m. to 3 p.m.

The Docksider Pub and Restaurant • *Next to Scandal Nightclub on Front St.; tel: 292–4089* • This pub boasts the island's largest selection of ales and lagers.

OUTSKIRTS OF HAMILTON

EXPENSIVE
Harley's • *Princess Hotel; tel: 295–3000* • A long wine list accompanies the menu of European specialties. A pianist entertains in the evenings. Lunch is served daily, and dinner is served every evening but Monday.

Once Upon A Table • *Serpentine Road; tel: 295–8585* • This former home, beautifully decorated with Victorian touches, has rounded archways, a sofa, and lace curtains. The atmosphere and service are warm and friendly. You'll be given sherbet between courses and sweets at the end of your meal. In addition, wine stewards, candlelit tables, and plentiful food make this continental restaurant one of the island's most pleasant places to dine. Stop by for afternoon tea with cucumber and watercress sandwiches, strawberries with cream, hot scones with jam, and homemade pastries. Once Upon a Table is closed on Mondays. *Major credit cards.* DA.

INEXPENSIVE
The Green Lantern • *Serpentine Road, between Pitts Bay Road and Rosemont Avenue; tel: 295–6995* • For some local flavor, stop by this casual, friendly restaurant for fish and chips, peas and rice, broiled fish, chicken, or pork chops. No alcohol is served. The Green Lantern

is closed Wednesday afternoons. It's about a 20-minute walk from the ferry dock.

Richardson's Chicken and Ribs • *North Shore Road; tel: 293–9577* • No longer is this the place to go for fish cakes, beef pies, and other Bermudian dishes. In its new incarnation Richardson's now specializes in fried chicken and shrimp and barbeque ribs. It opens for breakfast at 6 a.m. and closes at 10 p.m.

DEVONSHIRE

Restaurants are limited to dining rooms in the cottage colony and guest houses.

SMITH'S

MODERATE
The Inlet • *Palmetto Hotel, junction of Flatts Hill, North Shore, and Harrington Sound roads; tel: 293–2323* • While visiting the eastern side of Bermuda, you may want to stop at the small restaurant here for a lunch that includes a salad bar.

Specialty Inn • *Collectors Hill; tel: 236–3133* • This down-to-earth restaurant serves the kind of Bermudian and Italian food Mom used to make. Pastas include ravioli, spaghetti and meatballs, and fettuccine Alfredo. Pizza comes in several varieties. On the local side of the menu, consider the pan-fried fresh fish or deep-fried shrimp or scallops. Or try the roast turkey breast, Virginia baked ham, roast beef, or steak and mushrooms. For dessert, if you're not in the mood for ice cream (chocolate, vanilla, or strawberry, of course), the lemon meringue pie and the cheesecake are worth the calories.

HAMILTON PARISH

EXPENSIVE
Plantation Club • *Harrington Sound Road; tel: 293–1188* • When you surface from a visit to Leamington Caves, stop at this restaurant.

Its reputation as a *real* Bermudian dining place has grown dramatically. The menu includes steaks, chops, chicken, and seafood. You can dine outdoors in the summer and inside by a log fire on cool evenings. Dinner is served every night except Sunday and the restaurant closes from mid-December to the end of February. *Major credit cards.*

MODERATE TO EXPENSIVE

Tom Moore's Tavern • *Harrington Sound Road, Walsingham Bay (near Leamington Caves)* • The scenic grounds surrounding this gourmet restaurant are maintained by the Bermuda National Trust. Named after the Irish poet who lived on the island in the early-19th century, the tavern was built in 1652 as a private home. *Major credit cards.*

INEXPENSIVE

Half Way House • *Flatts Village; tel: 293–9200* • This popular spot was named for its location between the city of Hamilton and St. George's. It is not far from the Aquarium. The menu includes hamburgers, sandwiches, soups, fish cakes, chicken legs, and fountain drinks.

Bailey's Ice Cream Parlour • *Blue Hole Hill; tel: 292–3703* • In this Victorian-style spot, you can cool off with homemade ice cream. Across from the Swizzle Inn, this ice-cream parlor also serves swizzle sherbert.

Swizzle Inn • *Blue Hole Hill; tel: 293–9300* • This is a favorite stop among cyclists traveling between the city of Hamilton and St. George. Patrons have plastered their calling cards all over the restaurant. The home of the rum swizzle, a fruity drink that is more powerful than it tastes, the inn also serves swizzle burgers, shepherd's pie, sandwiches, and omelets, as well as Bermudian coffee (with Bermuda Gold liqueur). *Mastercard and Visa.*

ST. GEORGE'S

IN TOWN

EXPENSIVE

The Carriage House • *Water St.; tel: 297–1730 or 297–1270* • In the same building as the Carriage Museum, this restaurant is on the waterfront in the newly renovated plaza. The bare brick walls and arches retain the flavor of the 18th-century warehouse it once was. Beef and seafood dishes are on the menu. There is also a large salad bar. This is a good place to bring the family, especially for Sunday brunch. *Major credit cards.*

The Margaret Rose • *St. George's Club; tel: 297–1200* • This elegant hilltop restaurant overlooks the town and harbor of St. George's. Men are requested to wear jackets at dinner, which is served by candlelight. Menu selections might include fresh smoked river trout with cranberry cream, mushroom caps with tomato and herb stuffing, cream of onion soup, broiled double lambchops, or roast duckling. Reservations are suggested. The Margaret Rose is open daily for lunch and dinner. Brunch is served all day during the off season. *Major credit cards. DA.*

MODERATE TO EXPENSIVE

Wharf Tavern • *Somers Wharf; tel: 297–1515* • You'll find Bermudian, regional American, and Italian dishes on the eclectic menu here. Bermuda fish chowder or Portuguese red bean soup are good for openers. The avocado and shrimp salad is tasty. With more than a dozen toppings to choose among—from jalapeno peppers to pineapple or tuna—ordering a pizza can be a feat. Fresh fish comes broiled, pan-fried, or blackened Cajun style. For carnivores, liver and onions, ribs, and sirloin steak are also served. *M, V, D.*

MODERATE

Clyde's Cafe and Bar • *York Street; tel: 297–0158* • People come from all over the island for the fish sandwiches, fish and chips, and cole slaw served up in this neighborhood pub. Choose from the selection of beers and ales or try a dark and stormy (black rum and tangy ginger beer). Clyde's is open from noon until 1 a.m., except Tuesdays. *No credit cards.*

INEXPENSIVE

Pub on the Square • *King's Sq.; tel: 297–1522* • This British-style country pub serves sandwiches, pizza burgers, fish and chips, and has live entertainment at night. It's a good place to stop for lunch. *Major credit cards.*

White Horse Tavern • *King's Sq.* • The location on the harbor makes this extra special. A casual restaurant with indoor and outdoor dining, this is St. George's oldest tavern. The building was originally Government House. *Major credit cards.*

OUTSIDE TOWN

MODERATE

Gunpowder Cavern • *Government Hill; tel: 297–0904* • One of St. George's unusual restaurants, this was once a gunpowder cavern.

The menu includes filet mignon, lamb chops, veal, chicken, and seafood. Children's portions are available on request.

INEXPENSIVE TO MODERATE

Dennis' Hideaway • *St. David's Rd.; tel: 297–0044* • You will be hard-pressed to find two pieces of furniture that match in this somewhat ramshackle, family-operated restaurant on the water. However, many locals and visitors consider this an ideal place for fresh Bermudian dishes such as turtle steaks, seafood stews, conch fritters, and shark hash. No alcohol is sold.

Black Horse Tavern • *St. David's, between airport and St. David's Lighthouse; tel: 293–9742* • At the water's edge, the glassed-in outer dining room and grassy al fresco patio look out to bobbing boats. If you ask a Bermudian where to find the island's best local food, chances are you'll be directed here. Try the curried conch with rice, the fried fish and chips (not greasy in the least), or the shark hash on toast.

WHERE TO STAY

Not only does Bermuda offer a wide variety of accommodations from simple to luxurious, but it is also difficult to find a place to stay that is not well-kept, comfortable, and convenient to the rest of the island. No matter where you stay, you'll be close to beaches, water sports, tennis, golf, sightseeing, shopping, and restaurants. Many hotels that are not within walking distance of a beach provide complimentary transportation.

Rooms in most guest houses, cottage colonies, and small hotels are individually decorated. These homelike touches reflect the personal attention guests can expect from staff. In addition, evidence of Bermuda's rich history is apparent in the architecture and surroundings of many of these accommodations.

Many guest houses, which can be quite economical, are in former private homes in garden settings. Most have pools and some are on the waterfront. Some serve breakfast and other meals, but many don't have dining rooms. Visitors can also save money by renting rooms in private homes. Make arrangements by contacting the Visitors' Service Bureau, Front Street, Hamilton, Bermuda.

Housekeeping cottages and apartments, with full cooking facilities and limited maid service, are popular with families and those who want privacy as well as comfort. Cottage colonies are like housekeeping units, except that they have main clubhouses with dining rooms, lounges, and bars. Their kitchen facilities may be used for light snacks but not for full-time cooking. Most cottage colonies are on private beaches and have pools. During the summer season, some require a certain number of nights minimum stay and room rates generally include breakfast and dinner.

Bermuda has two luxurious private clubs, Coral Beach and Tennis Club and the Mid Ocean Club. Both require the introduction of a member. Visitors can investigate time-sharing at St. George's Club.

While resort hotels may be more impersonal than other accommodations, they offer the greatest number of facilities, including private beaches, indoor and outdoor pools, golf courses, tennis courts, scuba diving, waterskiing, snorkeling, sailing, bars, restaurants, night clubs, international and local entertainment, and planned activities. Many have cycle liveries, stores, barber shops, beauty salons, games rooms, and taxi stands on the premises. Though with less extensive facilities, smaller hotels all have beaches and/or pools. While most establishments will help guests make arrangements for babysitters, and some have high chairs, large hotels may be best for children since many also have shallow pools and other recreational facilities for children. Some also have children's summer programs that leave parents free to do their own thing.

All hotels and most guest houses are fully air-conditioned. (You may pay a daily surcharge, however, to use the air conditioners at some guest houses and housekeeping apartments.) The larger hotels have social desks where you can make arrangements to go on tours, or to take part in activities such as golf and scuba diving when they are not available at your accommodation. Most hotels and cottage colonies and some guest houses have nightly entertainment. Most will make arrangements for sports activities not available on the premises. Many serve complimentary high tea.

Most hotels and cottage colonies have MAP rates (Modified American Plan: the price of the room includes a full breakfast and dinner). Some hotels, particularly during the winter season, also offer BP (Bermuda Plan: full breakfast), and EP rates (European Plan: no meals). Except in a few cases, housekeeping apartments offer EP only. Guest houses offer MAP, BP, EP, and CP (Continental Plan: light breakfast). A daily service charge of about 10% (in lieu of tips) and a 6% government tax will be added to the cost of your room. *Note that most accommodations, even some large hotels, do not accept credit cards.* Some guest houses and hotels close for a few weeks during November, December, and January. See "Hotel Quick Reference Charts" for specifics.

RENTING PRIVATE HOMES AND CONDOMINIUMS

Especially during the late '80s, more than a few small tourist accommodations were converted into condominiums. Those who would like to rent private homes or condos can contact the Secretary of the Bermuda Chamber of Commerce Real Estate Division, c/o Visitors' Service Bureau, Front Street, Hamilton, Bermuda; (809) 295–4201. The following are some of the real estate agents you can also contact:

- Bermuda Realty Company Ltd., P.O. Box HM 724, Hamilton, Bermuda; (809) 295–0294
- L. P. Gutteridge, P.O. Box HM 1024, Hamilton, Bermuda; (809) 295–4545
- Kitson & Company, P.O. Box 449, Hamilton, Bermuda; (809) 295–2525
- Joy Lusher Estate Agent, Darrell's Wharf, Harbour Road, Warwick 7-17, Bermuda; (809) 296–5120 or (809) 296–0108

In the **Hotel Quick-Reference Charts,** you'll find more information about the following accommodations, which we highly recommend, as well as details about additional establishments.

RESORT HOTELS

☆☆☆ **The Belmont Hotel Golf and Country Club** • *Warwick* • On a 110-acre estate overlooking Hamilton Harbour, this resort also has wonderful views across Great Sound. The elegant lobby, chintzy like an English country house, welcomes guests with polished cedar pillars and paneling. Even elevator interiors are covered in cedar. There is a large L-shaped pool, and the hotel provides complimentary transportation to its south shore beach club. Electric golf carts are used on the private 18-hole championship golf course. Three all-weather tennis courts are lit for evening games. Rooms are furnished with Georgian pieces and TVs are hidden in imposing highboys. The ferry to the city of Hamilton, just a few minutes away, sails from the Belmont dock. Guests are offered exchange privileges with the Harmony Club. (Expensive)

☆☆☆ **Elbow Beach Hotel** • *Paget* • On a private section of one of Bermuda's most popular beaches, this south-shore hotel is centrally located, only 10 minutes from downtown Hamilton. Guests can stay in balconied rooms in the main hotel, duplex cottages, lanais overlooking the free-form pool and ocean, and surfside lanais. Some ground-floor guest-rooms in the main building may be noisy since they are on a main hallway with shops and much activity. Some of the hotel's rooms have been redecorated, and new rooms have been added by the pool. Another addition is a shopping promenade. The marbled lobby is now an atrium with sun streaming from its skylight. The pool is heated and has a fountain and a shallow play area for children. Two of the five tennis courts are lit for evening games and there is a health club. Note that Elbow Beach is the center of activities during College Weeks in March and April. (Expensive)

☆☆☆ **Grotto Bay Beach Hotel & Tennis Club** • *Hamilton Parish* • The 21 acres of beautifully landscaped hillside on the water's edge make this a particularly pleasant place to stay. Located in nine cottages, all rooms have balconies with panoramic sea views. Some have color TV, refrigerators, coffee makers, and all have hair dryers. The decor throughout is bright and attractive, especially the sunny garden room where guests can have breakfast. There are two beaches, a pool, tennis courts, and a putting green. Prospero's, a night club, is only one of the illuminated grottos on the property and there are nightly shows in the Rum House Lounge. Grotto Bay has many activities for children including a summer "day camp." (Expensive)

★★★★★ **Marriott's Castle Harbour Resort** • *Tucker's Town* • This impressive luxury hotel stands on a high bluff overlooking Castle Harbour and Harrington Sound. Behind the unpainted limestone walls, which are truly castlelike, lies the beautifully elegant round lobby, with gleaming marble and terracotta tile floors. The 250 acres of well-tended grounds include an 18-hole Robert Trent Jones golf course, seven tennis courts, three heated swimming pools, and two sandy beaches. Guests are able to indulge in a number of water sports such as windsurfing, waterskiing, and snorkeling. Sunfish and mopeds can also be rented on premises. Guests rooms, suites, and public spaces are decorated with Queen Anne and Chippendale furnishings. Most rooms, some of which have balconies or patios, face the ocean. The Harbour Wing spills down a steep cliff to the waterside. At the entrance, the arresting view of the ocean through the tall windows is overwhelming. Instead of taking the elevator *up* to your room, you'll ride *down*. The six restaurants include Bermuda's only Japanese restaurant, The Mikado. Blossom's is the resort's popular night club. Guests not wanting to go into Hamilton for shopping will find that branches of some of the city's best shops are located in the hotel with merchandise at the same prices as in town. (Expensive)

★★★★ **The Princess** • *Pembroke* • This luxury resort on Hamilton Harbour is at the edge of the city's main drag. The Princess is one of the island's first hotels. A few of the more famous guests during its 100-plus years of service have been Mark Twain, Prince Charles, and Muhammad Ali. From the elegant lobby, a marble staircase leads up to an indoor balcony with a striking view of the harbor. Hotel photos and menus dating back to the 19th century decorate the balcony wall. People having drinks in the back of the lobby can gaze at a fish-filled pond bordered by trees, moss, and small waterfalls. Floor-to-ceiling windows surround most of the Gazebo Lounge. Many rooms have private balconies. There are two oceanside pools—one freshwater, the other salt. Guests have exchange privileges with the Southampton Princess, and complimentary transportation is provided to the private south-shore beach club and 18-hole golf course.

Special arrangements are made for repeat guests, such as business travelers. Through the Princess Club, members are guaranteed rooms and take advantage of express check-in and check-out. They receive a corporate rate, complimentary continental breakfast, and afternoon wine and cheese. Rooms for club members have TV sets, terry robes, toiletry kits, suit and skirt hangers, and desks with telephones. Golf- and tennis-playing executives are given a discount and there is same-day laundry and cleaning service. Checks up to $200 may be cashed and companies may be billed directly. Applicants may call (809) 295–2254. (Expensive)

★★★★ **Sonesta Beach Hotel** • *Southampton* • After being closed for several months for a $3 million renovation, this modern, beach-front hotel located on 25 acres of landscaped grounds reopened in early 1991. All rooms have balconies with views of the ocean. One of the three beaches is enclosed in a sheltered bay. Popular with honeymooners, the Sonesta Beach has a moongate through which newly married couples walk for good luck. The lawn overlooking cliffs and crashing surf is a dramatic place for sitting and relaxing. There are two pools—one enclosed in a bubble; the other, outdoors, is heated. In addition to tennis, windsurfing, scuba diving, and snorkeling, guests can play shuffleboard, croquet, and Ping-Pong. Golf courses are nearby. The European health spa has a universal gym and separate facilities for men and women including exercise and massage rooms, whirlpools, saunas, and steam baths. (Expensive)

★★★★★ **The Southampton Princess Hotel** • *Southampton* • A luxurious Georgian-furnished hotel on a 60-acre estate, the Southampton Princess has two pools, one indoors and the other outdoors, a nearby private beach club (transportation provided), an 18-hole executive golf course, and 11 tennis courts. It is perched on a hill and the spacious rooms with walk-in closets all have balconies with panoramic views. In addition to its gourmet restaurants, the hotel has other rooms for dining, as well as for dancing and entertainment. The Whaler Inn, a restaurant at the south shore beach club, and the Waterlot, a more formal dining spot on the north shore, are both run by the hotel. Transportation is provided. Inquire about the 54-room Newport Club, with special amenities for guests, which has opened in a wing of the 6th floor. Guests can take advantage of exchange privileges with the Princess Hotel at the edge of Hamilton. (Expensive)

SMALL HOTELS

★★★ **Glencoe Harbour Club** • *Paget* • Many guests, particularly avid boaters, return year after year to this waterfront owner-operated hotel. The main house is more than two centuries old. There are two heated freshwater pools and a (very) small manmade beach. With water on three sides, Glencoe is perfect for those who want to go windsurfing (lessons are given), deep-sea fishing, scuba diving, waterskiing, and sunfish sailing (free to guests). The bar on the large patio overlooks the small inlet where boats always seem to be coming and going. Guests eat meals on the lively patio or in the attractive indoor dining room. Meals range from pepper pot or chilled avocado soup to codfish cakes with banana chutney, roast duckling, and chocolate brioches with raspberry cream. Small winding outdoor stairways lead to guest rooms, each refreshingly distinct, on different levels. The colorful rooms and suites have sitting areas or living rooms, patios or balconies, wicker furniture, and old-fashioned dark exposed-beam ceilings or high wooden tray ceilings. Some also have fireplaces, double balconies, and round bathtubs. In the newest wing, the conference room has a view of the second pool, which doubles as a Jacuzzi. Located in scenic Salt Kettle, where salt was stored during the 1800s, Glencoe is a short walk from the ferry. Guests receive discount ferry tickets to Hamilton as well as complimentary copies of the *Royal Gazette,* Bermuda's daily newspaper. The hotel provides a free taxi ride to the cycle livery for those who want to rent mopeds. (Expensive)

★★★ **Harmony Club** • *Paget* • This all-inclusive resort caters to couples. Although the clientele is much younger than during the days when it was the Harmony Hall Hotel, some things haven't changed: the columned walkway to the entrance, the rich cedar paneling in the lobby, and the gorgeous flowerbeds throughout the grounds. The rate covers three meals a day, unlimited drinks, afternoon tea, evening cocktails, and one two-seater moped per room for your entire stay. In March and November, those who forego mopeds can opt for unlimited public bus transportation. You'll be greeted with a bottle of champagne when you arrive. Rooms, luxuriously decorated with Queen Anne furniture, are equipped with terry-cloth bathrobes or kimonos, hair dryers, and other welcome amenities. Palm Court, the bar/lounge, is the place to go for live entertainment every night but Wednesday. Recreational facilities include tennis courts, a swimming pool, whirlpool, and exercise room. Golfers should ask about the package deals that allow them to play on a different course every day. Guests are transported to the beach and they are admitted free to Oasis and The Club discos in nearby Hamilton. (Expensive)

Mermaid Beach Club • *Warwick* • Readers have written to us complaining about poor maintenance of rooms and facilities and staff indifference. However, the boisterous young folks who descend on this beachfront hotel during College Weeks don't seem to mind. Individual rooms as well as two- and three-bedroom suites with kitchens are available. Most have balconies, and some have televisions. Miramar Restaurant is on the grounds. Room service is available for continental breakfast and light supper. (Expensive)

★★★ **Newstead** • *Paget* • Especially during spring and summer race weeks, sailing enthusiasts flock to this harborside hotel. With the sparkling pastel buildings of Front Street just across the water, the city of Hamilton is a brief ferry ride away. From the patio where lunch is served, guests have a perfect view of waterfront activity. In addition to the heated salt-water pool, where playful dolphins are frozen in a sculpture, there are two all-weather tennis courts, a putting green, and sauna baths. Two private docks are good for deep-water swimming. Brick pathways crossing many small staircases lead throughout the property. One of Newstead's most arresting public rooms is the bar/lounge in the main house, a 19th-century mansion. With blood red walls and plush couches and chairs, this room is a pleasant place to relax. Tea is served every afternoon and English antiques, oriental rugs, a grand piano, and wing chairs decorate the spacious living room and library. Cedar cabinets and dark ceiling beams are set off by stark white walls in the dining room.

Guest rooms are in the main house and in surrounding former private homes. The two huge guest rooms in the main house have sitting areas, large patios, and panoramic views of the water. Two fanlight windows are at the foot of the stairs that lead up to these rooms. Some of the rooms in other buildings share sitting areas and face the gardens or road. Many are decorated with an oriental theme: handsome teak and rosewood chests and chairs from Hong Kong, lamps with abacuses as their bases, Chinese wall hangings. Framed *Vogue* posters from the twenties and earlier add to the visual feast. Rooms have coffee makers and hair dryers. Refrigerators will be provided upon request at an additional cost. Newstead's guests have exchange privileges with the private Coral Beach Club, and with Waterloo House and Horizons and Cottages, among other hotels. (Moderate)

☆☆ **Palm Reef Hotel** • *Paget* • This centrally located low-rising hotel sprawls along the edge of Hamilton Harbour. Some of the balconied rooms overlook the water, where guests can sail, waterski, or swim from the main terrace. Other rooms have views of the large heated pool. The hotel has tennis courts, and complimentary transportation is provided to the beach. On the wall in the tiny coffee shop, a drink menu transports guests to 1927, when a martini could be had for 35¢ and Spanish sherry cost $3 a quart. Off the lobby is a comfortable sitting room with a fireplace. Nightly entertainment includes leading bands and international performers. (Moderate)

☆☆ **Palmetto Hotel & Cottages** • *Smith's* • Sailing, snorkeling, and other watersports are available at this hotel on Harrington Sound that has a small manmade beach, a pool, and a sun terrace. From the entrance to the main house, where a sprawling 200-year-old mahogany tree stands, there is a fabulous view of boat-studded Flatts Inlet. The hotel's original buildings were once a vicarage. The Inlet Restaurant serves a memorable brunch, as well as lunch and dinner. Afternoon tea is served in the lounge. A circular staircase near the lounge in the main house leads to small guest rooms decorated with wicker furniture. Rooms are also in waterside cottages. One unit has a tiny extra room that is good for a child. Unlike in most small hotels, room service is available. Free transportation is provided to a nearby south-shore beach. Located at the edge of pretty Flatts Village, Palmetto Hotel is a 10-minute ride from downtown Hamilton. The aquarium and zoo are within walking distance, and other sightseeing attractions are also nearby. (Moderate)

★★★ **Pompano Beach Club** • *Southampton* • This family-owned and -managed hotel is a cluster of pink, white-roofed buildings on a bluff overlooking the Atlantic. Pompano opened as Bermuda's first fishing club almost forty years ago. Fishing from the private dock is still popular here (particularly bone fishing) and sailing is available. While Pompano is the only completely American-owned hotel in Bermuda, it has a personalized Bermudian atmosphere, from the friendly, helpful staff to the Bermuda cedar in the clubhouse. The managers make a special effort to get to know their guests by name. Viewed from the dining room, bar/lounge, or any of the guest rooms (which all face the ocean), the sunsets are a real treat. For a front-row seat, slip into the Jacuzzi, overlooking the Atlantic. Two late check-out rooms are nearby, each with private bath and telephone. The bay windows in the dining room look out to a cliff above the water and the neighboring golf course. Breakfasts are really special here, with waffles topped with kiwi fruit, honey, coconut, and whipped cream; shrimp and guacamole omelets; kippered herrings; and chocolate chip muffins.

Enclosed by rocky cliffs, the small beach makes for ideal swimming and snorkeling among coral reefs in the clear depths. (Just be careful as you enter the water, since rocks are hidden by the waves.)

At low tide guests can walk 250 yards out to sea on a smooth sandbar. The kidney-shaped pool, with a mosaic pompano on the bottom, overlooks the ocean. A championship clay tennis court is on the premises and the Port Royal Golf Course is right next door. In separate cottages in the hilly grounds, rooms are decorated in a variety of styles, all with patios or balconies where you can arrange to have breakfast served. They are available as studios, cabanas, and suites. Terra-cotta tiles and floral bedspreads and curtains are features of some rooms. Others are decorated with area rugs on parquet floors, Queen Anne furniture, oak nightstands, and ginger jar lamps. Some have fireplaces and dressing rooms. There are telephones, clock radios, irons and ironing boards, and refrigerators in all. Complimentary transportation is provided from the bus stop down the hill from Pompano. (Expensive)

★★★ **The Reefs** • *Southampton* • This hotel is built into a cliffside overlooking its private, secluded south-shore beach. The pool is heated, and guests can fish or play tennis and shuffleboard. All facing the water, rooms are lanai and cabana-style, with wicker furniture, dressing areas, and ceiling fans. Many guests enjoy having tea in the attractive, comfortable lounge filled with natural rattan furniture. Lush hanging plants adorn the dining room, which has a sloping exposed-beam ceiling. On Saturday nights, the Reefs is alive with guests dancing to a combo in the lounge, drinking at the brass-trimmed cedar bar in the adjoining room, and feasting on the elaborate weekly buffet. The music floats through the louvered doors into the main dining room, where the spread might include curried chicken, ribs, pates, steamed mussels, smoked salmon, and a variety of salads. Coconuts is the name of the casual open-air waterview restaurant. On a bulletin board near the front desk, the names of arriving guests are posted along with names and photos of the friendly staff. For guests whose planes leave much later than check-out time, there are five courtesy rooms with showers so that they can spend more time on the beach. (Expensive)

☆☆ **Rosedon** • *Pembroke* • Although several wings with modern rooms have been added, the main building at Rosedon has retained the feeling of an old mansion. On a hill across from the Princess, it is often mistaken for a private home. Overlooking beautifully manicured flowerbeds, the tiled veranda in the front is the locale for weekly cocktail parties. The four guest rooms with the most character are in the original mansion. The rooms in the new wing, around the large heated pool out back, are more motel-like and don't get much light. Guests may have breakfast in their rooms or on the shared balcony outside their doors. Lunch, tea, and light suppers are served in sitting rooms in the old part of the hotel, where rounded floor to ceiling windows border the stairway. Lawns and gardens surround this small hotel, which is in easy walking distance of Hamilton's shops, ferry, and restaurants. Guests have the use of the beach and facilities at the Elbow Beach Hotel in Paget. (Moderate)

★★ **Royal Palms** • *Pembroke* • This large old Bermudian home is in a quiet, residential neighborhood within walking distance of downtown Hamilton. The shuttered windows and the tall curving palm trees out front in the lush, colorful gardens set Royal Palms apart from the surrounding houses. There is a restaurant and a bar off a patio where weekly barbecues are given during the summer season. Most of the spacious guest rooms have two double beds. At press time, this accommodation was up for sale. (Moderate)

☆☆ **Somerset Bridge Hotel** • *Sandys* • Water enthusiasts are attracted to this family-run housekeeping apartment hotel because it offers dive packages and has a freshwater pool. In addition, there is a popular restaurant and bar, the Blue Foam. All guest rooms are air conditioned and have balconies overlooking the bay. Close by are the Hamilton ferry (each guest receives one complimentary round-trip ticket), glass bottom boat tours to Sea Gardens, and the unique Somerset bridge. (Moderate)

★★★ **Stonington Beach Hotel** • *Paget* • Just a 10-minute ride from downtown Hamilton, this luxury hotel overlooks a beautiful private southshore beach. Facilities include a freshwater pool and tennis courts. The public rooms and guest rooms are a pleasing combination of the modern and the traditional. At the entrance, sunlight filters through the fronds of a palm in a tiled atrium. Wicker furniture adorns the modern airy lobby, with its arched windows and high open-beam ceilings. Tea is served every afternoon, and the comfortable library, decorated with an oriental rug, has a wood-burning fireplace. The Norwood Room, with its chandeliers and elegant table settings, is one of Bermuda's best restaurants. Guests who are so inclined may help prepare memorable dishes in the kitchen. Ceiling fans, cedar furniture, Italian terra cotta tile floors, refrigerators, and balconies or patios are features of guest rooms. The best views of the ocean are from those on the second floor. One of the island's newest hotels, Stonington has a guest room and special walkways designed for people in wheelchairs. Visitors may be surprised to learn that nearly half the staff members are students of the Bermuda Department of Hotel Technology. (Expensive)

★★ **Waterloo House** • *Pembroke* • An intimate hotel filled with antiques, Waterloo is on the harbor just outside downtown Hamilton. The entrance is an archway that leads to an inviting, greenery-filled courtyard. Tea is served in a cozy sitting room. The elegant dining room has high-backed chairs, chandeliers, and china cabinets. Sunny hallways in the main building look out to flower-filled courtyards. One sitting area is decorated with white rattan chairs, straw mats, and summery floral wallpaper. All air-conditioned, guest rooms have modern baths, attractive area rugs, and large closets. Most have dressing rooms and some have porches and sitting areas with comfortable couches. Televisions will be provided upon request. There is a small heated pool and a private dock. Guests are transported free to a private south-shore beach. Tennis and golf can be arranged. (Moderate)

☆☆ **White Sands** • *Paget* • Built in the 1950s, this pleasant hotel retains some of the feeling of that decade in its homelike public rooms and guest rooms decorated with old wooden chests, tables, and chairs. Oriental rugs cover the brick floor in the lobby. The dark, publike bar is decorated with old photos, such as the one of Front Street in the days when there was a railroad and horse-drawn carriages instead of cars. A huge skylight allows sunshine to pour into the dining room, which resembles that of a cruise ship. Opening to a sun porch and a grassy patio, the large lounge has a fireplace topped by a long cedar mantelpiece. Found in the main building, an adjacent wing, and separate cottages, rooms differ in size and decor. The nicest guest room in the main building, up a curving staircase from the lobby, is huge and extremely sunny, since it has windows on all six walls. The Bermuda-style tray ceiling, the heavy armoire and other old furniture, and the attractive modern bath further enhance a stay here. Some rooms have balconies and refrigerators. A short path will take you to the beach, and Hamilton is just two miles away. (Expensive)

COTTAGE COLONIES

☆☆☆ **Ariel Sands Beach Club** • *Devonshire* • Guest cottages sit along a slope that leads to the long private beach. In the clubhouse, a wrought-iron gate separates the dining room from the spacious sitting room, which has a piano, a large fireplace, and oriental rugs. Guests may dine inside or on the sunny indoor/outdoor patio that faces the pool and the ocean. Small comfortable rooms, some with two double beds and two sinks, have large closets and modern baths, and come equipped with coffee makers. The newest rooms have much more character than the older units. Entertainment includes calypso singers, piano music, and weekly barbecues during the summer season. Ariel Sands has three all-weather tennis courts. Guests have dining exchange privileges with Palmetto Bay and White Sands. (Expensive)

★★★★ **Cambridge Beaches** • *Sandys* • Tucked away on a peninsula in the pastoral western end of the island, Cambridge Beaches is on a 25-acre garden estate. This was Bermuda's first cottage colony and some guests have been returning here for more than 20 years. The cottages, one of which was built three centuries ago by a pirate, overlook Mangrove Bay, Long Bay, and the Atlantic. Some of the suites are huge. While most rooms are tastefully decorated with antiques or reproductions, a few are due for refurbishing. The sitting rooms in the main building, with a wonderful view of the boats in the water, are separated by archways and have antiques and fireplaces. Secluded coves are found along the private beaches. This is a great area for day sails, whether you rent a Boston whaler to explore nearby uninhabited islands on your own or take one of the organized cruises to St. George's, Hamilton, or a reef for snorkeling. Waterskiing, fishing, and other watersports are also available in addition to tennis courts, a putting green, and a large heated pool. Take tennis, windsurfing, scuba diving, or waterskiing lessons or learn to use a kayak. Mangrove Bay and Somerset Village are within walking distance and Hamilton is a ferry ride away. (In season, Cambridge Beaches provides its own ferry service to town twice a week. Complimentary ferry tokens are available the rest of the year.) Room service is offered from 7 a.m. to 6 p.m. (Expensive)

★★★ **Fourways Cottage Colony** • *Paget* • Guests of this posh harborview cottage colony don't have to travel far to dine at one of the island's most celebrated restaurants. Intimate Fourways Cottage Colony is located on the grounds of popular Fourways Inn. Continental breakfast is served in the cottages. The ground-floor suites can be connected to the double rooms upstairs. When you check in, you'll be greeted with a basket of fruit. You'll find fresh flowers; mini bars; balconies or patios; remote control color television; radios; telephones with extensions in the baths; and kitchenettes stocked with orange juice, milk, tea, and coffee. The huge baths have "his" and "hers" sinks, and terrycloth robes are provided. Marble floors in all rooms add to the elegance. Room service is available for three meals and snacks, and there is nightly turn-down service. You can also arrange to have your laundry done. Although not on a beach, Fourways has a freshwater swimming pool, and guests may use a private beach club. (Expensive)

★★★ **Horizons and Cottages** • *Paget* • A circular driveway around a towering cedar leads to the entrance. In the main building, a former mansion, guests are cooled by a ceiling fan while they check in and out at the glistening cedar front desk. The homelike public sitting rooms have wing chairs, handsome side tables, a grandfather clock, china cabinets, and Victorian love seats. A game room is to the right of the entrance. Overlooking the pool and the ocean is a grassy patio with weathered wooden tables, where lunch is served. Guests also eat in the dining room, decorated with hanging plants, or just outside on the brick patio with cast-iron tables and chairs. Horizons is Bermuda's only *Relais et Chateau*. Since it is set into a hillside, there's a breathtaking view of white rooftops nestled in trees, a plot of farmland, and the Atlantic in the distance.

Some of the wonderfully attractive guest rooms, which are equipped with built-in safes, are more modern than others. Over a dozen have fireplaces. Rooms in the cottages are larger than those in the main house. Done in pinks and other pastels, they have appointments including white wicker furniture, terra cotta tiles, dressing areas, and large closets. Most are air conditioned. The four-bedroom "Casuarinas" cottage has a whirlpool and a spacious living room. Visitors staying in cottages have breakfast served on their terraces. Nightly turn-down service is a special plus. Sports facilities are 3 all-weather tennis courts, a 9-hole pitch-and-putt golf course, and an 18-hole putting green. (Expensive)

★★★★ **Lantana Colony Club** • *Sandys* • This family-run hideaway is among the most sumptuous resorts in Bermuda. Plush cottage units, done in pastel colors, have private quarry-tiled patios, aromatic cedar chests, and extensive views of the Great Sound. There are split-level suites as well as units with separate living rooms and two bedrooms. Most have the latest in baths. However, some rooms are in need of upgrading. Guests staying in the Pool House cottage may use the owner's private pool. Those who forgo continental breakfast served in their cottages may have a full breakfast in the clubhouse. The main dining room, with ceiling beams hand-painted in floral designs, is where guests eat when they first arrive. After they have spent several days at Lantana, they'll be seated in the dazzling solarium dining room, where sunlight spills over plants, antiques, and polished Bermuda cedar tables. The menu, which changes daily, might include dishes such as steamed asparagus, gazpacho, and sauted calves liver with apple rings and onion. After dinner, guests move to the lounge, decorated with oil paintings, for demitasse or liqueurs.

On land that was once a Bermuda onion farm, Lantana's 22 acres are rich in spectacular plantings, including orchids, antheriums, and other tropical flowers, all growing around fountains and life-size bronze sculpture. The Canary Island date palms resemble overgrown pineapples. Many people are amused by the bench where there's a statue of a woman reading a newspaper. The umbrella of a huge almond tree provides a shady spot for relaxing. Another highlight of the property is a bridge over the old railway right-of-way now used only by joggers, cyclists, and, occasionally, horses. In addition to tennis courts, a fresh-water pool, a small beach, and a private dock where watersports are available, there are a croquet lawn and a shuffle board. The Port Royal Golf Club is not far away. (Expensive)

★★★★ **Pink Beach Club** • *Smith's* • The two south-shore beaches make Pink Beach Club an especially pleasant place to stay. And, yes, the sand really does have a pink cast, from pulverized coral and shells. The club was built as a home by Americans during the Depression and opened as a hotel in 1947. Some of the friendly staff members have worked here for more than 25 years. Hilly pathways lead through the hotel's extensive gardens. Guests may relax in wing chairs in the lounge, which has a fireplace. The spacious main dining room, with a menu that changes daily, overlooks the water and guest cottages. The longer guests stay, the closer they are seated to the picture window when they dine. A full breakfast is served in the dining room or in the cottages. While some rooms get little light, they are attractively decorated with dark wood furniture and have modern baths (some of which are huge). Second-story rooms are topped by open beam or tray ceilings. All have radios, televisions, and balconies or patios, and some have views of the boulders in the ocean. When the water is clear, parrot fish are visible. Sports facilities include a large freshwater pool and two tennis courts. Golf can be arranged at the nearby Mid Ocean Club. Nightly entertainment takes place by the pool or the bar. The club does not take children under 5 and it closes from December through February. (Expensive)

★★★ **The St. George's Club** • *St. George's* • This combination cottage colony/time-sharing resort sits on a hill overlooking the town of St. George's and its picturesque harbor. Modern one-bedroom cottages are available along with two-bedroom, two-bath duplexes. In the two-bedroom units, you'll dine on Wedgwood china and crystal. Terra-cotta tiles the kitchen, which is separated from the living room by a cedar bar. The spacious living room is decorated with Haitian cotton couches and dark wood tables and chairs. Off the living room and guest room is a patio. Upstairs, the plush master bedroom makes lingering easy. Two steps up are all that divides the bedroom area from the huge sunken tub, by a window, and the two sinks. The toilet and stall shower are enclosed, however. Bright lights trim the vanity mirror. Ceiling fans or air conditioners cool the air. At night, curl up in bed with a book from the selection of *New York Times* best-sellers. In addition to Margaret Rose, the gourmet restaurant, there are a pub, a lounge, and a gourmet food shop. Sports facilities include three freshwater pools, complimentary transportation to a private beach, all-weather tennis courts, and an 18-hole golf course. (Expensive)

☆☆ **Willowbank** • *Sandys* • To enter this cottage colony, guests pass through a stone moongate. Although Willowbank is an international Christian retreat, with daily devotional hours and no bar service, anyone is welcome. (Guests may have their own liquor in their rooms.) In the main building, the fireplaces, cedar-paneled walls, high ceilings, and well-worn comfortable furniture give the library and lounges a homelike feeling. The guest rooms are somewhat plain. Facilities include two beaches, tennis courts, and a freshwater pool. Except on barbecue nights during the summer, guests are asked to wear formal attire to dinner. Some have complained that portions at meals are far from generous. (Moderate)

GUEST HOUSES

Loughlands • *Paget* • This gracious mansion built in 1920 is set on nine flourishing acres. The tennis court sits on the terraced front lawn. White cast-iron garden furniture decorates the front porch and the entrance is shaded by a balcony. Enter the wide foyer and you'll be stepping back in time. The grandfather clock is over a century old. In the lounge, whose floors are covered with thick carpets brought from China, you'll see a mirrored Victorian chest and a hearth where cedar fires burn on cool winter nights. Breakfast is served in the dining room, across from the lounge. A window seat on the landing halfway up the stairs may tempt you to sit a while on your way to your room. Many guests admire the old tapestry and paintings on the walls. Most of the rooms contain English antiques. All have coffee makers and radios. Some share baths. A bus stop is nearby and Elbow Beach is a 10-minute walk away. (Inexpensive)

Edgehill Manor • *Pembroke* • This beautiful colonial-style mansion with high ceilings and a handsome wooden staircase is in a residential area on the outskirts of the city of Hamilton. Each bright, airy room has its own character. Most have balconies and two have their own kitchens. Some are air conditioned, while others are cooled by ceiling fans. You can have breakfast served in your room or in the cheerful dining room. Arriving guests are greeted with pots of English tea. The personal attention of the owner and staff makes a stay here particularly pleasant. Set in a secluded garden, Edgehill Manor has a small freshwater swimming pool. (Inexpensive)

Fordham Hall • *Pembroke* • If you're looking for convenience and a relaxed setting, consider Fordham Hall. Although breakfast is the only meal served here, restaurants and stores in Hamilton are within easy walking distance. Staying here will put you close enough to the capital to take advantage of downtown attractions whenever the spirit moves you, yet you'll feel pleasantly removed from city life. While eating your morning meal on the glass-enclosed veranda, you'll be able to watch the activity in Hamilton Harbour. Some of the comfortable, homey rooms, cooled by ceiling fans, also have views of the water. The harborview corner rooms, with their lacy curtains fluttering in the breeze, are popular with guests who've stayed here before. Although the sound of mopeds, cars, and horse-drawn carriages can be noisy at times, the view is excellent. (Inexpensive)

Greene's Guest House • *Southampton* • Half of the eight warmly decorated rooms, which vary in size and decor, look out to the water. All are equipped with refrigerators, telephones, coffee makers, TV, and VHS. The cozy dining room where breakfast is served adjoins the large open kitchen. Known for her curried goat and rice, Ms. Greene (originally from Trinidad) will prepare a four-course dinner on request for an additional charge. Across from the dining room, a short staircase leads past a plant-filled passageway to the large sitting room. Here you'll find a radio, books, and a working fireplace. Nearby is a games room with a dart board. Overlooking the sound, a large swimming pool and bar are out back. A five-minute walk will take you to the beach. (Inexpensive)

Hillcrest Guest House • *St. George's* • A family-operated guest house more than two centuries old, Hillcrest is on the edge of the 17th-century town of St. George's. It has spacious verandas, lawns and gardens, and is convenient to restaurants and shopping. A Robert Trent Jones golf course is a 10-minute stroll away. From the balcony off the upstairs sitting room, there is a breathtaking view of the town and St. George's Harbour, where yacht races take place. Although no meals are served here, Hillcrest is within walking distance of the restaurants in town. This eclectically furnished home has been in the family of its current owners since 1914. The owners, who boast a lot of repeat business, give guests as much personal attention as they need. Half-price bus tickets are provided. (Inexpensive)

Hi-Roy • *Pembroke* • Just off North Shore Road, Hi-Roy is located in the residential Princess Estate. You'll get a lot for your money at this six-room guest house run by Hyacinth ("Hi") and Everard ("Roy") Jones. Rates include breakfast and dinner, served in the petite window-enclosed dining room. Hi-Roy is popular with visiting college students. The shared refrigerator is used to store lunch fixin's and snacks. At least one room (all have private baths) has a closet in the bathroom—so with steam from the shower, there's no need to worry about ironing your clothes! All rooms come with satellite TV. Guests have the run of the house. Mr. Jones, a jazz lover, says that sooner or later most visitors find their way to his sound room. He welcomes company as he listens to music and watches one of his 300 video tapes of concerts featuring jazz greats such as John Coltrane, Dizzie Gillespie, Miles Davis, and Milt Jackson. Bus stops are nearby. (Inexpensive)

Little Pomander Guest House • *Paget* • On the edge of Hamilton Harbour, this old Bermuda cottage has a waterfront patio with a barbecue, and is close to beaches, as well as to downtown Hamilton. (Inexpensive)

The Oxford House • *Pembroke* • This old townhouse is within walking distance of downtown Hamilton. The entrance to the handsome building is bordered by two columns supporting a small balcony over the arched doorway. A gracious curving staircase just inside leads to comfortable spacious rooms. This family-operated guest house has the atmosphere of a friendly private home. (Moderate)

Pleasant View Guest House • *Pembroke* • Located in the residential Princess Estate off North Shore Road, Pleasant View has a pool and six comfortable bedrooms of varying sizes. You'll find books in all rooms and refrigerators in some. All have private baths, ceiling fans, telephones, clock radios, and televisions. Guests are welcome to use the washer, dryer, iron, and ironing board. Making visitors feel like part of the family, owner Uriel Griffin serves a full breakfast in the homelike dining room. (Inexpensive)

Que Sera • *Paget* • The grounds here are very attractive, with a bird bath, wrought-iron garden furniture, a pool, and patio. In the largest unit, a fireplace keeps guests warm during the winter if necessary. With a pullout bed, this apartment can sleep four. Most units come with kitchenettes, and some have spacious modern baths. TVs and radios are provided in rooms. (Inexpensive)

Royal Heights • *Southampton* • At the top of a driveway that would almost be vertical if it were any steeper, Royal Heights is aptly named. Not far from Henry VIII Restaurant, this guest house is poised high on a hill. Balconies run the width of the three-story, crescent-shaped house. The view of the surrounding hills and houses and the boat-studded Great Sound is so breathtaking that you'll feel as if you're seeing it for the first time every time you look. Continental breakfast is served in the handsomely furnished dining room with wide windows. Nearby is the comfortable living room with a decorative fireplace. A circular staircase leads down to pool-level rooms. With two double beds and a long balcony, room #3 is the largest of the seven guest rooms. The sunken tub and the walk-in closet help make it extremely popular among repeat guests. All rooms have televisions, refrigerators, and clock radios. Russell and Jean Richardson are your amiable hosts. Royal Heights is near south-shore beaches. (Inexpensive)

Salt Kettle House • *Paget* • This quiet, modern guest house with cottages is just across the road from the harbor and has a private dock. Some rooms have kitchenettes. Close to the ferry, Salt Kettle boasts 80% repeat guests. Discount ferry tickets and room service are provided. (Inexpensive)

LARGE HOUSEKEEPING COTTAGES AND APARTMENTS

Astwood Cove • *Warwick* • In a residential neighborhood near south-shore beaches, these well-kept apartments provide maximum privacy and comfort. The cluster of attractive buildings surrounding a pool are painted sparkling white. Guests are welcome to use the barbecue grill in the communal outdoor tiled courtyard. In the enclosed TV room, the health-conscious can work out on the exercycle. The main house dates back to about 1710 and was part of a dairy farm before guest apartments were built in the 1960s. Facilities include a sauna. (Moderate)

Brightside • *Smith's* • Located in Flatts Village, one of Bermuda's most attractive areas, this homelike accommodation looks out to Flatts Inlet. Out front, tall palms rise from a grassy area with flower beds. The brightly furnished one- and two-bedroom apartments, cooled by ceiling fans, have modern kitchens. Shady verandas hide behind handsome columns. Many guests park themselves at the spacious, very sunny pool patio. Walk across the bridge to the aquarium, or hop into one of the public buses that stop nearby. (Inexpensive)

Clairfont Apartments • *Warwick* • Close to bus stops, entertainment, and restaurants, Clairfont is in a residential area and has a pool and sundeck. (Inexpensive)

Clear View Suites • *Hamilton Parish* • Overlooking a rocky shore where guests can swim, these cottages are also near a sandy beach. There are two pools on the premises. Joggers take advantage of the picturesque trail along the water. The large balconied guest rooms, some with kitchenettes and sitting areas, all have high ceilings and are equipped with radios and televisions. Cribs and high chairs are available. A bus stop right outside the entrance makes transportation around the island very convenient. Clear View is midway between Flatts Village and the town of St. George. (Moderate)

Longtail Cliffs • *Warwick* • These cheerful apartments on the south shore all have balconies with ocean views. Rooms are appointed with white wicker upholstered furniture and straw mats on the tiled floors. Most units have two bedrooms, two baths, and a kitchen. There is a swimming pool, and guests can use Mermaid Beach facilities. The beaches in this area are pale pink. (Expensive)

Munro Beach Cottages • *Southampton* • Getting to this quiet locale is part of the fun. The road snakes through the wonderfully scenic Port Royal Golf Course. Perched high above the water, the eight cottages house the 16 plain but comfortable air-conditioned units. Each has a modern full kitchen, a couch, table and chairs, a ceiling fan, phone, and clock radio. Sliding glass doors open to patios facing the ocean and great sunsets. Guests may arrange to have groceries delivered at no extra charge. Have breakfast at the Port Royal Club House when you're not in the mood to cook. The Port Royal tennis courts are a five-minute walk away. A path leads down to the beach. (Moderate)

Pretty Penny • *Paget* • Near Fourways Inn, Pretty Penny is a good choice for travelers who like privacy in a personalized setting. Four cottages house nine upscale guest rooms, all with private patios and kitchenettes. Hibachis are also provided. Varying in size and decor, the units are accented with throw rugs, tile floors, and wicker or cane furniture. Two have fireplaces, one of which works. Weekly cocktail parties take place on the wooden deck surrounding the small pool. White cast-iron garden furniture and a plant-covered archway make the flourishing grounds even more pleasant. (Inexpensive to Moderate)

Rosemont • *Pembroke* • This group of housekeeping units has a large pool area with a stunning view of Hamilton Harbour and the Great Sound. The grounds are nicely landscaped with colorful flowers and thatch palms, and there is a citrus orchard. Each self-contained unit has a private entrance and some have private balconies. Double beds will be provided upon request. Some apartments have been specially designed to accommodate wheelchairs. The newest addition—the penthouse suite—contains three units, each with a living/sleeping room, a complete kitchen, and a private balcony. Rosemont is within walking distance of downtown Hamilton. Guests are given complimentary newspapers. (Moderate)

The Sandpiper • *Warwick* • In a residential neighborhood of South Shore Road, these attractive apartments have a garden and pool. Buses, beaches, hotels, and entertainment are all nearby. (Moderate)

Surf Side • *Warwick* • The small lobby is decorated with rattan, floral-cushioned chairs and couches, and rich wood. Your unit might come with a large kitchen separated from the living room by a spacious counter, cane-back chairs around the dining table, a Haitian cotton couch, and a patio with a view of the ocean. Some apartments have vinyl bar stools and twin beds, but most are spacious and brightly appointed. The swimming pool gazes down on the Atlantic. (Moderate)

SMALL HOUSEKEEPING COTTAGES AND APARTMENTS

Angel's Grotto • *Smith's* • Among Bermuda's nicest small accommodations, these housekeeping cottages hug the waterfront at Harrington Sound. The circular driveway surrounds a sprawling tree. Guests check in in the owner's grandmother-esque living room, crowded with china, porcelain statues, and other knickknacks. The studios and one- and two-bedroom units all have kitchens or kitchenettes. Some are decorated with Queen Anne reproductions. The beach at John Smith's Bay is about a five-minute walk away and after 20 minutes on a bus, you'll end up in Hamilton. (Inexpensive to Moderate)

Barnsdale Guest Apartments • *Paget* • A moongate leads to the inviting pool and patio at this small, family-run accommodation. Banana trees and other vegetation add to the attractive grounds. The large units, complete with kitchens and living and sleeping areas, can be combined as suites for families. (Inexpensive)

Burch's Guest Apartments • *Devonshire* • With a small garden, these apartments have panoramic views of the north shore and are close to Hamilton by bus. (Inexpensive)

Garden House • *Somerset Bridge, Sandys* • Owner/manager Rosanne Galloway, originally from Britain, sees to it that guests are well taken care of here. Whether they need a cookbook or would like to be driven to the grocery store, the Port Royal Golf Course, or a tennis court, all they have to do is ask. Arrangements will also be made for fishing and scuba excursions. A swimming pool and citrus trees, from which visitors may pluck their own fruit, are on the grounds. The separate cottages come with magazines, books, televisions, irons, ironing boards, hair dryers, and fully equipped kitchens. (Inexpensive)

Granaway • *Warwick* • Built in 1734, the seaside Granaway sits with its back to the water. This is because the captain who built it had spent his life at sea and wanted the house to face the gardens. Through the years, the house has been a wedding gift from a privateer to his daughter and has been rented to artists, writers, and schoolteachers who took in "wayward" boys. Noel Coward, a frequent guest of one of the owners, liked staying in the "Slaves Quarters," a small cottage adjacent to the main house. With its own fireplace, kitchen, and solarium, this cottage is still a popular unit. Guest rooms have exposed cedar ceiling beams. One room has a kitchen-style fireplace and bread oven. Breakfast is served in the rooms on trays, with china that matches each room's color scheme. Another special touch is the silver tea/coffee service. The two Bermuda stone love seats are popular with honeymooners, and there is good swimming and snorkeling. (Inexpensive)

Grape Bay Cottages • *Paget* • Run by Pretty Penny, these two cottages live up to the same high standard. This is a perfect place for honeymooners or others seeking seclusion in a tranquil setting. Beach House, high above the water, has a working fireplace for cool winter nights, rattan furnishings, a wood and tile-topped coffee table, a hardwood floor, ceiling fans, and a large eat-in kitchen. Windows are on three walls of the two bright, spacious bedrooms (with double beds), set off by peacock chairs and ginger jar lamps. The front porch has a great view of the Atlantic, and the beach is a brief walk downhill. A five-minute drive will take you to Hamilton. (Moderate to Expensive)

Marley Beach Cottages • *Warwick* • This secluded cluster of cottages and studio apartments is set among lawns and gardens. You can arrange to have groceries delivered prior to your arrival. From the small pool, you'll have a striking view of the south shore and the rocks below. The owners are proud of the fact that the movie *The Deep* was filmed here. Marley Beach is more expensive than most housekeeping accommodations. Nearby is Astwood Park where you can relax on benches overlooking the south-shore beach. (Moderate)

Ocean Terrace • *Southampton* • Located at Scenic Heights, Ocean Terrace has three modern, air-conditioned units. They all have full kitchens, ceiling fans, satellite TV, clock radios, and telephones. There is a pool on the premises and Horseshoe Bay beach is about a 10-minute walk away. Hop on a moped, and the shops and restaurants at the Southampton Princess are five minutes away. (Moderate)

Robin's Nest • *Pembroke* • You'll find this quiet guest house up a hill near the juncture of Cox Hill and North Shore roads. The three units are appointed with wicker headboards, ceiling fans, air conditioners, telephones, TV, and clock radios, and have full kitchens. When you check in your refrigerator will be stocked with complimentary wine, beer, and soft drinks. The pool patio is a good place to relax. A glossy

Bermuda cedar door leads to the two-bedroom apartment, complete with an eat-in kitchen with a window over the sink. (Inexpensive)

Valley Cottages • *Paget* • Shading various sitting areas, fragipani, Portuguese lily, and other blossoms splash color around this multi-level collection of cottages. Ranging in size from very small studios with kitchenettes to two comfortable two-bedroom apartments with spacious eat-in kitchens, the units all have a homelike feel. They all come with TVs and radios. Inlaid on the outer walls of cottages are blue and white plates from the 12-place setting of china that belonged to the owner's grandmother. Oleander Cycles and the bus stop are just across the road, and both a grocery store and liquor store are found at the end of the block. The ferry dock (for boats to Hamilton) is about a 20-minute walk away. (Inexpensive)

Whale Bay Inn • *Southampton* • This is a wonderful place to stay, especially if you want to be way off the beaten path. In each unit, etched glass panels divide the bedroom from the kitchen/dining area, with its glass and rattan table and sitting area. Carpeted bedrooms have two double beds or a double and a single; blond wood headboards, chests, and louvered closet doors; radios; and telephones. In the modern baths, smoke-colored glass doors slide open to the shower and tub. Enclosed by cliffs, nearby Whale Bay Beach is one of the island's most picturesque coves. (Inexpensive to Moderate)

HOTEL QUICK-REFERENCE CHARTS

Key

Facilities

BP	Beach Privileges: complimentary transportation to a private beach	T	Tennis
		L	Laundry (washing machines available)
BT	Boating	P	Swimming Pool
F	Fishing	MP	Mopeds rented on premises
G	Golf	S	Waterskiing
PB	Private Beach	M/D	Marina-Dock
SC	Scuba	Ba/B	Barber-Beauty Salon
PDF	Physically Disabled Facilities		

Meal Plans

AP	American Plan: Three Meals Daily	CP	Continental Plan: Light breakfast
MAP	Modified American Plan: Full breakfast and dinner	EP	European Plan: Room only
BP	Bermuda Plan: Full breakfast		

Credit Cards

A	American Express	M	MasterCard
C	Carte Blanche	V	Visa
D	Diners Club		

Note that the following hotel room prices are approximate. The rates we quote are for two people sharing a standard double room during high season (summer). Unfortunately, rates for single travelers are often quite a bit higher than half the cost of a double room. In addition to the 6% hotel occupancy tax and the service charge, some accommodations are now adding an energy surcharge to room rates.

Rates are EP unless otherwise noted.

For MAP rates, add about $40 per person, per night.

Resort Hotels

Page	Establishment, Mailing Address, Telephone	Meal Plans Offered	No. Rooms	Price of double (in season)	Credit Cards	Facilities	Other
96	The Belmont Hotel Golf and Beach Country Club (Warwick) P.O. Box WK 251, Warwick WK BX Bermuda/Tel: (809)236–1301 from U.S. and Canada: (800)225–5843; fax: (809)223–7434	MAP, BP, AP	154	$200 (BP)	M, V, D, A, C	BP, R, Ba/B, G, T, P, BT, F, S, M/D, MP, PDF	shops, games room, nightly entertainment, transportation to private beach club
	The Bermudiana Hotel, Tennis and Beach Club (Pembroke) P.O. Box HM 842, Hamilton 5, Bermuda/Tel: (809)295–1211						closed indefinitely
96	Elbow Beach Hotel (Paget) P.O. Box HM 455, Hamilton HM BX Bermuda/Tel: (809)236–3535/ (800)223–7434; fax: (809)236–8043	MAP, BP	298	$220 (BP)	M, V, A, D, C	PB, P, T, Ba/B, MP, PDF	shops, games room, pool w/ shallow play area for kids, beach club, nightly entertainment
97	Grotto Bay Beach Hotel & Tennis Club 11 Blue Hole Hill Hamilton CR 04, Bermuda/Tel: (809293–8333/ (800)225–2230 Massachusetts: (800)982–4770	MAP, BP, EP	201	$185	major	2PB, P, G, T, BT, M/D, L	games room, library, caves, summer "day camp" for children

Resort Hotels (cont.)

Page	Establishment, Mailing Address, Telephone	Meal Plans Offered	No. Rooms	Price of double (in season)	Credit Cards	Facilities	Other
97	Marriott's Castle Harbour Resort (Tucker's Town, Hamilton Parish) P.O. Box HM 841, Hamilton HM CX Bermuda/Tel: (809)293–2040 US and Canada: (800)228–9290; fax: (809)293–8288	MAP, BP, EP	402	$225	M, V, A	2PB, G, T, 3P, BT, M/D, Ba/B, S, SC, MP	shops, nightly entertainment, yacht club & marina, Japanese restaurant, TVs
97	The Princess (Pembroke) P.O. Box HM 837, Hamilton HM CX Bermuda/Tel: (809)295–3000 or US: (800)223–1818; Canada: (800)268–7176	EP, BP, MAP	456	$180	M, V, D, A	PB, P, SC, T, G, 2P, BaB, MP	shops, games room, beach club, miniature golf, nightly entertainment, 5-min. walk Hamilton, exchange privileges w/Southampton Princess
98	Sonesta Beach Hotel (Southampton) P.O. Box HM 1070, Hamilton HM EX Bermuda/Tel: (809)238–8122 or (800)343–7170	MAP, BP, EP	403	$200	A, M, V, D	2P, 3PB, T, SC, Ba/B, MP	children's program during summer
98	The Southampton Princess Hotel (Southampton) P.O. Box HM 1379, Hamilton HM FX Bermuda/Tel: (809)238–8000; US: (800)223–1818; Canada: (800)268–7176	MAP	600	$310 (MAP)	M, V, D, A	PB, 2P, G, MP, Ba/B, PDF	shops, games room, nightly entertainment, exchange priv. w/ Princess Hotel, comp. transport to nearby beach club

118

99	Glencoe Harbour Club (Paget) P.O. Box PG 297, Paget PG BX Bermuda/Tel: (809)236–5274 Direct: (800)468–1500 US: (800)468–1500; Canada: (800)268–0424; fax: (809)236–9108	MAP, BP	41	$210 (BP)	M, V, A	P, BT, S, PB, F	near ferry, free sun-fish sailing, some entertainment
99	The Hamiltonian Hotel and Island Club (Pembroke) P.O. Box HM 1738, Hamilton HM GX Bermuda/Tel: (809)295–5608	MAP, EP, BP	75	$175	M, V, A	P, T, M/D	time-sharing units
99	Harmony Club (Paget) P.O. Box PG 299, Paget PG BX Bermuda/Tel: (809)236–3500; US and Canada: (800) 225–5843	AP	72	$370 (AP)	M, V, D, A, C	P	comp. transport. to south shore beach, one free moped per room, unlimited drinks, TVs
100	Mermaid Beach Club (Warwick) P.O. Box WK 250, Warwick WK BX Bermuda/Tel: (809)236–5031/ (809)236–5031; (800)441–7087; Canada: (800)544–8478	MAP, BP, EP	67	$200	M, V, A, D	PB, P	gift shop, French cuisine in restaurant
100	Newstead (Paget) P.O. Box PG 196, Paget PG BX Bermuda/Tel: (809)236–6060 (800)468–4111	MAP, BP	50	$190 (BP)	none	P	heated pool, sauna, deepwater swim-ming, near ferry

Small Hotels (cont.)

Page	Establishment, Mailing Address, Telephone	Meal Plans Offered	No. Rooms	Price of double (in season)	Credit Cards	Facilities	Other
100	The Palm Reef Hotel (Paget) P.O. Box HM 1189, Hamilton HM EX Bermuda/Tel: (809)236–1000. NJ: (609)354–8113; US and Canada: (800)221–1294	MAP, BP, EP	94	$145	major	BP, P, T, BT, S, Ba/B	gift shop, nightly entertainment, good dine-around program with gourmet restaurants
101	Palmetto Hotel and Cottages (Smith's) P.O. Box FL54. Smith's FL BX Bermuda/Tel: (809)293–2323 (800)982–0026; fax: (809)293–8761	MAP, BP, EP	42	$150	A	PB, P, M/D	water sports, coffee machines in rooms
101	Pompano Beach Club 32 Pompano Beach Road Southampton SB 03 Bermuda/Tel: (809)294–0222/ (800)343–4155; Massachusetts or Canada (collect): (617)358–7737; fax: (809)234–1694	MAP, BP	56	$246 (BP)	none	PB, P, BT, M/D, SC	fresh-water pool, games room, new marina
102	The Reefs (Southampton) 56 South Road, Southampton SN 02 Bermuda/Tel: (809)238–8372 US: (800)223–1363; Canada: (800)268–0424; fax: (809)238–8372	MAP, BP	65	$258 (BP)	none	PB, P, T	heated pool, fishing, nightly entertainment, children on advance request only

No.	Hotel	Plan	Rooms	Rate	Cards		Notes
102	Rosedon (Pembroke) P.O. Box HM 290, Hamilton HM AX Bermuda/Tel: (809)295–1640; (800)225–5567; fax: (809)295–5904	BP, EP	43	$135	none	P	near ferry, tv room, comp. transport. to beach, no children under age 10, use of Elbow Beach Hotel facilities.
103	Royal Palms Club Hotel (Pembroke) P.O. Box HM 499, Hamilton HM CX Bermuda/Tel: (809)292–1854; (800)441–7087; fax: (809)292–1946	EP	12	$125	major	P	
103	Somerset Bridge Hotel (Sandys) P.O. Box SB 149 Sandys SB BX Bermuda/Tel: (809)234–1042 (800)468–5501; NY: (212)535–9530	EP, MAP, CP	24	$155	M, V	P, PB, M/D	watersports, near ferry, pool w/Jacuzzi; good restaurant
103	Stonington Beach Hotel (Paget) P.O. Box HM 523, Hamilton HM CX Bermuda/Tel: (809)236–5416; US: (800)223–1588; Canada: (800)268–0424	MAP, BP	64	$230 (BP)	M, V, D, A, C	PB, P	staffed by hotel training students supervised by professional management team
103	Waterloo House (Pembroke) P.O. Box HM 333, Hamilton HM BX Bermuda/Tel: (809)295–4480/ (800)468–4100; US: (800)468–4100; Canada: (800)268–9051; fax (809)295–2585	MAP, BP	34	$155 (BP)	none	P, BP	heated pool
104	White Sands and Cottages (Paget) P.O. Box 174, Paget PG BX Bermuda/Tel: (809)236–2023; (800)548–0547; fax: (809)236–2486	MAP, BP, EP	35	$205 (BP)	M, V, A	P	family-owned cottages available

Cottage Colonies

Page	Establishment, Mailing Address, Telephone	Meal Plans Offered	No. Rooms	Price of double (in season)	Credit Cards	Facilities	Other
104	Ariel Sands Beach Club (Devonshire) P.O. Box HM 334, Hamilton HM BX Bermuda/Tel: (809)236–1010 (800)468–6610; fax (809)236–0087	MAP, BP	51	$200 (BP)	none	PB, P, T, PDF	heated pool
105	Cambridge Beaches (Sandys) 30 King's Point, Sandys MA 02 Bermuda/Tel: (809)234–0331 (800)468–7300; fax: (809)234–3352	MAP	78	$265 (MAP)	none	PB, BT, S, F, P	heated pool, some nightly entertainment, pets allowed on request
105	Fourways Cottage Colony (Paget) P.O. Box PG 294, PG BX Paget, Bermuda (809)236–6517; (800)962–7654; fax (809)236–5528	CP	10	$230 (CP)	A, M, V, D	P	freshwater pool; 1- and 2-BR suites
105	Horizons and Cottages (Paget) P.O. Box PG 198, Paget PG BX Bermuda/Tel: (809)236–0048; (800)468–0022; fax (809)236–1981	MAP, BP	50	$225 (BP)	none	P, G	most units air-conditioned, heated pool, children under age 6 on request
106	Lantana Colony Club (Sandys) P.O. Box SB90, Sandys SB BX Bermuda/Tel: (809)234–0141 (800)468–3733; fax (809)234–2562	MAP	65	$270 (MAP)	none	P, PB, BT, S, M/T	complimentary ferry to Hamilton, children under age 10 on request; closed Jan.–mid-Feb.

#	Name	Plan	Rooms	Price	Cards	Bath	Notes
107	Pink Beach Club (Smith's) P.O. Box HM 1017, Hamilton HM DX Bermuda/Tel: (809)293–1666; US except NY: (800)372–1323; fax: (809)293–8935	MAP	81	$285 (MAP)	none	PB, P	no children under age 5; closes early December through February
107	St. George's Club P.O. Box GE 92 St. George's GE BX Bermuda (809)297–1200; US and Canada: fax: (809)297–8003	EP	61	$260	V, M, A, D	P, G, T, BP	time-share units available, cottages
108	Willowbank (Sandys) P.O. Box MA 296, Sandys MA BX Bermuda/Tel: (809)234–1616	MAP	60	$150 (MAP)	none	2PB, P	optional daily devotional time

Guest Houses

#	Name	Plan	Rooms	Price	Cards	Bath	Notes
108	Edgehill Manor (Pembroke) P.O. Box HM 1048, Hamilton HM EX Bermuda/Tel: (809)295–7124; fax (809)295–3850	CP	9	$105 (CP)	none	P	some rooms air-conditioned, others with ceiling fans
108	Fordham Hall (Pembroke) P.O. Box HM 692, Hamilton HM CX Bermuda/Tel: (809)295–1551; (800)537–4163	CP	12	$105 (CP)	M, V		children on advance request only
	Greenbank and Cottages (Paget) P.O. Box PG 201, Paget PG BX Bermuda/Tel: (809)236–3615; fax: (809)236–2427	EP, CP	9	$90	major	M/D	swimming, water sports, near ferry, air-conditioning on request, pets on request

Guest Houses (cont.)

Page	Establishment, Mailing Address, Telephone	Meal Plans Offered	No. Rooms	Price of double (in season)	Credit Cards	Facilities	Other
109	Greene's Guest House (Southampton) P.O. Box SN 395, Southampton SN BX Bermuda/Tel: (809)238–0834 or (809)238–2532; fax (809)238–8980	BP, MAP, EP	6	$110 (BP)	none	P	
109	Hillcrest Guest House (St. George's) P.O. Box GE 96, St. George's GE BX Bermuda/Tel: (809)297–1630	EP	11	$70	none		children on advance request only
109	Hi-Roy Guest House (Pembroke) 22 Princess Estate Road, Pembroke HM 04 Bermuda/Tel: (809)292–0808	MAP, BP	6	$80 (BP)	none		children on advance request only
110	Little Pomander Guest House P.O. Box HM 384 Hamilton HM BX Bermuda/Tel: (809)236–7635	CP, EP	5	$105 (CP)	none		Apartment available
108	Loughlands Guest House (Paget) 79 South Road, Paget PG 03 Bermuda/Tel: (809)236–1253	CP	24	$95 (CP)	none	P	some shared baths

124

Mazarine-By-The-Sea (Pembroke) P.O. Box HM 91 AX, Hamilton HM AX Bermuda/Tel: (809)292–1659; (800)441–7087; Pennsylvania: (800)292–9695	110	EP	7	$90	none		good deepwater swimming from cliffs
Oxford House (Pembroke) P.O. Box HM 374, Hamilton HM BX Bermuda/Tel: (809)295–0503	110	CP	12	$110 (CP)	none		children on advance request only
Pleasant View (Pembroke) P.O. Box HM 1998 Hamilton HM HX Bermuda/Tel: (809)292–4520	110	BP, EP	6	$95	none	P	
Royal Heights Guest House (Southampton) P.O. Box SN 144, Southampton SN BX Bermuda/Tel: (809)238–0043; (800)247–2447, telex 3507 SCAT BA	110	CP	6	$105 (CP)	major	P	children on advance request only
Salt Kettle House (Paget) 10 Salt Kettle Road, Paget PG 01 Bermuda/Tel: (809)236–0407	111	BP	6	$75 (BP)	none		some kitchen facilities
Que Sera (Paget) P.O. Box HM 1, Hamilton HM AX Bermuda/Tel: (809)236–1998	110	EP	3	$75	none	P	
South View (Warwick) P.O. Box HM 515, Hamilton HM CX Bermuda/Tel: (809)236–5257; fax (809)236–3382	110	EP	3	$85	M, V		sun deck on roof, apts.; one air-conditioned apt., two with fans

Guest Houses (cont.)

Page	Establishment, Mailing Address, Telephone	Meal Plans Offered	No. Rooms	Price of double (in season)	Credit Cards	Facilities	Other
	Wainwright (St. George's) 2 Slip Road, St. George's GE 02 Bermuda/Tel: (809)297-0254	EP	4	$65	none		
	Woodbourne (Pembroke) P.O. Box HM 977, Hamilton HM DX Bermuda/Tel: (809)295-3737	CP	4	$95 (CP)	major		children on advance request only

Large Housekeeping Cottages and Apartments

Page	Establishment, Mailing Address, Telephone	Meal Plans Offered	No. Apartments	Price of double (in season)	Credit Cards	Facilities	Other
111	Astwood Cove (Warwick) 49 South Road, Warwick WK 07 Bermuda/Tel: (809)236-0984; (800)225-2230; fax (809)236-1164	EP	18	$100	none	P	sauna, apartments
111	Blue Horizons (Warwick) 93 South Road, Warwick WK 10 Bermuda/Tel: (809)236-6350	EP	10	$65	none		near public pool
111	Brightside Apartments P.O. Box FL 319 Smith's FL BX, Bermuda (809)292-8410 or (809)293-1788	EP	11	$88	A, V, M		adjacent to aquarium
111	Clairfont Apartments (Warwick) P.O. Box WK 85, Warwick WK BX Bermuda/Tel: (809)238-0149	EP	8	$75	major	P	sun deck

126

	Name / Address	Plan	Rooms	Rate	Cards	Cat.	Notes
111	Clear View Suites Sandy Lane Hamilton Parish CR 02 Bermuda/Tel: (809)293–0484; (800)468–9600	EP	12	$175	none	P	cribs and highchairs available; close to beach, apartment available
112	Longtail Cliffs (Warwick) P.O. Box HM 836, Hamilton HM CX Bermuda/Tel: (809)236–2822; fax (809)236–5178	EP	13	$185	none	P	use of Mermaid Beach facilities, apartments
112	Munro Beach Cottages P.O. Box SN 99, Southampton SN BX Bermuda/Tel: (809)234–1175; US: (800)223–5581; NY: (212)535–9530; Canada: (800)346–8480	EP	16	$155	none	PB	better for couples than singles
112	Paraquet Guest Apartments (Paget) P.O. Box PG 173, Paget PG BX Bermuda/Tel: (809)236–5842; fax (809)236–1665	EP	9	$100	none	R	good home-style restaurant
112	Rosemont (Pembroke) P.O. Box HM 37, Hamilton HM AX Bermuda/Tel: (809)292–1055; (800)367–0040; fax (809)295–3913	EP	37	$120	none	P	roof sun deck, near ferry
112	Sandpiper Apartments (Warwick) P.O. Box HM 685, Hamilton HM CX Bermuda/Tel: (809)236–7093; fax (809)236–3898	EP	14	$115	M, V, A, D	P	
	Sky Top Cottages (Paget) P.O. Box PG 227, Paget PG BX Bermuda/Tel: (809)236–7984	EP	11	$80	M, V		

Large Housekeeping Cottages and Apartments (cont.)

Page	Establishment, Mailing Address, Telephone	Meal Plans Offered	No. Rooms	Price of double (in season)	Credit Cards	Facilities	Other
113	Surf Side Beach Club (Paget) P.O. Box WK 101, Warwick WK BX Bermuda/Tel: (809)236–7100; (800)553–9990; fax (809)236–3255	EP	35	$170	none	P	coffee shop

Small Housekeeping Cottages and Apartments

Page	Establishment, Mailing Address, Telephone	Meal Plans Offered	No. Rooms	Price of double (in season)	Credit Cards	Facilities	Other
113	Angel's Grotto P.O. Box HS 62, Smith's HS BX Bermuda/Tel: (809)293–1986	EP	7	$105	major		snorkeling, swimming
113	Barnsdale Guest Apartments P.O. Box DV 628, Devonshire DV BX Bermuda/Tel: (809)236–0164; (800)514–7426; NY: (212)535–9530; fax (809)236–4709	EP	5	$85	major		
113	Burch's Guest Apartments (Paget) 110 North Shore Road, Devonshire FL 03 Bermuda/Tel: (809)292–5746	EP	10	$80	none		no children under age 3
113	Cabana Vacation Apartments P.O. Box FL 40 Smith's FL BX Bermuda/Tel: (809)236–6964	EP	7	$85	major	P	club room, 200-year-old home, transportation from airport with tour

113	Garden House (Sandys) 4 Middle Road, Somerset Bridge, Sandys SB 01 Bermuda/Tel: (809)234–1435	EP	5	$85	none	P	deepwater swimming; air conditioning at extra charge
	Glenmar Holiday Apartments (Paget) P.O. Box PG 151, Paget PG BX Bermuda/Tel: (809)236–2844	EP	5	$65	major		
113	Granaway Guest House and Cottage P.O. Box WK 533, Warwick WK BX Bermuda/Tel: (809)236–1805	EP, CP	8		M, V	M/D	close to ferry
114	Grape Bay Cottages (Paget) P.O. Box PG 137, Paget PG BX Bermuda/Tel: (809)236–1194; fax: (809)236–1662	EP	3	$185	major		some cottages on Grape Bay Beach
114	Marley Beach Cottages (Warwick) P.O. Box PG 278, Paget PG BX Bermuda/Tel: (809)236–1143; fax (809)236–1984	EP	13	$155	none	PB, P	
114	Ocean Terrace P.O. Box SN 501, Southampton SN BX (809)238–0019; fax (809)238–8489	EP	3	$125		P	
114	Pillar-Ville P.O. Box SN 2, Southampton SN BX Bermuda/Tel: (809)238–0445	EP	7	$65	none		some air conditioning, children on advance request only

Small Housekeeping Cottages and Apartments (cont.)

Page	Establishment, Mailing Address, Telephone	Meal Plans Offered	No. Apartments	Price of double (in season)	Credit Cards	Facilities	Other
112	Pretty Penny Guest House P.O. Box PG 137, Paget PG BX Bermuda/Tel: (809)236–1194 (800)541–7426; fax: (809)236–1662; fax (809)236–1662	EP	9	$100	major	P	near ferry, complimentary newspapers, family-run
114	Robin's Nest Apartments (Pembroke) 10 Vale Close, Pembroke HM 04 Bermuda/Tel: (809)292–4347; US: (800)223–6510; Canada: (800)268–0424	EP	3	$90	none		not air-conditioned; each unit has fan, heater, TV, radio
115	Syl-Den Apartments (Warwick) 8 Warwickshire Drive Warwick WK 02 Bermuda/Tel: (809)238–1834	EP	5	$90	major	P	sun terrace
115	Valley Cottages (Paget) P.O. Box PG 214, Paget PG BX Bermuda/Tel: (809)236–0628; fax (809)236–3895	EP	9	$75	major		no children under age 12
115	Whale Bay Inn P.O. Box SN 544 Southampton, Bermuda SN BX (809)238–0469	EP	5	$105	none		near Port Royal Golf Course; free for children under age 10

130

King's Square, St. George's, Bermuda   GORDON CHRISTMAS

Mangrove Bay, Somerset Village, Sandys Parish, Bermuda   MEL WRIGHT

Dockyard, Sandys Parish, Bermuda   MEL WRIGHT

Shopping lane in Hamilton, Bermuda   GORDON CHRISTMAS

Flatts Inlet, Smith's Parish, Bermuda   MEL WRIGHT

A traditional moongate, the Belmont Hotel, Warwick Parish, Bermuda   MEL WRIGHT

Gibb's Hill Lighthouse, Southampton, Bermuda   BERMUDA NEWS BUREAU

Beach at Driggs Hill, Southern Andros, the Bahamas   GORDON CHRISTMAS

One of Harbour Island's trademark cottages, Eleuthera, the Bahamas
RACHEL JACKSON CHRISTMAS

Shelling conch is a social event, Bimini, the Bahamas   GORDON CHRISTMAS

Snorkeler off the beach at Bluff House hotel, Green Turtle Cay, Abaco, the Bahamas   MEL WRIGHT

A hammock with a view, Abaco Inn, Elbow Cay, Abaco, the Bahamas

RACHEL JACKSON CHRISTMAS

Dogs and human take in the Dolphin Experience, during which people swim with Flipper's cousins, Freeport, the Bahamas   RACHEL JACKSON CHRISTMAS

Out for a sail, Cargill Creek,
Andros, the Bahamas
MEL WRIGHT

Fruit stand,
Potters Cay Dock,
Nassau, the Bahamas
GORDON CHRISTMAS

Giggly residents of Cockburn Town, San Salvador, the Bahamas

RACHEL JACKSON CHRISTMAS

A hibiscus grows in Nassau, the Bahamas   GORDON CHRISTMAS

Diver with dinner, Green Turtle Cay, Abaco, the Bahamas   MEL WRIGHT

THE BAHAMAS

WHY THE BAHAMAS?

This year marks the 500th anniversary of Christopher Columbus' arrival in the "New" World. The Bahamas is where it all began. While historians disagree on exactly which island was his first landfall, most point to San Salvador, which today remains one of the least developed parts of the country.

The variety of its islands, breathtaking coastlines, and different lifestyles is what makes The Bahamas special. From the international city of Freeport and its neighboring Lucaya to the pink sand beaches of tiny Harbour Island, The Bahamas offers a wide choice of vacation opportunities. Its islands sprawl southeast from the tip of Florida to the fringes of the Caribbean. Unlike Bermuda, much of which can be seen by moped in a day, The Bahamas, with its many islands and cays, could take months of exploration.

Contrary to a widespread impression, The Bahamas, a country of more than 200,000 people, is actually in the Atlantic Ocean, not the Caribbean Sea. Its islands and islets are an archipelago strung out on the northern side of Cuba, Hispaniola, and the Lesser Antilles, those islands that arc toward South America to enclose the Caribbean Sea.

Visitors looking for the excitement and conviviality of casinos, a vibrant night life, and varied dining opportunities have Nassau and the adjoining Paradise Island, as well as Freeport. Some of the larger resorts here are quite self-contained and cater to guests not interested in exploring much beyond their hotels. Vacationers who do wish to get to know Nassau and Freeport during their stay can begin with bus or taxi tours available through hotels and the tourist bureau. Those with a more

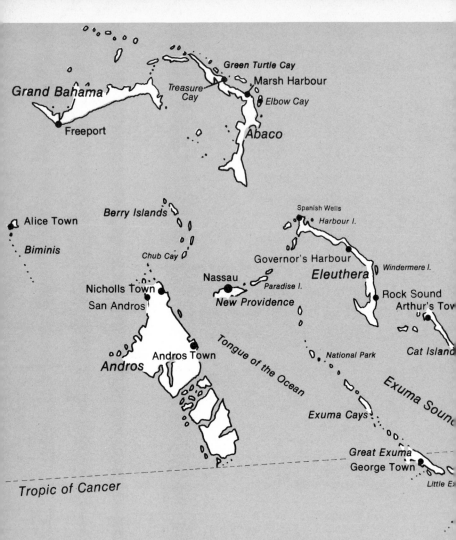

Grand Bahama

Freeport

Treasure Cay

Green Turtle Cay

Marsh Harbour

Elbow Cay

Abaco

Alice Town

Biminis

Berry Islands

Chub Cay

Spanish Wells

Harbour I.

Governor's Harbour

Eleuthera

Windermere I.

Nassau

Paradise I.

New Providence

Rock Sound

Arthur's Tow

Nicholls Town

San Andros

Tongue of the Ocean

National Park

Cat Island

Andros Town

Andros

Exuma Cays

Exuma Soun

Great Exuma

George Town

Little Ex

Tropic of Cancer

ATLANTIC OCEAN

Ragged Island

Duncan Town

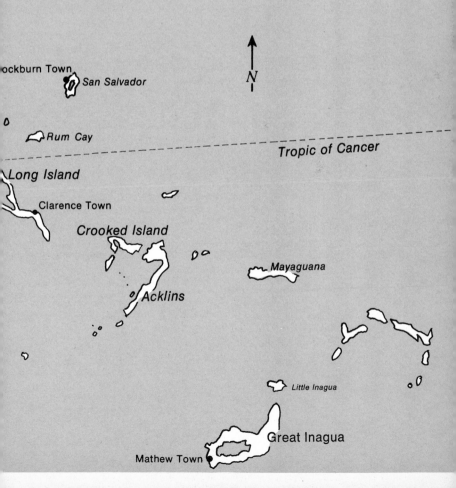

The Bahamas

ATLANTIC OCEAN

N

ockburn Town, San Salvador

Rum Cay

Tropic of Cancer

Long Island

Clarence Town

Crooked Island

Mayaguana

Acklins

Little Inagua

Great Inagua

Mathew Town

adventurous spirit can attempt tours on their own using local transportation. This can be fun and gives the flavor of what life is like for residents.

Through its popular People-to-People Program, which operates in Nassau, Freeport, and now Eleuthera, the government sponsors a means of getting acquainted with its citizens. This free program enables visitors to meet Bahamians, go to their homes, and take part in local activities that would otherwise be missed by most tourists.

Visitors seeking a slower pace, fewer fellow tourists, and more serene surroundings should definitely consider one of the Family Islands. Also called the "Out Islands," these more reclusive spots are often striking in their beauty. They bring visitors closer to the natural wonders of Bahamian land and sea and introduce them to friendly people not jaded by the tourist trade.

For all, there is swimming, tennis, boating, fishing (including big game), diving, snorkeling, windsurfing, parasailing, and, especially in Nassau and Freeport, golf. Those whose idea of a vacation is to sit lazily on a terrace, read, sunbathe, or beachcomb can find plenty of desirable hideaways for these quieter pursuits. Through some hotels and resorts, you can even arrange to be "marooned" on your own "X-rated" island beach, where you and a friend, well provisioned, are left alone all day.

If you like to explore, the islands can introduce you to caves, deserted and pristine beaches, old churches, mysterious ocean holes, plantation ruins, early local architecture, undersea caves, wrecks and marine life, lacy gingerbread manor houses, bird sanctuaries, salt flats, eerie pine forests, old fortresses, international research centers, sun-drenched lighthouses, wild boars, and much more. None of these sights is ever too far from the incredibly colored and ever-changing sea.

You may hear some rumors about the drug trafficking that is said to be responsible for the profusion of gold chains that decorate many a neck and the expensive cars and houses owned by people barely two decades old. However, unless you make a point of searching out drug dealers, you are unlikely to be affected by whatever behind-the-scenes action there might be. The Bahamian government has come under attack by the U.S. (which certainly has its own drug problem) for not doing enough to control its borders. The Bahamas has responded that, with so many uninhabited islands and so much coastline, putting an end to the drug trade here would be a mammoth task for any government. They have joined forces with the U.S. in an attempt to come up with more effective solutions.

Nassau/Paradise Island and Freeport/Lucaya

The best-known city in The Bahamas is Nassau, the capital. It is located on the island of New Providence, where more than 135,000 Bahamians live. In the past it was one of the playgrounds for the international rich. Just before World War II, the Duke and Duchess of Windsor were in residence, while the duke served as governor general. Their presence helped to attract the world's affluent, especially Americans. International conferences and meetings are frequently held in Nassau and jet-setters, entertainers, and politicians still find their way here to enjoy the beaches, posh hotels, secluded hideaways, and casinos. Some, such as British royalty, find seclusion in more remote spots, like Windermere Island and some of the private cays spattered among the islands.

Nassau is also full of the nation's history. Visitors can explore the sites of both intact and crumbling fortresses and see legendary homes and monuments. They can wander through settlements such as Grant's Town, Carmichael, Adelaide, and Fox Hill, founded by or for freed slaves after emancipation. They can bask on beaches where buccaneers once strolled and see rocky coasts where ships were deliberately wrecked for plunder. At the New Year, the Junkanoo Festival, with roots reaching back to slavery, erupts throughout the islands, but nowhere as sizzlingly as in downtown Nassau.

For shoppers, Bay Street and some of its tributaries in downtown Nassau are full of stores with bargains in linens, woolens, china, crystal, perfumes, cameras, and watches. The Straw Market offers a wide variety of "native" crafts. Bahamians often surprise visitors by their use of the word "native" to describe their food, crafts, and some customs. Visitors are cautioned not to use the word themselves in describing Bahamians, as some people consider it demeaning.

Nassau has enough restaurants to satisfy the dining whims of any visitor. The cuisine ranges from continental to local, and from elegant to inexpensive and homelike. Settings range from seaside to poolside.

Connected to Nassau by an arched toll bridge, Paradise Island is a long, narrow sand bar dotted with hotels and restaurants, a casino, and a variety of nightspots. Communities of condominiums and private homes also share the island. The beaches attract visitors from the island's hotels and condos as well as from Nassau.

Freeport, the second city of The Bahamas, has fewer hotels than Nassau and is less compact. It is located on the island of Grand Bahama, which has a population of about 35,000. Built during the sixties, Freeport lives in its dazzling present, making its history now, since, unlike Nassau, there is very little evidence of its past. Carefully planned and landscaped, the city adjoins Lucaya, the beach area, merging as Freeport/Lucaya, with wide, palm-lined boulevards and gleaming white buildings. The island's main attractions are the casinos, one of which is entered through a domed, Moorish archway, the two shopping and dining plazas, the 10-acre International Bazaar, and the waterfront Port Lucaya, and The Dolphin Experience, a program through which visitors can swim with Flipper's cousins.

Outside the Central Mall and Lucaya beach area, there are some good restaurants in appealing settings at the water's edge. Especially toward the West End are settlements of local Bahamians whose families have lived on the island since long before an American, Wallace Groves, began its development. Wealthy individuals with financial stakes in the area have created tourist attractions such as the Garden of Groves, named for Groves and his wife, and the Rand Memorial Nature Centre. Beyond the resort area, in addition to the waterfront restaurants and small settlements, you'll come across oil refineries, pharmaceutical factories, and other manufacturing plants that give a glimpse of the day-to-day life of Bahamians not associated with tourism.

The Family Islands

Except for some game fishermen, confirmed boaters, and dedicated divers, most visitors know little of The Bahamas beyond Nassau and Freeport. But away from those bustling tourist centers is the serenity, calm, and beauty of the Family Islands, where 40,000 Bahamians live and work in more sparsely settled communities. Some residents, young and old, have never been to Nassau. Still also called the "Out Islands," the Family Islands are largely undeveloped. Only a handful have tourist accommodations. Many are breathtaking reminders of Winslow Homer watercolors. They make no demands for activity, and you can organize your day or let it go to pot with no pangs of guilt.

Most of the islands have few large trees. The thick vegetation that stretches for miles between towns consists mainly of shrubs and bushes. The flat terrain of many of the smaller islands encourages walking when venturing out to explore and see the sights. You may come upon unexpected settlements, discover a small fishing colony, or be awed by a natural wonder peculiar to the islands such as a cave, unusual flora or an inland pool teeming with sea creatures. You'll see chickens, donkeys, sheep, and goats wandering freely through yards and on roads. Should you find nature too close, you can always flee to one of the islands' more up-to-date resorts with comfortable, often luxury appointments and services for the less rugged.

Since Family Island towns are small, it is easy to meet and socialize with locals, most of whom are farmers, fishermen, craftspeople, or service workers at resorts. With tourism a seasonal business, many islanders combine resort service with one or more other occupations. Some of the older people will say "God bless you" instead of good-bye. The numerous churches (there is at least one in even the tiniest of towns) are another indication of the importance of religion here. While the majority of people adhere to Christianity, on the more remote islands some still practice the voodoo or obeah of their African ancestors.

The buildings in the islands' villages and settlements, formerly constructed of wood, limestone, and coral, are now mainly of concrete block. You may see some that seem abandoned, with weeds, grass, and shrubs growing within the windowless, roofless walls. These are homes in progress, which grow as their owners can afford building materials. When the house is finally finished, the owner is secure in an unmortgaged home.

Some villages seem transported from New England, such as Dunmore Town on Harbour Island and Hope Town on Elbow Cay. Striking examples of colonial manor houses and native thatched-roof stone houses remain. You can see outdoor ovens for baking bread in Gregory Town in northern Eleuthera. There are underwater caves, grottos, and reefs to attract divers, including one of the longest reefs in the world. Many divers are fascinated by the sunken railroad train parts off Eleuthera.

Especially in the Family Islands, visitors will encounter islands called "cays," pronounced "keys" as in Florida's Key West. Chub Cay, Pigeon Cay, and Green Turtle Cay are just a few of these islets.

A Bit of History

In his 1492 voyage to the New World, Christopher Columbus is said to have landed at San Salvador, a southerly Family Island. Later research has placed the landing at Samana Cay, also in the Bahamas but farther south. San Salvador was once known as Guanahani by the Indians who lived there. The Bahamas was first called the Lucayans, after the Indian tribe that, with the Arawaks, inhabited the islands. The name was later changed to Bahama, derived from "baja mar," meaning shallow water or shallow sea in Spanish.

The islands remained in the possession of the Spanish until 1647, when what is now Eleuthera was taken over by a group of English refugees in search of religious freedom. Later, another band of British, who were fleeing Bermuda and also escaping religious restrictions, arrived here. They chose the name "Eleutheria," meaning freedom in Greek. As time went on, the *i* was lost.

During the next two centuries, The Bahamas, near the much-used shipping lanes connecting Europe with the New World, became a lucrative haven for pirates seeking treasure. The marauders found endless hiding places, entrapments, and points of attack among the many inlets and cays. Piracy was not suppressed until 1718, when Woodes Rogers, a much more ruthless governor than those who had preceded him, was able to bring about order and stop the plunder.

As the American Revolution came to a close, thousands of Americans, loyal to the British crown, settled with their slaves in The Bahamas. Also seeking a new life, freed American slaves found these shores as well. As in Bermuda, slavery was abolished in 1834 in The Bahamas, almost 30 years before Emancipation in the United States.

After years of racial, political, and economic strife, the accumulation of grievances in this predominantly black country came to a head during the Fifties and Sixties. Bent on majority rule, black leaders formed the Progressive Liberal Party (PLP) in 1953. When the new International Airport opened in 1957, taxi drivers were furious over the government's plan to provide low-cost buses to take tourists to hotels. Drivers parked their cars on roads leading to and from the airport, closing it down for several days. But the drivers' demands were not met and trade union leaders called a general strike. After three weeks, the unionists won. Bolstered by the surge in the power of workers, people joined black political parties in droves. You'll note that there is still no public bus service to and from the airport.

In 1961, those who did not own property were finally granted the right to vote, and women won the right to vote for the first time. Eight years later, the islands became a commonwealth nation and PLP leader Lynden Pindling became the country's first prime minister. Despite reluctance on the part of Her Majesty's government and resistance by the "Bay Street Boys," independence from Britain was gained in 1973.

Government

Now a member of the British Commonwealth of Nations, The Bahamas is a parliamentary democracy with a two-chamber parliament, an independent judiciary, and a government headed by a Prime Minister. The British Queen appoints the Governor General. The first Bahamian-born Governor General was appointed in 1977. In 1979, the government of The Bahamas celebrated its 250th year of uninterrupted parliamentary democracy.

Economy

Tourism accounts for the greatest part of the Bahamian gross national product, about 70%. Oil and pharmaceuticals, based on Grand Bahama, are also important contributors to the GNP. Other significant areas supporting the economy are finance, based primarily in Nassau, and to a lesser degree, fishing and agriculture. Bahamians pay no sales tax or income tax.

The Bahamians

In a country that is more than 80% black, it was not until 1956 that black Bahamians could legally patronize theaters, hotels, and restaurants. The populations of several islands (Spanish Wells, Man-O-War Cay, and Elbow Cay among them) are still exclusively or predominantly white. However, it can now be said that Bahamians of all colors like to regard themselves simply as Bahamians. Some will assure you that animosities and prejudices based on race are behind them and that, as a nation, they are moving confidently forward to a more enlightened time.

With tourism the major industry, black people, historically the poorest members of the nation, were once restricted to service jobs. Since independence, increasing numbers of black people have found their way into hotel administration and management. Some have opened their own small hotels and guest houses. Young Bahamians continue to leave the Family Islands, attracted to Nassau and Freeport by employment opportunities in the nation's largest industry. The heritage of British habits and culture persist, along with African, Caribbean, and traces of indigenous Indian influences.

When spoken by Bahamians, English, the national language, may sound West Indian to some ears. But it actually has its own lilt, intonation, syntax, and idiom. You'll hear accents ranging from upper-class British to those where the letters *v* and *w* are interchanged. "So you wisitin', eh?", translates into "So you're visiting, are you?" Some words even sound as if they were imported from Brooklyn: "woik" is what you do "fuh" a living and a waiter will "soive" you.

If a Bahamian tells you he's going "spilligatin'," he means that he is planning to "carry on bad." In short, he intends to "party," "paint the town red," or have an all-out good time. Some Bahamians, Harbour Islanders and people from Abaco, for example, add or drop *h*s. Harbor becomes " 'Arbor" and the name Anderson becomes "Handerson."

The church plays a major role throughout The Bahamas. Churches, representing the leading religions and their denominations, are very visible. Structures run the gamut from almost cathedral in size to one-room shacks. Great numbers of the smaller churches are scattered throughout the poorer residential neighborhoods. On the Family Islands, no village or settlement is complete without at least one place of worship. As in small towns of the American South, Sunday mornings bring the comforting sounds of hymns and gospel from the islands' many churches. Itinerant preachers travel from island to island for local services as well as large revival meetings.

It is against the law for Bahamian citizens to gamble in the country's casinos. Some visitors have suggested that this is paternalistic, that adults should be able to decide for themselves whether or not to gamble.

However, most Bahamians seem to agree that the law is good, especially since the purpose of casinos is to bring in new money, not to recirculate Bahamian money. Besides, they add, Bahamians who want to gamble find other means: witness the many domino games, regattas, and other sporting events where more than a few bets are placed.

Meeting the People

The free People-to-People Program, sponsored by the government in Nassau and Freeport through the Bahamas Tourist Bureau and with hundreds of volunteers, gives visitors unique opportunities to meet, socialize with, and get to know Bahamian families and individuals. Besides meeting Bahamians in their homes, visitors can participate in local social and cultural events.

Visitors can be invited to activities such as performances of the local theater group, civic and sporting events, and local receptions not generally open to tourists. On several occasions, visitors have gained access to behind-the-scenes political events. What you do and see depends on you and your host.

Information about the People-to-People Program is available at the Bahamas Tourist offices on Market Square in downtown Nassau and at Prince George Dock. Other offices are on Rawson Square, just west of the fountain, and at the arrival and departure points of Nassau International Airport. In the Freeport/Lucaya area, you can make arrangements to participate at the International Bazaar tourist office.

Music and Festivals

Most of the music you will hear on the radio and in discos and night clubs will be calypso (sometimes called merengue), reggae, and American pop or rock. One type of indigenous Bahamian music, played with goatskin drums and West African rhythms, is called "goombay." (The Bermudian version is "gombey.") The name has been adopted for the July and August "Goombay" festival, with its street dancing, music, and other activities for tourists during the off season.

The biggest and most popular of the Bahamian festivals is Junkanoo, celebrated on Boxing Day (Dec. 26), and on New Year's Day. As in pre-Lenten carnivals in the Caribbean, celebrants dance through the streets in colorful and fantastic costumes, masks, and intricate headdresses, blowing whistles and jangling bells, creating Junkanoo music. In Nassau, Bay Street truly comes alive during Junkanoo celebrations. The parade begins at 4 a.m., followed by a "boil fish" and johnny cake breakfast at 9:00.

The origin of Junkanoo remains in dispute. It is variously attributed to West Africa, indigenous Indians, and the American south, among other sources. Some say the name comes from a West African called "Jananin Canno," others, the American folk hero "Johnny Canoe," and still others, someone called *l'inconnu,* meaning "the unknown" in French. Whether this figure was a god, a slave, a Mayan Indian, or an African prince, there is a move to develop Junkanoo into the primary Bahamian music.

Eating and Drinking

The ubiquitous sea is the main source of Bahamian food. Chief among the varieties of fare available is conch, pronounced "conk", said to be an aphrodisiac. High mounds of discarded conch shells indicate that the meat has gone into delicacies such as cracked conch (beaten and fried), conch salad (raw, with vegetables and lime juice), and conch fritters. You can watch fishermen on docks prepare scorched conch, eaten raw from the shell after being spiced with salt, hot pepper, and lime.

Fish, especially grouper, which turns up for dinner, lunch, and even breakfast, is also a staple, along with varieties of shellfish. Lobster is usually what Americans call crayfish. Minced lobster, a favorite, is shredded crayfish cooked with tomatoes, green peppers, and onions, then served in the shell. Among other local specialties are crab and rice, chicken and dough (dumplings), mutton, turtle steak, wild boar, and souse (pig's feet, chicken, sheep's tongue, or other meat in a savory sauce). Everything comes with heaping portions of peas and rice, potato salad, or cole slaw—sometimes all three. Mildly sweet johnny cake is also often served on the side.

Don't let the various ways of preparing seafood confuse you. "Boil fish" (a popular breakfast item served with hominy grits) is cooked with salt pork, onions, green peppers, and spices. Also eaten as the day's first meal, stewed fish has a rich brown gravy. Steamed fish (which may sound bland, but is far from it) isn't eaten before noon and is cooked with a tomato base. Of course, you'll also find beef, lamb, and pork, but they are imported.

Guava duff, a rich and delicious dessert, is to Bahamians what apple pie is to people in the U.S.A. It is made by spreading guava jelly on dough, rolling it, boiling it for about 90 minutes, then topping the warm slices with a white sauce. Benny (sesame) cake is another popular local treat (the benny seeds are boiled with sugar).

Because most food is imported, it tends to be expensive. Restaurants serving Bahamian specialties and Bahamian diners can save you money and introduce new tastes. Salads and greens are not much in evidence, but you'll also discover such dishes as roti, curried chicken, and plantain, inspired by Caribbean neighbors.

While local restaurants, especially in the Family Islands, stress traditional Bahamian fare, American and continental cuisine are available almost everywhere. Thirst is quenched with beer, beer, and more beer, some of it imported directly from Germany and the Netherlands. The Bahamas now brews its own (high quality) brew, called Kalik (which is the sound cowbells make in Bahamian Junkanoo music). Fruity concoctions such as Goombay Smashes, Bahama Mamas, and Yellowbirds, all with a rum base, are also popular drinks.

THINGS TO KNOW

COSTS • In season, from December through April or May, double-room rates range from about $45 per night at a small guest house to $200 or more at a resort. Off-season rates are appreciably lower. Meal plans offered by hotels are FAP (room and three meals), MAP (room, breakfast and dinner), FB (room and full-American breakfast), CP (room and light breakfast), and EP (room only). If you plan to stay at an accommodation where you can prepare your own meals, you should be aware that although supermarkets may be nearby (in Nassau and Freeport), food prices may be quite high. This is because many foods are imported.

Travel agents can advise you on economic package deals. Many packages have specific requirements for day and time of departure and return, and a limited choice of hotels and locations. However, particularly if you plan a trip to the more remote Family Islands, you may want to design your own vacation. The accommodations charts in the back of the book will help you make your own reservations should you choose to do so.

Hotels charge a 10% tax on rooms and many also add an energy surcharge. There is no sales tax. Most restaurants and hotels add a 15% service charge to cover gratuities for food and drink. The smaller, locally operated restaurants specializing in homestyle cuisine are the least expensive and often serve better food than hotel dining rooms. Taxi drivers and tour guides are also given tips of at least 15%. Bellmen and porters are tipped 50¢ to $1 for each bag. Some hotels and restaurants add a surcharge if you pay with travelers checks or an American Express card.

It is best to arrive with enough film and books or magazines to last for the duration of your stay. Film and imported books are sold at inflated prices compared to those back home.

TRAVELING WITH CHILDREN • Ships, planes, and hotels all go out of their way to help make traveling with children as simple, safe, and enjoyable as possible. Most hotels offer free accommodations for children up to about age 12, provide small-fry menus, and, sometimes, special recreation programs, as well as baby-sitting. Some of the larger hotels, such as the Holiday Inn Lucaya Beach Resort and Princess Towers in Freeport, have small playgrounds.

TRAVEL FOR THE DISABLED • With rising concern for improving and extending leisure-time facilities and services for the physically disabled, many cruise ships and hotels in The Bahamas, including some resorts in the Family Islands, have made their accommodations more accessible to this group of visitors. Nassau's Crystal Palace Hotel, for instance, has set aside a number of specially designed rooms for people confined to wheelchairs. The Bahamas Paraplegic Association, based in Nassau, has made a survey of hotels and resorts throughout The Bahamas where ramps, elevators, dining areas, baths, and other facilities can also serve those with limited mobility. Contact the association at (809) 322–2393 or (809) 323–1392. Renal House, a dialysis facility, recently opened in Nassau. Visitors needing dialysis may make arrangements with this modern professional clinic by calling Princess Margaret Hospital at (809) 322–2861.

SPECIAL SERVICES • Members of **Weight Watchers** need not postpone or forgo a trip for fear of interrupted regimens. For the latest information on Weight Watchers programs in The Bahamas, call (212) 896–9800.

Chapters of **Alcoholics Anonymous** meet in The Bahamas in the following areas: Nassau; Freeport; George Town, Exuma; Hope Town, Abaco; and Moxey Town, Andros. For specific information, contact Alcoholics Anonymous at 468 Park Avenue South, New York, NY, 10016; Tel: (212) 686–1100.

WHEN TO GO • **Weather** • The winter season (from December through April) is considered the ideal time to visit The Bahamas. Daytime temperatures average in the 70s with cooler evenings. Swimming is often comfortable in January and February, but some days and most evenings may be quite cool, making a jacket or heavy sweater necessary. While there is more rain at times during the summer, rates are lower and the government sponsors enjoyable ''Goombay'' festivities. Showers are usually brief and the temperature averages in the 80s.

Most hotels have air conditioning, but trade winds make it unnecessary in some hotels. On the Family Islands, some visitors prefer the more romantic and relaxing ceiling fans that stir the already refreshing air. Nassau and Freeport, both north of the Tropic of Cancer, are in the cooler climate zone. Warmer weather is found in the more southerly islands.

Holidays and Special Events • Junkanoo and Goombay are two festivals that may help determine when to visit The Bahamas. Junkanoo is a festival that occurs during the Christmas/New Year's season. Goombay is an annual series of special events to attract visitors during

	Average Temperature Fahrenheit/Centigrade		Average Rainfall Inches
January	70°	21°	1.9
February	70°	21°	1.6
March	72°	22°	1.4
April	75°	24°	1.9
May	77°	25°	4.8
June	80°	27°	9.2
July	81°	27°	6.1
August	82°	28°	6.3
September	81°	27°	7.5
October	78°	26°	8.3
November	74°	23°	2.3
December	71°	22°	1.5

the summer season, when the weather is hotter and somewhat wetter. Other special events such as those for boaters, sports fishermen, and divers will also help you decide when and where to go.

In anticipation of the 500th anniversary of Columbus' arrival in the New World, a fall promotion called "Discover It," lasts from September through December, previewing the all-out celebration in 1992. Events include culinary festivals, walking tours, and tea parties at Government House.

Event	Month	Location
Junkanoo Parade*	Jan. 1	All Islands
Supreme Court Opening	2nd Wed. in Jan.	Nassau
Annual Miami-Nassau Boat Race	Feb.	Nassau

Event	Month	Location
Annual Nassau Yacht Cup Race	Feb.	Nassau
International 5.5 Metre World Championships	Mar.	Nassau
Annual Bacardi Snipe Winter Championship	Mar.	Nassau
Annual Abaco Fishing Tournament	Apr.	Abaco
Family Island Regatta	Apr.	George Town Exumas
Supreme Court Opening	1st Wed. in Apr.	Nassau
Annual Walker's Cay Billfish Tournament	May	Walker's Cay Abaco
Penny Turtle Billfish Tournament	May	Marsh Harbour, Abaco
Long Island Sailing Regatta	June	Long Island
Cat Cay Billfish Tournament	June	Cat Cay
Bimini Big Game Blue Marlin Tournament	June	Bimini
Labour Day Parade	1st Fri. in June	Nassau & Freeport
Supreme Court Opening	1st Wed. in July	Nassau
Abaco Regatta	July	Abacos
Independence Day	July 10	All Islands
Pepsi-Cola Independence Open Golf Tournament	July	Nassau
Commonwealth Exhibition and Fair	July	Nassau
Chub Cay Blue Marlin Fishing Tournament	July	Chub Cay Berry Islands
Emancipation Day	1st Mon. in Aug.	All Islands
Bimini Local Fishing Tournament	Aug.	Bimini
Cat Island Regatta	Aug.	Arthur's Town Cat Island
Fox Hill Day Celebration	2nd Tues. in Aug.	Nassau
Supreme Court Opening	1st Wed. in Oct.	Nassau
Discovery Day Regatta	Oct.	Nassau
Discovery Day	Oct.	Nassau & San Salvador

Event	Month	Location
Remembrance Day	Nov.	Nassau
Abaco Week Festival	Nov.	Abaco
Annual Bahamas Bonefish Bonanza	Nov.	George Town Exumas
Annual International Pro-Am Golf Championship	Nov.	Nassau
Boxing Day Junkanoo Parade*	Dec. 26	All Islands
Adam Clayton Powell, Jr. Memorial Fishing Tournament	Dec.	Bimini

*Visitors may join in the Junkanoo Parades by applying before Dec. to the Bahamas Tourist Office.

GETTING THERE BY AIR

Airlines fly to The Bahamas from the U.S., Canada, the Caribbean, Great Britain, and Europe. Some small airlines in addition to those listed below fly from Florida to Freeport, Abaco, Eleuthera, and Exuma. The only non-stop flight from the U.S. west coast to the Bahamas is a package run by GoGo Tours to Nassau for 8 days and 7 nights at a choice of hotels; (800) 252–0408 (California).

Airline	From	To
Air Canada	Toronto; Montreal	Nassau; Freeport
Air Jamaica	Jamaica	Nassau
American	New York, Raleigh/Durham; Miami	Nassau; Freeport
Bahamasair	Miami; Tampa; Atlanta; Ft. Lauderdale; Orlando; Washington, D.C.; Philadelphia	Nassau; Freeport; Family Islands*
British Airways	London; Bermuda; Kingston, Jamaica	Nassau; Freeport
Carnival Airlines	Miami; Ft. Lauderdale; Newark; Nashville; Cleveland; Cincinnati; Baltimore; New Orleans	Nassau
Chalk's International	Miami; Ft. Lauderdale; West Palm Beach	Paradise Island; Bimini; Cat Cay

Airline	From	To
Delta	Atlanta; Chicago; New York; Newark; Ft. Lauderdale	Nassau; Freeport
Midway	Chicago; Ft. Lauderdale	Nassau
Pan Am	New York; Miami	Nassau; FreeportTreasure Cay; Abaco; Governer's Harbour; Eleuthera
Paradise Island Airlines	Miami, Ft. Lauderdale, West Palm Beach	Paradise Island
USAir	Baltimore, Charlotte, Philadelphia, Ft. Lauderdale	Nassau; Freeport

*Bahamasair has daily flights from Nassau to the Abacos, Andros, Eleuthera, and Exuma. Flights to other Family Islands leave from Nassau several times a week.

Private Planes and Yachts: Private planes and yachts are free to enter and leave The Bahamas at their own convenience. Aircraft pilots, however, should contact the Bahamas Tourist Office for the Air Navigation Chart or Flight Planner Chart, or contact the Bahamas Private Pilot Briefing Center at 1 (800) 327–3853.

Private plane pilots must also file declaration forms with customs officials. A copy is retained by the pilot as a cruising permit when visiting other islands. U.S. Airmen's Certificates are recognized flying credentials in The Bahamas, but an extension of the aircraft's insurance may be needed to include the islands. Declaration forms are obtainable from Fixed Base Operators at points of departure, or at Bahamian ports of entry.

Charter Planes: Charter flights are frequently used to reach resorts not served by regularly scheduled airlines. Charter planes are available for hire in several southern Florida cities. Following are some Bahamian inter-island charter services:

Pinders Charter Service
Nassau International Airport
P.O. Box N–N799
Nassau, Bahamas
(809) 327–7320

Bahamas Air Charter
P.O. Box N4881
Nassau, Bahamas
(809) 327–8223

Nixon Aviation Service
P.O. Box EX–29003
Georgetown, Exuma, Bahamas
(809) 366–2104

Trans Island Airways, Ltd.
P.O. Box CB–10991
Nassau, Bahamas
(809) 327–8777

Abaco Air Ltd.
Marsh Habour, Abaco,
Bahamas
(809) 367–2266–2205

Four Way Charter
Nassau International Airport
Nassau, Bahamas
(809) 327–5139

GETTING THERE BY SEA • A popular way of traveling to The Bahamas is to go by cruise ship. For those who don't live near a departure point, some lines include bus or air transport to the port as part of the package. A few cruises even include stopovers at Florida's Disney World. Small children are often put up in their parents' stateroom without additional cost. Some ships have recreational areas, baby-sitters, and special activities for youngsters. An increasing number are adding facilities for the handicapped, including wheelchair accessibility in cabins and corridors and the installation of ramps.

The well-appointed ships that cruise to The Bahamas have so many amenities that travelers need never leave the vessel. In response to the current physical fitness vogue, exercise rooms, jogging areas, and spas have burgeoned. Now more than ever, sumptuous and almost continual dining, formal as well as in snack bars and soda fountains, is a feature of shipboard life. Young people can dance until all hours in discos, and some ships even put on lavish nightclub extravaganzas. Passengers with the itch can visit the ships' casinos. Those who prefer a more relaxed trip have the choice of libraries, lounges, in-cabin television, sun decks, and indoor and outdoor pools.

Ships carry from several hundred to more than 1000 passengers. Some voyages tend to be sedate, while others are marked with continual activity. Carnival Cruise Lines, for example, calls its vessels "Fun Ships" and tends to attract a younger and more budget-conscious crowd. However, on the same ships, Carnival also offers posh suites with private decks. For all lines, extras usually include bar service, sightseeing tours, and on-board tipping.

Some cruise lines have added Cashphones, so that passengers may call the United States as well as other countries. On most lines, calls to the U.S. range from $11 to $15.50 per minute, with calls to other countries costing more.

A hallmark of ships of the Royal Caribbean Line, Viking Crown Lounges are glass-enclosed public rooms circling the ships' funnels, to give a 360-degree, panoramic view of the sea and the decks below.

A very different and delightful way to reach Bimini, Chub Cay, and Cat Cay, three quiet Family Islands, is to sail from Miami on a real sailing ship, the 440-foot *Windstar*. This 150-passenger ship has a mere 74 staterooms, all outside, giving carefree passengers the feel of a luxury yacht. That feeling is enhanced even more when travelers find that they can eat when they want and make their own recreation and entertainment.

Tropicana Cruises runs a daily cruise to Bimini from Miami (800–999–1958), and *Discovery I* sails once a day from Miami to Freeport. SeaEscape, Ltd. (1080 Port Blvd., Miami, FL 33132; (800) 327–7400), offers a one-day cruise from Miami or Fort Lauderdale to Freeport for a day of shopping, gambling, or hitting the beach.

Except for military personnel, the U.S. Immigration and Naturalization Service has imposed a $5 inspection fee for all U.S. cruise passengers arriving in the U.S. on ships that have stopped at foreign ports. In most cases, the fee is collected from the cruise line, which adds it to the passenger fare.

Embarkation points for The Bahamas are primarily Miami, Fort Lauderdale, and Port Canaveral. One line, American Canadian, departs from Nassau in The Bahamas for a 7-day cruise to cays in the Family Islands. Because most Bahamian cays do not have landing docks, the line's 72-passenger *New Shoreham II* has a landing ramp in its bow permitting direct access to the cays and their beaches. *The Sea Fever,* a 90-foot, air-conditioned, aluminum boat, departs Miami for diving cruises that visit Andros and the Berry Islands. Dive equipment is provided and dress when not in bathing suits is extremely casual. Cruises range from four to six nights with prices starting at about $789. For information on sailings and costs, call (305) 531–3483 or (800) 443–3873.

Because schedules, ships and prices change from season to season, it is advisable to call the ship line or check with your travel agent when planning a cruise.

Following are lines that provide service to The Bahamas:

Cruise Line	Destination	No. Passengers	Facilities	From
Admiral Cruises 1220 Biscayne Boulevard Miami, FL 33132 (305) 374–1611				
Emerald Seas	Nassau, Freeport	980	OP, C	Ft. Lauderdale
American Canadian Lines P.O. Box 368 Warren, RI 02885 (401) 247–0955, (800) 556–7450				
New Shoreham II	Nassau	72		Caicos

Cruise Line	Destination	No. Passengers	Facilities	From
Carnival Cruise Line 5225 N.W. 87th Avenue Miami, FL 33166 (305) 599–2600				
Fantasy	Nassau, Freeport	2000	3 OP, S, C, TK	Miami
Mardi Gras	Freeport Nassau	906	2 OP, IP, C	Port Canaveral
Carnivale	Freeport Nassau	950	4 OP, IP, C	Port Canaveral
Jubilee	Nassau	1486	3 OP, C	Miami
Chandris Fantasy Cruises 900 Third Avenue New York, NY 10022 (800) 621–3446				
Britanis	Nassau	960	OP, C	Miami
Costa Cruises 1 Biscayne Tower Miami, FL 33131 (305) 358–7330, (800) 447–6877				
Costa Riviera	Nassau	1000	OP, C	Ft. Lauderdale
Crown Cruise Lines 2790 N. Federal Highway Boca Raton, FL 33431 (800) 841–7447				
Crown del Mar	Nassau	486	OP, C	Palm Beach
Dolphin Cruise Line 1007 North American Way Miami, FL 33132 (305) 358–2111				
Dolphin IV	Nassau	664	OP, C	Miami
Seabreeze	Nassau	800	OP, C	Miami
Holland America Lines, Westours 300 Elliott Avenue West Seattle, WA 98119 (206) 281–3535, (800) 426–0327				
Rotterdam	Nassau	1114	OP, IP, C	Ft. Lauderdale
Westerdam	Nassau	1494	2 OP, S, C,	Ft. Lauderdale

Cruise Line	Destination	No. Passengers	Facilities	From
Norwegian Caribbean Lines 1 Biscayne Tower (Suite 3000) Miami, FL 33131 (305) 358–6670, (800) 327–7030				
Norway	Stirrup Cay	1864	IP, 2 OP, C, CPh	Miami
Sunward II	Nassau, Stirrup Cay	696	OP, C	Miami
Princess Cruises 2029 Century Park East Los Angeles, CA 90067 (213) 553–7000				
Sky Princess	Nassau	1212	3 OP, C	Ft. Lauderdale
Premier Cruise Lines P.O. Box 573 Cape Canaveral, FL 32920 or 101 George King Blvd., Port Canaveral, FL (305) 783–5061, (800) 327–7113				
Majestic	Abacos	950	C, W	Port Canaveral
Star/Ship Atlantic	Nassau	1600	2 IP, C	Port Canaveral
Star/Ship Majestic	Treasure Cay, Green Turtle Cay (Abaco)	950	C, W	Port Canaveral
Star/Ship Oceanic	Nassau, Salt Cay	1500	2 OP, C	Port Canaveral
Royal Caribbean Cruise Line 903 South America Way Miami, FL 33132 (305) 379–2601				
Nordic Empress	Nassau	1610	2 OP, C, S	Miami
Nordic Prince	Nassau	1038	OP, C	Miami
SeaEscape, Ltd. 1080 Port Blvd. Miami, FL 33132 (800) 327–7400	1-day cruises Miami, Fort Lauderdale			Freeport
Sitmar Cruises 10100 Santa Monica Blvd. Los Angeles, CA 90067 (213) 553–1666				
Fairsky	Nassau	1212	2 OP, S, YC, C	Ft. Lauderdale
Fairwind	Nassau	925	2 OP, YC, C	Ft. Lauderdale

Key

IP	Indoor Pool
OP	Outdoor Pool
C	Casino
CPh	Cashphone
S	Spa or Exercise Facilities
YC	Youth Center
T	Theater
W	Whirlpool
TK	Track

ENTRY AND DEPARTURE REQUIREMENTS • Travel Documents • To enter the Bahamas, you must have proof of citizenship and an onward-bound ticket. While Bahamian Immigration accepts either a valid passport, birth certificate, voter's registration card, or driver's license as proof of citizenship, the U.S. government now requires that you have a passport to reenter the country.

Citizens of Canada and the United Kingdom visiting for three weeks or less may enter upon showing a passport or the same items required for U.S. citizens. Citizens of Commonwealth countries do not need visas for entry.

All visitors must fill out and sign immigration cards. Vaccination certificates for smallpox and cholera are needed only for people coming from areas where such diseases still occur.

Departure Tax • Upon departure by air, travelers are required to pay a $13 tax. Children under age 3 are exempt.

Customs • Although no written declaration is required, baggage is subject to customs inspection. For dutiable items such as furniture, china, and linens, a declaration is necessary. New items should be accompanied by sales slips. Any used household items are subject to assessment by the Customs Officer.

Each adult visitor is permitted 50 cigars or 200 cigarettes or one pound of tobacco and one quart of alcohol duty free, in addition to personal effects. Purchases of up to $25 are allowed all incoming passengers.

Duty-Free Allowances • United States residents, including children, may take home duty-free purchases up to $300 in value if they have been out of the United States for more than 48 hours, and have not taken such an exemption within 30 days. The exemption includes up to 32 ounces of alcohol per person over 21, and families may pool their exemptions.

Canadians absent from their country for 48 hours or more may take home up to $50 (Canadian) worth of duty-free merchandise, which must accompany the passenger.

Personal items such as jewelry, cameras, and sports equipment may be brought in duty-free.

Pets • The Bahamian Ministry of Agriculture and Fisheries, with headquarters in Nassau, requires a permit for all animals entering the country. Written applications for permits should be submitted to the Ministry of Agriculture and Fisheries, P.O. Box N–3208, Nassau, telephone (809) 32–21277. Forms are available at the Bahamas Tourist Offices. Although most hotels exclude pets, several accept them when arrangements are made in advance and a permit has been obtained.

Drugs, Alcohol, and Firearms • Possession of marijuana, cocaine, or other such drugs is an extremely serious and punishable offense. If you indulge here or attempt to bring narcotics into the country, you are looking for trouble, especially since the government has been cracking down on drugs more than ever lately. The minimum drinking age is 21.

Under no circumstances may firearms be brought in without a Bahamian gun license.

BEING THERE • Language • The language of The Bahamas is English, accented with West Indian, Scottish, and Irish influences. Like Bermudians, Bahamians often substitute *w*s for *v*s. This is thought to date back to 18th-century English.

Dress • In The Bahamas, dress is generally casual although, in season, most hotels and restaurants request that men wear jackets and ties for evening meals. Dress is more relaxed during the off season. At some of the larger hotels and posher resorts, long skirts or cocktail attire are preferred for women during the evening. Out in the Family Islands, dress is much more casual, except in one or two resorts.

Beachwear is discouraged in the public rooms of hotels, and wearing short shorts in town is frowned upon for both men and women.

Business Hours • In Nassau, banks are open 9:30 a.m.–3 p.m. Monday through Thursday, and on Friday from 9:30 a.m.–5 p.m. Stores are open 9 a.m.–5 p.m. every day except Sunday and holidays.

Banks in Freeport are also open 9:30 a.m.–3 p.m. Monday through Thursday and from 9:30 to 5 p.m. on Friday. Most stores are open 9 a.m.–6 p.m. except Sundays and holidays. Many shops in the International Bazaar and Port Lucaya stay open until 9 p.m. on Saturdays during the winter season. Some banks on the Family Islands are open only several days a week, with limited hours. Many stores close for an hour or two for lunch.

Accommodations • The large hotels and resorts have daily activities and many facilities such as shops, restaurants, large dining rooms, cycle rental stations, and water sports equipment. Most also have nightly entertainment. When not located on a beach, many provide complimentary transportation. Most establishments that have few or no sports facilities will arrange sporting activities for their guests elsewhere. All large accommodations are fully air conditioned. Smaller hotels and guest houses have fewer facilities and many are partially air conditioned, if at all. Particularly in the Family Islands, many establishments rely on fans and trade winds. Some of the smaller guest houses are in former private homes and have shared baths. In the Family Islands, with power generators in wide use at hotels, visitors may sometimes find themselves without electricity for short periods of time. It is therefore a good idea to note the location of candles that are put in most guest rooms.

Hotels add a 6% room tax to rates. Many also add a 15% service charge. High season runs from about December through April. During the summer (or "Goombay") season, rates are about 20% to 50% lower.

In the **Hotel Quick Reference Charts** at the back of the book, you'll find more information about the accommodations described in each island section as well as details about other establishments.

Renting Private Homes • Following are some real estate agencies that handle private homes throughout The Bahamas:

- Caribbean Management, Ltd.
  P.O. Box N–1132, Nassau, The Bahamas; (809)322–8618/1356
- Ingraham's Real Estate
  Hospital Lane North, P.O. Box N–1062, Nassau, The Bahamas; (809)325–2222/3433/8930
- Jack Isaacs Real Estate Co., Ltd.
  25 Cumberland St., Nassau, The Bahamas; (809)322–1069/325–6326
- Plot Realty Co., Ltd.
  P.O. Box N–1492, Nassau, The Bahamas (809)322–2460

Money • Bahamian money is pegged to the American dollar, with the same designations for bills and coins and exchanged at the same rate. Visitors are likely to receive change in mixed American and Bahamian dollars and coins. Travelers checks are accepted throughout the islands and are cashable at banks and hotels. However, banks and some restaurants will add a service charge. Credit cards are widely accepted, but you may have to pay a service charge if you use American Express.

In Nassau and Freeport, commercial banks are open from 9:30 a.m. to 3 p.m., Monday through Thursday, and until 5 p.m. on Friday. Most banks will cash verifiable personal checks. Nassau's American Express office for check cashing and cash advances is conveniently located downtown at the Playtours office, upstairs at the intersection of Shirley and Parliament streets. In Freeport, American Express is located in the Kipling Building, off Kipling Lane in Churchill Square.

Getting Around • *By Taxi:* Taxis are available in New Providence, Grand Bahama, and most of the Family Islands. In Nassau and Freeport, as well as the Family Islands where there are no tour buses, drivers will serve as island guides. The rates, often negotiable, are about $16 an hour. Some Family Island roads are not in the best of repair. A bumpy ride with a friendly driver can be an adventure in itself.

In Nassau and Freeport, taxis, which are metered, wait for passengers at airports and hotels. From Nassau International Airport to a hotel on Cable Beach, two people should expect to pay about $10 from the airport to Paradise Island, the ride will be about $19, including the $2 bridge toll. From Freeport's International Airport to the hotel districts, the fare will range from about $6 to $9. Taxis in the Family Islands are not metered and tend to be more expensive than in Nassau or Freeport. On most Family Islands taxis (sometimes simply the cars or vans of local residents) meet planes. However, to be on the safe side, check with your accommodation about land transportation before arrival.

By Car: Visitors with valid U.S. or Canadian driver's licenses can rent cars in the Bahamas. *Note that driving is on the left.* Daily rates range from about $45 to $72. You'll save renting by the week. Rental agencies in Nassau and Freeport are at airports, hotels, and downtown locations. During high season, a reservation is suggested before leaving home. In addition to local companies, Avis, Budget, Dollar Rent-A-Car, and National also have offices in The Bahamas. An Avis agency is in back of Nassau's British Colonial Beach Resort and National agencies are on nearby Marlborough Street and at the Crystal Palace Hotel. Budget has an office at the Paradise Island airport. You'll also find an Avis office in Freeport's International Bazaar. You can rent cars in the Family Islands (sometimes from taxi drivers), but many of the models are battle scarred by years of use on bumpy roads. Be sure to check your car's condition before pulling off. You can import your own car for touring, duty-free, for up to 6 months. A deposit of up to 70% of the vehicle's value is required, but it is refunded if the car is shipped out within 6 months. The value is assessed by Customs upon arrival.

By Cycle: Cycles are a popular mode of travel in The Bahamas and visitors take to them with a passion. At most hotels and resorts, you can rent mopeds on the premises or at nearby cycle shops if you are 16 or older. No driver's license is necessary. Wearing a helmet, which you are given with the moped, is required by law. Until you become accustomed to motorized bikes, it is best to practice driving in a low-traffic area. Renting a moped ranges from about $15 a day, $8 a half day to about $30 a day, $18 a half day, including insurance. You'll be asked to leave a deposit of about $20. Bicycles are about $12 a day. *Remember, Bahamians drive on the left.*

By Bus: Visitors can take advantage of public transportation in getting around Nassau and Freeport. Bahamians will come to the rescue with directions if you seem uncertain. Nassau has jitneys (about 75¢) you can pick up at bus stops, and they go to Cable Beach, downtown Nassau, public beaches, and other points in the city. To go east, toward the Paradise Island bridge, pick up jitneys downtown at Frederick Street at the corner of Bay Street; to go west to Cable Beach, pick up jitneys in front of the British Colonial at Bay Street. Some hotels run complimentary buses to downtown Nassau and to the casino on Cable Beach. Buses on Grand Bahama (about 75¢) connect Freeport with Lucaya and all hotels with beaches, the International Bazaar, and Port Lucaya. Vacationers traveling on package deals generally get pre-paid vouchers for bus transportation between the airport and hotels.

By Ferry: Ferries run between downtown Nassau and Paradise Island from Prince George Dock. These "water taxis" also operate in the Family Islands to various offshore cays.

By Mail Boat: Inter-island mail boats travel between Nassau and the Family Islands. The mail boats leave for the outer islands from Potter's Cay, next to the Paradise Island bridge, East Bay Street in Nassau. Boats leave once a week, stopping at one or two islands, in a trip that takes almost a day, and is usually made overnight.

Mail boats are an economical way of traveling, if only for the more adventurous visitor. Decks are crowded with local commuters, freight, varieties of cargo, produce, and livestock. Schedules are constantly revised and there are often postponements. Passage cannot be arranged in advance. Bookings can only be made after arrival.

Information on mail boats may be obtained at the Dock Master's office on Potter's Cay in Nassau (809) 323–1064.

Casinos • Gambling at the casinos of The Bahamas is legal for all visitors over the age of 21. Bahamian citizens, however, are not permitted to play. Two casinos are located in Nassau: one on Paradise Island, and the other on the mainland in Carnival's Crystal Palace. Two more are found in Freeport, Grand Bahama—one between the Princess Tower Hotel and the International Bazaar, the other at the Lucayan Beach Resort and Casino.

Time • Eastern Standard Time is in use throughout The Bahamas. Eastern Daylight Saving Time is used during the summer months coinciding with the U.S. changes, so when it is noon in New York, it is noon in The Bahamas, year round.

Electricity • American electrical appliances can be used in The Bahamas without adapters.

Medical Concerns • There are excellent medical services in The Bahamas. Hospital, public and private medical facilities, and personnel are available in Nassau and Freeport. There are also health centers and clinics in the Family Islands. In medical emergencies, patients are brought to Princess Margaret Hospital, a government-operated institution in downtown Nassau. The government also operates the 58-bed Rand Memorial Hospital in Freeport.

The water throughout The Bahamas is potable. However, on most Family Islands it is best to drink bottled or filtered water, if only because tap water can be quite salty.

Communications • Nassau's two newspapers are the *Nassau Guardian,* published Monday through Saturday, and the *Tribune,* an afternoon paper. Freeport's paper, the *Freeport News,* is published afternoons, Monday through Friday. *The New York Times,* the *London Times,* the *Daily Telegraph,* and the *Wall Street Journal* are available at most of the larger hotels and newstands, but sometimes a day late. Radio Bahamas operates two radio stations in New Providence, ZNS1 and ZNS2, and ZNS3 in Grand Bahama. Its television station, TV-13 ZNS, operates out of New Providence.

Visitor Information • The address of The Bahamas Ministry of Tourism is P.O. Box N–3701, Nassau, The Bahamas. Contact the Family Islands Promotion Board at 1100 Lee Wagener Boulevard, Suite 206, Fort Lauderdale, FL 33315, (305) 359–8099, or The Grand Bahama Promotion Board, P.O. Box F650, Freeport, Grand Bahama. Following are the locations and phone numbers of The Bahamas Tourist Offices in the United States and Canada:

Atlanta
2957 Clairmont Rd., Suite 150
Atlanta, GA 30345
(404) 633–1793

Chicago
875 North Michigan Avenue
Chicago, IL 60611
(312) 787–8203

Dallas
2050 Stemmons Freeway
Dallas, TX 75201
(214) 742–1886

Los Angeles
3450 Wilshire Boulevard
Los Angeles, CA 90010
(213) 385–0033

Coral Gables
255 Alhambra Circle
Coral Gables, FL 33134
(305) 442–4860

New York
150 E. 52 St.
New York, NY 10022
(212) 758–2777

Boston
1027 Statler Office Building
Boston, MA 02116
(617) 426–3144

Philadelphia
437 Chestnut St.
Philadelphia, PA 19106
(215) 925–0871

Detroit Area
26400 Lahser Road
Southfield, MI 48034
(313) 357–2940

District of Columbia
1730 Rhode Island Avenue, NW
Washington, DC 20036
(202) 659–9135

Toronto
85 Richmond Street West
Toronto, Ontario M5H2C9
(416) 363–4441

Montreal
1255 Phillips Square
Montreal, Quebec H3B3G1
(514) 861–6797

The United States Embassy is located in Nassau in the Mosmar building on Queen St. (322–1181). **The Canadian Consulate** is in the Out Island Traders building on East Bay St. in Nassau (323–2124); and the **British High Commission** is in the Bitco building on East St. in Nassau (325–7471).

WHAT TO DO AND WHERE TO DO IT

For most visitors, having a good time in The Bahamas revolves around watersports and just being outdoors. Because the islands are surrounded by some of the clearest, most beautiful, and game-stocked waters in the world, fishing, boating, and undersea exploration are very popular. Nassau, the adjoining Paradise Island, and Freeport offer lively nightlife, including their casinos, and the Family Islands are paradise for those looking for real escape. For more specific information on sports, nightlife, shopping, tours, or dining, refer to the individual islands.

SPORTS

You can get further information about exactly where and when various sports are available before leaving home. Contact The Bahamas Sports Information Center at 1 (800) 32–SPORT for answers to any sports-related question.

Bare Boating • The marinas, ports, and harbors of almost every island are thronged with pleasure boats making use of the extensive

Bahamian boating facilities. Those sailing have a wide choice of marinas throughout the Family Islands as well as in New Providence and Grand Bahama, where Nassau and Freeport are located. Visitors without boats can charter bare boats and, if needed, a captain and crew. Provisions, fuel, and instruction are all at hand on the islands. Ask at your accommodation how to make arrangements.

Game Fishing • The Bahamas cannot be mentioned without a discussion of fishing. Its Bimini Islands are known as the fishing capital of the world, and locals as well as visitors are addicted to this pastime. Andros is loved for its bonefishing. Walker's Cay in the Abacos and Chub Cay in the Berry Islands are both excellent for deep-sea and shore fishing. Scores of world-record catches have been made in The Bahamas. Fishing tournaments are held throughout the islands at various times of the year and attract fishing enthusiasts from around the world. Even those not aspiring to take part in tournaments can be bitten by the fishing bug on almost any island. Arrangements can be made through your accommodation.

Golf • Most courses are in and around the cities of Nassau and Freeport/Lucaya. Courses designed by such luminaries as Robert Trent-Jones and Dick Wilson are also at the Cotton Bay Club in Eleuthera and Treasure Cay in the Abacos. Grand Bahama's Lucayan Park Golf and Country Club is the oldest in the country. The newest is at the Crystal Palace Hotel & Casino in Nassau. The best is said to be the one at the Divi Bahamas Beach Resort. The Emerald Course in Grand Bahama is considered less challenging than the Ruby Course. Bahamian courses play host to several tournaments, including an annual Pro-Am, and an Open to celebrate Independence Day.

Horseback Riding • In Freeport you can go horseback riding at Pine Tree Stables and in Nassau, at the Paradise Island Riding Stable.

Jogging • For some barefoot joggers, the hard-packed sand near the waterline of beaches throughout The Bahamas can be sufficient. Those who run in shoes, however, prefer places like the wide, tree-lined, traffic-free esplanade of Nassau's Cable Beach area. There is also the cool, tree-vaulted Casuarina Walk on Paradise Island that leads to the dock and to Chalk's seaplane terminal. In Grand Bahama's Freeport/Lucaya area, there is a choice of streets in a broad, landscaped, well-paved network. The Bahamas Princess Resort & Casino has a 10-km (6.2 mile) jogging course, dedicated to world marathon champion Grete Waitz. On the Family Islands, most joggers blaze their own paths, using either the beaches or the paved roads.

Parasailing ● If you've ever had the urge to be strapped to a brightly colored parachute that is tied to a boat, then gently lifted into the air as the boat takes off, parasailing is for you. In Nassau, you can enjoy this sport at the Crystal Palace Hotel & Casino, the Ambassador Beach Hotel, and the Nassau Beach Hotel; on Paradise Island, at the Sheraton Grand Hotel and at Paradise Island Resort and Casino, and in Freeport, at the Atlantik Beach Hotel, the Lucaya Holiday Beach Resort and the Lucaya Beach Resort.

Scuba Diving and Snorkeling ● The Bahamas' magnificent undersea attractions have helped to encourage the growth of scuba and snorkeling. Centers such as the Underwater Explorers Society (UNEXSO) in Freeport and Treasure Cay, Abaco, have sprung up for trained divers as well as beginners. The centers give instruction and lead expeditions to the undersea wrecks, special marine life, and coral formations. UNEXSO offers a week-long course in underwater photography. It also hosts The Dolphin Experience (in Freeport), a program that allows people to swim with several of those friendly mammals.

Most hotels will make arrangements for snorkeling and diving if facilities are not on the premises. The Family Islands are major attractions for those fascinated by underwater spectacles such as the sunken train off Eleuthera. One of the largest barrier reefs in the world is just off the coast of Andros. Excellent diving programs are run by Small Hope Bay Lodge in Andros; the Green Turtle Club in the Abacos; the Stella Maris Inn on Long Island; Riding Rock Inn on San Salvador; and the Rum Cay Club, on a tiny island between Long Island and San Salvador (see San Salvador/Rum Cay).

By merely donning a helmet, novice divers of any age can take an undersea walk to see fish, coral, and other marine life through Hartley's at the Nassau Yacht Haven.

Tennis ● Nassau and Freeport have many courts and you can also play on a number of Family Islands, such as the Abacos, the Berry Islands, Eleuthera, and Exuma. The larger resorts have pro shops for players. The first-class tennis facility at the Crystal Palace Hotel & Casino has 10 courts, five of them lighted, as well as a stadium for tournament and exhibition games. Next door is an indoor complex with three courts each for **squash** and **racquetball.** A junior national tennis championship for youngsters 10–18 years old is sponsored annually in Nassau to encourage the sport among young Bahamians.

Waterskiing ● This sport is available at most large beach hotels throughout The Bahamas.

Windsurfing • Seeing several windsurfers at once is as thrilling as watching one of The Bahamas' popular regattas. In addition to Nassau and Freeport, windsurfing is available in Walker's Cay, Treasure Cay, Marsh Harbour, and Elbow Cay in the Abacos; Nicholls Town in Andros; and Harbour Island and Rock Sound in Eleuthera.

NIGHTLIFE

Nassau and Freeport/Lucaya are the places to see and enjoy Bahamian nightlife in its most elaborate and sophisticated form. Entertainment tends to run to what Bahamians refer to as "native." Native shows include some elements common to countries in the Caribbean like calypso, limbo dancing, and steel drums. A difference is that a goombay beat alters these rhythms, transforming them into Bahamian music. The Bahamas' casinos are located in Nassau's Cable Beach, Paradise Island, and Freeport/Lucaya. They are open to the small hours.

The larger hotels have discos and present revues and single acts in their night clubs, lounges, and sometimes in dining-room areas. Performances can be loud, lavish, and brassy at the casino theaters, or smooth, refined, or intimate as when a single player strums a guitar and softly croons songs of the tropics. Discos and nightclubs are also found away from the hotels in places such as the Bay Street area in Nassau and the International Bazaar area in Freeport. Visitors should venture out for Bahamian entertainment away from their hotels and resorts for another aspect and flavor of life in the islands. On the Family Islands you can see the same kind of entertainment, but on a smaller scale. Some performances are so understated that they gain even more in overall effect.

SHOPPING

Although The Bahamas is not a duty free territory, bargain hunters can be roused by the wares offered along Nassau's Bay Street, in some Paradise Island shops, and in Freeport. Prices can be 25 to 45% lower than in the U.S. for things such as crystal, china, woolens, linens, perfumes, watches, clocks, cameras, and liquor. You don't even have to leave the larger hotels to dip into your purse or wallet. Many have arcades filled with tempting shops and boutiques. Most visitors agree, however, that it's more fun (and usually less expensive) to venture out and rub elbows with resident shoppers.

Seeming to jostle for attention, shops line Bay Street, Nassau's main thoroughfare and several tributary streets on both sides. Arcades such as the International Bazaar, Beaumont House, and Colony Place run from Bay Street out to Woodes Rogers Walk. For Seiko and Rolex watches, clocks; jewelry; English, Meissen and Limoges porcelain, and much more, stop in at **John Bull** between East Street and Elizabeth Avenue. The **Brass and Leather Shop,** on Charlotte Street off Bay, sells wallets, belts, Bottega Veneta luggage, and the like. French, American and local perfumes are available at the **Bahamas Fragrance and Cosmetic Factory** on Charlotte Street, which makes its own, and at **Lightbourn's** on Bay Street. **Marlborough Antiques,** across from the British Colonial Beach Resort on the street of the same name, has beautifully displayed antique items, and **Balman Antiques** specializes in old maps.

In Freeport, many shops, boutiques, and restaurants are clustered in the International Bazaar. **Midnight Sun** is where you'll find a wide selection of Scandinavian bargains, and the **Discount Bazaar** is worth checking out. The multimillion dollar **Port Lucaya** is an exciting shopping, dining, and entertainment complex, across from the Lucaya Holiday Beach Resort and the Lucayan Beach Resort & Casino.

Handmade straw goods are sold on most Bahamian islands, but the greatest variety is found in Nassau and Freeport. The largest straw market in The Bahamas is on Bay Street in Nassau. On Nassau's Cable Beach, a straw market is located across from the Ambassador Beach and Crystal Palace hotels. Shoppers can pick up straw hats to keep the sun off, or straw bags and baskets for overflow on the way home. Don't be shy about bargaining—no one expects you to pay the first price quoted.

Throughout The Bahamas you'll find bright resort wear made of Androsia batiks. These colorful bathing suits, shirts, shorts, shifts, head ties, and dresses come from the factory begun by the owners of Small Hope Bay Lodge on Andros. At the Andros Beach Hotel in Nicholl's Town on Andros, the proprietor in the on-premises boutique will run you up a shirt or a dress overnight made of an Androsia fabric or another material.

TOURS

In Nassau and Freeport, bus, taxi, and boat tours can be arranged at hotel tour desks, or at Bahamas tourist offices. From Rawson Square in Nassau, you can also take 30-minute horse-drawn carriage tours for about $5 per person. Horses rest from 1 p.m. to 3 p.m. from May to

October and from 1 p.m. to 2 p.m. November through April. In the Family Islands, taxi tours can be arranged through resorts or guest houses. Bus, boat, and horse-drawn carriage tours run most frequently during the winter season. In Nassau, avoid nightclub tours, which usually aren't much fun.

DINING OUT

Especially in Nassau and Freeport, restaurant reservations are generally required for dinner during the winter season. Men are expected to wear jackets at night at the more expensive restaurants. Off season, these requirements are relaxed at most places. While Nassau and Freeport have many restaurants, those in the Family Islands are mainly limited to hotel and resort dining rooms and small locally operated restaurants. On some islands, such as Abaco, there are individuals who prepare elaborate Bahamian feasts for visitors who call ahead. Hotel staff members and other residents can tell you how to find these chefs. (Also see Eating and Drinking, page 153.)

NASSAU

ATTRACTIONS AT A GLANCE

	Place	Page
Forts		
*Fort Charlotte	Off West Bay Street	185
Fort Fincastle	Bennett's Hill	186
Fort Montagu	East Bay Street	186

	Place	*Page*
Gardens, Parks, & Nature Reserves		
Ardastra Gardens	Near Fort Charlotte	184
Royal Victoria Gardens	Near Government House	188
*Versailles Gardens	Paradise Island	182
*Botanical Gardens	Near Fort Charlotte	185
Government Buildings		
*Government House	Blue Hill Road	186
Historical Sights		
Blackbeard's Tower	Fox Hill Road	185
Queen's Staircase	Shirley Street	186
Gregory Arch	Near Government House	186
Museums & Animals		
*Seafloor Aquarium	Near Ardastra Gardens	188
Roselawn Museum	East Street & Bank Lane	188
*Sea Gardens	East End of Nassau Harbor	188
*Coral World	Silver Cay	185
*Hartley's Undersea Walk	East Bay Street	188
Nautilus Submarine	Marina	186
Local Sights		
Water Tower	Bennett Hill	189
Potters Cay	Under Paradise Island Bridge	186
Straw Market	Market & Bay Streets	188

First Impressions

One of the first places most visitors see upon arrival in The Bahamas is the 7-by-21-mile island of New Providence, where Nassau, the capital, is located. The island has an international airport, and gleaming white cruise ships dock at its busy harbor. Some of the largest and most luxurious hotels and restaurants serve its visitors, and the city is rich in Bahamian beauty and history. If you arrive at the International Airport, your taxi takes you along a scenic drive, with glimpses of surf, exotic blossoms, ancient trees and leafy, overhung roads, dappled with sunlight. You see pastel-colored, shuttered houses, some from colonial times,

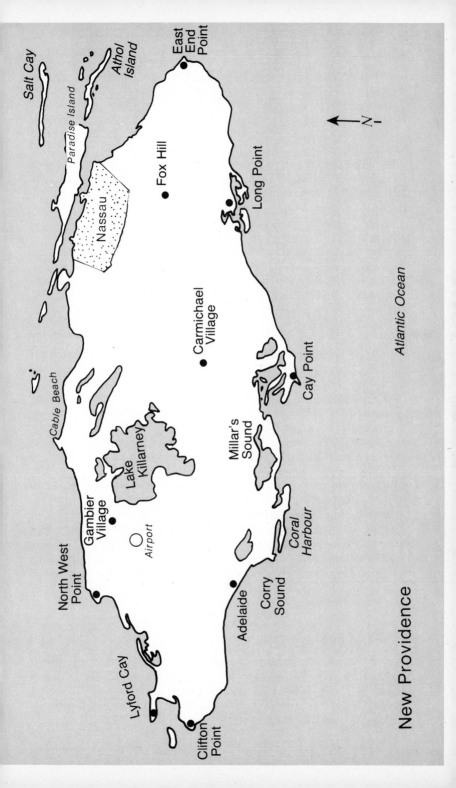

Salt Cay

Paradise Island

Athol Island

East End Point

←—N—

Nassau

Fox Hill

Long Point

Cable Beach

Carmichael Village

Atlantic Ocean

Cay Point

Lake Killarney

Millar's Sound

Gambier Village

Airport

North West Point

Coral Harbour

Corry Sound

Adelaide

Lyford Cay

Clifton Point

New Providence

with flowers and shrubs spilling in abundance over their walls. As you turn onto Bay Street, you'll see two low, gaping caves on the right side of the road. Historians believe that they were once inhabited by Indians, but the government doesn't have the money to conduct an archaeological study. Aptly named Caves Beach is across the way, not far from Orange Hill Beach. Nearby Sandy Point is a community of attractive villas. The condominiums and hotels along Cable Beach are followed by historic downtown Nassau. If you're bound for one of the Paradise Island hotels, your taxi turns off Bay Street and takes you over the toll bridge.

Unfortunately, too few visitors venture much beyond Cable Beach, downtown Nassau, or Paradise Island. To see more of New Providence you can take part in the popular free **People-to-People Program,** where Bahamians will be your hosts. You might be taken on a personalized sightseeing tour. Your host might also give you the opportunity to join in some local event to which visitors are seldom privy, such as a church picnic or local beach party. In any case, you will learn about The Bahamas from people who know the islands intimately. Arrangements can be made through one of the Bahamas Tourist Bureau offices.

Some Bahamians and visitors get to know each other in another way: it's been *de rigeur* in the last few years for visiting women (and even some men) to have all or part of their hair cornrowed and beaded by Bahamian women on the beach or in the straw markets. Depending on the number of braids, this can take anywhere from a few minutes to over an hour. The price, which varies greatly from braider to braider, is negotiable. Be forewarned: If you don't have much melanin in your skin, put some sunscreen on the exposed scalp between braids!

While taxis are available for traveling between Cable Beach, downtown Nassau, and the foot of the Paradise Island bridge, and some of the larger hotels provide complimentary bus service, riding jitneys is much more fun. For about 75¢, with the radio playing loud reggae or calypso, you'll pass sights most visitors miss—tiny churches, homes with lush banana trees growing in their front yards, local stores and bars, wide-trunked silk cotton trees, a bakery decorated with huge red polka dots, a row of tiny clapboard houses painted bright blue or yellow with pink and green or orange shutters. If you call out "Bus stop!" as you approach your destination, you might even pass for Bahamian.

A Bit of History

New Providence was settled in 1656 by a colony of Britons, some of whom came from Bermuda, looking for a better way of life. The new colony was supposedly ruled from the Carolinas on the North American mainland, but supervision was lax and the new and remote Bahamians were pretty much on their own.

Spain, in an effort to end the incessant and irksome raids on its ships by pirates based in the Bahamas, attacked the settlement called Charles Town, named for Britain's Charles II. Spain's occupation of the town was short lived and she left almost immediately, because there was a new king in England. The settlement was renamed Nassau, after William III, of Orange-Nassau.

The pirates, notably Blackbeard, the alias for Edward Teach, remained there along with his cohorts, "Calico" Jack Rackham, Major Bonnet, a Frenchman, and the notorious women pirates, Mary Reed (who was eventually hung) and Anne Bonney, Rackham's mistress.

The marauders were not driven out until the ruthless Captain Woodes Rogers was appointed governor. In tribute to his feat, a statue stands before the British Colonial Hotel, and a waterfront road bears his name.

Nassau was once an acknowledged playground for the rich. The height of that period was probably during the tenure of the Duke of Windsor, the abdicated King of England, just before World War II. The wealthy still come to Nassau, many finding their way to Lyford Cay, a private resort where foreign notables often stay.

Cable Beach

With one of the most beautiful (but busy) strips of beach in The Bahamas, this area was named in 1892 after the laying of a telegraph cable from Jupiter, Florida, to The Bahamas. For the first time, messages could be sent directly from The Bahamas to the United States and England. Horse racing, all the rage with officers of the British West India Regiment stationed in Nassau, was once Cable Beach's prime attraction. In 1933 an annual racing season began, lasting until 1975 when the track closed. In the past, pineapples to be exported to the United States were grown in much of the Cable Beach area.

New Providence's first luxury beach resorts began springing up here after World War II. Meridien's Royal Bahamian Hotel, formerly the Emerald Beach, was one of the first in the area to be restored. Then the lavish 700-room Cable Beach Hotel & Casino was built. Now called the Rivieria Tower, it has been absorbed into Carnival Cruise Line's even more elaborate Crystal Palace Resort & Casino, which dominates the area with its painted Pompidou Center–like pipes and eye-catching colors. With the smaller Cable Beach hotels joining in, the area is being touted as the Bahamian Riviera. Between downtown and Cable Beach, Coral World Villas on Silver Cay is included when describing Riviera resorts as is even the Lighthouse Beach Hotel, which is downtown. Across from the Crystal Palace complex is the headquarters of the Hotel Corporation of the Bahamas. An added diversion for the Cable Beach area is Discovery Island, which lies just offshore. Boats leave every half hour for its beaches, sunning areas, and refreshment places. Information is available at any of the hotels along the strip.

Runners jog along tree- and flower-lined West Bay Street in front of the hotels. **Delaporte Beach,** at the western end of the area, is never crowded. **Goodman's Bay** and **Saunders Beach,** on the way to downtown Nassau, are other pleasant beaches, and are popular with locals for cookouts as well as swimming.

Downtown Nassau

Bay Street, full of all sorts of shops and restaurants, is in the heart of Nassau. The annual Junkanoo Parade, rivaling Caribbean carnivals and New Orleans' Mardi Gras, passes rhythmically along this thoroughfare. Here you'll find bargains in a variety of items from china and crystal to liquor and cameras, and you can visit Nassau Art Gallery By the Waterfront. At one end of the street is the dignified British Colonial Beach Resort. The busy straw market in the open-air Ministry of Tourism building sells T-shirts and jewelry in addition to countless straw products. Off the waterfront, from Cumberland east to Church Street, Bay Street brings back memories of the "Bay Street Boys." This notorious group of businessmen ruled The Bahamas from Nassau, and are alleged to have divided the spoils among themselves and their enterprises. The Duke of Windsor was tainted by their scheming during his tenure as wartime governor.

Nearby Rawson Square is really a palm-shaded circle full of bright flowers where horse-drawn carriages wait to give tours. It sits between Prince George Dock and the government buildings across Bay Street. Visitors from cruise ships pour out into the square heading for restaurants and bargains on Bay Street. Tourists from town compete with the cruise passengers for the taxis and surreys that line up at the square. The 45-minute surrey trips are about $7 per person.

Prince George Dock is the busiest point in Nassau. Cruise ships dock here. Freighters, tugs, charter boats, sightseeing boats, pleasure boats, fishing craft, and mail boats to the Family Islands all use this wharf. It teems with pedestrians coming and going, mirroring the activity of the harbor. Facing the water is a statue by Randolph W. Johnston of Little Harbour, Abaco, in tribute to the Bahamian woman. It was dedicated in 1974 by the prime minister, and the inscription begins, "In grateful tribute to the Bahamian woman whose steadfast love and devotion sustained our nation through countless years of adversity."

Woodes Rogers Walk, bordering the waterfront, is a colorful place for a stroll. Near the Straw Market, across from the towering cruise ships, women sell home-cooked meals from pots in the trunks of their cars. You might see a man hawking conch salad from a jar and someone else trying to attract customers to a shopping cart full of ripe bananas. Near Parliament St., ferries depart for Paradise Island and Coral World marine park. Off Bay Street by the British Colonial Hotel you can catch local jitneys or minibuses to Cable Beach. Buses depart for the Paradise Island bridge and elsewhere from nearby Frederick Street, off Bay. Small boys with sacks slung over their shoulders will sell you peanuts through the window of your bus as you wait for it to take off.

In Parliament Square, with its statue of a slim, young queen Victoria, visitors can watch ceremonial parades or attend the solemn opening of the nation's Supreme Court. Also housed in the colonial government buildings here are the House of Assembly, the Supreme Court, the office of the Colonial Secretary, the Central Police Station, and the public library, formerly a prison. Spend some time at the garden of Remembrance, where a monument honors the war dead. As well as being the capital and the seat of government, Nassau is the financial center. It is also the hub of air and boat traffic to the outer islands.

Paradise Island

Paradise Island is connected to New Providence Island by a dramatic arching bridge that gives a spectacular view of the harbor. As you cross the bridge (25¢ by foot, 75¢ by bike or moped, $2.00 by car, round trip), you will see colorful fruit and vegetable stands on the Nassau side next to piles of conch shells.

Ferries run between downtown Nassau and Paradise Island (about $2.50 each way, depending on your hotel location). Shuttle buses (about 50¢) connect Paradise Island hotels and restaurants.

Lavishly landscaped and stocked with deluxe hotels, restaurants, sports facilities, condominiums, and a transplanted ruin, Paradise Island went by the unglamorous name of Hog Island when it was farmland.

The original concept to develop Hog Island came from a Swedish millionaire, Axel Wenner-Gren. He purchased the old Lynch estate on the island and set about digging canals to connect a lake with the Nassau harbor. He then proceeded to rebuild the estate, the former home of the Edmund C. Lynch of Merrill, Lynch fame. During World War II, it was discovered that Mr. Wenner-Gren's munitions works in Sweden were allied with and partially owned by the Nazi-controlled Krupp works. Despite a boycott, the war made him even wealthier, but he sold his Hog Island holdings to another millionaire, Huntington Hartford, the A&P heir.

After a few false starts, the island's serious development was begun again by Hartford, who planned to make it a showplace. A medieval cloister had been dismantled earlier and brought stone by stone from France by William Randolph Hearst and stored with the rest of his Old

World treasures. Hartford took it off Hearst's hands and had it reassembled in Versailles Gardens, where it now stands, an ancient attraction for the new Paradise Island.

The island continued its ascent toward prestige and glamour even after the departure of Hartford. Other hotels sprang up to take advantage of the new space and its attractive beaches. World renowned statesmen, politicians, jet setters, and European royalty came to sample the enticements of this fashionable new playground.

The casino, operated by Resorts International (now owned by Merv Griffin), is connected to the Britannia Towers and the Paradise Towers, part of the Paradise Island Resort. Between the towers are many shops and boutiques, the Folies Bergere–like Cabaret Theatre, and a selection of pleasant places to dine and drink.

Guests from nearby hotels as well as those from adjacent and more remote island locations find their way to the casino, including those at the island's self-contained Club Med. The only visitors who seem to shun the casino are patrons of the Yoga Retreat, who prefer contemplation, vegetarianism, exercise, and work.

A shopping center, Paradise Village, serves hotel guests as well as residents of the island's apartment hotels and condominiums. The center includes a bank, fast-food shops, and the inevitable souvenir stores.

The Ocean Club, one of the small luxury hotels, began as a vacation home for Hartford. Operated by Resorts International, it remains one of the preferred hostelries for those with deep pockets. Not far away is quiet, secluded Cabbage Beach.

Restaurants that have achieved the widest reputations are the Cafe Martinique, the Courtyard Terrace of the Ocean Club, the Villa d'Este, and Julie's in the Sheraton Grand Hotel. Because of confusion with the Courtyard Terrace and the Terrace at the Britannia Towers, the Terrace Restaurant in downtown Nassau has added its address, 18 Parliament Street, to its name.

Athletic-minded visitors at Paradise Island resorts take advantage of an almost unlimited choice of sports. Windsurfers and parasailers splash the landscape with the bright colors of their sails and parachutes. Fringed with beaches, the island has many swimming pools, an 18-hole golf course, and tennis courts. Romantics who have dreamed of going horseback riding along a beach can have that fantasy come true at the stables near the Ocean Club.

Chalk's International Airlines has an amphibious terminal on the island for flights to Bimini, Cat Cay, and Miami. While waiting for your plane, try some fresh conch salad or have a drink at the Island Restaurant. Paradise Island Airlines now flies 50-passenger planes from Miami and Ft. Lauderdale into the island's airstrip.

Beyond the Resorts

To get the scoop on current social issues stop by the Bahamian Forum, the weekly gathering that is a cross between a town meeting and a cultural happening. You might hear a historian spinning tales about the African roots of Junkanoo, a local playwright discussing his craft, or a debate about whether the Bahamas should institute a national lottery. The forum meets every Wednesday at 5:30 p.m. at the Roman Catholic Sisters Convent on West Hill St. in Nassau.

As far as a Bahamian lottery goes, by the way, some people believe that there is far too much gambling in these islands as it is. They rue the day in 1920 when the first casino opened in Nassau. Others say that Bahamians already spend a great deal on lotteries—by sending their money to the U.S. so that friends can purchase state lottery tickets for them. Why allow so much cash to leave the country? they argue. With a Bahamian sweepstakes, these tidy sums could be kept at home.

On Watch Night, otherwise known as New Year's Eve, you'd think the Zion Baptist Church on East and Shirley streets was giving away money instead of conducting services. Hundreds of people, no matter what their denomination, begin to fill the pews at around 11 p.m. for the exhilarating sermon and the energetic countdown to midnight. As in Freeport, most folks go straight from church to their favorite night club and from there to the frenetic pre-dawn Junkanoo parade. On other evenings throughout the year the stage is set at the Dundas Center for the Performing Arts for plays, instrumental or vocal concerts, and other local entertainment. Check newspapers for details. Pick up tickets at Nassau Stationers, on Rosetta Street, around the corner from the theater.

Some neighborhoods outside downtown Nassau and Cable Beach are poor and studded with ramshackle buildings. Yet the ghosts of their rich history creep out between the weathered wooden or cinderblock houses, churches, bars, and mom-and-pop shops. In addition to the dominos and checkers played religiously in many front yards, you'll see people deeply involved in *warri,* a game brought over by enslaved Africans.

One area seldom visited by tourists begins just beyond the most frequented streets of the capital. Gregory Arch, on Market St. and visible from downtown Bay St., is one of the gateways to this populous region. Locally known as Over-the-Hill, this area contains settlements such as Grant's Town and Bain Town. A 19th-century Black Bahamian businessman, Charles H. Bain, purchased a land grant to found the town bearing his name.

South of here, Fox Hill was once divided into four villages. In the beginning, three of these had populations consisting of freed people who had been born in Africa. The other was settled by Bahamian-born people of African descent. Every year in Freedom park and on the Village Green, in the center of Fox Hill, residents celebrate Emancipation Day (the first Monday in August) and Fox Hill Day (the second Tuesday in August) with food, music, and other festivities.

Carmichael Village, further southwest, was one of the earliest settlements of freed slaves. At a farm near the Carmichael Chicken Farm, about a 15-minute drive from the Divi Bahamas Beach Resort, you can pick your own vegetables, juicy grapefruit, and other citrus. Another place to gather your own goodies is Claridge Farm, on Harold Road, about five miles from downtown Nassau, near the Bacardi distillery. This fresh produce is especially welcome for those staying in time-share units, condos, and housekeeping apartments.

Down on the southwestern coast, the settlement called Adelaide was named for Queen Adelaide, consort of William IV of England. Its first settlers were Africans captured by the Portuguese in the early 1800s and headed for enslavement. Their vessel, the *Rosa,* was taken by the British, and the 150 or so Africans landed in Nassau as free men since slavery had already been abolished in the British colonies. As late as the 1960s, more than a few thatched-roof houses remained in this town, which was reminiscent of 19-century African villages.

Gambier Village sits on the northern coast, west of Cable Beach. Its original settlers were freed Africans who arrived in 1807 with the British Royal Navy. One of its best known residents was Elizah Morris, a former slave, who helped bring about the 1841 Creole Mutiny off the coast of Abaco.

Visitors can see some of these areas by taxi or in inexpensive jitneys. These minibuses take circular routes, so you'll have no trouble returning to your point of departure.

WHAT TO SEE AND DO

SIGHTS AND ATTRACTIONS

New Providence is one of the Bahamian islands that was settled early and has a number of points of historical interest, most of which can be reached in a day's tour. Nassau, as the seat of government, has reminders of former British rule, and remnants of slavery.

Ardastra Gardens • *Near Fort Charlotte off Columbus Avenue and Chippingham Road (323–5806)* • The national bird of The Bahamas, the flamingo, is used to put on a show for visitors to the gardens. Among the attractions is a precision parade of the pink birds to the command of their trainer. Visitors are invited to pose for photographs with the birds. *Open 9 a.m.–4:30 p.m. Admission $7.50. Children under 12 $3.75.*

Blackbeard's Tower • *East of Fox Hill Road* • The climb to Blackbeard's Tower is worth the trip if only to view the sweep of the Nassau harbor and the city stretching east and west. However, what remains of the tower itself is not as spectacular. The structure was supposedly used as a lookout point by the pirate Edward Teach, alias Blackbeard, to watch for approaching ships during the period when he was a marauder in Bahamian waters.

*Botanical Gardens • *Near Fort Charlotte, off Columbus Avenue* • This protected area has 18 acres of 600 species of tropical flowers and plants. There is a lily pond, a cactus garden, and a children's playground. *Open daily 9 a.m.–4 p.m. Admission: Adults $1, Children 50¢.*

*Coral World • *Silver Cay, between Cable Beach and downtown Nassau (328–1036)* • At least a couple of hours are needed to take in this marine park not far from Fort Charlotte. Built by the developers of Coral World in the U.S. Virgin Islands, the Bahamian version also has a natural undersea observatory. At the Pearl Bar, select an oyster guaranteed to contain a pearl. Flamingos, macaws, and other rare birds flutter about the grounds. Sharks, in their tank, can be seen from above and below. There are morays, rays, parrot fish, huge sea turtles, and many other creatures. A crow's nest, 85 feet above sea level, gives photographers a breathtaking panorama of Nassau. A souvenir shop, snack bar and a restaurant are on the grounds. Groups of giggling Bahamian schoolchildren on education excursions are admitted without charge. *Open daily from 9 a.m. to 6 p.m., with extended hours during Daylight Saving Time (Apr.–Oct.); Admission $12 adults; $8 children aged 3–12; free for children under 3. A round-trip boat departs from Woodes Rogers Walk every half hour, $18 including admission. Free shuttle bus service from Cable Beach hotels, 9 a.m.–5 p.m.; and free boats from Paradise Island hotels, 9:15 a.m.–3:30 p.m.*

*Fort Charlotte • *Off West Bay Street overlooking Nassau harbor* • This is the largest fort in The Bahamas. Built in 1788, it guards the entrance to Nassau's harbor. Like Blackbeard's Tower, it also affords a panoramic view of the harbor. Of special interest are its moat, dungeon, and gun emplacements. The guide often waits to collect a group and expects a tip at the tour's end. *The tourist office in Nassau has information on the frequency of tours, since they are not regularly scheduled; tel. 322–7500.*

Fort Fincastle • *On Bennett's Hill overlooking Nassau harbor* •
This ship-shaped fort also sits above downtown Nassau overlooking the
busy harbor. It served primarily as a signal tower and is now largely in
ruins. Nearby is a souvenir shop.

Fort Montagu • *Off East Bay Street* • Fort Montagu is the oldest
of Nassau's remaining forts. Facing the eastern entrance to the harbor,
it was built in 1741 to ward off an attack by Spaniards that never came.
The fort, however, was occupied for a short time by Americans during
the Revolutionary War. The nearby park, with lawns, shade, and vendors, is a pleasant place to stop.

*Government House • *Off Blue Hill Road* • The official residence
of the British-appointed Governor General stands on one of the island's
highest points. In front of the colonial mansion is a statue of Christopher Columbus wearing a broad-brimmed hat, draped in a cloak, and
carrying a staff. Every other Saturday morning, the changing of the
guard takes place here. The mansion's grounds are thick with lush tropical foliage and plants. Visitors can sign the guest book in a small house
located near the exit gate.

Gregory Arch • *East of Government House at Market Street* •
This arch marks the entrance to Grant's Town, just over the ridge from
the Nassau harbor. The town was established at Emancipation on land
given to ex-slaves to build homes and set up farms.

Nautilus • *New Mermaid's Tavern Marina* • This glass-bottomed
submarine, which shows undersea life at night as well as during the
day, departs the marina at 9:30 a.m., 1:30 p.m., 3:30 p.m., and 9:30
p.m. *Cost: $20.*

Potters Cay • *Under Paradise Island Bridge* • At this colorful
market, you can buy fresh fish, fruit, and vegetables, and watch fishermen shell conch.

Queen's Staircase • *Across Shirley Street, toward the rise away
from the harbor and beyond Princess Margaret Hospital* • These 65
steps-of-stone have come to represent the number of years Victoria ruled
the British Empire. One hundred and two feet high, the staircase is said
to have been hewn by slaves from solid limestone, and leads to the now
crumbling Fort Fincastle at the top. When the weather and/or water
supply permit, a cascade spills down next to the staircase, causing an
iridescent mist when the sun hits the enclosure. At the top of the stairs,
small boys wait to give you the well-memorized history of the staircase
in exchange for a small fee.

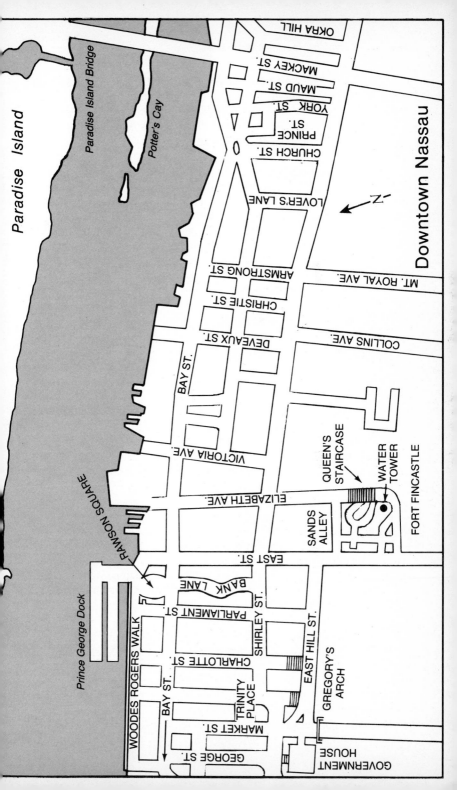

Downtown Nassau

Paradise Island

Paradise Island Bridge

Potter's Cay

Prince George Dock

OKRA HILL

MACKEY ST.

MAUD ST.

YORK ST.

PRINCE ST.

CHURCH ST.

LOVER'S LANE

N

ARMSTRONG ST.

CHRISTIE ST.

DEVEAUX ST.

MT. ROYAL AVE.

COLLINS AVE.

BAY ST.

VICTORIA AVE.

ELIZABETH AVE.

SANDS ALLEY

QUEEN'S STAIRCASE

WATER TOWER

FORT FINCASTLE

RAWSON SQUARE

EAST ST.

BANK LANE

PARLIAMENT ST.

SHIRLEY ST.

EAST HILL ST.

CHARLOTTE ST.

WOODES ROGERS WALK

BAY ST.

TRINITY PLACE

MARKET ST.

GEORGE ST.

GREGORY'S ARCH

GOVERNMENT HOUSE

Roselawn Museum • *East Street and Bank Lane* • In a house built in 1820, The Roselawn museum displays memorabilia from Nassau and the Family Islands, including Bahamian coins, maps, stamps, parts of shipwrecks, old bottles salvaged from the sea, and Junkanoo costumes. *Open 9 a.m.–5 p.m. Free admission.*

Royal Victoria Gardens • *Across Shirley Street and up toward Government House* • The sprawling Royal Victoria Hotel was built during the American Civil War and was used as the headquarters of Bahamians who ran arms for the Confederacy. Part of the building is now used for government offices. In its time, the hotel was the showplace of The Bahamas, and its gardens reflected its grandeur and opulence. The gardens contain about 300 kinds of tropical plants. Although the grand old hotel was closed in 1971 and rumors of its reopening persist, the gardens remain open to the public.

*Hartley's Undersea Walk • *Nassau Yacht Haven, East Bay St.; tel: 325–3369* • This 3½-hour cruise on the yacht *Pied Piper* includes a safe, escorted undersea walk to see varieties of tropical fish, coral formations, and other undersea life. Even kids, the elderly, and nonswimmers can enjoy the experience. The trick is the helmet you wear. Take a bathing suit. The yacht leaves at 9:30 a.m. and 1:30 p.m. daily. Check-in time is a half hour before departure. *About $30 per person.*

*Sea Gardens • *Eastern end of Nassau harbor* • This fantastic underwater attraction covers 40 acres of coral, fern, and all the colorful marine life found in tropical waters. *($15 from Prince George Dock)*

*Seafloor Aquarium • *West of Columbus Avenue near Ardastra Gardens* • Also close to downtown Nassau, the aquarium presents underwater tropical marine life including giant turtles, sharks, manta rays, and myriads of sea creatures that inhabit coral reefs. A performance is put on by trained sea lions and dolphins. Tortoise-shell jewelry, made on the premises, is for sale along with other Bahamian souvenirs. *Open 9 a.m.–5:30 p.m. Shows every 2 hours weekdays. Closed Sun. Admission: Adults $5, children $2.50.*

Straw Market • *Bay and Market Streets* • Everything that can be rendered in straw—plus much more—is on sale here. Market women may beckon you to examine their handicrafts. They may quickly slip a necklace over your head in an attempt to convince you to buy. The wares include hats and baskets, which are much in evidence, along with objects of shell, bead jewelry, wood sculpture, and T-shirts. Many items are fashioned on the spot. The merchants are aggressive and bargaining is spirited. In addition to the beach, this is the place to go to get your hair cornrowed and beaded.

Water Tower • *On Bennett Hill near Fort Fincastle* • While on Bennett Hill seeing Fort Fincastle, also stop at the Water Tower. It is the highest point on New Providence, 216 feet above sea level. An elevator takes you to the observation deck for an unusual view of Nassau and points beyond. *Open 9 a.m.–5 p.m. Admission: 50¢.*

SPORTS

Diving • Make diving arrangements through your hotel or by contacting Bahama Divers (322–8431), Nassau Dive Supply (322–4869), South Ocean Beach Hotel & Golf Club (326–4391/6), Sun Divers (326–3301), or Underwater Tours (326–3285).

Fishing and Boating • Arrange fishing and boating trips through your hotel or by contacting Bayshore Marina (326–8232); East Bay Yacht Basin (326–3754); Lyford Cay Marina (326–4267); Nassau Harbour Club (322–1771); or Nassau Yacht Haven (393–8173), all in Nassau; or Hurricane Hole Marina (326–5441) on Paradise Island.

Nassau offers a variety of sightseeing **cruises** as well as sailing trips to other islands for swimming and snorkeling. For example, the *Keewatin* sailing schooner, which departs from the British Colonial hotel dock at 9:45 a.m. and the Harbour Cove Inn dock on Paradise Island at 10:15 a.m., goes to Rose Island for **snorkeling,** swimming, and lunch (about $30; 326–2821). The Sea Island Adventure excursion goes to another Family Island and also includes snorkeling, swimming, and lunch (325–3910). Operated by Powerboat Adventures of Nassau (day: 322–3724; eve. and weekends: 359–3631), the speedy, 41-foot *Midnight Express* zips out toward Exuma, visiting some of the islands in that chain. Passengers can see undersea marine life through the clear waters, and spot friendly iguanas when they reach Allan's Cay. Lunch is served on a beach and snorkeling gear is available. The boat departs at 9:30 each morning, Monday through Friday.

Glass-bottom boats go from Prince George Dock to Paradise Island for all-day swimming. A catamaran cruise, with a Goombay band and a picnic lunch, also leaves from this dock, as well as daily schooners. *Hotel tour desks have further details.*

Golf • Courses are at the Crystal Palace PGA Course, 18 holes, (327–8231); the Coral Harbour Golf Club, 18 holes, (326–1144); the Divi Bahamas Beach Resort, 18 holes, (326–4391); and the Paradise Island Golf Club, 18 holes (326–5925).

Horseback Riding • *Paradise Island* • Rates at the Paradise Island Riding Stables are about $20 an hour (326–1433).

Tennis • Most of the large hotels have tennis courts. The sports complex at the Crystal Palace has **squash** and **racquetball courts** as well. You can also play these sports at the Nassau Squash and Racquet Club (Independence Drive; 322–3882).

Parasailing • Enjoy this sport on Cable Beach at the Ambassador Beach Hotel, the Crystal Palace, and the Nassau Beach Hotel, and on Paradise Island at the Sheraton Grand Hotel.

Waterskiing • Most of the larger beach hotels offer waterskiing.

Windsurfing • The Ambassador Beach Hotel, the Crystal Palace, and Coral Harbour Beach Villas all have windsurfing.

NIGHTLIFE

In the 800-seat Palace Theater at the Crystal Palace, visitors can see elaborate musical productions. This resort also sports the high-tech **Fanta-Z** disco. Many other hotels have night clubs and discos. **Club Pastiche** in Paradise Island's Casino and **Trade Winds Lounge** in the adjoining Paradise Towers attract many Bahamians as well as visitors, and feature rock and roll, disco, and sometimes Bahamian music. **The Paon,** in the Sheraton Grand, has a computerized sound system that will shame any New York disco.

In Nassau, **Peanuts Taylor's Drumbeat Club** on West Bay Street features an Afro Bahamian Revue with a fire ritual and limbo. Dinner is served during the first show of the evening. **The Palace** on Elizabeth Avenue has a live band that plays a mix of calypso, reggae, and disco. **The Ritz Waterside Nite Club,** on Bay and Deveaux streets, is an indoor/outdoor disco behind **Captain Nemo's Restaurant.** Another popular disco is **Club Waterloo,** on East Bay Street. **Club Mystique** hosts a well-attended Friday happy hour. However, check the status since it is located in the Cable Beach Inn, which is up for sale.

The casinos in Nassau and Paradise Island are two of the most popular places to be after dark—and for some, during the day as well. The Crysal Palace casino gives visitors a bright, modern alternative to the more traditional-looking Paradise Island Casino. Glittery Las Vegas–style performances are put on in the Paradise Island Cabaret Theatre.

Avoid the nightclub tours offered by some companies—you'll have much more fun doing the clubs on your own.

DINING OUT

Cable Beach/Nassau

EXPENSIVE

Sole Mare • *Carnival's Crystal Palace Resort & Casino, Cable Beach; tel: 327–6200* • Although this gourmet restaurant is located in the casino building, you don't have to be a gambler to enjoy the delicious Northern Italian food. The Sunday buffet brunch is popular. Seafood and veal are served in addition to a variety of pasta dishes. *Open Tues.–Sun. Major credit cards.*

The Riveria • *Carnival's Crystal Palace Riviera Towers, Cable Beach; tel: 327–6000* • Located on the hotel's fourth floor, the Riviera serves seafood and variations of Bahamian dishes. The restaurant is open for dinner only (Tues. through Sun.). *Reservations recommended. Jackets required. Major credit cards.*

Buena Vista • *Delancy St., downtown Nassau; tel: 322–2811* • A circular driveway leads to the gourmet restaurant in an old mansion. The candlelit dining areas are decorated with paintings and hanging plants. At night, a pianist plays. *Major credit cards.*

Roselawn • *Bank Lane, downtown Nassau; tel: 325–1018* • This restaurant is a stone's throw from Rawson Square. Pasta is made on the premises and Bahamian seafood as well as Continental cuisine is served. There is entertainment at dinner. Roselawn is closed on Sunday, and reservations are a must. *Major credit cards.*

Da Vinci • *10 West Bay St., downtown Nassau; tel: 322–2748* • For good Italian and French cuisine not far from the main drag, Da Vinci, which serves dinner only, is the place to go. It has a fine cellar to match its excellent Italian entrees. *Major credit cards.*

Graycliff • *West Hill and Blue Hill Rd., downtown Nassau; tel: 322–2796* • This is considered one of the finest restaurants in The Bahamas. It is located opposite Government House in a beautiful old mansion, and meals are served in charming and tasteful settings that include antiques, Royal Copenhagen china, and British silverware. Although the cuisine is elegantly Continental, the chef also knows his way around Bahamian cooking. Visiting celebrities as well as ordinary mortals beat a path to Graycliff's at least once before leaving the island. Reservations are required. *Major credit cards.*

Sun And . . . • *Lakeview Dr., off East Shirley St., downtown Nassau; tel: 393–1205 or 393–2644* • In an old mansion not far from Fort Montague, this restaurant serves French and Bahamian dishes including conch chowder, braised duckling, and sweetbreads with asparagus tips. Guests, who are asked to dress up, may dine al fresco or on a palm-shaded patio or in the indoor-outdoor areas around the pool. Sun And . . . is closed on Mondays. Reservations are requested. *Major credit cards.*

MODERATE

Poop Deck • *Nassasu Yacht Haven Marina, East Bay St., downtown Nassau; tel: 393–8175* • The busy water traffic of Nassau's harbor can entertain while you dine outdoors. There is also a bar inside if you are just stopping for a drink. If you are not in the mood for a heavy lunch, a burger or a bowl of sea food chowder might be satisfying. Cracked conch, grouper, and chicken are also on the menu. *Major credit cards.*

Three Ladies • *Pilot House Hotel, East Bay St., downtown Nassau; tel: 322–8431* • This dining room has a fine waterfront view. Diners look out on the hotel's marina and off to the busy harbor with its cruise ships. The service is prompt, the food is both Bahamian and American, and the atmosphere is cheerful. Lunch is the best time to enjoy the harbor. *Major credit cards.*

The Mansion • *West Hill St., downtown Nassau; tel: 326–8028* • In an attractive colonial-style former house called Postern Gate, this restaurant serves local dishes such as cracked conch, peas and rice, and stewed fish. It is popular with families.

Bon Homme Richard • *Nassau Harbour Club; tel: 323–3771* • British favorites like steak and kidney pie are found at the Bon Homme Richard. The restaurant also caters to those who like Bahamian or Continental dishes.

Del Prado • *El Greco Hotel, West Bay St., downtown Nassau; tel: 325–0324 or 325–1121* • Despite the Spanish name, the accent is on French cuisine, with some Bahamian specialties thrown in. At dinner, candles flicker in the pleasantly decorated room. The flambed dishes are especially good. Herbs and spices used in cooking are grown by the chef himself. Del Prado is one of the few places where visitors can sample guava duff, a wonderfully rich Bahamian dessert usually reserved for special occasions. *Jackets recommended.*

Europe Restaurant • *Ocean Spray Hotel, downtown Nassau; tel: 322–8032* • In the small, downtown Ocean Spray Hotel, the Europe Restaurant, is as intimate as the hotel. At night is warmly lighted, and the American and Bahamian dishes are well served. The restaurant is proud of its German specialties. It has a good selection of wines and, of course, beer. *Major credit cards.*

Androsia Restaurant • *Henrea Carlette Hotel, Cable Beach; tel: 327–7805* • The restaurant is a pleasant room with wicker chairs and napkins rolled in tall glasses. There are ship's lanterns on the walls and other reminders of the sea. Among the house dishes are lobster thermidor, conch chowder, gazpacho, veal, and duck. *Major credit cards.*

MODERATE TO INEXPENSIVE

Green Shutters Inn • *Parliament St., across from the Royal Victoria Gardens, downtown Nassau; tel: 325–5702* • Green Shutters has all the flavor of an English pub. From its decor to its fish and chips, steak and kidney pie, and beer, it is all British and good for a luncheon stop. *Major credit cards.*

Corona • *Hotel Corona, Bay St. and Dunmore Lane, downtown Nassau; tel: 326–6815* • This restaurant has a reputation for tasty Bahamian dishes at moderate prices. It is conveniently located in the thick of downtown activity and is well worth a try. The lunchtime buffet draws Bahamians from all over the island. Upstairs is a lounge for drinks, and there is entertainment in the evening.

The Terrace (18 Parliament Street) • *Parliament Hotel, downtown Nassau; tel: 322–2836* • Because of confusion with two other Nassau restaurants with similar names, this downtown establishment has added its address to its name. In the evening, torches flare at the entrance to the outdoor dining area. Candlelit tables are covered in bright African prints and the waiters wear colorful dashikis. The managers emphasize Bahamian cuisine. *Major credit cards.*

Tony Roma's • *East Bay St., east of Paradise Island bridge, downtown Nassau: tel: 393–2077 or 393–1956* • Most people come here for the barbecued ribs, but barbecued shrimp and chicken as well as conch fritters and broiled lobster are also good choices. Be sure to try a side of onion rings. *Open daily, 11 a.m. to midnight. Major credit cards.*

Marietta's Restaurant and Lounge • *Marietta's Hotel, Okra Hill, downtown Nassau; tel: 322–8395* • Not far from the Paradise Island bridge, this warm, friendly restaurant is certainly worth a visit, if only to sample the crab soup, the house specialty. Other Bahamian dishes are just as delicious.

Round House • *Casuarinas Apartment Hotel, Cable Beach; tel: 327–7921* • With the owners on the premises, the restaurant does admirable Bahamian cooking, and capably ventures into other cuisines. *Major credit cards.*

Ivory Coast Seafood & Steak Restaurant • *East Bay St., top floor of Nassau Harbour Club, downtown Nassau; tel: 393–0478 or 393–0771* • Colonial Africa is brought to life at this pleasant spot where patrons may sit on a porch overlooking the harbor. Stuffed wild animals gaze at diners and walls are hung with masks from the Ivory Coast and colorful fabrics. Waiters are decked out in safari-style khaki and pith helmets. Fish and meat are served smoked, broiled, and grilled. Before or after the evening meal, spend some time in the Casablanca Piano Bar. *Reservations recommended.*

Tamarind Hill Restaurant & Music Bar • *Village Rd., Nassau; tel: 323–1306* • Dine al fresco or sit inside by one of the tall windows at this hilltop restaurant that specializes in Bahamian and West Indian cuisine. Good choices are the roti (East Indian bread filled with curried meat or vegetables), barbecued ribs, cracked conch, and broiled grouper. Happy hour (Monday through Friday from 5 to 7 p.m.) is a popular time to make an appearance. The Tequila Sunrise Party livens up Saturday afternoons and evenings (4 to 7 p.m.), and the Reggae Sunsplash Party is the place to be on Sundays. *Open noon to midnight Monday through Friday and 4 p.m. to midnight on Saturdays and Sundays.*

Prince George Roof Top Cafe Restaurant & Lounge • *Prince George Plaza (upstairs), Bay St., downtown Nassau; tel: 322–5854* • There's no charge for the view of the harbor at this appealing restaurant in the heart of downtown Nassau. Diners are seated both downstairs in the cafe and outdoors on the rooftop overlooking busy Bay Street. The menu is thoroughly international, featuring Greek, Continental, and Bahamian dishes. Local boil fish and Johnny cake move quickly at breakfast, while the lunch buffet offers everything from soups and salads to pizza. Dinner selections include stuffed broiled lobster, shrimp kebab, skewered scallops with bacon, steak, barbecued ribs, and blackened snapper. *Open from 11 a.m. to 11 p.m. Closed Sundays.*

Grand Central • *Charlotte St., off Bay St., downtown Nassau; tel: 322–8356* • This attractive restaurant and bar in a small, Greek-owned hotel near the straw market makes a convenient lunch stop during a day of shopping. The cheerful decor is highlighted by blond wood, floral wallpaper with matching curtains, and a Day-glo blackboard scrawled with the daily specials. Bahamians highly recommend the cracked conch, steamed grouper, pork chops, turtle steak, and minced lobster, all served with peas and rice or yellow rice. The restaurant usually closes early (8 p.m.), but may stay open later during the busiest seasons, so check before coming.

Big Daddy's Seaside Lounge • *Potter's Cay Dock, East Bay St., just west of the Paradise Island bridge, downtown Nassau; tel: 393–4702* • For a real local breakfast, try stew fish with grits and Johnny cake. Popular selections for lunch and dinner are grouper fingers, conch patties, and steamed lobster. Memorable desserts, such as Key Lime pie, are all baked daily. *Open 7 a.m.–11 p.m.*

The Palm • *Bay St., opposite John Bull, downtown Nassau; tel: 323–7444* • This cheerful restaurant in the heart of Nassau's shopping district draws just as many locals as tourists. Perhaps this is because of the homestyle cooking. The very spicy conch salad is excellent here, and the grouper fingers, peas and rice, cracked conch, pasta, soups, and sandwiches are also delicious. Wash it all down with an ice cream soda. *Major credit cards.*

INEXPENSIVE
Basil's • *Blue Hill Rd., Nassau* • Basil's, slightly off the beaten track, caters very much to a local clientele. Visitors would do well to sample its conch fritters.

The Fish Net • *Ernest St., Nassau; tel: 323–2568* • Just a step off Bay Street, this is another restaurant that caters to locals, but visitors would do well to stop by to get a taste of what Bahamian cooking is all about.

Larry's Pub No. 2 • *Thompson Blvd., Nassau; tel: 322–3800* • This spacious restaurant and bar is popular for lunch accompanied by television soap operas. The food is tasty and plentiful. House specialties include such dishes as steamed and cracked conch, lobster salad, okra soup, most of which come with side dishes of peas and rice and fried plantain. To get here from the Cable Beach area, take a jitney going downtown. You can also take a minibus from downtown, but you'll have to go all the way through Cable Beach before arriving. *American Express.*

The Shoal & Lounge • *Nassau St., Nassau; tel: 323–4400* • Few Bahamians talk about the Shoal without mentioning the delicious boil fish served here. Attracting quite a few families, this casual local restaurant is also celebrated for its crawfish salad, grouper fingers, steamed or cracked conch, steak, and mutton. Fried plantain and mountains of peas and rice come on the side. The lounge adjoining the dining room is a good place to mingle with Bahamians.

Coco's Cafe • *Marlborough St., across from the British Colonial Hotel, downtown Nassau; tel: 323–8778 or 323–8801* • Three meals a day are served here amid bright art-deco decor. The Bahamian and American fare includes broiled fish, steaks, veal, hamburgers, pasta, and large salads. *Major credit cards.*

Johnson's Take-Away • *Shirley St. and Ball's Alley; tel: 393– 0071* • You might be mistaken for a resident at this unassuming eatery known for its generous portions of tender cracked conch, chicken, potato salad, cole slaw, and peas and rice. *Open Mon. through Sat. from 9:30 a.m. to 12:30 a.m.*

Mandi's Conch • *Arundel and Mount Royal Ave., Palmdale, Nassau* • Bahamians prepare mild-flavored conch in countless ways, and you can sample a variety of incarnations here. Try the conch fritters, conch chowder, stewed conch, conch salad, and of course good old cracked conch, all accompanied by cole slaw and french fries. *Open daily (except Sun.) from 11:30 a.m. to 11:30 p.m.*

Mondingo Restaurant & Lounge • *Mondingo Inn, Nassau Village; tel: 324–3333* • Mondingo's is across Prince Charles Street. This is an area that visitors often miss. The walk can be worth it since the Bahamian dishes offered are the ones cooked for locals.

Piggily Viggily • *Gambier Village; tel: 327–7439* • This restaurant's name plays with the way Bahamians pronounce the letter *w*. There is no playing with the way good, inexpensive food is served up, accent and all, in this relaxed local restaurant.

Swanks Pizzeria • *Cable Beach Shopping Center; tel: 327–8749* • No, none of the many varieties of pizza served here—from regular to deep dish and French bread—tastes like what you'd find in New York or Chicago. But this casual restaurant, with several locations, packs 'em in from 11 a.m. to midnight and even delivers to nearby accommodations. Entrees also include lasagne and spaghetti and meatballs. Other branches are at Village and Bernard roads (393–4000 or 393–4001), open from 11 a.m. to midnight; and at the Paradise Island Shopping Center (363–2765), serving three meals a day from 8 a.m. to midnight.

Choosy Foodss • *Market St., off Bay St.; tel: 326–5232* • Near the Straw Market, this local dining spot serves good seafood lasagne, conch salad, conch burgers, and fruit-stuffed grouper.

Traveller's Rest • *West Bay St., near airport; tel: 327–7633* • As you approach this popular restaurant across the road from a narrow beach, you might find children selling cantaloupes or other fruit out front. Many people enjoy dining on the patio, near the tall palm trees on the front lawn. Inside, wicker lamp shades hang from the ceiling and paintings of colorful aquatic scenes decorate the walls. Your gracious hostess is likely to be owner Joan Hanna, a former schoolteacher from Canada, whose Bahamian husband is a local politician and head of the musician's union. Scribbled on the chalkboard menu, you'll see "smudder" (smothered) grouper, steamed conch, turtle steak, grouper fingers, minced lobster, and the like. If you happen by on a weekend, you might be treated to conch salad. *Major credit cards.*

The adjacent **Sea Grape Boutique** sells bright Androsia resortwear, fashioned into skirts, shirts, shorts, dresses, and bathing suits. Straw hats are also on sale, along with belts, shoes, jewelry, stuffed animals, and other toys. This tiny boutique even accepts American Express, MasterCard, and Visa.

Other good casual restaurants specializing in homestyle cooking are the **Bahamian Kitchen** on Trinity Place off Market Street; **F & S** in Beaumont House on the Waterfront; **Frank's Place** on Mackey Street South; **Lum's** on Bay Street; and **Three Queen's** on Wulff Road.

Paradise Island

EXPENSIVE

Cafe Martinique • *opposite Britannia Towers at the Paradise Island Resort & Casino; tel: 326–3000* • As its name implies, the cuisine emphasis is French. The popular restaurant is situated in a palm-shaded spot across from the Britannia Towers. With tall windows facing the lagoon, the setting invites dining at what some consider one of the best Continental restaurants in The Bahamas. The candlelight, the linens, and the romantic music add to the elegant atmosphere. Since the elaborate dessert souffles are so tempting and time-consuming to prepare, the dessert menu precedes the dinner menu, and your waiter will ask you to order your last course when you place your dinner order. Men are required to wear jackets. *Major credit cards.*

The Courtyard Terrace • *the Ocean Club; tel: 363–3000 or 363–2501 (after 4 p.m.)* • At this elegant al fresco restaurant, white cast-iron garden furniture sits at the edge of a long rectangular pool with a fountain, surrounded by palms. Meals are served on Wedgwood china, with crisp Irish linen. Candles flicker in the breeze. Try such treats as goose liver pate with truffles, Bahamian conch chowder or cream of asparagus soup, and hearts of palm salad. The filet of beef stuffed with crabmeat comes baked in a puff pastry. The pan-blackened red snapper is deliciously seasoned. For dessert, good choices are pear belle Helene (pears with vanilla ice cream and chocolate sauce) and coconut cake. Live music floats down from the balcony above the central staircase that leads to this outdoor restaurant. *Major credit cards.*

The Rotisserie • *The Sheraton Grand; tel: 362-2011* • This is the hotel's upscale dining room overlooking the ocean. Only dinner is served. Specialties are meat, fish, and poultry grilled or broiled over open flames. *Major credit cards.*

Villa d'Este • *Paradise Island Resort & Casino, Britannia Towers; tel: 325–5441* • This restaurant, serving delicate Italian specialties, is situated in the casino area. It is open for dinner nightly and features entertainment. It attracts much of the casino crowd. *Major credit cards.*

Le Cabaret Theatre • *Paradise Island Resort & Casino, Britannia Towers; tel: 326–3000* • Here the show is more exciting than the food. The nightly revue, much like the Folies Bergere, presents women dancers, often innocently bare-breasted, in spectacles with performers ranging from comedians and acrobats to animals. *Major credit cards.*

MODERATE

Boat House • *opposite Britannia Towers at the Paradise Island Resort & Casino; tel: 326–3000* • Next door to the Cafe Martinique, the Boat House is also open only for dinner. It has gained a reputation for steaks and seafood Bahamian-style. Food is cooked on grills at your table and the decor, as the name implies, has the sea as its theme. *Major credit cards.*

The Coyaba • *Paradise Island Resort & Casino, Britannia Towers; tel: 326–3000* • For lovers of Polynesian and Chinese cuisine, this room in a South Pacific design with impressive rattan furniture sets the proper atmosphere. The drinks echo the tropical mood of this restaurant, which is open only for dinner. *Major credit cards.*

Blue Lagoon • *Club Land'Or; tel: 363–2400* • Overlooking the Paradise Island lagoon, which sparkles with lights in the evening, this restaurant specializes in seafood. Dinner only is served Monday through Saturday, 5–10 p.m. *Major credit cards.*

Neptune's Table • *Pirates' Cove Holiday Inn; tel: 325–6451* • Patrons are enthusiastic about the seafood and hearty Bahamian specialties of this restaurant. It is the Inn's top dining place and features gourmet delicacies. *Major credit cards.*

The Terrace Garden • *Paradise Island Resort & Casino, Britannia Towers; tel: 325–5441* • This indoor-outdoor dining spot overlooks the quiet and pleasant lagoon. Quick meals are available, enabling guests to get back to whatever pleasures were being pursued. It is also possible to enjoy a more leisurely meal while people-watching and enjoying the view. *Major credit cards.*

WHERE TO STAY

Nassau's variety of accommodations gives visitors a wide choice. There are hotels, housekeeping apartments, and guesthouses to suit almost any need and pocketbook. Places to stay are located along Cable Beach, in downtown Nassau, out on Paradise Island, and at a sprawling, self-contained resort at the island's southwestern end. Carnival's Crystal Palace, Nassau Beach, and Ambassador Beach hotels are all within easy walking distance of each other. The British Colonial Beach Resort is the only downtown hotel on a beach. During spring break, the more modest hotels in Cable Beach, downtown Nassau, and Paradise Island often cater to the American high-school and college student crowd. Unless you plan to join the (often noisy) fun, this may not be the best time to book a room at these hotels.

Cable Beach

EXPENSIVE

☆☆☆**Wyndham Ambassador Beach** • Across from the Crystal Palace golf course, this modern 385-room hotel welcomes guests with inviting public rooms done in subdued pastels. The pleasant guest rooms have ample tiled baths and are done with cheerful carpeting and dressing areas. Guests have a choice of restaurants and bars, including a dining room with Italian cuisine. Sun worshipers gravitate either to the pool or step out to the hotel's beach. Water sports facilities are available and guests can perfect their tennis, raquetball, or squash skills at the nearby Sports Centre.

★★★**Carnival's Crystal Palace & Casino** • This lavish, multi-colored extravaganza is the latest addition to the Cable Beach area. With the absorption of the Cable Beach Hotel, now called Carnival's Riviera Tower, Carnival's Crystal Palace is the largest hotel in the Bahamas. Some guests have complained that it's too big for its own good—that checking in and out can take forever and that the staff is impersonal. Its five towers are striped with pinks, purples, mauve, magenta, and turquoise, really bloom when lit at night. While somewhat startling for the outside, the colors are much better when used attractively in room decoration for walls, carpeting, sconces, and other furniture. However, as chic as the art-deco decor of rooms is, the workmanship leaves something to be desired. A bathroom cabinet door fell off its hinges when a guest opened it during a recent visit. Also, the neon bedside lights are too dim for reading. Rooms have floor-to-ceiling windows with balconies overlooking the ocean. Public corridors, facing atriums or the street receive natural light. A two-level swimming pool has a waterfall and a curling slide. A health spa features a sauna, a steam room, massage, and aerobics. Tennis, racquetball, and golf on an 18-hole course are also available. There are in-hotel boutiques as well as a straw market.

A profusion of restaurants cater to all tastes and include Japanese, delicatessen, and Mexican cuisines. There are, of course, seafood and continental restaurants. Unfortunately, most of these eating spots are frightfully expensive. The Palace Theater puts on the expected colorful Las Vegas–like revue with feathers, sequins, and bare breasts. The two-level, laser-lighted Fanta-Z disco sweeps on until the small hours. The casino seems to extend into infinity, offering the gamut of gaming attractions, including slots, blackjack, craps, roulette, and baccarat.

For really high-livers, there are 30 theme suites, some duplexes, with powder rooms, marble baths, wet bars, king-sized beds and two-person Jacuzzis. If even this is not enough, for $25,000 a night, you can book a computerized suite where doors open by voice command and lights come on mysteriously by other electronic miracles.

★★★★**Nassau Beach Hotel** • This elegant hotel has well-appointed and decorated rooms, its own beach, pool, a small spa, and a landing dock, the latest in watersports, tennis, and a pro shop. A number of dining rooms cater to varied tastes, and Cinnamon's, a nightclub and disco on the premises, can provide an evening on the town. A renovated wing has been added for an all-inclusive program called the Palm Club. Its guests are met at the airport by limousine and taken to the hotel where a chilled bottle of champagne awaits and a concierge handles any entertainment and/or recreational needs.

★★★**Le Meridien Royal Bahamian** • For a pampered stay in a serene and posh setting without the hordes and noise of a large hotel, this is the place. The columned six-story pink main house with its marble-floored, Georgian-furnished entrance lobby opens onto a courtyard with a fountain. One end of the paved courtyard leads to an area of pink villas, some with their own pools, set among attractive landscaping. The pampering continues with plush rooms, some with balconies overlooking the sea and the hotel's secluded private beach. There are dressing areas, and an array of toiletries. Beds are turned down at night, and a helpful concierge is at hand to take care of any special needs. Afternoon tea is served off the lobby of the main building. Guests can have drinks in the Palm Bar or on its terrace. Breakfast and lunch are served either indoors or outside on the patio of the Cafe de Paris, which is adjacent to the pool. Luncheon drinks are available at the Pool Bar, which also has sandwiches. Tennis courts are on the grounds, and the hotel's Spa has the latest in the universal gym equipment and exercise rooms, which are free to guests. Massages and mud baths, arranged by appointment, are the only spa services for which there is an extra charge.

MODERATE

☆☆ **Cable Beach Manor** • This pink, 2-story apartment hotel surrounds a swimming pool. All rooms and suites have housekeeping facilities, and a shopping center, including a restaurant, is across the street. Daily maid service is available and, for small children, baby-sitting. There are 34 apartments and the hotel has its own beach. The dining in the neighboring hotels and restaurants is varied and, of course, there is the nearby casino. The hotel is convenient to the airport as well as to downtown Nassau, either trip taking about 15 minutes.

Casuarinas • Located on two sides of the road, Casuarinas has a flower-filled courtyard and two swimming pools. Paintings of local and island scenes decorate the lobby walls and the adjoining bar. There are 1- and 2-bedroom units with kitchenettes, and some studios also have kitchens. On the oceanside is the Round House, the more expensive restaurant, which is open for dinner only and closed on Tuesday. Organic vegetables grown in the proprietor's own garden are often served. Across the street, Albrion's serves light meals such as conch fritters, fish and chips, pizza, omelets and hamburgers. Note that readers have complained to us that the service and maintenance of facilities at this modest hotel leave a lot to be desired.

Silver Cay
EXPENSIVE

★★★**Coral World Villas** • *between downtown Nassau and Cable Beach* • This small and unusual hotel is at the Coral World Undersea Observatory and Marine Park. Each of its 22 rooms is really a suite with living, dining, and kitchen areas. The baths, with extensive glassed areas, provide privacy even though they look out to the nearby ocean crashing in against the jagged rocks. Each unit has a lush planting area near the entrance. With one end of the suite facing the dramatic sea, the other end opens to a quiet, fenced-in, private swimming pool. A restaurant is on premises and, of course, there is the Marine Park with its shops and other attractions. A bridge takes guests to the mainland for shopping, dining and gambling and there is free ferry and bus service to downtown Nassau, Cable Beach, and Paradise Island.

Downtown Nassau

EXPENSIVE

★★★**Graycliff Hotel** • This historic mansion, set behind a wall opposite Government House, has become a sought-after accommodation. The columns at the entrance, the wide porch, and the latticework set it apart from the run-of-the-mill hotel. It houses a five-star restaurant that boasts a world-wide reputation. A plaque celebrating its five stars and its *Relais et Chateau* designation, is affixed to its outside wall. Staying as a guest in one of the 14 rooms is like accepting an invitation to the home of a wealthy friend. Each large room is different and each bears a name, such as Pool Cottage, Yellowbird, or Hibiscus. Some have walk-in closets and dressing rooms, and many have beautiful tile floors. All are furnished with a melange of comfortable, eye-pleasing pieces, including well-polished antiques. The varied bathrooms are commodious and invite lingering showers or bubble baths. A stone walkway and lush greenery surround the pool. The hotel seems to have endless dining areas, including porches, patios, and poolside. One dining room off the main sitting room has bamboo growing outside the window. Resort additions include a jacuzzi, sauna, gym, and solarium.

MODERATE

☆☆☆**British Colonial Beach Resort** • The largest downtown hotel and the only one directly on a beach, the British Colonial is an impressive-looking structure. It stands at the end of Bay Street and spreads over eight acres of gardens. The large rooms face the city, the harbor, and the ocean. The private beach is great for watching incoming and departing cruise ships. The hotel is a vivid reminder of Blackbeard, the pirate, who lived on the site when it was Fort Nassau and hid from the Royal Navy in a well that is still on the grounds. The hotel's steak and seafood grill is called Blackbeard's Forge.

☆ **The Pilot House** • For being in the center of things, the Pilot House is the place. Just across the bridge from Paradise Island, this hotel has a harbor view and is steps away from the action on the island

and in the square. It was erected on the site of a pilot house which had stood for 150 years. Guests have an ever-changing view of the harbor's activity.

★★ **Buena Vista** • After crossing the veranda of this nineteenth century mansion near Government House, and entering the reception area, it seems as if you have stepped into a comfortable, lived-in, private home and well-used living room. Everything spells comfort. A staircase leads up to the second floor and six, spacious, eclectically furnished rooms. The Buena Vista dining room rivals the best and most elegant of eating places, ranging from candlelight to fine china and crystal in the several dining areas hung with paintings and plants.

☆ **El Greco Hotel** • Despite its Spanish decor, with its huge ornate wrought-iron chandelier in the lobby, El Greco serves excellent Bahamian and European food. Its restaurant, Del Prado, opens at 5 p.m. There are 26 rooms and a pool. The hotel faces a beach and is within walking distance of Bay Street shopping.

INEXPENSIVE

★**The Parliament** • *18 Parliament Street* • For those who dislike large, bustling hotels, the Parliament, at the hub of town, may be the answer. Located across the street from Government buildings, near the venerable Victoria Gardens and the Cenotaph, it has pleasantly decorated rooms. No two are alike and all 11 are comfortable in size. The hotel has its own restaurant, The Terrace—18 Parliament Street, which attracts visitors as well as the hotel's guests. It is several blocks from a beach. Bay Street shopping and Rawson Square and its attractions are also nearby.

☆ **Lighthouse Beach Hotel** • Formerly the Mayfair, the Lighthouse Beach is a comfortable hotel across the street from a beach, yet close to the heart of downtown Nassau. While the rooms are small, they are pleasantly decorated and have color satellite TVs. Some have ocean views and private balconies. A swimming pool is on the roof. In addition to the weekly manager's cocktail party, a moonlight cruise and a Rose Island picnic several times a week are complimentary to guests. In the lobby, the sign on the door that leads to Franco's Original Italian Restaurant and Pizzeria reads, "No shoes, no shirts, no service."

Olympia Hotel • Within walking distance of Bay Street shopping and the beach, the Olympia has comfortable rooms that vary in size. They overlook the beach, Paradise Island across the harbor, and the street. The back rooms are quietest. All are air conditioned and most have balconies. The five rooms on the main floor are good for the elderly or wheelchair-bound (there is a ramp at the entrance for wheelchairs). The small, dimly lit English-style pub serves pizza and sandwiches, and guests can watch satellite TV or play darts or backgammon. The Olympia is next door to Da Vinci restaurant and across the road from Lighthouse Beach.

☆ **Ocean Spray Hotel** • Many Europeans have been coming to this hotel for years. Located across the street from Peanuts Taylor's Drumbeat Club, a popular nightspot, Ocean Spray is fully air conditioned and has a sun roof. The beach and the stores of downtown Nassau are short walks away. The cozy Europe restaurant/bar serves continental and Bahamian food.

☆ **Marietta's Hotel** • Marietta's is near the Paradise Island bridge and the Potter's Cay fish and vegetable market. Rooms are plain and practical. The restaurant is a magnet for guests and outsiders looking for exceptional Bahamian cooking. Marietta's was begun by a former hotel maid. Some of the better known guests have included members of Count Basie's band.

☆☆**Dolphin Hotel** • Across West Bay Street from the beach, this hotel does a land-office business during spring break. The students descend upon Nassau, and life is not the same for those nearby. The rooms all have balconies and look out to the beach. The lobby is modern with ceiling fans and paneled in horizontally laid wood.

Paradise Island
EXPENSIVE
☆☆☆ **Pirate's Cove Holiday Inn** • This high-rise structure looms over the casuarinas and palms of Paradise Island and serves as a landmark for wanderers. There are bars, restaurants and a variety of shops. The hotel has one of the nicest self-contained beaches on the island and the guest rooms overlooking it have magnificent ocean views. The free-form pool has a bar, reached by a bridge for those who are clothed and by water for swimmers. An outdoor restaurant overlooks the pool. All sports are at hand and the hotel bustles with much leisure time activity organized by its enthusiastic staff.

★★★★★**Ocean Club** • This posh resort was once the home of A&P heir, Huntington Hartford. Guests checking in are offered rum punches in crystal goblets while seated at an antique desk. From there, the concierge escorts them to their rooms. Rooms are furnished with double beds, television, dining areas, patios or balconies and ceiling fans for those who eschew air conditioning. Some rooms have garden views while others face the ocean. Villas are also available, some of which have marble whirlpool baths. The Courtyard Terrace can be a romantic dining spot at night. The lavishly landscaped grounds bring vistas that include the terraced Versailles Gardens and a filagree gazebo overlooking the harbor. Teatime is every afternoon except Sunday. The long, broad white sand beach is wonderful for swimming and sunbathing. Water sports and tennis are always on tap for the energetic.

☆☆☆☆**Paradise Island Resort & Casino** • The two main buildings of this lavish resort were once separate hotels. Paradise Towers and Britannia Towers are part of the largest resort/gaming complex in the world. The busy, sprawling lobbies of the buildings connect with the 30,000-square-foot casino. A short walk to the beach takes guests to the pool, shuffleboard, afternoon balloon dances, and snorkeling. Offshore are windsurfers, parasailers, and pleasure boats making for a lively and colorful tropical vista. Ferries to downtown Nassau pick up and drop off at Britannia Towers. The casino is open from 11 a.m. until 4 a.m., but the slot machines go on forever. A Las Vegas–type revue at Le Cabaret Theatre plays every night except Sunday. A beachfront building is reserved for Club Paradise guests. This luxury, all-inclusive program provides airport transportation, breakfast at a selection of dining places and dinner at any one of the resort's restaurants. Wine is served with meals and there are amenities from open bar cocktail parties to hot and cold hors d'oeuvres in the Lounge. For the athletically minded there are unlimited greens fees, tennis clinics, complimentary use of health club and aerobic classes. Guests receive terry robes in the Paradise Concierge program, $20 in match play chips for the casino, newspapers in rooms, and they can book a vast suite with a matching price tag of $3000 per night during the winter season, complete with a butler. Note that throughout the year, weekday room rates are lower than weekend.

☆☆ **Paradise Paradise** • The atmosphere of this 100-room hotel is relaxed. Rooms have mini bars, television, and double or king-sized beds. Some have balconies. Young people in pink T-shirts with the letters AE (for achievers of excellence) are ever-present to see to your needs. Because the emphasis is on sports here, the ratio of activity directors to guests is higher than at the larger hotels. There is a bicycle tour every morning and all activities are included in the room rate. The inviting beach is seldom crowded and changing rooms are at the disposal of guests who arrive early or stay around after check-out.

☆☆☆**Sheraton Grand Hotel & Towers** • All rooms in this beige high-rise have balconies which look out to the ocean. The lobby's focus is a fountain and waterfall which empty into a pool surrounded by lush foliage and other plantings. High backed rattan chairs are arranged before the floor-to-ceiling windows and there are hanging baskets and lazily revolving ceiling fans. Last visit, the plastic cushions were in need of replacement but, in all, the lobby is impressive and welcoming. The rooms are tastefully decorated and the latest disco innovations lure stay-up-late guests from other Paradise Island evening attractions, most of which are within walking distance. An excellent beach stretches in front and all water and other sports are on tap, including tennis. Two upper concierge floors are given over to more luxury living. Those guests are provided with a maid and butler, a private elevator, an outdoor Jacuzzi and a sunken bath tub with gold fixtures.

☆☆ **Bay View Village** • The rooms in these red roofed white buildings with dark wood balconies are more plain than the flower-filled grounds might lead you to expect. There are rental units as well as units for sale. There is a mini-market for those who cook in and lunch and snacks are served at the bar of one of the three pools. Tennis is free during the day and one dollar for 45 minutes at night. Paths through the grounds are planted with a profusion of blossoming flowers and fruit trees. There is bougainvillea and more than 20 varieties of hibiscus. The villas and duplexes are 1, 2 and 3 bedroom units, each with a terrace or patio garden. There are even some penthouses with roof gardens.

MODERATE

☆☆☆ **Harbour Cove Inn** • This hotel stands tall, just south of the humpbacked Paradise Island bridge to overlook all of Nassau and its waterfront bustling with cruise ships, pleasure and excursion boats, ferries, and the spectacular sight of Chalk's seaplane as it takes off and lands. Cabbage Beach is a stone's throw and the palm-shaded pool overlooks the harbor. All water sports can be had along with such games as tennis, table tennis, and shuffleboard played near the hotel's petite, man-made beach. All rooms, furnished in wicker, have two double beds, television, and some have balconies. The Buccaneer Lounge is a popular night spot. A complimentary water taxi takes guests to Nassau every day except Wednesday and Sunday.

★★ **Club Land'or** • The main focus of this resort is time sharing, but some hotel rooms are available. Affiliated with the Xanadu Hotel in Freeport, it is a part of Resorts Condominiums International. All units have living-dining areas and kitchenettes and rattan furnishings. Some of the rooms have balconies. The beach is about 10 minutes away and the pool overlooks the lagoon. Each day except Sunday there is a happy hour in the Oasis Lounge and the Blue Lagoon restaurant serves breakfast and dinner on the third floor. There is a once a week trip to Rose Island and the ferry to Nassau or the island tour boat are just outside.

Southwestern New Providence

EXPENSIVE

☆☆☆**Divi Bahamas Beach Resort & Country Club** • Formerly the South Ocean Club, this sprawling resort is about a 10-minute drive from the airport. By 1992 the hotel is expected to have over 1000 rooms. New guests are greeted with rum punches as they enter the circular lobby decorated with potted ficus, banana trees, and exotic, colorful birds in domed cages. Rooms are smartly decorated with wicker and dark wood. Most have louvered doors leading to balconies or patios. However, those on ground level, whether facing the pool-area cafe or the gardens, have little privacy and can be noisy if you want an afternoon nap. It is best, therefore, to request a second-story room. The glass-enclosed Papagayo restaurant overlooks the golf course and is a pleasant alternative to the rather standard main dining room. Papagayo is Italian/American gourmet.

Video tapes are for rent to play in your room, and the hotel has an extensive video library. The in-room safe-deposit boxes are good for passports, tickets, jewelry, and cash, but too small for 35mm cameras and the like. Front-desk safes are available for a small fee. There are 4 tennis courts and scuba certification courses as well as windsurfing and other watersports. Room keys come on rubber coils that fit your wrist for swimming. Complimentary transportation is provided to downtown Nassau (about 30 minutes each way). This is a good thing, since taxi drivers either groan or quote exhorbitant rates upon discovering that you want to go all the way to Divi. The last hotel shuttle leaves Nassau at midnight. You can also take the local jitney for about $1.75 each way. Divi owns the nearby beachfront Sandpiper timeshare units.

FREEPORT

ATTRACTIONS AT A GLANCE

	Place	Page
Shopping and Dining Plazas		
International Bazaar	Torii gate at West Sunrise Highway	214
*Port Lucaya	Lucaya	215
Local Industries		
Straw Market	Next to International Bazaar	215
Perfume Factory	Near International Bazaar	215
Bahamas Arts and Crafts Market	Near International Bazaar	212
Gardens, Parks, and Nature Reserves		
*Rand Memorial Nature Centre	Settlers Way East	215
*Garden of the Groves	Off Midshipman Road	214
*Lucayan National Park	Eastern End	214
Hydroflora Garden	East Beach Drive	214
Museums		
Underwater Explorers Society Museum	Across from Lucayan Beach Resort	216

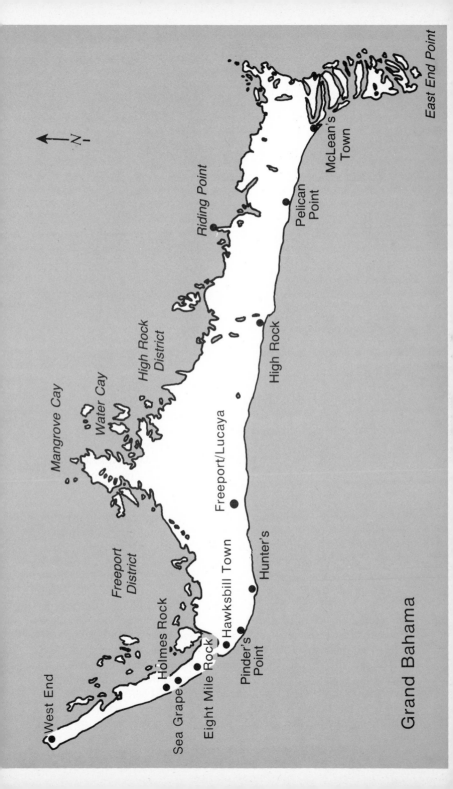

Grand Bahama

	Place	*Page*
Grand Bahama Museum	Garden of the Groves	214
Animals		
*The Dolphin Experience	UNEXSO Dock, Lucaya	212

The Second City

Freeport, with an array of restaurants, clubs, sports, and two vast casinos, is located inland on Grand Bahama. This island of about 35,000 people has taken its place after New Providence as the second most important in the Bahamas chain. An orderly city with excellent roads and broad, landscaped highways bordered by stately palms and pines, Freeport is scarcely three decades old. Since it is shy on historical attractions and sightseeing shrines, those who thrive on sunbathing, watersports, fishing, golf, gambling, dining, and nightlife will find it made to order. For theatergoers, the Regency Theatre on East Mall often presents local and imported plays.

High-rise hotels, apartment buildings, condominiums and time-sharing complexes stand against the cerulean sky and sparkling waters. Residents of Freeport and adjoining Lucaya (the islands' beach resort), have attractive homes surrounded by well-kept lawns and flowering shrubs. The many Europeans, Canadians, and Americans now living in Free-port/Lucaya make it a truly international city. Many Americans have spilled over from Florida and other states for retirement and vacation homes. The late American band leader Count Basie lived in Bahamia, an exclusive neighborhood popular with sightseers.

As you enter Freeport along West Sunrise Highway, the lofty Princess Tower and the casino next door become unmistakable landmarks. Through Moorish domes, minarets, and intricate tilework, they strive for the exotic. Along with the low-rise Princess Country Club across the road, they form the Bahamas Princess Resort & Casino.

Alongside the Princess Resort's tower, a Japanese torii gate welcomes you to the sprawling International Bazaar with its shops and decor representing countries around the world. Visitors may purchase international wares and dine on a wide selection of international cuisines. The Bahamas Tourist Office is also in the busy bazaar. Here, through the government's free **People-to-People Program,** you can arrange to do things with individual Bahamians or families who volunteer their time to make your stay more enjoyable. Whether or not you participate in the People-to-People Program, you may want to check the local newspaper for the weekend barbecues or beach parties sponsored by churches, lodges, or schools to raise money. There is always music as well as spirited domino games, and you'll have an inexpensive home-cooked meal of treats such as conch fritters, curried chicken, and ribs.

If you're staying at a hotel or guest house with cooking facilities, you can buy fresh seafood at the Harbour Fish and Lobster House in Freeport's downtown industrial area. Fresh fruits and vegetables are sold in the market outside the grocery store in the downtown shopping area and fresh-baked goods can be found at Mum's and Western bakeries.

In the Lucaya area, across from the Lucayan Beach Resort & Casino, the Atlantik Beach Hotel, and the Lucaya Holiday Beach Resort is the Port Lucaya shopping complex. Spread along the marina, the various buildings and plazas house shops, a marina, restaurants, a bandstand, and other attractions. At UNEXSO, near Port Lucaya Marketplace, a not-to-be-missed experience for visitors is swimming with playful dolphins. The Lucayan Beach Resort & Casino is a three-hotel complex, having incorporated the Lucayan Marina Hotel and the Lucayan Beach Hotel. Guests of each unit have reciprocal privileges of all facilities. A ferry connects the hotels and condos along the channel to those along the beach. A peaceful, pleasant stroll along Royal Palm Way will take you past some attractive private homes bordered by Cook Island pines, casuarinas, and colorful flowers—but no royal palms.

Local buses running among Lucaya, Freeport's International Bazaar area, and downtown Freeport cost about 75¢. Near Pub on the Mall restaurant you can get a bus to the Lucaya Holiday beach for windsurfing or waterskiing. Rent a car or a moped through a hotel for a short trip to one of the uncrowded Lucaya beaches, such as beautiful Taino and others off Midshipman Road. The 40-acre Lucayan National Park, about 25 minutes by car east of downtown Freeport, has a wide, secluded beach with high dunes. The lush Garden of the Groves is also worth a visit. Another pleasant nature reserve is the Rand Memorial Nature Centre, not far from the International Bazaar area. A drive along the western coast will take you through tiny old settlements and to restaurants overlooking the ocean.

The Early Days

Until the sixties, Grand Bahama had developed in fits and starts, beginning at its west end. Then Wallace Groves, an American from Virginia, saw trade and other growth possibilities. With loans and the enthusiastic encouragement of the colonial government, he began building the city of Freeport and developing its deepwater harbor for the expected boom in trade and commerce. Since the 1964 opening of its first tourist hotel, the Lucayan Bay, Freeport/Lucaya has blossomed with hotels and resorts. Sensing that his new city could not thrive on tourism alone, Groves set out to attract industry as well. His foresight has resulted in an industrial area that now supports oil refineries, cement production, pharmaceuticals, and other types of manufacturing.

Most of what little history there is can be found in the small settlements such as Pinders's Point, Eight Mile Rock, and Seagrape, along the western coast. Before the advent of tourists, and when there was Prohibition in the United States, this section of Grand Bahama was notorious. It was an important operating point for smugglers and rum runners who used the area much as their predecessors, the pirates, did.

When it appeared that tourism would develop at the western end of the island, the Grand Bahama Hotel and Country Club was erected. This expansive resort with lush plantings, a golf course, tennis courts, a giant pool, a marina, and countless other amenities, fell upon hard times when growth took place at Freeport, some 25 miles to the east. It was resurrected as the now closed Jack Tar Village.

~~~~~~

WHAT TO SEE AND DO

SIGHTS AND ATTRACTIONS

A number of buses take visitors on tours of Freeport/Lucaya and the vicinity. Tour attractions are celebrity homes, the historical West End, several beaches, nature reserves, and the industrial area. Some tours stop for shopping and lunch or a snack. One of the tours is aboard a red, double-decker bus from London. Prices range from about $10 to $15 for adults. Check hotel tour desks for details.

Bahamas Arts and Crafts Market • *Behind the International Bazaar* • The various booths here sell locally made jewelry, paintings, and other crafts. This market, too often overlooked by visitors, deserves a stop.

*The Dolphin Experience • *At the UNEXSO dock across from the Lucayan Beach Resort & Casino; tel: 373–1244* • While some animal lovers are disturbed by the idea of dolphins in captivity, others won't pass up the chance to swim with them in this special program. You get right into the water with these playful acquatic mammals, who allow you to stroke and hug their powerful 6- or 7-foot bodies, and caress their smooth skin. Children are welcome. In the regular program, up to six participants swim with the dolphins for about 20 minutes after the orientation. Participants wear flippers. Life jackets, masks, and snorkels are also available. Afterwards you can view your performance on video and purchase a copy for about $30. Originally from Mexico, the dol-

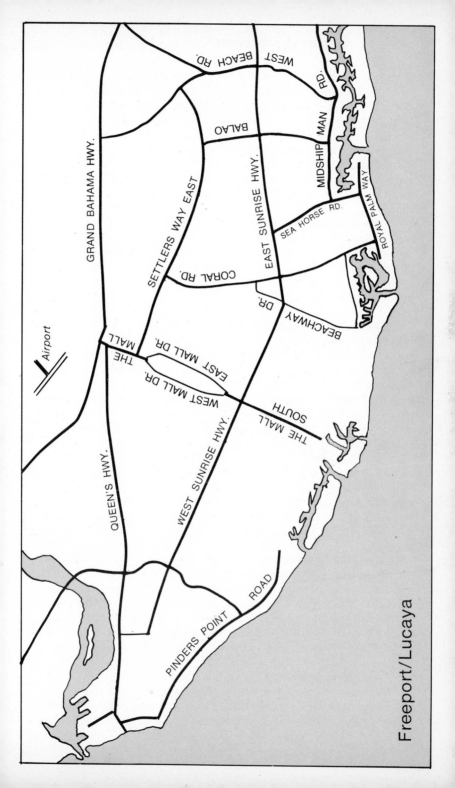

Freeport/Lucaya

phins now reside in a large pen at the UNEXSO dock. They are part of an experiment in human/dolphin interaction. After being taught to follow a boat back and forth between their enclosure and a reef a mile away, they are now released into the open sea regularly to swim with scuba divers and snorkelers. The trainers periodically test the dolphins' ability to use sonar and to retrieve objects from the divers. *Call for reservations. $50 per swim session; $10 for orientation only; $95 to spend day as an assistant trainer, $100 to scuba dive; $60 to snorkel. Make reservations several weeks ahead.*

***Garden of the Groves** • *Off Midshipman Road, about 8 miles east of downtown* • This 12-acre garden is named for Freeport's founder, Wallace Groves, and his wife. The garden has a thousand species of flowers, ferns, shrubs, and trees. Among its attractions are waterfalls and hanging gardens. *Open daily (except Wed.) 9:30 a.m.–5 p.m. Free admission.*

Grand Bahama Museum • *Garden of the Groves* • This museum is just inside the entrance to the Garden of the Groves. Here you'll find artifacts of the Lucayan Indians, who came by canoe from South America and inhabited the island when Columbus arrived. You'll learn that English words such as canoe, hurricane, potato, and barbecue were taken from the Lucayan language. Also on display are colorful costumes worn for the Bahamian traditional Junkanoo parades on New Year's Day, Boxing Day, and Independence Day. *Admission: $2.00 for adults; $1.00 for children.*

Hydroflora Garden • *East Beach Drive* • This garden demonstrates hydroponics, the growing of plants in water. Visitors are given complimentary Bahamian flowers, and they learn the history of the conch shell, which has its own museum here. *Open daily 9:30 a.m.–5 p.m. Admission: Adults, $1, Children under 12, 50¢.*

***Lucayan National Park** • *Eastern End* • This 40-acre park made up of four different ecological zones has coca plums, seagrape, ming trees, wild tamarind, mahogany, and cedar, among many other types of vegetation. Gold Rock Creek flows through the park to the ocean and there is a beautiful, wide, secluded beach. Two cave openings are accessible by stairways and ramps, and there is over a mile of footpaths and elevated walkways. *Free admission.*

International Bazaar • *Entrance through Torii gate on West Sunrise Highway, next to Princess Tower Hotel and casino* • This is a complex of international shops, boutiques, and restaurants with architecture, goods, food, and souvenirs reminiscent of a variety of countries. Most

Freeport/Lucaya visitors eventually find their way here. Unfortunately, this bazaar has become somewhat tattered around the edges over the years. Although its shops are more expensive, Port Lucaya has a more pleasant atmosphere. *Open daily (except Sundays) until midnight. No admission charge.*

Perfume Factory • *Near International Bazaar* • Perfumes, made from local flowers, are manufactured here, and the entire process may be seen in operation. Visitors may make purchases, selecting from among several fragrances.

*Port Lucaya • *Near UNEXSO dock* • Pleasing to the eye, Port Lucaya is a cluster of pastel, shingle-roofed buildings filled with shops and restaurants. Guests dine and relax on balconies overlooking the water. Food ranges from Chinese to English pub and Bahamian. Strolling through, you can buy everything from imported gold jewelry, leather goods, and perfumes to antique bottles and old coins and handmade crafts. At some of the stalls, women (and men) can have their hair cornrowed. Count Basie, the legendary jazz pianist and band leader, who lived on Grand Bahama until his death, first had the idea for this attractive plaza and promenade. Live music spills out of a lacy gazebo both by day and night. A steel band plays every evening except Sunday. Many of the shops and restaurants stay open late and can be pleasant spots for sunset watching.

*Rand Memorial Nature Centre • *Settlers Way East* • Named for and financed by James H. Rand, a former president of Remington-Rand, this 100-acre park has 200 species of birds, and more than 400 varieties of plants. On the guided tour, you are followed by friendly birds. You can photograph the national bird, the pink flamingo, in all its glory at a tropical pool. You will also learn where the "straw" at the straw markets really comes from, and you'll see how bubble gum grows. *Open Mon. through Fri. and Sun. Guided tours at 10:30 a.m., 2 p.m., and 3 p.m. and on Sun., 2 p.m. and 3 p.m. $2.00.*

Straw Market • *Next to the International Bazaar* • Freeport/Lucaya's Straw Market carries the same kinds of handcrafted items found in straw markets throughout The Bahamas. Items include hats for both sexes, baskets, and place mats, as well as wood carvings, necklaces, and a variety of objects fashioned from the ubiquitous conch shell. *Open daily.*

SPORTS

Diving • Divers gravitate to Freeport/Lucaya to take advantage of the services and facilities offered by the Underwater Explorer's Society (UNEXSO), which gives diving lessons, leads expeditions to several diving sites, operates a diving museum and library, and runs a snack bar where visitors can grill their own hamburgers. Across from the Lucayan Beach Resort & Casino, UNEXSO offers a course in underwater photography. UNEXSO personnel are happy to give advice on diving sites on other islands. The "resort course" is about $80 and the 5-day certification course runs about $295. A single dive in the tank will be about $30. Dive packages range from about $75 for 3 dives to about $200 for 10 dives. (Call UNEXSO at (809)373–1244 in the Bahamas, (305)761–7679 in Florida; and 1–800–992–DIVE toll-free from the rest of the U.S.) The UNEXSO store sells the latest in wet suits, snorkels and fins, and other underwater gear as well as shorts, bathing suits, T-shirts, dive books, and underwater videos.

Fishing and Boating • For deep-sea fishing, boats leave daily from the marina adjacent to the Lucayan Bay Hotel at 9 a.m. and 1 p.m. Bait and tackle as well as soft drinks and ice are included in the price. Make reservations through your hotel tour desk or bell captain. The cost is about $40 (or $20 for spectators).

Cruises include sightseeing trips as well as **snorkeling** excursions for beginners or those with experience. The *Mermaid Kitty,* said to be the world's largest glass-bottom boat, leaves from the Lucayan Bay Hotel dock at 10 a.m., noon, and 2:30 p.m. and visits tropical fish–filled coral reefs and a shipwreck. You can also see a diving show. The cost is about $10 for adults and about $6.50 for children. Other cruises allow time for swimming and lunch on a deserted beach. Sailing trips can be arranged through hotels. *Check hotel tour desks for further details.*

Golf • There are six golf courses in Freeport/Lucaya: Bahama Reef, 9 holes, is not far from the Holiday Inn; Lucayan Park Golf & Country Club, 18 holes, caters to guests of the Atlantik Beach Hotel; Fortune Hills Golf & Country Club is a 9-hole course; Princess Ruby is one of two courses operated by the Princess hotels and has 18 holes; Princess Emerald, the other one, was designed by Dick Wilson and has 18 holes; and Jack Tar Village, a 27-hole course, is in the West End resort 45 miles outside Freeport.

Horseback Riding • Pinetree Stables takes groups out at 9 a.m., 11 a.m., and 2 p.m. every day except Monday. Riders have a choice of English or Western saddles. *Adults $20 per hour.*

Tennis • Courts are at the Princess hotels, the Holiday Inn, the Shalimar Hotel, Silver Sands Sea Lodge, and Jack Tar Village.

Parasailing and Windsurfing • These sports are available at the Atlantik Beach Hotel and the Holiday Inn.

Waterskiing • The Princess hotels and Lucaya Holiday Beach Resort offer waterskiing.

NIGHTLIFE

Freeport Inn is the nightspot to go to if you want to party with an almost completely Bahamian crowd. The live band plays Bahamian music as well as disco, and the club attracts mainly young people. While people tend to dress up to go dancing at **Studio 69** on Midshipman Road, jeans and sneakers are the attire for many at **Sultan's Tent** in the Princess Tower, which plays more calypso than most other clubs. **Yellow Bird,** at Castaways Resort, features Bahamian music. You can listen to live jazz at **Skipper's Lounge** in the Bahamas Princess Country Club. With potted plants and a gleaming black bar, snazzy **Club Estee,** in Port Lucaya, is a newcomer to Freeport's after dark scene. Happy Hour here is a good time to mingle with other vacationers. Also check out **Club La Chic,** a disco on East Sunrise Highway.

There is always a flurry of activity in The **Princess Casino,** adjoining the tower of the Bahamas Princess Resort. Visitors to the casino's nightclub are treated to a Las Vegas–style act complete with magicians, comedians, and glittering, scantily dressed male and female dancers. Although not as busy, the **Lucayan Beach Hotel Casino** attracts many guests from the beach area.

DINING OUT

NOTE · · · Some restaurants will add a service charge to your bill if you pay with traveler's checks.

EXPENSIVE
Luciano's • *Port Lucaya; tel: 373–9100* • Residents rave about the Bahamian and continental steak and seafood served here amid sophisticated surroundings. Save this one for a special night out. *Jackets required. Closed Sundays.*

The Rib Room • *Bahamas Princess Resort & Casino; tel: 352–6721* • The atmosphere of this restaurant is warm in the evening, with candlelight against dark beams, and there is a variety of gourmet dishes on the menu. *Major credit cards.*

MODERATE TO EXPENSIVE

Big Buddha • *Port Lucaya; tel: 373–8499* • This Japanese and Chinese restaurant is a fun place to eat, not only because of its waterfront dining patio, but also because patrons get to watch the chefs work their magic on the meat, seafood, and vegetable dishes at tableside hibachis. There's also a sushi bar. If you arrive between 5 and 7 p.m., you'll save money with early bird specials.

Fat Man's Nephew • *Port Lucaya; tel: 373–8520* • Upstairs from the Pusser's Pub, this restaurant continues the legacy of the late Fat Man, who ran a popular local eatery for years. Bahamian favorites served here include conch fritters, turtle steak, grouper fingers, and peas and rice. From the balcony, you'll have a wonderful view of the Bell Channel Waterway.

Guanahani • *Bahamas Princess Resort & Casino; tel: 352–6721* • Guanahani was the Indian name for San Salvador when Columbus "discovered" this Bahamian island. Near the pool, this glass-enclosed, elegant restaurant featuring American, French, German, Italian, Japanese, Mexican, and Bahamian cuisine is surrounded by lush plants and is attractively lit at night. *Major credit cards.*

Ruby Swiss • *West Mall and West Sunrise Highway; tel: 352–8507* • Down the street from the Princess Tower, this restaurant has American, German, and Swiss entrees on its extensive menu. The crab meat Rockefeller is a good choice. Live calypso music accompanies dinner. Reservations are necessary.

Pub on the Mall • *Ranfurly Circle; tel: 352–5110* • Right across from the International Bazaar, this lively pub serves English, Bahamian, and American food as well as a variety of imported beers. Closed Sundays. *Major credit cards.*

The Stoned Crab • *Taino Beach; tel: 313–1442* • In addition to crab dishes, this seafood restaurant on one of Freeport's most beautiful beaches specializes in lobster and steak. Only dinner is served.

MODERATE TO INEXPENSIVE

The Brass Helmet Restaurant and Bar • *Upstairs from UNEXSO, Lucaya; tel: 373–1244* • Among the most popular menu items are cracked conch, steak, and burgers (which you can grill yourself out on the balcony). An unusual piece of decor, the head of a huge, fierce looking shark has "burst" through one of the walls of the restaurant. An old copper diving helmet sits atop an aged wooden crate. Other antique diving gear is hung on walls. A large screen TV plays underwater videos.

Cafe Valencia • *International Bazaar; tel: 352–8717* • When the manager asks, "How's everything?" she really seems to mean it at this cafe specializing in homestyle cooking. Try the cracked conch with peas and rice or the chicken. Portions are generous. Keeping one eye on the soap operas on the TV above the bar during lunch, the waitresses are friendly and efficient.

The Pusser's Co. Store & Pub • *Port Lucaya; tel: 373–8450* • Dine inside or al fresco on the patio at this upscale pub. Outside, instead of mundane brands of condiments, you'll find goodies such as Coleman's Hot English Mustard on the marble-topped, cafe-style tables. Inside, the dark wood tables and paneling create a warm atmosphere. Sandwiches, burgers, fish, and other pub fare are on the menu. The adjoining store sells sportswear (for men, women, and children), model ships, scrimshaw chess pieces, oversized mugs, and other items.

Japanese Steak House • *International Bazaar; tel: 352–9521* • The Japanese Steak House is a welcome find in the labyrinth of the International Bazaar. It has a pleasant atmosphere, and food is dramatically prepared at hibachi tables. Closed Sundays.

Harry's American Bar • *Queen's Highway at Deadman's Reef* • This little restaurant, with a view of the sea, becomes a favorite of visitors once they discover it. Fourteen miles out of Freeport, it is away from the heart of tourist activity. Having a drink or a steak, chicken, or seafood meal here can be a welcome break in a day or an evening's rounds.

The Buccaneer Club • *Queen's Highway and Deadman's Reef; tel: 348–3794* • This restaurant is a good reason for getting out of town. It is on the beach and its grounds have lush palms and other foliage. The menu consists of European and Bahamian selections. From November through April, when the restaurant is open, it sponsors beach parties with food, volleyball, and other activities for an all-inclusive price. Call for free transportation from your hotel. Open only for dinner, the Buccaneer is closed on Mondays.

Churchill Pub • *Near International Bazaar; tel: 352–8866* • This English-style pub, named for Sir Winston Churchill and next to the straw market at the International Bazaar, serves dishes such as roast beef with Yorkshire pudding, but it is also known for its cracked conch. In addition to a Happy Hour Monday through Friday, there is entertainment several nights a week. The pub is open until 4 a.m.

La Phoenix • *Silver Sands Sea Lodge; tel: 353–3373* • The menu here ranges from Indian curry dishes, seafood kebabs, and chicken Kiev to conch chowder, steak, and lobster. Early-bird specials are served from 5–6:30 p.m. *Major credit cards.*

Marcella's • *East Mall at Kipling Lane; tel: 352–5085* • Before digging into an Italian meal here, try a frozen daiquiri. Many people consider Marcella's the best place to find authentic Italian food in Freeport. It has also become a popular evening hangout.

Captain's Charthouse • *East Sunrise and Beachway Dr.; tel: 373–3900* • In this restaurant the hearty fare runs to steaks, chops, shrimp, lobster, and the like. The decor is tropical, and island music adds to the lively atmosphere. *Major credit cards.*

INEXPENSIVE

Papa Charlie's • *Port Lucaya; tel. 343–1451* • This is a good choice for Bahamian conch salad, conch fritters, hot dogs, sandwiches, and other light fare.

George's Restaurant and Disco • *Port Lucaya; tel. 373–8513* • Try George's for an authentic Bahamian breakfast of boiled or stewed fish, chicken souse, or corned beef and grits.

The Office • *Logwood Rd.; tel: 352–8997* • The Bahamian specials at this casual dining spot that serves three meals a day include okra soup, curried chicken, steamed mutton, chicken souse, and barbecued ribs. The Office, open daily from 8 a.m. to 5 a.m., has a live band and a disco.

The Pancake House • *East Sunrise Highway; tel: 373–3200* • This popular restaurant specializing in Bahamian home-style cooking has nothing to do with the American chain with a similar name. In addition to 12 different kinds of pancakes, the menu includes stewed fish and grits, shrimp, steak, and sandwiches. Breakfast is served all day.

Kristi's • *West Atlantic Drive; tel: 352–3149* • Open for breakfast and lunch, this eatery whips up great homestyle soups and quiches. A variety of sandwiches and salads is also served, along with hot daily specials.

Scorpio's • *Explorer's Way and West Atlantic; tel: 352–6969* • Cracked conch, steamed grouper, and minced lobster are just a few of the dishes served at this restaurant recommended highly by Bahamians. Take-out service is available from 7 a.m. to 3 a.m. every day. *Major credit cards.*

Freddie's • *Hunters; tel: 352–3250* • Open from 11 a.m. until 11 p.m., Freddie's serves grouper, steak, minced lobster, pork chops, cracked conch, and other local dishes. Early-bird specials are on the menu from 5 p.m. to 6:30 p.m. Freddie's is closed on Sundays.

Blackbeard's • *Fortune Beach; tel: 373–2960* • The location, right on the beach, makes this an especially pleasant place to have a drink, mingle with locals, and sample Bahamian specialties like peas and rice and cracked conch.

Traveller's Rest • *William's Town, off Beachway Dr.; tel: 353–4884* • This informal restaurant, overlooking a narrow beach, is off the beaten track. Conch is served in burgers, fritters, and salads. Hearty chowders, rice and peas, and fish are also on the menu.

Other good restaurants for Bahamian cuisine are the **Native Hut** on Sergeant Major Drive and **Peace & Plenty** in Eight Mile Rock (353–1814).

WHERE TO STAY

Freeport

EXPENSIVE

★★★**Xanadu Beach & Marina Resort** • Readily recognizable as the pyramid-topped high-rise with a cluster of villas at its base, Xanadu was once the hideaway of multi-millionaire recluse Howard Hughes. Today's hotel is a modern refurbished accommodation with comfortable, well-furnished, balconied rooms and set on a peninsula formed by its own beach and its 72-slip marina on the canal waterway. When not basking on the beach, guests may use the pool where there is a bar and drink service. All water sports are offered, with golf at the Ruby or

Emerald courses short trips away. Tennis is on premises. Dining is offered at several locations. Pre-dinner cocktails can be had at one of the bars in either the tower building or the pool wing.

MODERATE

★★★**Bahamas Princess Resort & Casino** • This large resort, on both sides of West Sunrise Highway, results from the combining of Freeport's two Princess hotels. Guests enjoy the ample facilities of both establishments, which include dining at nine restaurants, sports, other recreation and, of course, the casino. Two golf courses are on tap and guests not using either of the two pools have free transportation to Xanadu beach. The winding, shop-filled streets of the busy International Bazaar are a step away and the new Port Lucaya shopping center is a short bus ride away. The two hotels, the Princess Tower (adjacent to the casino), and the Princess Country Club are pleasantly landscaped and are an imposing sight seen together. The domed tower building has a Middle Eastern theme brought together in a lavish, blue tiled Moorish lobby with a grand piano in the center. The Country Club buildings (where the less expensive guest rooms are located) are spread out, with much activity centered around the pool with its waterfall and swim-under bridge. All rooms are cheerfully furnished, equipped with television, and those in the tower have panoramic views of the city. However, some Country Club rooms are a long walk from the lobby and a few of the others get little sunlight and have uninspiring views.

Windward Palms Hotel • This modest hotel is just across from the International Bazaar, near a number of good restaurants, and a short walk to the casino. There is an inviting pool area lush with trees and colorful flowers. Guests are provided with free transportation to the beach in Lucaya.

Caravel Beach Resort • This small apartment hotel, near the Xanadu Beach Resort, consists of 12 two-bedroom villas, each with a kitchen and dining area. There is also a small restaurant and lounge, and free transportation is provided to the International Bazaar in the morning and evening. The beach here is rocky. Since Caravel has become quite run down, only those on a very limited budget should consider staying here.

Freeport Inn • This downtown hotel is not far from the International Bazaar and straw market. Guests have a choice of air-conditioned rooms, with or without kitchenettes. There is free transportation to Xanadu beach and arrangements can be made for golf and a variety of water sports. After being destroyed by fire, the restaurant has been rebuilt.

This no-frills hotel attracts visiting college students during spring break, when the disco becomes even more popular than usual.

INEXPENSIVE

Castaways Resort • Castaways is next to the International Bazaar and close to the casino. This four-story, 138-room hotel has a bright, pagodalike roof, and its disco, the Yellowbird, attracts dancers from far and neare. Guests who tire of the swimming pool and sun deck can be transported free to a nearby beach.

Lucaya

EXPENSIVE

★★★**Silver Reef Health Spa** • *Williamstown* • Owned and run by a Bahamian couple, this 13-room health spa at the edge of a canal was born in October, 1990. It is by far the accommodation with the most character in Freeport, in part because the main building used to be the home of the owners. With time on her hands after raising five children, Andrea Gotlieb decided to enter the spa business. Her father-in-law, Grand Bahama's first physician, and her sister-in-law, a physical therapist, provide advice and moral support. The staff includes doctors, manicurists, exercise trainers, acupuncturists, and masseurs. Guests pamper themselves with facials (in a converted stable), herbal wraps, mud treatments, hydrotherapy, and designer hair styling. Most stay a week to ten days. A dietician is on hand. No red meat is served and supervised fasts can be arranged.

The beach is not far and the spa has its own boat for taking guests fishing, snorkeling, and cruising. Kayaks, paddleboats, and bikes are also available, at no extra charge. In addition to tennis and volleyball courts, there are a hot tub, sauna, swimming pool, weight room, and aerobic deck. Painted in bold, textured colors, the air-conditioned guest rooms, which also have ceiling fans, are all individually decorated. Terra cotta tile floors, wicker and antique furniture, walk-in closets, and French doors are features of the waterfront villa rooms. With wonderfully patterned Mexican ceramic tiles and painted sinks in the baths, the rooms in the main house are fabulous. Some of the terra cotta floor tiles in this building have coyote paw prints in them! Upstairs in the huge living room, along with a fireplace, oriental rug, wing chairs, and floor to ceiling windows, is a Steinway piano that used to belong to Count Basie. A TV and games amuse guests in the nearby library. With a king-sized brass bed, an antique love seat, and a giant bath sporting a Jacuzzi and a skylight, the penthouse (the old master bedroom) is a real knockout.

MODERATE

Atlantik Beach Hotel • At press time, major renovations are underway at this resort hotel. Inviting facilities are its broad beach and large swimming pool bordered by terra-cotta tiles. The Swiss management blends a continental approach with the local ambience for a happy meeting ground. There are four newly redone restaurants including one that looks out on the pool, and the Sunday buffet remains popular. The Port Lucaya Marketplace and its attractions is just across the road. The gamut of water sports, including windsurfing and parasailing, is available on premises, as well as a variety of other activities. A bus delivers guests to the hotel's Port Lucaya Golf & Country Club. Although rooms are comfortable and well furnished, they are reached by climbing or descending a short flight of stairs after leaving the elevator. We have yet to figure out the logic of this architectural feature. Cars for island exploration can be rented across the road at Avis and National.

★★★**Lucayan Beach Resort & Casino** • This upscale hotel is set on a beautiful section of Lucaya's long beach. It sprawls low along the beach and is noted for its lighthouse tower, which soars above the two- and three-story wings. Rooms are spacious, with generous walk-in closets and terry robes. The large baths are marble, but the over-the-counter lighting could be brighter for makeup and shaving. All rooms have TV and king-size or oversize twin beds, with terraces or balconies, depending upon location. The casino is large and bright with all the traditional games of chance, along with a bar and cocktail area. It is never as noisy or crowded as the one at the Bahamas Princess. Tennis courts are across the road as is the complimentary ferry to the Lucayan Marina Hotel, and Reef Tours, which offers boating, sailing, and fishing trips on a glass-bottom boat. Right across the road is the Port Lucaya Marketplace, the waterfront array of restaurants and shops. The Lucayan Marina Hotel, the resort's modest sister property across Lucaya Bay shares its facilities. However, we've heard complaints about the service and rooms of this poor relation.

☆☆**Lucaya Holiday Beach Resort** • One of the best features of this former Holiday Inn is its excellent beach where parasailing, waterskiing, and windsurfing are often in evidence. The hotel has been redone, inside and out, with added facilities for the outdoor area. On the way to the beach you pass the pool where entertainment always seems to be under way, with guests making merry. A welcome addition is a health center. In the busy lobby there are a number of shops and lounge areas that are studded with comfortable chairs. The Panache Disco is open until all hours. Be sure to request a room well away from the laundry exhaust system. The constant hum can be heard even with the balcony door closed and the TV and air conditioner on. Port Lucaya

Marketplace is across the road as is UNEXSO, the dive center, and car rental offices.

☆☆ **Silver Sands Sea Lodge** • Modest studio and one-bedroom apartments are available here; all have balconies overlooking the pool, the ocean, or the marina. The beach is within easy walking distance and the lodge has two tennis courts as well as paddleball and shuffleboard courts. The hotel's restaurant, La Phoenix, is popular among both locals and visitors. This hotel is isolated from the group of Lucaya hotels near the casino, but a few condos are nearby.

INEXPENSIVE
☆☆☆ **Coral Beach Hotel** • Only a few of the studios and one-bedroom apartments in this condominium complex are rented to guests. Facilities include a pool and a stunning beach, where guests can sail and snorkel. Fishing is also available, and golf can be arranged. The Sandpiper, a popular nightspot, is in this hotel.

Channel House • This apartment hotel is near Port Lucaya. Not far from the beach, it has its own swimming pool. There are 19 units, each with a kitchen, and a snack bar is at the pool for a quick bite. Tennis is on premises and the casino is a short stroll away.

Off East End
EXPENSIVE
☆☆**Deep Water Cay Club** • This small lodge, a short flight from Freeport, is the perfect place for divers and fishermen who want to enjoy their sports in seclusion. In addition to great bonefishing, a 20-mile barrier reef offshore, and blue holes to be explored, there are quiet unspoiled beaches where guests can snorkel over shallow reefs. Diving and fishing package deals are available. In a recent renovation the dining room and front patio have been extended, and a game room for cards and backgammon has been added.

THE FAMILY ISLANDS

Many visitors as well as Bahamians consider the Family Islands the most beautiful part of The Bahamas. These islands include all those other than New Providence and Grand Bahama, where Nassau and Freeport are located, and Paradise Island, which is connected to New Providence by a bridge. The government changed the name from "Out Islands" to show that these islands are indeed part of the Bahamian family.

Except for small towns here and there and a few large-scale resorts, nature in these islands has been left almost intact. Countless palm-shaded beaches lapped by clear turquoise waters lie undisturbed. Where there are roads, they are often bordered by nothing but wind-blown pines and bushes for miles. Bahamian waters maintain their crystal clarity because they are virtually unpolluted, especially in the Family Islands. Also, the islands are without streams and rivers and no silt or sediment collects to cloud them. While most fun for visitors revolves around watersports, there are also some natural and historical attractions. For seeing the sights, you can rent bicycles or cars or take taxi tours, but be prepared for bumpy roads and large old rattling cars in some areas.

Visitors to the Family Islands have more of a chance to meet and socialize with islanders than those who travel only to Nassau or Freeport. Some experiences have reinforced a belief among visitors that Family Island Bahamians are some of the most pleasant and hospitable people ever encountered during their travels. Many hotels are the centers of activity for their areas and locals are invited to hotel parties and other events. By the same token, residents often invite visitors to town happenings, such as beach parties, parades, dances, and other celebrations. There is not much nightlife during the week, but on weekends something is always going on somewhere nearby. The Family Islands are not for those who are looking for casinos or hotel boutiques and beauty parlors. Don't expect phones, radios, or televisions in most guest rooms. Many hotels and restaurants communicate by VHF or CB radio instead of phones.

Boats, bikes, mopeds and golf carts are far more popular than cars on some islands. Many hotels do not use keys for rooms, but safety deposit boxes are available. Some accommodations have an honor bar system during the day—leaving it up to guests to write down the drinks they fix for themselves. Visitors may find that, even in the larger resorts, tap water may taste a bit salty, but most hotels supply filtered or bottled water for drinking. Although brief power "outages" are not uncommon, guest rooms usually have candles. Some Family Island accommodations close for several weeks during September and October. Although many of the hotels and guest houses have little or no air conditioning, most visitors are perfectly comfortable with ceiling fans and sea breezes. Most Family Island restaurants are in hotels and guest houses, although there are some good, locally operated eating spots.

On smaller islands, people usually wear several hats, appearing as drivers, waiters, fishermen, carpenters, guides, or hotel workers. One of the popular social events is helping unload mailboats, which arrive every week or ten days. At airports, where planes fly in once or twice a week, there is also a gathering of onlookers watching their baggage-laden friends and family arriving and departing. After flights from the Family Islands, a tricycle or a carton of green bananas might come down Nassau or Freeport's baggage conveyer belt in between overstuffed cardboard boxes and suitcases tied with rope. Religion and superstition go hand-in-hand in the Family Islands. For instance, when local people kill a snake, they put it in the middle of the road, even if they end its life in the bush. This way everyone can see that Adam's enemy has been done in.

The most developed islands are Abaco, Eleuthera, and Exuma. Off the coast of Eleuthera, Harbour Island is known for its pink sand beaches, picturesque Dunmore Town, reminiscent of New England, and its exceptional small hotels. Green Turtle Cay, in the Abacos, is another pretty island. Many travelers are surprised to find that the populations of some islands (such as Spanish Wells, off Eleuthera, and Man-O-War and Elbow Cay, in the Abacos) are predominantly or almost exclusively Caucasian. Along with other areas, these islets were settled around 1648 by white Bermudians seeking religious and political freedom. They were later joined by British Loyalists fleeing America after the Revolutionary War. In the beginning, some of these Loyalists were against slavery and therefore did not keep enslaved Africans. However, as new generations cropped up, these sentiments were transformed into a desire to maintain the all-white status quo.

In April, George Town, in Exuma, is alive with the colorful Family Island Regatta. Many divers make their way to Andros, where one of the world's largest barrier reefs is just offshore, and Long Island, where they can learn to scuba dive among sharks. With its huge colony of pink flamingos, Inagua is great for birdwatching. Bimini attracts dedicated fishermen. The other Family Islands with tourist accommodations offer visitors even more opportunities for rest and relaxation.

The Hotel Corporation of the Bahamas has plans under way to

expand tourism in the Family Islands. For Andros, the largest yet least developed of the islands, a hotel and marina are under construction at Fresh Creek. Another hotel and marina are slated for Morgan's Bluff and a third resort for Driggs Hill in South Andros. Plans for Exuma include a new hotel and marina at George Town and, for Eleuthera, expansion of the Winding Bay area, a yacht club and marina at Hatchet Bay, and a new beach hotel near Governor's Harbour.

Resorts on some islands will pick up guests in Florida or Nassau and fly them in on private planes. While some commercial airlines have direct flights from Florida to a few Family Islands, **Bahamasair** flies daily or weekly from Nassau to all of them. You may end up spending more time than planned between connecting flights because Bahamasair flights are often delayed. Bahamians are fond of saying, ''If you have some time to spare, be sure to fly Bahamasair.'' However, Family Islands are worth the wait.

Attractions at a Glance

	Place	Page
Abacos		
*Manjack Cay	North of Green Turtle Cay	244
*Albert Lowe Museum	New Plymouth, Green Turtle Cay	245
Memorial Sculpture Garden	New Plymouth Green Turtle Cay	246
Hope Town Lighthouse	Elbow Cay	246
Wyannie Malone Museum and Garden	Elbow Cay	246
*Tahiti Beach	Elbow Cay	246
Local Shipbuilding	Man-O-War Cay	245
*Sea and Land Park Preserve	Fowl Cay	245
Great Guana Cay	Between Treasure Cay and Marsh Harbour	245
Tilloo and Pelican Cays	South of Elbow Cay	244
Art Colony at Little Harbour	South of Marsh Harbour	245

	Place	*Page*
San Salvador		
Observation Platform	Near Riding Rock Inn	324
San Salvador Museum	Cockburn Town	324
New World Museum	North Victoria Hill	325
Columbus Monuments	Long Bay, Fernandez Bay, Crab Cay	324
Grahams Harbour	Northern San Salvador	325
Father Schreiner's Grave	Grahams Harbour area	325
Fortune Hill Plantation	Eastern San Salvador	326
East Beach	Northeast Coast	326
Dixon Hill Lighthouse	Dixon Hill	326
Watling's Castle	Sandy Point Estate	326
Farquharson's Plantation	Pigeon Creek	326
Big Well	Sandy Point Estate	327
Dripping Rock	Sandy Point	327

THE ABACOS

Often referred to as Abaco, this is actually a cluster of islands and islets, forming the second-largest grouping in the country. With some 650 square miles of land and many scenic coves, these islands are extremely popular among boaters. Each year in late June and early July, everyone is caught up in Abaco Regatta fever, which envelops Marsh Harbour, Elbow Cay, Green Turtle Cay, and Treasure Cay. While the

April Family Island Regatta in Exuma draws mainly locals, this event has traditionally attracted more tourists.

Despite growing development to lure vacationers, much of the untouched beauty of Abaco remains. The islands are thick with tropical pines, especially the feathery-needled casuarinas. Wild boar still roam some of the forests, providing meat for local tables and often for festive barbecues at resorts. Islands including Elbow Cay, Great Guana, and Manjack Cay are graced with some of The Bahamas' most scenic beaches. There are long stretches of tropical trees and flowering shrubs. Bearing trays of fruits and vegetables on their heads, local women still stroll along quiet lanes. Most settlements have sprouted on the east side of the main island, which faces the Atlantic but is protected by offshore cays and reefs. Many visiting families enjoy renting private homes or staying in accommodations with housekeeping facilities.

Days Gone By

The early Spanish explorers called these islands Habacoa, probably a corruption of *haba de cacao,* which describes the Abacos' rugged, bumpy limestone base. They found these islands of little value, except when it came to capturing and enslaving Indians to replace those who had been killed off by excessive work and smallpox on Cuba and Hispaniola. By 1550, The Bahamas' Lucayans were completely wiped out. For years, piracy flourished amid the Abacos' many tiny cays.

As in nearby Eleuthera, 18th-century colonial Loyalists from New England, New York, the Carolinas, and other parts of the Colonies settled here after the American Revolution. Believing that democracy and republicanism would be detrimental to their property and pocketbooks, they decided to move a piece of the British Empire to the Abacos. They chose these islands because promotional literature of the day claimed that endless agricultural and commercial opportunities awaited them. However, they discovered that there was little fertile soil, and long droughts further thwarted their farming efforts. Many turned to fishing, developing communities on the smaller cays closer to reefs, and to salvaging the cargo and wreckage of ships that fell victim to reefs and shallows.

In a country where some 85% of the population is of African descent, the Abacos are about 50% white. In 1967, the Abacos opposed the attempts of the black-dominated Progressive Liberal Party (PLP), led by Lynden Pindling, to gain a majority in the House of Assembly. But the PLP was victorious and formed a new government. Residents of Abaco were further put out when the PLP carried The Bahamas to independence from the British Crown in 1972. They tried to enlist the support of Queen Elizabeth II in their attempt to separate from The Bahamas to continue as a British Crown Colony. However, their request

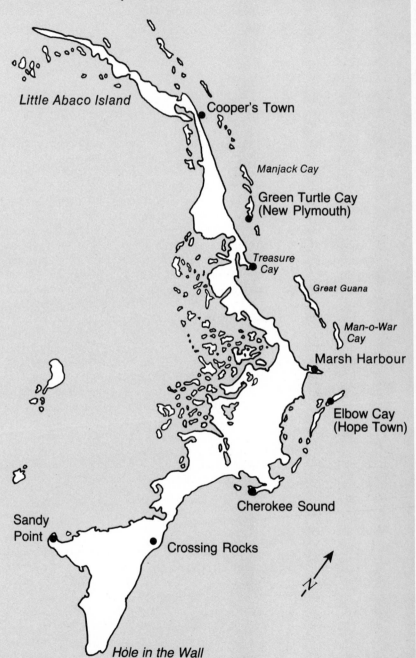

The Abacos

Walker's Cay
Grand Cay

Little Abaco Island

Cooper's Town

Manjack Cay

Green Turtle Cay
(New Plymouth)

Treasure Cay

Great Guana

Man-o-War Cay

Marsh Harbour

Elbow Cay
(Hope Town)

Cherokee Sound

Sandy Point

Crossing Rocks

Hole in the Wall

N

was denied. Although some areas in the Abacos remain predominantly white, these islands seem to have come to terms with progress, for the most part.

Getting Around

Airports in the Abacos are at Walker's Cay, Treasure Cay, and Marsh Harbour. Ferries from Marsh Harbour take passengers to Elbow Cay, Man-O-War Cay, and Great Guana Cay. Those headed for Green Turtle Cay catch the ferry near the Treasure Cay airport. If you plan to explore the Abacos, note that Green Turtle Cay is about a 45-minute powerboat ride from Elbow Cay, and Treasure Cay is about a 45-minute bumpy drive from Marsh Harbour or a pleasant sail away.

To get from the Marsh Harbour airport to Albury's Ferry Station (367–3147 or 365–6010) you'll need to take a taxi (about $12 for two people). Ferries depart two or three times a day for Elbow Cay, about 15 minutes away. Adults are charged about $9 one way or $13 for same day round trip, and children under age 12 pay half price. For about the same price, ferries leave Marsh Harbour for Man-O-War Cay (which has no hotels) twice a day (about a 15-minute ride). If you arrive after the last ferry (around 4 p.m.), pray that you run into others going your way because you'll have to charter a ferry ($40 and up, per boat). A one-way ride between Marsh Harbour and Great Guana Cay will cost about $10 per person ($12 for same day round trip). Guana Beach Resort & Marina picks up guests twice a day from Mangoes Restaurant in Marsh Harbour. A charter will be about $70 for one to five passengers, plus $12 for each additional passenger. You can also charter boats to Little Harbour, Treasure Cay, and Green Turtle Cay, among other islands. Note the "Tips cheerfully accepted" signs in the ferries.

The taxi from the Treasure Cay airport to the dock for ferries to Green Turtle Cay will cost about $7 per couple. Plan to pay about $9 per person for the brief ferry ride. Again, if you arrive after the last ferry your taxi driver will have to radio for a charter, which will run you considerably more.

Marsh Harbour

Most of the boaters on craft of all sizes streaming into the Abacos wind up at Marsh Harbour for rest, food, and fuel. The town is also a center for chartering bareboats (fully equipped yachts without crews), or boats with captains, crews, or fishing guides. The Bahamas Yachting Service (BYS) does a brisk business among veteran sailors as well as novices, who can take a BYS sailing course. Trainees are never sent out alone until fully ready, and even then, fast boats are just a radio call away if trouble arises. If you visit in late April or early May, you'll be just in time for the annual Penny Turtle Billfish Tournament, which is accompanied by all kinds of parties.

Nearly centrally located on the "mainland," Marsh Harbour is the Abacos' chief town. Twice a week, the mailboat from Nassau ties up, bringing passengers, replenishing stores, and unloading materials for building, furnishing, and merely carrying on life in the Abacos. A few shops have sprung up that are clearly geared to tourists. Next to A & K Liquor on Queen Elizabeth Drive, the main drag, you'll find **The Perfume Bar,** where prices for name-brand fragrances are generally much lower than in the U.S. Near the Conch Inn Hotel (pronounced "conk") and Lofty Fig Villas are **John Bull** and **Little Switzerland,** which also has a larger branch in a huge building down the road where the Great Abaco Beach Bazaar shopping center is being developed.

In addition to the hotels in Marsh Harbour, there's a time-sharing development called Abaco Towns. Along with the upscale Great Abaco Beach Hotel & Villas, this Mediterranean-style complex offers a touch of luxury in the midst of this mostly boating and fishing settlement. The 140 slips at **Boat Harbour Marina** (VHF Channel 16; tel: 809/367–2736, 305/359–2720 in Florida, or 800/468–4799; fax: 809/367–2819), adjoining the Great Abaco Beach Hotel, draw yachts up to 125 feet long, with seven or eight foot drafts. Complete services are available for crews. Here **Harbour Lights** restaurant, specializing in Bahamian and American-style seafood, hangs over the edge of the water. The marina pool has a swim-up bar. **Penny's Pub** is for those who'd rather drink dry. Consider renting a Boston Whaler at the marina to spend a day visiting some of the Abacos' varied cays. Many people enjoy the cocktail and dinner cruises as well as the sightseeing trips and sails to deserted beaches. A night club featuring live entertainment keeps boaters occupied after dark.

Arrange to scuba dive through **Dive Abaco** (P.O. Box 555, Marsh Harbour, Abaco, Bahamas; tel. 809/367–2014 or 809/367–2787), based at the Conch Inn. If you'd like to take a sightseeing and/or snorkeling cruise to some of the nearby islands, contact **Albury's Ferry Service** (367–3147 or 365–6010). Some trips leave from the ferry dock at The Crossing, a mile northeast of Boat Harbour Marina, and others from the 67-slip marina at the Conch Inn. This hotel makes a popular lunch stop for locals who drop in from various cays to conduct business in town.

Wally's, one of the Bahamas' most attractive restaurants, is down the road a piece. Run by Wally Smith, the former owner of the Conch Inn, it is housed in a two-story building that resembles a small mansion. Shaded by an awning, the outdoor dining area faces the smooth front lawn and the marina. The snazzy interior, cooled by ceiling fans, is decked out in Haitian-influenced paintings by the country's renowned Amos Ferguson. White peacock chairs sit on terra cotta tiles. Lunch fare ranges from burgers, buffalo chicken wings, and fish and chips to conch fritters and escargot. Try the lemon mousse cake or the butterscotch blizzard cake for dessert. Wally's is open for lunch and drinks from Monday through Saturday. Live music accompanies dinner—served Monday night only, by reservation (367–2074)—and Wednesday evening happy hours. The upscale boutique next door is open from Monday through Saturday.

Lunch and dinner are served daily except Sunday at nearby **Mangoes Restaurant,** which also has a boutique. Many people bypass the indoor dining room, decorated with potted plants, to sit on the breezy waterfront patio with its multi-colored captain's chairs and table cloths. Menu items include mozarella sticks, conch chowder, seafood, sandwiches, salads, and burgers. Popular for its Bahamian cooking, more modest **Cynthia's Kitchen** is in the center of town. The bar and dining room are informal, with hanging plants and plastic tablecloths. Try the curried goat or fried grouper. Other specialties are turtle steak, turtle pie, baked stuffed crabs, and Cynthia's own johnny cakes. At **Mother Merl's,** between Dundas Town and Murphy, about a 10-minute drive from Marsh Harbour, you might find wild boar, goat, and turtle on the menu along with fish and chicken.

After dark, the main local hangouts are **The Jib Room,** across the water from the Conch Inn (you can get there by boat or over land); **The Ranch,** in Marsh Harbour; and **The Oasis** in Dundas Town.

Man-O-War Cay

While you might see frigates (Man-O-War birds) gliding overhead, you won't find any hotels, liquor, or police here. Residents take their religion even more seriously than in some other parts of the Bahamas, so be sure not to offend by walking around in your bathing suit or other skimpy attire. Like Spanish Wells in Eleuthera, the population of this island is almost exclusively white. It was settled in the 1820s by a sole couple, who came to be called Mammy Nellie and Pappy Ben. A poll conducted some hundred and fifty years later showed that 230 of the 235 residents of Man-O-War were descendants of this pair.

Here in the boat-building capital of the country, yachts and sailboats cluster in the harbor. The marina is bordered by gaily painted buildings, many housing boat yards. Residents note sadly that nowadays wooden boats are being replaced by those made of fiberglass. However, if you find one of the older artisans to talk to, he may tell you all about the good old days, when creating wooden boats was a craft very much in demand.

Along the dock trees are hung with fish nets and buoys, like overgrown Christmas ornaments. In the shade of one such sea grape, you'll see the huge rocklike vertebrae of a killer whale. Nearby is **Albury's Harbour Store,** a grocery where you can overhear the local gossip.

The prices here are generally better than those at groceries on neighboring Elbow Cay. Everyone seems to be an Albury on Man-O-War. As one young woman put it, "I know I can't marry anyone on this island."

When you're ready for a snack, try **Arlene's Hide-away Restaurant** (365–6143), which serves both Bahamian and American food. Drop by for lunch or make reservations for dinner. In addition to bread and pies, **Albury's Bakery,** located in a private home, sells conch fritters. At **The Sail Shop,** on the waterfront at the northern end of town, sturdy handmade canvas bags come in all shapes, sizes, and colors. While for generations sail making by hand has been in the families of the women who work here, they no longer carry on the tradition. As they sit behind sewing machines whipping up everything from pouches to overnight bags, they joke, "Call us the bag ladies. We don't make sails anymore—just S-A-L-E-S." A sign on the door at the edge of the harbor reads, "Fish-a-holic: A person obsessed with rods, reels, lures, and baits . . . who casts, trolls, and exaggerates."

To see sails being made or repaired, visit **Edwin's Boat Yard.** In the loft, you might happen upon a craftsperson sewing a portion of the canvas while the rest of the huge, unwieldy-looking cloth sprawls across the floor. Completing one sail can take up to a week. Along the dock, you'll see signs advertising half models—the glossy wooden miniature boats sold to be mounted flat on walls. You might be able to watch an artisan or two at work. Along with half models, **Joe's Studio,** decorated with old nautical gear, sells ceramics, watercolors, wind socks, jewelry, T-shirts, and postcards, among other merchandise. At **Seaside Boutique,** custom-made clothing can be fashioned from Androsia, the bright batik cloth created on Andros. **Aunt Mady's Boutique** offers a variety of resort wear.

Elbow Cay

Long slim Elbow Cay, a serene stretch of land, lies off Marsh Harbour. It is noted for its New England-esque Hope Town, its gorgeous empty beaches, and its much-photographed red-and-white striped lighthouse. Some of them backed by sandy dunes, the island's long ivory shores are among the most picturesque in The Bahamas. In the early 1900s, Hope Town was the largest and wealthiest settlement in the Abacos. The main street, Queen's Highway, curls through Hope Town, following the island's configurations and passing pastel-trimmed clapboard houses with a profusion of purple and orange bougainvillea and other blossoms tumbling over stone and picket fences. Were it not for the palms and other tropical vegetation, Hope Town might be mistaken for a Cape Cod fishing village. The sea is never far from view, whether it is the pounding, crashing ocean, the calmer bay, or the placid harbor with its bobbing forest of masted boats. Some travelers, especially serious boaters, have been so bitten by the Elbow Cay bug that they now return annually and rent private houses. Many of the largest and most impressive homes are owned by Americans, Canadians, and Europeans.

Cars are restricted from the center of town, so bikers and pedestrians have the narrow paved roads (with names such as Lovers' Lane) to themselves. As they pass each other in the street, residents are quick to greet strangers. Spend some time browsing through the gift shops or chatting with locals. You'll learn interesting tidbits about the island's past and present. Margaret Sweeting, whose family runs both a grocery store and Benny's Place (housekeeping apartments) outside of town, remembers well the day Elbow Cay residents first got telephones. It was way back in . . . 1988. The phones were turned on the night her daughter-in-law gave birth to a baby in Nassau, and Grandma Sweeting got to talk to the new mother in the hospital. Before the advent of telephones on Elbow Cay and other Family Islands, everyone communicated the way many still do: by VHF.

Most islanders are white, the descendants of British Loyalists. In their distinctive accent, *h's* pop up in and disappear from words unexpectedly. You might run into the old man who looks for new faces in town so that he can point out the site of the Methodist church that was destroyed by fire. He delights in telling the story of its preacher, who "didn't know 'is hass from a 'ole in the ground." It seems that the minister gave his sermons while facing the window that overlooked the ocean. His congregation sat with their backs to the water. One day he saw a shipwreck and decided to claim the booty. He told the congregation to kneel and pray. He then jumped out of the window, intending to land on his jackass and take off for the ship down the beach. Instead, he fell into a hole. The old man says the preacher ended up claiming the loot anyway.

Stores in Hope Town are shut tight on Sundays, and the various churches are in full swing. You can stand on a corner and hear two different sermons at the same time. An outdoor Catholic service is held in waterfront Jarret Park Playground, next to the main dock (often called the post office dock, since it's overlooked by the P.O.). After parking their bicycles at the entrance, people crowd the benches in the shade of huge overhanging trees—and some even find perches in the branches. If you ask why the priest must stand in the hot sun while the congregation enjoys the shade, residents will answer, "So he won't talk so long." During the service, people rise one by one to read Biblical selections. A child or two often uses the swings and the priest may have to compete with a radio from a nearby house. Behind the white-robed clergyman, a group of boaters in skimpy bathing suits might disembark at the dock.

Down the street, the aroma of baking bread floats out of **Harbour's Edge** restaurant. Topped with wooden tables and benches, the deck here provides a perfect view of the candy-cane lighthouse and the boat-packed harbor. The gullywings (chicken wings), conch chowder, crawfish salad, and fish sandwiches are all eagerly gobbled up. A pool table, juke box, and satellite television entertain the young folks who pour in after dark, especially on Wednesdays (reggae night). Lunch and dinner are served daily except Tuesdays, when only the bar is open (in the evening). Note that this restaurant is strict about its hours: if you arrive just a few minutes after 2 p.m., when lunch ends, for instance, you won't be served anything but drinks.

Neighboring **Whispering Pines** specializes in Bahamian dishes, such as the usual conch, peas and rice, and chicken or fish and chips. But the menu might also include less common selections such as stir-fried beef and vegetables with rice. The South American wall hangings reflect the Ecuadorian origins of Tanny Key, the owner, who also works at **Native Touches Gift Shop.** Selling T-shirts and other beach- and sportswear, this nearby store takes credit cards. You can spend more money at **Edith's Straw Shop,** where hats and bags are handmade, or **Kemp's Souvenir Center.**

For delicious, freshly baked bread and pound cake, stop at **Vernon's,** the general store across the way. The indefatigable Vernon Malone is not only a grocer, baker, taxi driver, artist, and minister, but he's also a descendant of Wyannie Malone, Elbow Cay's most celebrated historical figure. You can learn all about her role in the Abacos' past at the Hope Town museum bearing her name. Not far from town, **Bessie's Bakery** is the place to go for key lime pie. At **Albury's Fish Market** in Hope Town, people staying in rented houses can pick up crawfish, conch, and fish filets. If you have a boat, your best bet for groceries is another **Albury's,** on nearby Man-O-War Cay, where the wide selection of merchandise is somewhat less expensive than on Elbow Cay.

Next door to Hope Town's stark white St. James Methodist Church is **Ebb Tide,** which sells everything from jewelry and books to Androsia (colorful batik clothing made on Andros). For a truly Bahamian breakfast, try waterfront **Cap'n Jacks,** which serves boiled fish and homemade bread on Sunday mornings and cornbeef and grits on Mondays. At other times you might be able to sample turtle burgers here, along with fish, chicken, conch, and burgers.

The garden of the Wyannie Malone Museum is filled with greenery. Set within the low, stone-walls are coconut palms, hibiscus, Norfolk pine, crotons, and sea grape, among other plants. After all this vegetation, it is startling to see an empty area here, Cholera Cemetery, which was closed during the 19th century after a cholera epidemic. Graves and headstones are no longer in evidence. A nearby park, sporting a gazebo and filled with flowers, overlooks the beach. This is a wonderfully tranquil setting for cooling out.

At first glance, Hope Town Harbour Lodge seems just another of the clapboard houses along Queen's Highway. Then you notice that one wing has three stories, probably making it the tallest building in the Family Islands. An informal poll among conch fritter addicts reveals that this is the best place in town for these Bahamian snacks. The Sunday champagne brunch here also receives high marks. At night, the dart board in the bar is often the center of attention among the lively young crowd. Across the road, near the swimming pool on the ocean side, is the hotel's early 19th century Butterfly House, often rented by families.

Club Soleil, a restaurant across the harbor from town, will pick up diners at the post office dock and ferry them over. You can arrange transportation through your hotel or at Vernon's store. Rudy Malone, who runs Club Soleil with his wife, Kitty, happens to be Vernon's brother. As a matter of fact, the driftwood wall sculpture of Hope Town that adorns the breezy, pine-panelled dining room was done by Vernon. Windows all around provide spectacular views of the harbor. The confit of duck, poached red snapper with dill and white wine sauce, and the steak with herb butter are all highly recommended. Bring your meal to a close with Bahamian, Jamaican, Spanish, or Irish coffee. Club Soleil is closed on Mondays and serves only brunch on Sundays.

Rudy's Place and the dining room at **Abaco Inn,** both outside Hope Town, also provide complimentary transportation, from hotels and private homes. Abaco Inn is known for its multi-course gourmet meals. Many people renting private homes gather on the oceanview patio for cocktails before dinner. Serving dinner only, rustic wood-panelled Rudy's is closed on Sundays. Here the filling meals include conch fritters, soup (perhaps lima bean, potato, or broccoli), salad, warm freshly baked bread (maybe cinnamon raisin), and dessert. Entrees might include New York strip steak, lamb chops with mint jelly, and turtle steak sauteed with mushrooms. But the most popular choice is the crawfish, which is removed from its shell, lightly battered, fried, replaced, and baked with Parmesan cheese. Wine is available from France, Germany, Portugal, and the U.S. The night you dine, a child—the very serious son or daughter of one of the other workers—might be waiting tables. Rudy himself will periodically take a break from the kitchen to ensure that all is well in the dining room. A sign by the door reads, "All of our guests bring happiness—some by coming, others by going."

Near the Hope Town public dock, **Hope Town Dive Shop & Boat Rentals** (366–0029), which also sells ice, will see to your aquatic needs. Other operations to try for boat rentals or fishing guides are **Island Marine** (366–0282 or fax: 809/366–0281), **Day's Catch Charters** (366–0059), and **Sea Horse Boat Rentals** (367–2513 or fax: 809/366–0189). For exploring the island by land, rent bicycles in town or at Abaco Inn (where the use of bikes is gratis for guests). Be sure to take a ride or a walk outside town. Except for the occasional car and the distant motors of boats, the only sounds you'll hear in many areas will be birds conversing, the sudden scuttle of a curly-tailed lizard in the bushes, or the buzzing of a stray fly.

Just north of the center of town, a sandy road, cushioned by pine needles, is bordered by calm waters on one side and private oceanfront homes high on a bluff on the other. You'll pass a tiny offshore island topped by a sole house. Although the homes along the other side of this narrow strip of land obscure the view of the open ocean and the long white beach, you'll hear the crashing surf. Take a left where the road forks and you'll come to a small calm beach—if the tide is in, that is.

While Hope Town Harbour Lodge is right in town, the two other main accommodations, Abaco Inn and nearby Sea Spray Resort, are about two miles south in White Sound. At the southernmost tip of Elbow Cay, quiet palmshaded Tahiti Beach yields all kinds of shells and sand dollars.

Many people enjoy the bike ride from Abaco Inn to town. Take the bumpy dirt road parallel to the beach, keeping the ocean to your right. Turn left at the corner by the two houses with a row of 11 palms out front. (If you see a "NJ Turnpike" sign in front of a house, you'll know you've gone too far—unless you don't mind taking the longer route.) Not far from Abaco Inn, you'll pass Terry's Auto Repair. Terry's wife, Wanda, prepares homecooked take-out meals for vacationers upon request (366–0069). On the same street as the auto repair shop, **Sweeting's Grocery Store** is a good place to buy apple bananas (the miniature, exceptionally sweet variety), oversized avocados, and other produce.

The dirt road then curves to the right into a perpendicular paved road. Take the fifth right (back toward the sound of the ocean). You'll pass a small inlet on the left where a boat or two may be docked. The road curves left, now bordered by a low stone wall with bright fuschia and orange bougainvillea spilling over it. Then suddenly to your left, a spectacular view opens up of the red-and-white striped lighthouse and the boat-filled harbor. To your right is the harborside entrance to Hope Town Harbour Lodge, which gazes down on the road from its lofty perch.

If you'd rather walk to town, take the shorter route (which is too rugged even for mountain bikes). Instead of turning onto the street with Sweeting's Grocery and Terry's Auto Repair, continue straight, and you'll come to the narrow path that eventually intersects with the paved road to town.

Treasure Cay

Despite its misleading name, Treasure Cay is on the mainland and is second to Marsh Harbour as an Abaco entry point. Like Marsh Harbour, it is easily reached from most of the Abacos. The Treasure Cay Beach Resort, with its inviting coastline, is the out-island center for golf and tennis enthusiasts. From the dock, a brief taxi ride from the airport, ferries depart for Green Turtle Cay.

Treasure Cay was the first part of the Abacos to be settled after the Lucayan Indians were killed off by European explorers. Founded in the early 1780s, the town of Carleton was built by American colonists loyal to Britain. It stood near the northern end of Treasure Cay Beach. However, less than 90 days after the settlement was born, the 600 or so residents fell to fighting over when and how each person should work in the communal provisions store. Unable to come to an agreement, most of the population pulled up stakes, moving about 20 miles southeast, where they founded Marsh Harbour. Carleton eventually died out, after only a few years.

Green Turtle Cay

Green Turtle Cay, northwest of Marsh Harbour, is one of the most charming islands in The Bahamas. Unless they arrive by boat, travelers fly into Treasure Cay, then take a taxi to the nearby ferry. Like Hope Town on Elbow Cay, Green Turtle's tiny town of New Plymouth resembles areas of Cape Cod. During the 1800s, it was the most prosperous settlement in the Abacos. It brings to mind those British Loyalists who would not face the consequences of the American Revolution. It was to this island that the notorious pirate Vain the Great fled around 1717 after Woodes Rogers, the first royal governor, was sent to Nassau to wrest it from the buccaneers.

Although you can walk most places on the island, people usually get around by boat. When you arrive at the dock in New Plymouth, you'll be greeted by a row of small, handsome clapboard houses trimmed in pastel pinks, blues, and greens. Bushy palms and tropical flowers decorate streets and front yards enclosed by white picket fences. Away from the waterfront, you'll see goats and roosters as you walk along narrow, paved roads and you might hear children spelling in unison in a one-room schoolhouse. Barclay's, the lone bank, opens only once a week. Lobsters trapped offshore have become a thriving local export business for American restaurants. If you're staying somewhere with kitchen facilities, this is a good place to buy fresh lobster for dinner.

At **Sea View Restaurant,** you can have a hearty, inexpensive Bahamian meal before strolling down to the beach. The casual, friendly restaurant has patrons' business cards, photographs of visitors, and dollar bills plastered on the walls. Another popular local restaurant is **Rooster's Rest,** where the Gully Rooster band plays on weekends. At **Laura's Kitchen,** which sells conch, fish, chicken, and ice cream, you can order at the window, then eat on the breezy porch. Light meals are served between 9 a.m. and 3 p.m. at **Plymouth Rock Liquors & Cafe,** next to **Ocean Blue Gallery.** When in the mood for pastry, cool drinks, or local snacks, stop at **The Wrecking Tree Restaurant & Bar.** (The island's fanciest restaurants are found at **Bluff House** and the **Green Turtle Club** hotels, outside town.) For T-shirts, try the **Loyalist Rose Shoppe** or the **Sand Dollar Shoppe.**

Visitors who like to be enveloped by history may stay at the restored New Plymouth Inn, a former private home dating back to the mid-19th century. The inn's lively restaurant is a popular spot. More history is found at the Albert Lowe Museum, which has a collection of hand-carved ships as well as information about the little island's early settlers, and at the Memorial Sculpture Garden.

About a 15-minute walk from Bluff House and 5 from the Green Turtle Club, Coco Bay is one of the most beautiful crescents in the Bahamas. Shaded by casuarinas and lapped by calm waters, this long beach is often empty. The Green Turtle Club plans to build additional accommodations here. We hope they make the new structures as unobtrusive as possible. Farther along, the frothy waves thrash the island's Atlantic beach. The intense blue of the ocean here is set off by the stark white surf and sand. Unfortunately, however, in recent years this expansive ocean beach has become increasingly trash-strewn, with bottles and cans lying amid the pine needles at the edge of the sand. Pristine shores are found on nearby uninhabited islands such as Manjack Cay. Both Bluff House and the Green Turtle Club take guests there for picnics.

Walker's Cay and Grand Cay

Walker's Cay and Grand Cay are two tiny islands seemingly cast off by Abaco and left to drift into the Atlantic. Walker's Cay attracts fishermen who come in search of the abundant variety of marine life and boaters who pass through these small islands and others in the Bahamas chain. Most visitors stay at the lone hotel on Walker's Cay.

The vegetation here is markedly different from that of other Family Islands. You'll see few casuarinas, and many of the kind of gnarled old trees that are more common in the U.S. One surprise near the hotel is the ficus with its trunk growing around the trunk of a tall palmetto tree.

Take a guided tour of Aqualife, not far from the island's one hotel. This commercial operation produces tropical fish that will eventually end up in pet stores. The marine life, which comes mainly from the Pacific, is in various stages of development. The black fish with iridescent bright blue and purple stripes or orange and red tiger stripes are something to see. Swarming in black tanks, they look like thin neon lights flashing back and forth.

Most of the hotel's workers live across the water on Grand Cay, where everyone has a boat instead of a car. The popular **Island Club Bar and Restaurant,** also known as Rosie's, attracts visitors in their own boats for lunch and dinner, or transports them by water taxi. Rosie Curry owns the restaurant as well as a modest motel. Also on the island is the **Seaside Disco and Bar,** near a cut bordered by a tangle of mangroves. The bar's walls are decorated with the nicknames of such patrons as "Thatch," "Hitman Rev," 'T'he Sea Wolf," and "Flash Dancers." When they want a good beach, the locals, again by boat, take off for nearby Whale Bay Island, another minuscule dot in the Atlantic.

WHAT TO SEE AND DO

Sports • Serious divers go to Marsh Harbour, Walker's Cay, Elbow Cay, Green Turtle Cay, and Treasure Cay. Anglers and boaters have the run of the cays, with rewarding deep-sea fishing and convenient marinas. While boats can be rented in most areas, Marsh Harbour is the main sailing center. Tennis buffs can choose among Marsh Harbour, Treasure Cay, Green Turtle Cay, and the tonier Walker's Cay up north. Treasure Cay also has an 18-hole Dick Wilson–designed golf course. Windsurfing is available on Walker's Cay, Great Guana Cay, Elbow Cay, and Treasure Cay.

Sailing Destinations

*Manjack Cay • *north of Green Turtle Cay* • Through Bluff House, the Green Turtle Club, or on your own boat, take a day trip to this uninhabited island surrounded by some of The Bahamas' most beautiful sandy shores. The guide from Bluff House spears lobster, catches fish, and then cooks it right on the pine-rimmed beach along with other lunch goodies. The guide at the Green Turtle Club also prepares a great meal on the beach. There's plenty of time for swimming, jogging, relaxing, and drinking rum punch. Most visitors get a kick out of watching the baby nurse sharks that appear when the guides clean the fish and throw the entrails into the water.

Tilloo and Pelican Cays • *south of Elbow Cay* • Especially if you're based on Elbow Cay, excellent targets for a day's sail are pencil-thin Tilloo Cay and the tiny Pelican Cays, with their irresistible deserted beaches. The waters around Tilloo Cay, packed with grouper and conch, are particularly good for both fishing and swimming. In the Pelican

Cays Land and Sea Park, Sandy Cay Reef is one of the most colorful dive sites in the region. The area is protected, so line fishing, spearfishing, crawfishing, and shelling are all taboo.

Art Colony at Little Harbour • *south of Marsh Harbour, Great Abaco* • At this small, picturesque anchorage, you'll find the studio and home of Margot and Randolph Johnston, who run an art colony here. Margot's forte is ceramics while Randolph specializes in lost wax casting in bronze. Their creativity has been passed down to their son, Pete, who makes jewelry, among other items. Look for the sign by the dock that tells when the studio is open to visitors. Whether you stop by the art colony or not, be sure to stroll over to the old lighthouse and the ocean side of the narrow peninsula.

Local Shipbuilding • *Man-O-War Cay* • This cay was once one of the strongest contributors to the Bahamian economy as a center for shipbuilding. Although that industry has waned, some shipbuilding continues, and visitors may watch craftsmen at work. A sunken ship of the Union Navy, the U.S.S. *Adirondack,* lies off Man-O-War Cay. It was wrecked on a reef in the middle 1800s and can now be explored by divers.

*Sea and Land Preserve • *Fowl Cay* • North of Man-O-War Cay, Fowl Cay is a Bahamian government sea and land park reserve. Divers can explore undersea caves and the shallow reefs that are also accessible to snorklers.

Great Guana Cay • *northeast of Treasure Cay* • Divers and snorklers are enthusiastic about Great Guana Cay for its beaches and the coral and marine life seen in its clear water. The Treasure Cay Resort uses part of the island as a playground.

Green Turtle Cay

*Albert Lowe Museum • *New Plymouth* • This museum is housed in one of the village's historic buildings. Exhibits go back to the early Loyalist settlers and include much other Bahamian history. There is a collection of model ships built by the late Albert Lowe, for whom the museum is named. In a workshop at his nearby home, Vertrum Lowe, a son of Albert, carries on his father's nautical craft. The artwork of another son, Alton Lowe, one of the Bahamas' best-known artists, is on display at the museum, and you can purchase prints of his paintings. Also on sale here are silk scarves in hard-to-resist colors, Bahamian straw goods, and books on local history.

Memorial Sculpture Garden • *across from New Plymouth Inn* • Laid out in the pattern of the British flag, this garden honors residents of the Abacos, both living and dead, who have made historical contributions to the Bahamas. Busts sit on stone pedestals with plaques detailing each person's accomplishments. You'll learn about some of the American loyalists who came to the Bahamas from New England and the Carolinas, their descendants, and the descendants of the people who were brought as slaves. You'll see everyone from Albert Lowe—whose ancestors were among New Plymouth's first European-American settlers—to Jeanne I. Thompson—a black Bahamian, a contemporary playwright, and the country's second woman to practice law.

Elbow Cay

Hope Town Lighthouse • *Elbow Cay* • Before the installation of the lighthouse in 1863, many of Hope Town's inhabitants made a good living luring ships toward shore to be wrecked on the treacherous reefs and rocks so that their cargoes could be salvaged for cash. To safeguard their livelihoods, residents tried in vain to destroy the lighthouse while it was being built. Today people can climb the 130-foot red-and-white striped tower for sweeping views of the harbor and town. If you can't hitch a ride across the harbor to the lighthouse, arrange a visit through Dave Malone's Dive Shop in Hope Town or Abaco Inn in White Sound. Or if you take the morning ferry from Marsh Harbour to Elbow Cay, ask about being dropped off, then picked up a little while later.

Wyannie Malone Museum and Garden • *Hope Town, Elbow Cay* • The museum is a tribute to the South Carolinian widow who founded Hope Town in 1783. It gives some interesting details of the cay's history. The garden displays indigenous plants and trees. *Open 10 a.m.–noon.*

Tahiti Beach • *southern Elbow Cay* • This curving sandy stretch got its name from its thick wall of palms. At low tide, the shelling can be excellent. Bonefishing is also rewarding in these shallow waters. Picnics are periodically held here, and some residents have chosen this site for wedding receptions. Unfortunately, at one end of the otherwise pristine beach, someone has built a house so large and rambling that it looks like a resort. However, you can round a bend and put this intrusion out of sight. Across the cut, you'll see uninhabited Tilloo Cay and the thrashing waves of the Atlantic in the distance.

The beach is a pleasant, though up and downhill, bicycle ride from Abaco Inn (about 20 minutes) or the closer Sea Spray Resort & Villas. You might have to walk the bike up and down a few of the small but very rocky rises. Along the way, you'll pass seagrape trees, fluffy long-needled pines, and other varied roadside vegetation. Turn left when you come to a corner with a house on a bluff to your left. Go all the way to the end of this path, and you'll see the ocean crashing at Tilloo Cut in front of you. Turn right and follow that road past houses with barbed wire fences enclosing banana groves and pink and orange bougainvillea bushes. Walk through the dense palm grove to the beach. Since you'll be headed for the shore, which is public, ignore the "Private. No Trespassing" signs.

WHERE TO STAY

If you're interested in renting a private home on Elbow Cay, contact **Malone Estates** (Hope Town, Elbow Cay, Abaco, Bahamas; tel. 809/366–0100; or 809/366–0157 phone or FAX). Some houses have their own docks and laundry is often included in rates. For beach houses or garden villas in the Treasure Cay area, try **PGF Management & Rentals** (P.O. Box TC 4186, Treasure Cay, Abaco, Bahamas; tel. 809/367–2570, ext. 127).

Marsh Harbour

EXPENSIVE

☆☆☆ **Great Abaco Beach Hotel** • This modern hotel adjoins Boat Harbour Marina, with its extensive facilities. Guest rooms in the main building and the two-bedroom, two-bath villas all face the beach, backed by a palm grove, or the marina. Decorated in wicker and colorful prints, each bedroom has either two queen sized beds or one king. All units are air conditioned, with satellite TV, telephones, and sliding glass doors leading to balconies. Dressing areas with well-lit mirrors and built-in vanities add to the pleasure of a stay here. Tennis courts and swimming pools keep people active when not out on the ocean. In the attractive marina pool, you can swim under a bridge or float up to the bar for a drink. On weekends, there's live entertainment at Below Decks Lounge.

INEXPENSIVE

☆☆ **The Conch Inn** • The entrance to the Conch Inn is lined with palms. Although this hotel is only 10 minutes from the airport, its most enthusiastic guests are the boaters who come to tie up, have a drink at the bar, and join in the "wollyball" game that sometimes takes place in the pool. In addition to using its 67 slips, boaters who do not take rooms get everything from berths to baths as well as laundry services, mail, and messages. The needs of guests are seen to under the watchful eyes of the managers, who are always nearby when needed. Most rooms, furnished in sunny yellows and apple greens, have small terraces overlooking the marina and its moored boats and, sometimes, a spectacular sunset. The pleasant dining room has a view of the harbor and its twinkling night lights. The homemade potato chips and the grouper are both delicious. Another good restaurant and several shops are right next door to the Conch Inn. The beach is about a ten-minute walk away.

☆☆ **The Lofty Fig Villas** • Conveniently located across the road from restaurants, shops, and a marina, these housekeeping cottages surround a bean-shaped swimming pool. The smooth lawns are set off by bursts of bougainvillea and other attractive plantings. Each cottage, air conditioned and with ceiling fans, has a large screened-in patio, full kitchen, and both a double and single bed. A ten-minute stroll will take you to the beach. Bicycles are available for rent.

Elbow Cay

MODERATE

★★★**Abaco Inn** • At this small resort on a narrow strip of Elbow Cay, the ocean's froth-crested surf washes the beach on one side while the tranquil waters of White Sound bathe the other. Overlooking the ocean is a sunbleached gazebo and a salt-water swimming pool. Tucked away a bit up the shore, a secluded area is reserved for guests who enjoy bathing in the buff. Hammocks wide enough for two are strung outside the various cottages where rooms are located. In the six oceanview units, vacationers fall asleep to the sound of crashing surf. Completely renovated in 1991, the six smaller harborside rooms look out to pines and a sliver of water. While the cottages are rustically furnished, they are perfectly comfortable, with a homelike feel. All have books left behind by previous travelers. Some rooms are air conditioned, while ceiling fans cool the air in others.

The focal point of Abaco Inn is the main building, where a stone fireplace commands the inner lounge. Before dinner, guests and vacationers renting private homes gather for cocktails here and at the bar on the screened-in harborview porch. Choices for the five-course evening meal might include cream of spinach soup; salad with raspberry vinaigrette dressing; warm freshly baked Bahamian nut bread; and chicken breast stuffed with mushrooms, onions, peppers, and cheddar cheese. Chocolate peppermint silk, hot apple coconut crisp, or key lime pie might be on the dessert menu. Calories can be burned off by riding the mountain bikes that are lent gratis to guests and rented to outsiders. Upon request, travelers can be driven by van to Hope Town, a couple of miles away. Those who rent boats or are sailing their own should be sure to visit nearby Shell Island, where the lovely beach is great for shelling.

Club Soleil Resort • Built by Rudy Malone and his Dutch wife Kitty, the owners of the popular neighboring restaurant by the same name, this waterfront hotel is nearly completed as we go to press. Lunch will be served on the deck surrounding the freshwater swimming pool. Guests will be ferried across the harbor into town. They can walk to the beach from there. Boat rentals will also be available.

Hope Town Hideaways • Another new establishment on Elbow Cay, this collection of brightly decorated, modern cottages sits across the harbor from the center of town. Panelled in white-washed wood, each unit has a large kitchen with a long counter and stools, two bedrooms, and two baths. Daybeds are in the sunny living rooms, which, along with bedrooms, open onto spacious decks. A freshwater swimming pool is being built. Rooms are cooled by ceiling fans. Club Soleil Restaurant is right next door.

INEXPENSIVE

☆☆☆**Hope Town Harbour Lodge** • Sandwiched between a gorgeous stretch of stark white beach and the harbor with its red-and-white striped lighthouse, this hotel is right in town. Perched on a bluff, it's a great vantage point for some of Elbow Cay's most appealing views. Originally from Boston, co-owner Mark Sullivan came to Hope Town Harbour Lodge as a chef in 1980. Ten years later, he married the woman who has owned the hotel since 1977, Laddie Wilhoyte Sullivan, who hails from San Francisco. Together they offer guests a welcome dose of personal attention. The lodge is known for its excellent dinners, served in the wood-panelled dining room off the bar and lounge. The Sunday champagne brunch is another popular meal here. Norris Smith, the young European-trained Bahamian chef, has been at the helm for years. At night, visitors and locals often play darts in the convivial bar.

Rooms are located in the main building, in cottages by the freshwater swimming pool, and in nineteenth-century Butterfly House, one of the oldest surviving buildings in Hope Town. This historic two-story house with hardwood floors sports a living room, bedroom, and full kitchen downstairs, and both a double and a single bed in the attic. The hotel's other guest rooms are plain but comfortable. Some have twin beds while others have queens or a double and a twin. The closets of those in the main wing are located in the bathrooms. Cross breezes usually make staying in rooms that aren't air conditioned perfectly pleasant.

★★★**Sea Spray Resort** • Here in White Sound, 3½ miles from Hope Town, the oceanside and harborside cottages range from one-bedroom, one-bath to two-bedroom, two-bath. Grounds are handsomely landscaped. Built in 1989, oceanside Sea Mist Villa is the newest, with blond wood panelling, a modern kitchen with generous counter space, a dining area, two bedrooms, two full baths, and a sunny living room with two day beds. Sea Grape is also especially nice. Although Sea Spray Villa was built around 1980, it was recently refurbished. All cottages have decks, barbecue pits, air-conditioned bedrooms, and ceiling fans. Oceanside units, on a bluff overlooking the somewhat rocky beach, all have queen-sized beds. Maid service is provided, and playpens and cribs are available.

Guests, as well as people staying elsewhere on Elbow Cay, can arrange to have meals catered by Belle Albury (366–0065), the mother of owner Monty Albury, who lives on the property with his wife. Among Belle's specialties are cracked conch, pork chops, fish, and all kinds of baked goods. The harborfront club house, where Monty and his father used to build boats, now houses a pool table. Docking is convenient for sailors, and 17′ to 22′ boats are rented here. Use of sunfish and windsurfers is free to guests, who can also take day sails with a captain. One free transfer is provided to and from Hope Town. Bikes can be rented at Abaco Inn, down the road a piece. A 20- to 30-minute hike will take guests to scenic Tahiti Beach. Sweeting's is the closest grocery store.

Benny's Place • On a steep unpaved road near Abaco Inn in the White Sound area, this large two-story wooden building houses modest housekeeping apartments. Many guests are young surfers and others on limited budgets. The breezy upstairs balcony overlooks the greenery that slopes down to the calm harbor. Although you can't see the ocean from here, you can hear the crashing waves. The tiny hillside swimming pool provides a marvelous view, but it may or may not be filled with water when you visit. This accommodation is run by Margaret and Roger ("Benny") Sweeting, whose family owns the grocery store down the road. Roger received his nickname because of his resemblance to the British TV character Benny Hill.

Great Guana Cay

MODERATE

☆☆ **Guana Beach Resort & Marina** • For total escape, book a room at this hotel on an unspoiled island near Marsh Harbour. Instead of telephones and cars, you'll find seven miles of virtually empty beaches, a freshwater swimming pool, and hammocks strung between palms. The hotel deck is great for sunset watching. Vacationers spend their time sailing (Sunfish are complimentary to guests), fishing, snorkeling, scuba diving, shelling, and simply soaking up sun. Each villa contains a kitchen, and rooms are all air conditioned, with ceiling fans as well. The hotel picks up guests twice a day from Marsh Harbour at Mangoes Restaurant, a brief taxi ride from the airport.

Treasure Cay

MODERATE

Treasure Cay Beach Hotel & Villas • We hope that now that this resort has reopened under new management, the wave of decline that washed over it since becoming all-inclusive will be history. At press time, there are big plans to refurbish. A small village in itself, Treasure Cay Beach Hotel & Villas is served by the island's northern airport, about fifteen minutes away. A deeply curved, 3½-mile, white sand beach offers such attractions as fishing, sailing, scuba, snorkeling and aqua biking. Near the boat-filled marina is one of the resort's three swimming pools. Next door is the dive shop providing the full range of watersports equipment. In addition to the 18-hole Dick Wilson-designed golf course, there are both hard and soft tennis courts, and four are lit for games after dark. A night club is on premises. Cars and bicycles can be rented for exploration of the island. Guests can find secluded beaches and colorful settlements nearby.

Green Turtle Cay

MODERATE

★★★★**Green Turtle Club •** Born as a yachtsman's hangout in the 1960s, Green Turtle Club now welcomes all kinds of travelers. After the beginning of a $2.7 million renovation, some rooms have been completely redone Colonial style, putting them among the most upscale in The Bahamas. Twenty-five thousand dollars was spent on each refurbished unit, and it shows: Mahogany headboards and dressers; oriental throw rugs and vases; oak floors; wood-trimmed doors; bedspreads, dust ruffles, and drapes imported from France; snazzy baths with dressing areas; and terra-cotta tiles on patios. Individual rooms, suites, and villas with private docks are available. All have air conditioning, ceiling fans, clock radios, and refrigerators or full kitchens.

In the bar/lounge in the clubhouse, yachting club flags hang from the ceiling beams and the walls are papered with dollar bills. During the days when commercial flights to the Family Islands were limited or nonexistent, private pilots, many of whom had flown in World War II, would write their names on dollars, paste them to the walls, and say, "If I don't come back, have a drink on me." Other visitors have carried on this old wartime tradition (and taken it a bit further). While people gather in the lounge for cocktails, it is not unusual to see a man hoist a woman onto his shoulders so that she may stick a bill on the ceiling. Managers Bill and Donna Rossbach run Green Turtle Club as if they were entertaining friends in their home. There is one seating for dinner, and Donna escorts guests into the elegant dining room, table by candle-lit table. The delicious food is beautifully presented. With live bands, the Wednesday night patio parties draw locals and visitors from all over the island.

The ocean beach is about a 10-minute walk from the clubhouse and the calmer beach at Coco Bay is about five minutes from the hotel. Plans are in the works to build additional rooms here. The reef just 50 yards off the hotel's shore makes for excellent snorkeling. Brendal's Dive Shop, which also rents bicycles, has a very good diving and snor-keling program. There is a large pool as well as tennis. Guests have free use of snorkeling gear, fishing tackle, and windsurfers. Those who aren't in the mood for the long walk into town may take the compli-mentary boat ride. The hotel can arrange for guests to play golf at nearby Treasure Cay.

★★★ **Bluff House Club & Marina** • Many people make a habit of returning to this beautiful hotel perched high above a beach. The view of the water from the main house and pool deck is breathtaking. Some say the wooded trails and dirt paths remind them of summer camp. Especially since wooden boardwalks and stairs lead up and down throughout the hilly property, this is not the place for heels or for people who have trouble walking. There are suites, villas with full kitchens, and individual rooms. Over the years, Bluff House has expanded from 8 guest rooms in the main house to more than 30 in various wings. All have private porches. Some of the modern, air-conditioned units are duplexes. Appointments include wicker chairs, floral conches, ginger jar lamps, weathered wood paneling, and wall-to-wall carpeting. The sunny split-level main house lounge, overlooking the pool and the ocean, is decorated with tiles, paintings, and framed posters. In the dining room, where guests get to know each other at large tables, many people ask to be seated at the huge round oak table in the center, with its high-backed chairs. The personal attention of the warm staff, the beautiful beach, and the good food create many repeat guests. Boat rides to the town of New Plymouth and to the Wednesday-night parties at the Green Turtle Club are free to those staying here. Tennis and rackets are also complimentary. The staff will arrange fishing and snorkeling excur-sions.

★★ **New Plymouth Inn** • Staying at this old home with high ceil-ings and antique furniture may make you think you've slipped back in time. The 10 inviting guest rooms, all with private baths, have old-fashioned quilts on the beds, attractive floral wallpaper, and handsome chairs and chests. Books line shelves in the hallway. A large octagonal Mexican brasero table sits in the center of the living room. Instead of coals in the center, you'll see fresh hibiscus. The shell of a giant turtle hangs on a wicker partition in the bar area. Paintings decorate the walls, and lanterns hang from the ceiling. The inn was once the home of Captain Billy Roberts, whose ghost is said to appear from time to time. But don't let that scare you away from this charming place. While New Plymouth is located in town, it has a pool, and beaches are not far. Guests can also arrange to go boating, diving, and fishing.

INEXPENSIVE

☆☆**Coco Bay Club** • These three rental cottages, with fully equipped kitchens, are in an excellent location. The land is so narrow here that guests are right near both the ocean and the bay. The two small two-bedroom cottages are paneled in dark pine. Louvered doors divide the bedrooms from the kitchens. Although the three-bedroom cottage is not always available for rent (the owners often use it), it's definitely worth asking about. It has a huge modern kitchen/dining/living room with bright white cabinets, rattan furniture, and a wonderful ocean view. Many fruit trees grow on the grounds, including those bearing sweet and sour oranges, mangos, papayas, and tangerines. Guests are welcome to help themselves (as long as they aren't gluttons, the managers say). Boat rentals and fishing trips can be arranged through Coco Bay.

★★**Linton's Beach and Harbour Cottages** • There are only two rental cottages here, with two bedrooms each, and they are on a long quiet beach. This is a good choice if privacy and complete comfort are what you want. With high-beamed ceilings, walls paneled in rich brown Abaco pine, ceiling fans, rattan furniture, and screened-in porches with hammocks, each is quite attractive. Linens and all kitchen utensils are supplied. Maid and cook service is available for an additional $45 a day. Many palmettos, seagrapes, white lilies, avocado trees, and huge casuarinas surround the cottages. Near the manager's house on the bay side you can relax in a hammock in a small screened-in cottage called "the Conch Out Lounge."

☆ **Sea Star Cottages** • These four housekeeping cottages are in extensive shady grounds along a long narrow beach. You'll see breadfruit trees, pigeon plum trees, and even bamboo. Fishing groups not looking for posh accommodations are attracted to these simple cottages, which are generally rented by the week. Town is about a 15-minute walk away.

Walker's Cay

MODERATE

☆☆**Walker's Cay Hotel & Marina** • This is the only hotel on this minute island. When the plane lands, it seems to be headed directly for the water on the other side of the island. Boaters and fishermen come to the hotel in droves. Other guests are not always as enthusiastic; the hotel is not on a beach and what beaches there are are unmemorable. The hotel has modern rooms in two buildings as well as separate villas. The rooms are spacious and comfortable, with balconies. Rooms in the Hibiscus wing are motel-like, while those in the Coral wing are more upscale. The fishing orientation is reflected in the bar-lounge, where the walls are adorned with giant barracuda, bonefish, sharks, and marlin. There are also photographs of fishermen posing with their catches. The energetic head for the two swimming pools, one salt and the other fresh, and the multipurpose Sport Court where guests can have a go at tennis as well as paddle tennis, pickle ball, basketball, hockey, "wacketball," and soccer tennis. The Lobster Trap—the bar, billiard room, and disco at the marina—is the place to go on weekends. The marina also has showers and a grocery and supply store for boaters.

ACKLINS & CROOKED ISLAND

Together Acklins and Crooked Island comprise an almost 200-square-mile area and are about 223 miles southeast of Nassau. The narrow Crooked Island Passage, separating the two islands and sprinkled with tiny cays, is still an important sea lane on the southern route. Twice a week, planes visit Spring Point on Acklins and Colonel Hill on Crooked Island.

The islands are a point of interest for fishermen, boaters cruising the southern Bahamas, and devoted divers, all of whom are attracted to the fishing and diving possibilities off Landrail Point on Crooked Island. Since the islands hardly swarm with tourists, those who do come can expect leisure and serenity at one of the few places of accommodation.

The first known settlers of these islands were Loyalists who arrived toward the end of the eighteenth century. Soon almost 50 plantations had sprung up, with hundreds of slaves working the fields. But by the

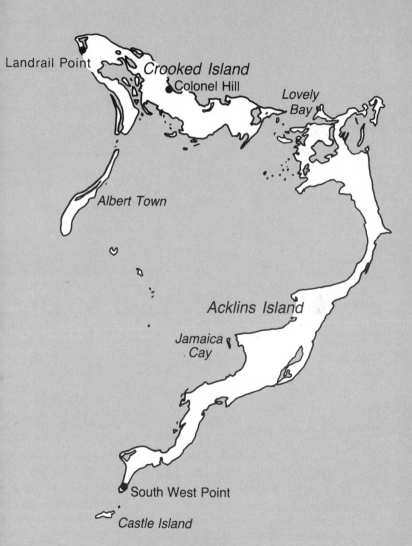

Acklins-Crooked Island

1820s most of the plantations lay in ruins, the crops having been destroyed by blight.

Most activity is centered on the smaller, 70-square-mile Crooked Island. This is where visitors find the one resort, Pittstown Point Landing, and a few guest houses. The mailboat from Nassau makes the overnight trip twice a month. Small farming and fishing are the principal industries and a fish processing plant is under development. There are few telephones and communication is mainly by CB and marine radio.

Crooked Island's capital is Colonel Hill, a small settlement with colorfully painted wood and cement buildings. In Church Grove stands tiny **Tiger Bar,** the first drinking establishment on the island. Every Friday night, dances are held at the **Bloom of the Valley** bar and pool hall, across the street from the **Hillside Grocery** store. There are other minute settlements, such as Cripple Hill, with about a dozen residents; Moss Town, with the houses clustered around the Anglican church; and, to the northeast, Landrail Point where nearly all the residents are Seventh Day Adventists.

Beyond Landrail Point are several private, beachfront homes owned by Americans and other foreigners. At a salt pond, just outside of town, you'll see flamingos, tropical birds with long, thin tails, mocking birds, finches, wild canaries, and humming birds. The 33 miles of barrier reef off the islands make for excellent diving and snorkeling. Boats are unnecessary for seeing the exciting coral formations and colorful fish. Masks and fins are all that are needed.

Pilots were the first to ''discover'' Crooked Island in the fifties and built some of the early beachfront homes. One American describes the island as ''the kind of place where, if I lost my wallet, someone would look inside to see who it belonged to, then walk two miles to return it.''

A government-provided ''ferry'' at the southeast tip of Crooked Island takes visitors across to Lovely Bay on Acklins. Driving from Pittstown Point Landing to the ferry takes about an hour and a quarter. Hard woods such as mahogany and lignum vitae are found on Acklins, as well as the bark used to make Campari. Many of the houses on the island have dirt-floored, separate kitchens. In some, a corn grinder, used for making one of the staples, grits, stands in the corner. Although weatherbeaten, some houses are painted startlingly bright shades of purple, green, blue, and orange. Built in 1867 off Acklins' southern tip, the Castle Island Lighthouse guides ships through a passage that was once used by pirates escaping pursuit.

WHAT TO SEE AND DO

Bird Rock Lighthouse • *Crooked Island Passage* • If there were more visitors, the gleaming-white Bird Rock Lighthouse guarding Crooked Island Passage would be as famed and photographed as the lighthouse at Hope Town in the Abacos. This is a popular nesting spot for ospreys.

*Crooked Island Caves • Like many other islands in The Bahamas, Crooked Island is riddled with caves. These look like majestic, ancient cathedrals, or medieval castles that have fallen into ruins. It is best to explore them with a Bahamian guide arranged through Pittstown Point Landing. Dark, narrow, low passageways suddenly widen into gaping chambers. Fingers of sunlight poke through holes high above. Clusters of harmless bats cling to the ceilings and begin squealing and crawling when flashlight beams hit them. No, you probably won't find drawings of the ancient Arawaks who once inhabited the caves. However, more recent visitors have certainly scratched their names into the stone.

*Southwestern Beaches • *Crooked Island* • Accessible only by boat, these shores are some of the island's best. As you approach, schools of flying fish, resembling flocks of birds, jump out of the water and sail through the air before dipping back in. Snorkelers head for Shell Beach, where coral heads loom beneath the clear water and large slabs of coral rock lie along the coast. In some areas, the layered rock looks strangely like ancient crumbling stone steps. At Bathing Beach, the light turquoise water reveals an immense expanse of sandy ocean floor, completely free of rocks and seaweed. Look for the inland freshwater springs. The location may still be marked by a pile of stones on shore. Make arrangements at Pittstown Point Landing to cruise to these beaches.

*French Wells • *Crooked Island* • It would be difficult to find a more serene part of the island. Flamingos often beach here, near a narrow passage lined with a jumble of mangroves. If you come by power boat, turn off the motor and listen to the quiet. You'll look through crystal water at barracudas and other fish. Sharks have been sighted in this area, so don't go swimming.

Marine Farm • *North end of Crooked Island Passage* • This is the ruin of a Bahamian fort. It was built by Britain to guard Crooked Island

Passage against marauding pirates. Although rusted, markings on the cannons are well-preserved.

Mayaguana • *across the Mayaguana Passage, and flanked by Acklins and Crooked Islands as well as Inagua* • The 24-mile long island has few more than 400 inhabitants, who are almost completely out of touch with the capital at Nassau. The forests are rich in hardwoods, especially lignum vitae. The U.S. has established a missile-tracking station on the island. There are two acceptable harbors, inviting beaches, and astounding vistas. Because there are no accommodations for tourists, Mayaguana is visited mainly by boaters. It remains quiet, undeveloped, and undisturbed.

WHERE TO STAY

INEXPENSIVE

☆☆☆ **Pittstown Point Landing** • This hotel is 16 miles from the Colonel Hill airport. If there are no taxis, by asking at the airport you'll find a driver who'll charge from $25 to $40 for the trip to the hotel. The hotel has its own airstrip and most guests arrive in their own private planes. The management will arrange for guests to be flown in from Florida, Nassau, or George Town in Exuma. The rooms, with two double beds, bright baths, and good reading lights, are comfortable but somewhat spartan. The bar, separated from the dining room by the kitchen, is built around what is said to be the first post office in The Bahamas. Guests get to know each other over meals, games, drinks, discussions about birds sighted during the day, and, of course planes. Guests also get to know the staff. The cook often doubles as a waitress; the bartender might take a group on an excursion to the caves, or the assistant manager might take guests bonefishing. The gift shop, where the register is signed, sells Androsia batik resort wear as well as T-shirts, books, film and toilet articles. Things are casual, although house rules are outlined in a booklet found in your room. In regard to proper dinner attire, for example, it says, "Hair on the chest and low cleavage are great but distract the attention from things on your plate."

Crooked Island Beach Inn • *Colonel Hill* • Owned and operated by Ezekial Thompson, a Bahamasair agent, this comfortable rustic inn has eleven rooms and is near the airport. Guests can arrange for meals, although there are kitchens, and cars can be rented for about $50 per day.

ANDROS

Andros, 108 miles long, about 40 miles across at its widest point, and covering 2300 square miles, is the largest of the Bahama islands. It is interlaced with channels, bays, bights, and inlets. These waterways—called creeks by locals but seeming more like bays, rivers, and open sea to outsiders—divide the island into three main sections.

Running almost parallel to the east coast is the awesome 120-mile-long Andros Barrier Reef, which is in the league of Australia's Great Barrier Reef and the one off Belize. Multicolored marine life of all kinds is found in these waters. Ocean blue holes, fathomless fresh-water columns of deep cobalt and ultramarine rising from the depths, are also offshore. Benjamin's Blue Hole is one that has attracted wide interest. In 1967 Dr. George Benjamin found stalactites and stalagmites 1200 feet under the sea. His conclusion was that The Bahamas are really the peaks of former mountains, since such formations never occur under water. Benjamin's Blue Hole and Uncle Charley's Blue Hole have been featured in the Jacques Cousteau television series on oceanic exploration. In addition, more than 100 inland holes have also been found on the island. Examples are Captain Bill's, near Andros Town and Evansville, not far from Nicholl's Town. The island is also riddled with intricate underground caves such as those at Morgan's Bluff.

Andros has the best farming land in The Bahamas as well as an abundance of plant life found nowhere else. It is said to be the home of nearly 50 kinds of wild orchids. A new species of peony, the white-petaled P. *mascula* subspecies *hellenica,* was recently discovered here, according to Niki Goulandris, a botanist and botanical painter.

Plans are in the works to increase tourism on Andros. As the largest of the islands, there is lots of room for development as well as some tourist-worthy sights and attractive, varied landscapes. A hotel is proposed for a site high on Morgan's Bluff, overlooking the channel from which, at night, the sparkling lights of Nassau can be seen. Near completion is the rebuilding of a superbly situated former luxury resort at Fresh Creek called Andros Town Lighthouse Hotel and Marina. In South Andros, Driggs Hill Club House & Marina is underway.

If on schedule, the mailboat stops weekly at Morgan's Bluff, Mastic Point, Stafford Creek, Fresh Creek, and Mangrove Cay. The boat brings supplies to the various points and returns with deliveries and passengers. The arrival of the mailboat is a signal for a social occasion, with locals suspending their activities to see who and what is arriving and to catch up on bits of news and gossip. Similar gatherings also take place at the airports of Andros, which are located in the north at San Andros, near the center of the island at Andros Town, and farther south at Moxey Town and Congo Town.

Fishing and Hunting

Andros is known as the bonefish capital of the world. Marlins and tarpons are found in the surrounding waters as well as reef-seekers such as snapper, amberjack, yellowtail, and grouper. Several fishing lodges are south of Fresh Creek. Three of the nicest are the upscale Cargill Creek Fishing Lodge and the Andros Island Bonefishing Camp, next door to each other near Cargill Creek, and Charlie's Haven in Behring Point. During the summer, land crabs crawl across the beaches to lay their eggs. Beachcombers can simply pick up the crabs and have one or two for dinner.

The forests are thick with pine, mahogany, and other tropical trees. These woods are an excellent habitat for quail, ducks, partridges, marsh hens, and parrots, which are hunted by enthusiastic nimrods during the September through March season. In September and October, hunters in camouflage fatigues hunt white crown pigeons in the forests of South Andros.

History and Folklore

Andros, then populated by Lucayan Indians, is said to have been visited by the Spaniards in search of slave labor to work in Hispaniola. Both during and after the Seminole Wars in the United States, Seminole and Creek Indians, African slaves, and escaped slaves who had intermarried with Native Americans fled Florida to northern Andros. They landed at Joulter Cays and later filtered south to the mainland at what is now Morgan's Bluff and Red Bay. Other former slaves, freed by the British, came from Exuma and Long Island on the other side of the Tongue of the Ocean, settled in southern Andros, and took up farming.

Later in the 19th century, sponging became a thriving and lucrative industry in Andros. This undersea organism was found in abundant supply off the mud flats of the southwest coast. Until then, the chief industry had been ship wrecking for often very valuable cargoes. Sponging continued until the late 1930s, when an unknown blight killed only the sponges and no other marine life. Another profitable industry was sisal production, the plant used in rope making. Sisal grew well in the Andros soil, but this industry also waned in the early 1920s. From the '60s until well into the '70s, the U.S. company Owens-Illinois harvested

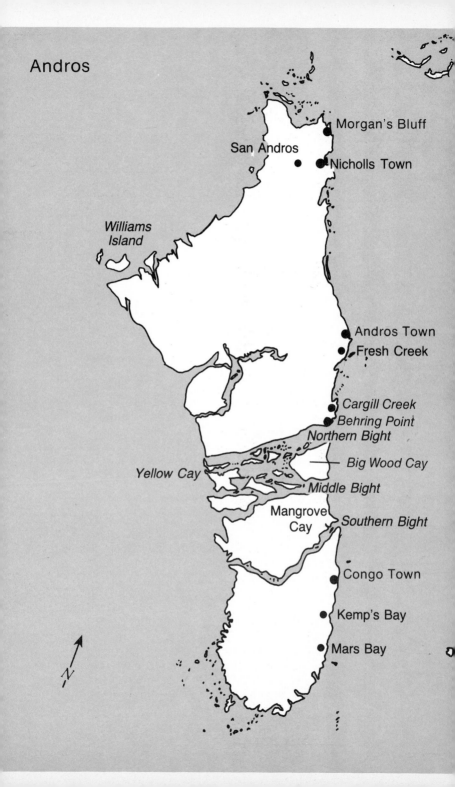

Andros timber for pulp production. To facilitate shipment, a system of crushed limestone roads was built by the company. The roads remain, now somewhat in disrepair, but that industry, too, departed leaving a pocket of unemployment.

Sir Henry Morgan, the notorious pirate, is said to have established his headquarters in north Andros at the point now called Morgan's Bluff, which looks out toward the Berry Islands. According to legend, Morgan buried some of his ill-gotten treasure near the site. However, searches both serious and frivolous have uncovered nothing.

Another persistent legend tells tales of chickcharnies. These are impish, mischievous, red-eyed, feathered creatures with three-toes and three-fingers and a long, prehensile tail. Some say chickcharnies have the ability to turn their heads completely around. They are said to live in the pine and hardwood forests of Andros and are not found on any of the other islands.

If a wanderer happens upon a chickcharney and treats it well, then blessings and good fortune follow. However, if the chickcharney is mistreated, the wanderer can be struck by the direst misery, which can last a lifetime. Having done its mischief, the chickcharney scampers merrily off into the forest. Today, locals with a twinkle in their eyes warn each other of the wrath of mischievous chickcharnies and frighten naughty children into obedience.

Red Bay Village is said to be near the home of a primitive people who maintain old tribal traditions, still use bows and arrows, and dwell in the forests. Although this belief persists, no evidence of such people has been found. Some believe that the legendary tribe are descendants of the mixed Africans and Seminoles who fled slavery and war in Florida.

Northern Andros

In North Andros the distinctive, unusually tall, straight pines look like telephone poles with trees stuck on top. Most of the action in this area is in Nicholl's Town. Many divers and other vacationers stay here at the Andros Beach Hotel, where the staff will be happy to arrange guided trips to see the tallest pines or to the caves in nearby Morgan's Bluff. The hotel bar is a popular hangout for locals and tourists. Formerly part of the hotel, the 40 modern villas bordering the two adjacent streets are now owned by Americans, Canadians, and other foreigners. A small shopping center, with a bank, a drugstore, a liquor store, and a grocery store, is just down the street.

The residential road leading to the tiny town is filled with the sound of roosters crowing to each other. The small, colorfully painted wooden houses are overhung with palm fronds and the bright green leaves of banana trees. A 15-minute walk to town will take you past stores such as **Curry's Grocery** and **Wellie's Variety,** and the popular **Picaroon Restaurant** near the beach. Mr. and Ms. Henfield have run the restaurant, affectionately called Picaroonie's by locals, for over 25 years. They serve chicken, ribs, and fish Bahamian style. Next door at the Henfield's gift shop, you can rent bicycles for about $12 a day.

Other good restaurants in town are **Hunter's** with a bar and satellite television, and **Donna Lee's.** Both also have inexpensive guest rooms and often give parties on weekends to which everyone, including tourists, is invited. If you didn't rent a car at the airport or through the Andros Beach Hotel, you can rent one at Hunter's. **Pinewood Cafeteria** and **Paula's Inn** also serve homestyle food. About two miles south of Nicholl's Town, at Conch Sound, is a tiny settlement devoted to fishing and boat repair. It was once the site of a thriving local boat construction industry. The boats were then used primarily for spongers.

Not far from Nicholls Town, in the Pleasant Harbour area, are nicely landscaped beachfront homes owned by foreigners. When the tide is low you can walk out to uninhabited Money Cay to collect colorful shells.

Some seven miles south of the San Andros airport is The Bahamas Agricultural Research Centre. Presently headed by Dr. Godfrey Springer, a Tuskegee Institute–trained veterinarian, BARC advises and assists local farmers in obtaining maximum production from their land. The center was established in 1973 through the cooperation of the U.S. agency for International Development and the Bahamian government. Visitors are welcomed to the facility and given informative tours. At the center's large packing house hangar, vegetables such as potatoes, okra, cucumbers, cabbage, tomatoes, and some grains are brought in for sorting, grading, packing, and shipment to Nassau. Other products grown on Andros are papayas, cantaloupes, strawberries, and a variety of citrus fruits. Another section of the center is devoted to breeding and raising improved strains of horses, cattle, and other livestock such as sheep, hogs, and poultry. Dr. Springer attests that there is no rabies in The Bahamas and that a rigid inspection program is in force for meats such as beef and mutton.

Andros supplies much of the nation's fresh water. The two-million gallon reservoir off Queen's Highway between Nicholl's Town and the San Andros airport produces more than six million gallons of potable water each day, a record for The Bahamas. Almost three million gallons of water are shipped by barge each day from the port at Morgan's Bluff to New Providence, just 20 miles across the channel. Because the deep Tongue of the Ocean divides the channel, barges are the only way of transporting fresh water across. One of the engineers says that bad weather sometimes interrupts water shipments and worries that continued development and growth in Nassau might soon overtax the supply.

Andros Town and Fresh Creek

Most visitors to Andros Town, south of Nicholl's Town, stay at Small Hope Bay Lodge. Before the lodge was built in 1960, this area had no roads, electricity, or running water, and only one telephone. While this part of Andros has come a long way since then, it is still mainly undeveloped, with just a few small settlements here and there. If you go bike riding, you'll notice that people in cars will wave to you as they pass.

Many locals consider the beaches in Staniard Creek, about 10 miles north of Andros Town, the nicest around. **Prince Monroe's** is a popular restaurant here. **Androsia Batik Works,** which began in 1973 at Small Hope Bay Lodge, is at the edge of nearby Fresh Creek. This factory, which produces brightly colored resort wear and decorative batiks, has been a real boon to the island's economy. It is on the grounds of the former Lighthouse Club, a luxurious resort built by a Swedish millionaire in the '50s. Although the club has been torn down, another one is rising in its place, on the shore of a wide creek where masted houseboats bob. In the old club's heyday, peacocks strolled through the attractive grounds. Royal palms and lush colorful plantings still remain.

Good local restaurants in Fresh Creek include **Papa Gay's** on the waterfront, which sells chicken in a bag; the dining room in tiny **Chickcharnie's Hotel; Skinny's Landmark Restaurant;** and the somewhat more upscale **Golden Conch.** At midday, you'll see people clustered around cars and trucks selling home-cooked beef stew, peas and rice, cole slaw, potato salad, and other local favorites. In this drowsy town where the quiet is punctured by crowing roosters, you'll also find stores such as **Turpi's Straw Market** and **Rosie's Gift Shop,** which sells T-shirts and other items.

The peaceful town of Calabash Bay is within walking distance of Small Hope Bay Lodge. On weekends, the Samson Center opens as a bar and disco, where many teenagers gather. On nights when the moon is full, the walk along the beach to Calabash Bay is especially pleasant. **Minnes' Diamond Bar** is one of the oldest bars in the area. Cyril Minnes, the owner, is nicknamed ''Twenty-Four Hours'' because he can almost always be seen sitting outside watching life happen. During the summer, there are church fairs practically every weekend to raise money for various causes.

On the way to the freshwater Captain Bill's Blue Hole from Small Hope Bay Lodge, you'll pass bushes that partially obscure ''pothole'' farms, where corn, cassava, pigeon peas, sugar cane, and bananas are grown. These farms are called potholes because the soil has accumulated in small depressions in the land. You'll also pass the pretty settlement of Love Hill, where there are several churches, but no bars (usually it's one for one). Here **L & S** is a local restaurant owned by taxi driver/

bartender Linwood Johnson, who often puts in appearances at the Cargill Creek Fishing Lodge. He claims his chicken or pigfeet souse, served for breakfast, will do wonders for a hangover. Also on the menu are cracked conch, peas and rice, and baked goods such as benny cake (made from sesame seeds), peanut cake, and coconut cake.

Divers appreciate the proximity of the Andros Barrier Reef to shore. Many are enthusiastic about the extensive dive programs offered by Small Hope Bay Lodge and the Andros Beach Hotel. So much marine life lies close to beaches that snorkelers get as excited as scuba divers.

A station of the Atlantic Undersea Testing and Evaluation Center (AUTEC) is located at Fresh Creek. This research station is jointly operated by the British and U.S. governments. It was established in 1966 as an antisubmarine research center and is protected from heavy ocean traffic by the offshore Tongue of the Ocean chasm.

Central and Southern Andros

The central and southern parts of Andros are even less built up than the north. Towns, few and far between, are smaller and quieter. In Cargill Creek, about 30 miles south of Fresh Creek, **Green View** restaurant specializes in cracked conch, lobster, and peas and rice. Not far from Cargill Creek Fishing Lodge and the tiny, quiet settlement of Behring Point, Bigwood Cay is the largest islet in Andros. Fishing guides charge about $50 to drop a group of people off at the long, wide, pine-shaded beach here and pick them up later. Manta rays glide through the clear, shallow water, and you can wade out to bonefish just off shore. Turning the Atlantic a pale turquoise, the sandbar known as Bigwood Cay Flat stretches nearly as far as you can see. Then the water becomes deep blue where the ocean floor abruptly falls away.

Nearby Steamer Cay is one of the places where sponge fishermen do their thing. You'll see (and smell) the mounds of sponges in various stages of preparation. They are black as they lie on shore drying in the sun. Then they are anchored in clumps in the water and later dried again so that they turn a golden brown. When they are ready, the sponges are sold in Nassau. Visitors are surprised that no one worries about anyone stealing them as they lie unattended. This area is also popular for lobster fishing between August and May. With jagged coral and a tangle of mangroves at the water's edge, this beach is not good for swimming. South of Bigwood Cay, a few accommodations are found in Mangrove Cay and Congo Town.

WHAT TO SEE AND DO

Sports • Small Hope Bay Lodge near Andros Town and the Andros Beach Hotel in Nicholl's Town both offer diving. For fishing and boating, the places to stay are the Cargill Creek Fishing Lodge and Andros Island Bonefishing Club, both near Cargill Creek; Charlie's Haven in Behring Point; and the Chickcharnie Hotel in Fresh Creek. Andros is in one of the world's most famous areas for bonefishing. For excellent guided fishing excursions in the Cargill Creek/Behring Point area, contact the **North Bight Bonefishing Service,** run by Andy Smith (write to him at Behring Point, Andros, The Bahamas, or call (809) 329–5261). Now in his twenties, Andy has been a guide since he was 16 and bonefishing for as long as he can remember. He'll take you to the best spots and teach you anything you don't already know. According to Andy, "You can fish all day and not see another boat. That's how many flats there are." High season for bonefishing is from September to June. The rest of the year Andy dives for conch and takes the occasional fisherman out.

*Andros Barrier Reef • *off the east coast* • At this natural wonder, the third largest reef in the world, divers can swim through caves and tunnels to get a close look at some spectacular marine life, including brilliantly colored (and friendly) fish and many kinds of coral and sponges. Small Hope Bay Lodge, outside Andros Town, specializes in diving excursions to a depth of from 10 feet on one side of the reef to 185 feet "over the wall," where the reef plunges into the 6000-foot Tongue of the Ocean.

*Blue Holes and Inland Ocean Blue Holes • *points throughout the coast and island* • Ocean blue holes, the 200 feet and more fresh water wonders arising from the briny deep, may be visited by either rented or tour boats. Some of these holes have been featured in a Jacques Cousteau TV program. Diving expeditions off Andros give visitors another way to see these majestic undersea phenomena in the waters surrounding the island. Inland ocean holes are tucked away in the woods throughout Andros. With steep, porous limestone walls that catch the dancing reflection of the sun on the water, Captain Bill's Blue Hole, near Small Hope Bay Lodge, is a tranquil place for a private swim. Many birds, including great blue herons, snowy egrets, and humming birds, come through this area.

Nicholl's Town Area

Morgan's Bluff • *North Andros* • This is a site where pirate Sir Henry Morgan's treasure is said to be buried. Visitors are not barred from seeking clues. At the Andros Beach Hotel, arrange to explore caves here.

Andros Town and Fresh Creek

***Androsia Batik Works** • *at the edge of Fresh Creek* • Started by Rosi Birch, the former wife of the owner of Small Hope Bay Lodge, Androsia began in the early '70s with a staff of three who worked out of bathtubs on the lodge's property. The batik factory employs about 70 people who design, dye, and sew the colorful wall hangings and resort wear that is sold throughout the Bahamas. The clothing, for both men and women, ranges from shorts, jackets, and dresses to bathing suits. Visit Androsia to see how the material is made.

Turnbull's Gut • *off Small Hope Bay Lodge* • This is a coral and sun-filled underwater tunnel that opens onto a thrilling vertical drop to the depths, where divers encounter awesome undersea life.

The Barge • *Small Hope Bay Lodge* • This navy landing-craft from World War II was sunk by the owner of Small Hope Bay Lodge to enhance underwater adventure for his guests. Curious fish join the divers in this protected area.

WHERE TO STAY

Northern Andros

INEXPENSIVE

☆☆ **Andros Beach Hotel** • *Nicholl's 'Town* • On a powdery four-mile stretch of beach, this casual hotel attracts many divers. Deep-sea and bone fishing, snorkeling, and trips to deserted islands can be arranged. By the pool area, which overlooks the beach, guests may relax in a hammock between two palm trees. Ten spacious ocean-front rooms with terraces and ceiling fans are available along with three private cottages. On short notice, sometimes overnight, the on-premises boutique will run you up a shirt or a dress in Androsia fabric or another of your choice. In the bar where people from town mingle with visitors, try your hand at the famous "Ring Game." Ask at the front desk about baby-sitting.

Movashti Hotel • *Lowe Sound* • Just north of Nicholl's Town, this 30-room hotel looks out on the sound. All rooms are air-conditioned and have TV. There is a restaurant and bar on premises. Because of the hotel's small size, guests get to know each other and often join up for sightseeing and beach trips.

Central Andros
EXPENSIVE

★★★ **Small Hope Bay Lodge** • *outside Andros Town* • Many guests have remarked that this family-run resort has the casual, convivial atmosphere of summer camp. Leave your jackets, ties, and evening wear at home when you come to this rustic beachfront lodge that specializes in diving. Less than 15 minutes from shore is one of the world's longest barrier reefs, and snorkelers need only swim under the dock to see some of the most exciting marine life around. Small Hope Bay Lodge was the first resort in the Bahamas to make diving the main attraction. Nondivers and nonsnorkelers don't have to miss the wonderful underwater displays. Expert dive masters will teach them how to snorkel or dive—at no cost—and will allow them to learn at their own pace. Because the reef is so extensive, dive masters are always finding new sites for visitors to explore.

The lodge's cabins (which aren't particularly soundproof) are spread out along an expansive beach shaded by tall coconut palms. Some have picture windows. All are cooled by ceiling fans and are colorfully decorated with wall hangings, pillows, and curtains made of the distinctive batik cloth created at the Androsia factory, begun by the former wife of the lodge's owner. Families with children often request the cabins with two rooms and a shared bath. No room keys are provided, but you can lock up your valuables in the office. Hammocks wide enough for two are strategically located throughout the grounds so that guests can stretch out while gazing at some of the best views. This is probably not the kind of place where you'd expect to find a hot tub, but one is right on the beach. You can even arrange to have a massage. Complimentary bicycles are available for trips to nearby settlements or Captain Bill's Blue Hole, a secluded inland body of fresh water about 5 miles away. Deep-sea fishing, birdwatching, shell collecting, examining unusual species of wild orchids, finding plants used in bush medicine, and shopping at the "batik boutique" are some of the ways guests spend their time when not diving. Cocktails, along with conch fritters that go quickly, are served every evening before dinner.

Young children, who are well taken care of while their parents are off diving, eat in the game room off the main dining room. On barbecue nights, meals are served on the waterfront by the outdoor bar. After dinner, there might be an impromptu party or a showing of underwater slides in the lounge, with its overstuffed pillows and gaping fireplace. Or a staff member might simply give guests directions to the disco in nearby Calabash Bay. The lodge runs a charter air service between Andros Town and Fort Lauderdale.

★★★**Cargill Creek Fishing Lodge** • *about 30 miles south of Fresh Creek* • "This place is too nice to be called a lodge," one guest told us. Owned by a Nassau businessman, this upscale waterfront resort opened in December 1989. Within its first year, the lodge had already had repeat guests. The vast majority of people who stay here are avid bone fishermen (yes, *men*), but reef fishing for grouper, snapper, barracuda, and jacks, and deep-sea fishing for marlin, tuna, sailfish, wahoo, and dolphin are excellent as well. While there is no real beach (there's an artificially created sandbar just across the channel), the small pool is fine for cooling off. All of the appealing rooms and cottages are air-conditioned, with televisions, double beds, and very chic baths. Fans hang from the high, sloping wooden ceilings that are set off by exposed beams. The attractive A-frame dining room is paneled in honey-colored wood and has a tile floor. Overhanging the water, the adjoining bar/lounge gives guests the feeling of being on a moving ship. Every afternoon when the fishing boats return, guests gather on the waterfront patio for cocktails and hors d'oeuvres. Cookouts are hosted on Saturdays. Located between the towns of Cargill Creek and Behring Point, this lodge is about 30 miles from the airport.

INEXPENSIVE

☆☆**Andros Island Bonefishing Camp** • *about 30 miles south of Fresh Creek* • Next door to the Cargill Creek Fishing Lodge, this seaside club is more rustic and low profile. There is no beach, but guests don't seem to mind, since they spend their days out on the water. Off the homelike lounge, the expansive oceanfront deck with heavy wooden chairs is a wonderful place for relaxing. On the grounds, hammocks hang between trees. Although the rooms aren't air-conditioned, they are modern and comfortable, with ceiling fans.

Charlie's Haven • *Behring Point, about 32 miles south of Fresh Creek* • After a fire in 1983, this fishing lodge has finally been rebuilt and is scheduled to reopen as we go to press. The stone fireplace is the highlight of the cozy bar/lounge, with its comfortable chairs and TV. The ceiling of the small dining room is paneled in wood. Off the lounge, there's a room reserved for tying flies and fixing fishing equipment. The walls are decorated with old photos of fishermen and their catch. Each of the 10 cheerfully done guest rooms is air-conditioned and has its own bath. Bigwood Cay, with its beautiful beach and good shore fishing, is a 3-mile boat ride away.

Nottages Cottages • *Behring Point, about 32 miles south of Fresh Creek* • Although you'll find some of the island's most attractive architecture and decor here, this hotel has remained only partially completed for years. In the one finished cottage. a TV, overstuffed chairs and couches, a bright modern kitchen done in yellow and white, and two bedrooms, each with a double bed, make guests feel right at home. Each of the 10 upscale double rooms comes with two double beds and a modern bath. Floor-to-ceiling sliding glass doors surround the sunny, spacious dining room in the main building. Potted plants and other lush vegetation add color to the grounds. Most of the guests are anglers, since there is little to do in the area besides fish.

Mangrove Cay

INEXPENSIVE

Bannister's Cottages • This small, no-frills accommodation is known for its good homestyle food, particularly the fresh seafood. Only one of the rooms in the group of stone buildings is air conditioned. Most of the guests are avid fishermen, hunters, and boaters.

Moxey's Guest House • Visitors are taken into the family at this six-room guest house. In the best Bahamian People-to-People tradition, you can become involved in local activities such as church suppers, barbecues, and chorales.

Congo Town Area

EXPENSIVE

★★★★**Emerald Palms by-the-Sea** • *Driggs Hill* • Formerly somewhat modest Las Palmas, this hotel has undergone a spectacular transformation. Rebuilt and refurbished, it still looks out to the sea and a magnificent beach fringed with palms and casuarinas. There's also a swimming pool. Stepping into the lobby, guests are greeted by a macaw that lords the room in a large ornate cage. Wicker sofas, pine bookcases loaded with books and magazines, and a discreet TV set invite relaxation. Many guests gather here for drinks before dinner. The gourmet meals, beginning with breakfast, are unsurpassed and the wine cellar is commendable. White tiles cover the floors of guest rooms, which are furnished with wicker and pale pine. The TV is housed in a pine armoire and video cassettes may be borrowed for in-room viewing. Four poster beds are festooned with filmy mosquito netting, and duvet covers are embroidered in white lace. From each room, french doors lead out to a small patio with hammocks and Adirondack chairs with footrests. Honeymooners and others looking for complete escape find Emerald Palms by-the-Sea ideal.

THE BERRY ISLANDS

The 12 square miles of the Berry Islands are a series of small cays, most of them privately owned, just north of Andros and New Providence. Some have colorful names such as Cockroach Cay, Crab Cay, and Goat Cay. Bebe Rebozo, remembered from the Nixon years, bought a home on Cat Cay. There's a private bird sanctuary on Bond's Cay and a private airfield on Hog Cay. The remnants of a farming community, established for freed slaves, can still be found on Whale Cay. Sponge fishermen live on many of the smaller islands. Sailors and fishing enthusiasts enjoy cruising around this area.

Chub Cay, the southernmost part of the Berry Islands and just across the channel from Andros, is where you'll find the archipelago's only hotel that is open to the public. This resort—which has hosted Bill Cosby and Quincy Jones—is called the Chub Cay Club, and sports a 76-slip marina, full boating services, and a commissary. Beyond fishing, boating, scuba diving, relaxing on beautiful beaches, and playing tennis (but only if you are a member of the resort's club or make special arrangements with the manager), there is little to do on Chub Cay. Every week, the Nassau mailboat docks at this island, which is home to the main airport. Another airport is found on Great Harbour Cay in the north, where the Berry Island's population (of little more than 500) is concentrated. At 7 miles long and 1½ miles wide, this is the largest chunk of the archipelago. After aggressive developers got hold of it, Great Harbour Cay began attracting the international wealthy. Where the monied set goes, golf seems to follow. The island's clubhouse sits on a rise overlooking the carpetlike fairways with the sea as a background. Douglas Fairbanks, Jr., was once chairman of the development company's board. His presence drew film people and jet setters eager to catch a glimpse of and be part of the new "in" place.

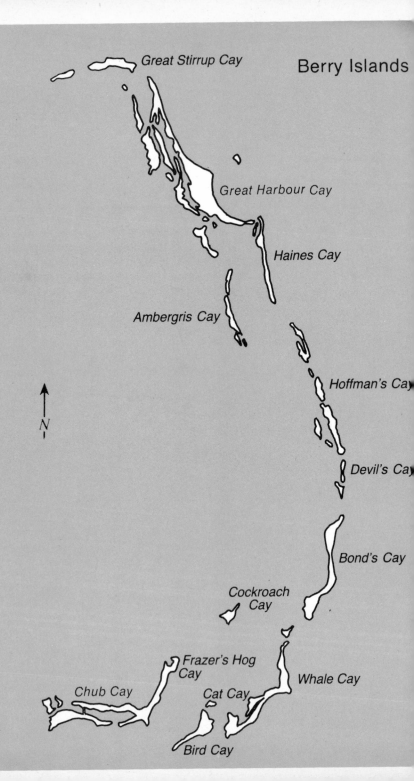

WHERE TO STAY

MODERATE

☆☆☆**The Chub Cay Club** • The beachfront rooms, one of the restaurants, and some of the other facilities are reserved for members of this expansive fishing and boating retreat. Members also get first priority on the tennis courts. However, nonmembers will certainly enjoy themselves in this tranquil, picturesque setting. Guest rooms, though plain, are perfectly comfortable, with TV and pots for making coffee or tea. Since most visitors spend their days out in their boats, this resort is the perfect place to find complete peace and quiet. The calmer of the two beaches is long and wide, and vacationers often have it to themselves. It is lined with bungalows for members as well as attractive private vacation homes. The other beach, where the frothy surf trims the electric blue water, is even more unpeopled. You'll find this one at the end of a sun-dappled, casuarina-shaded path cushioned with pine needles.

The members' pool overlooks the more placid beach, while the palm-shaded pool for nonmembers is near the marina. But no one seems to mind when nonmembers decide to take a dip in the private pool. Neal Watson's Undersea Adventures offers scuba lessons as well as trips for experienced divers. The scuba office is located in the T-shirt–packed gift shop, near the commisary and nonmembers' bar and dining room. The restaurant serves three meals a day, with selections including broiled fish with grits for breakfast, lobster salad and grouper fingers for lunch, and grilled lamb chops, chicken creole, and peas and rice for dinner. At night, those who don't turn in early play pool and dominoes, dance, and talk up a storm with the hotel workers who frequent the bar in the staff housing area. Through the resort, arrangements are made for charter flights between the Chub Cay Club and Nassau or Florida.

THE BIMINIS

Many avid anglers consider the Biminis *the* place for serious big-game fishing. These islands are definitely *not* for those in search of exceptional hotels or fine dining. Both visitors and residents seem more reserved than on other Family Islands. Some say this stems from the island's proximity to the U.S. and its relatively long history of American tourism. Beginning just 50 miles east of Miami, the Biminis are closer to the U.S. than the rest of The Bahamas. Yet, with only a handful of small fishing-oriented hotels, Bimini could hardly be considered overdeveloped. Hook-shaped North Bimini, where the action is centered, is trimmed by seven miles of mostly empty sandy shores on one side while marinas and docks line the other. Although there's an airport on nearly deserted South Bimini, most travelers arrive with a splash— by seaplane from Paradise Island or Miami—on North Bimini. It drops them off right in Alice Town, the capital.

The ocean is in view from just about all points along narrow North Bimini. Visitors can ride rented scooters or take taxis to the most picturesque beaches, which are found in the north. King's Road runs along one side of the island and Queen's Road claims the other. The story goes that the names of the roads are exchanged periodically depending on whether a male or female monarch is in power in England, with the larger road honoring the current ruler. Most hotels are within walking distance of the seaplane landing in Alice Town, but vacationers with heavy luggage can board mini-buses.

Across the road from the Bimini Big Game Fishing Club in Alice Town is the **Bimini Breeze** restaurant, which serves lunch and dinner. The Bahamian food at this neat, sparkling eatery is hearty and tasty. Always lining the bar, a lively, vocal group of local philosophers provides diversion for diners. Other hangouts along the main road are **Diandrea's Inn,** the dining room of a hotel; **Captain Bob's,** which whips up breakfast and box lunches for fishermen; and **Fisherman's Paradise,** which serves all three meals. **The Wee Hours Club** and **Edith's Cafe and Deli** are nearby. About three miles north of Alice Town, the paved road parallel to the beach ends, turning into a pine-needle cushioned dirt road. Leaning toward each other, the wispy branches of evergreens create a canopy overhead. Bailey Town, where **Pritchard's** sells the best freshly baked bread around, and Porgy Bay are quiet settlements north of the capital.

Bimini Lore

Folklore and legends, an integral part of the heritage of the Biminis, are happily shared with vacationers. Ponce de Leon visited the islands during his fruitless quest for the Fountain of Youth. A spot said to be the fountain, near Bimini's only airport, on South Bimini, is invariably pointed out to newcomers. Off Paradise Point on North Bimini, a group of large flat rocks juts from 20 to 30 feet out of the water. Because they appear to have been hand-hewn, some people believe they are remnants of the

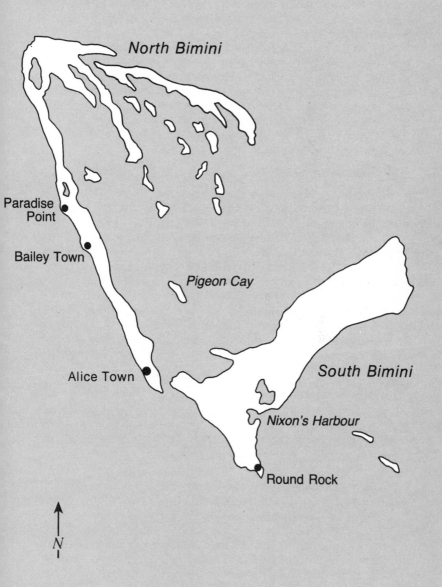

The Biminis

North Bimini

Paradise
Point

Bailey Town

Pigeon Cay

South Bimini

Alice Town

Nixon's Harbour

Round Rock

N

road system of the fabled Lost Continent of Atlantis. While the story behind these rocks is intriguing, they aren't worth a special trip. During U.S. Prohibition, the Biminis were a refuge for bootleggers and rum-runners who took advantage of the islands' closeness to Florida. They used the cays and inlets as shelters while they eluded their pursuers, as their piratical predecessors had.

If you'd like to visit Healing Hole Springs, whose watears are said to have medicinal powers, inquire about a guide at Brown's Hotel. We're told that only a few islanders know how to get there. Located near bonefish flats, the clear fresh water of these springs is hidden beneath a layer of muddy salt water. Your boat will pass through a cut bordered by gnarled mangroves before reaching this spot, which is some nine feet in diameter.

The Two Americans

Two Americans, Ernest Hemingway and Adam Clayton Powell, Jr., have put their stamps on the Biminis. Hemingway, an avid fisherman, spent his time away from the water at the bar of the Compleat Angler Hotel. At one time he lived in a cottage called Blue Marlin, which is now part of Bimini Blue Water Marina hotel. The lobby of the Compleat Angler Hotel is filled with Hemingway memorabilia, and there is a rentable guest room where sections of *To Have and Have Not* are said to have been written.

Adam Clayton Powell, Jr., the New York congressman, could be found in Alice Town's "End of the World" bar, where he was a favor-ite among residents who admired him as the black man who, with sat-ire, wit, and good humor, could tell off white Americans. Powell, too, fished enthusiastically. Every December, Bimini holds the Adam Clay-ton Powell Memorial Fishing Tournament.

WHAT TO SEE AND DO

Sports ● Deep-sea fishing records are held by many who have fished Bimini waters. The walls of the Bimini Hall of Fame are covered with photographs of fishermen displaying their catches. Veteran fishermen wax ecstatic about the seas swarming with giant tuna, tarpon, dolphin, snapper, bonefish, amberjack, bluefish, white and blue marlin, sword-fish, sailfish, bonito, mackeral, barracuda, grouper, and shark. Bonefish flats are also found in the Biminis. Make fishing and boating arrange-ments through the Big Game Fishing Club & Hotel, Bimini Blue Water

Ltd., Brown's Marina, or Weech's Bimini Dock. Brown's Hotel also has a dive program.

For diving, contact Bimini Undersea Adventures or Brown's Hotel. Tennis Courts are at the Bimini Big Game Fishing Club.

*Hemingway Memorabilia • *Compleat Angler Hotel, Alice Town* • The lobby of the Compleat Angler Hotel has a display of mementos associated with Ernest Hemingway, including manuscripts, photographs, and paintings.

Hall of Fame • *Diandrea's Inn, Alice Town* • Proud anglers, from around the world, pose in photographs displaying their prize-winning catches in this fisherman's hall of fame. Some of the beaming exhibitors are celebrities.

The *Sapona* • *Between South Bimini and Cat Cay* • During the first World War, the automobile magnate Henry Ford built a large, concrete ship, the *Sapona*. No longer his during Prohibition, it was anchored off South Bimini for a private club much used by rumrunners. In 1929, it was wrecked and blown toward shore during a hurricane. Now sitting upright in fifteen feet of water, it is a reminder of the Bimini's adventurous past.

WHERE TO STAY

MODERATE

☆☆**Bimini Big Game Fishing Club** • This hotel, with 35 rooms, 12 cottages, and two penthouses, is the largest in the Biminis. It is operated by Bacardi International, the rum people, and is headquarters exclusively for serious sport and game fishermen. This is where they find comfort after their boats are tied up in the hotel's marina. The marina accommodates up to 60 boats. There are also a swimming pool, tennis court, bar, and two dining rooms. The Fisherman's Wharf restaurant has an attentive maitre d' and colorful murals of local life. The beach is a step or two away. Guest rooms, which come with TVs, have tiled floors, area rugs, and some rattan pieces painted a cool, celadon green. Sportspeople are grateful for the out-of-the-way, built-in racks for boating, fishing, and scuba gear.

★★ **Bimini Blue Water Marina** • Nicely landscaped, with a picket fence out front, this 12-room establishment has a welcoming dining room and bar. It has its own beach and two pools. Most rooms overlook the sea and sunset views can be spectacular. Now accommodating guests of the hotel, Blue Marlin cottage is one of the places where Ernest Hemingway stayed during his frequent writing and fishing visits to the Biminis. Hanging over the stone working fireplace in the living/dining room is—what else?—a blue marlin. This spacious, wood-panelled room is also decorated with other fish and huge fish tails. With a kitchen, three bedrooms, and three bathrooms, this cottage also sports a large front patio. Bimini Blue Water Marina shares management and facilities with the Compleat Angler, next door.

INEXPENSIVE

☆☆**The Compleat Angler Hotel** • With its rich dark panelling and 12 cozy rooms, this three-story balconied building seems an overgrown private home. At the entrance, a huge tree shades a courtyard that doubles as an outdoor bar. Hemingway certainly seemed to feel at home here. Opening onto a balcony, the small room where he stayed is sometimes rented to visitors. Downstairs, the bar where he drank is fashioned from old rum barrels. Other public rooms—often filled with young folks partying to live music on weekends—are decorated with colorful U.S. license plates and old photos of Hemingway. This hotel has become part of the neighboring Bimini Blue Water Marina Hotel.

Brown's Hotel • At Brown's modest, somewhat run-down 28-room hotel and marina, divers will find Bimini Undersea Adventures, an enterprise working to popularize diving as an attraction in Bimini. It caters to guests at the Big Game Fishing Club as well as to others interested in scuba.

★★ **Diandrea's Inn** • The thirteen rooms in this small hostelry all have color televisions. Some have double beds and others, twin. The one-room "suite" with two double beds, is huge and the cottage has cooking facilities. There is a front porch and a sunny, outside reception area. The 30-room addition has a bar and dining room.

☆ **Seacrest** • This small hotel has ten rooms, all with television. Each room has a single and a double bed and rooms are surrounded by outside corridors. The spacious rooms, which can be adjoining, are good for families. There is neither a pool nor a restaurant, but the beach is across the road and good, local restaurants are nearby.

☆ **Admiral Hotel** • Farthest from the Alice Town seaport, the Admiral Hotel is in residential Bailey Town. Reached by taxi or mini-bus, the 24 rooms have television, air-conditioning, and two double beds. A favorite with vacationing Bahamians, the hotel offers doubles, suites, and efficiencies.

CAT ISLAND

Across the sound from the Exumas, Cat Island has the highest elevation of all The Bahamas. Like many Bahamian islands, it is long and thin. At 50 miles in length, it varies from one to 4 miles across. Despite its natural beauty and near pristine beaches, Cat Island is not a major stop on the tourist path. It is a nice island for mingling with residents, walking trips, and bicycling. The one airport is at Arthur's Town, in the north.

During the 1700s, Cat Island was known as San Salvador, the contemporary name for the Bahamian island to the southeast that is thought by many historians to be the first place Columbus visited in the Americas. So, because of its old name, some Cat Islanders believe that their home is really the original Columbus landing point. More than a few have grumbled that, with all the hoopla of 1992 cinquecentennial celebrations, they are being beaten out of their birthright. Thus, a bit of rivalry has developed between Cat Island and neighboring San Salvador, and a few pranks have resulted. In 1990, a foreign landscape architect was on her way to San Salvador. When the plane made its first stop, on Cat Island, the flight attendant announced, "Welcome to Arthur's Town, San Salvador." Believing that she had reached her destination, the architect climbed off and before she realized her mistake, the plane had taken off! To make matters worse, Bahamasair had only two flights a week in and out of Cat Island.

Atop the island's 206-foot Mount Alvernia is the Hermitage, built by Father Jerome Hawes, a revered Catholic missionary who died in 1956. As in many such communities, his untiring efforts did not succeed in wiping out century-old practices such as Obeah, a mixture of African and Caribbean ritual.

There are still the remains of colonial plantations on the island. One, built by the slaves of a loyalist from the colonies, Colonel Andrew Deveaux, lies in ruins near Port Howe.

Cat Island is slow-paced, far removed from the frenetic tourism of Nassau and Freeport. Some people have no electricity, cook outside, and draw water from wells, just as their ancestors did centuries before them. You might see people sitting on their front steps while they burn coconut halves in their yards to convince mosquitoes to go elsewhere. Cat Island's population, something over 4000, lives by limited farming and fishing. Young people tend to seek more lucrative ways of making a living on other islands or in the U.S. One of the island's native sons, the actor-director Sidney Poitier, did just that, leaving Arthur's Town as a youth.

As with other Bahamian islands, there are stories of pirates having come this way. But unlike other islands, treasure was actually found here. This gave rise to a belief that there is still more awaiting discovery somewhere on land or sunken offshore.

WHAT TO SEE AND DO

The Hermitage • *Town of New Bight* • This structure, at the 206-foot pinnacle of Mount Alvernia, is a small abbey with a miniature cloister and a round corner tower, all of gray native stone. The Hermitage commands a sweeping view of Cat Island, taking in the Bight as well as Fernandez Bay to the north. It is reached by turning off the main road at New Bight and following the dirt road to the foot of the rise. Here, you'll have to abandon your car. A free-standing arch marks the beginning of the foot path up the hill. Rubber-soled shoes are recommended for the tricky climb to the top. Where he could, Father Jerome Hawes, who built the abbey, carved steps into the existing stone and also carved stations of the cross along the way. Just to the right of the main road leading up to Mount Alvernia, standing like a forgotten movie set, is the ruined stone facade of a structure from the Ambrister Plantation.

Deveaux Plantation • *Town of Port Howe* • This plantation was constructed for Colonel Andrew Deveaux by his slaves when he settled on Cat Island after leaving the Colonies. It is reputed to have been beautifully furnished and the scene of much entertainment, but is now in ruins.

Armbrister Plantation • *Near Port Howe* • This is another reminder of colonial life in The Bahamas. Crumbling stone fences and the remains of walls are all that is left of this plantation.

WHERE TO STAY

EXPENSIVE
★★★**Fernandez Bay Village** • Charming, rustic, and laid-back, this resort is on a curving stretch of dreamed-of beach, fringed with

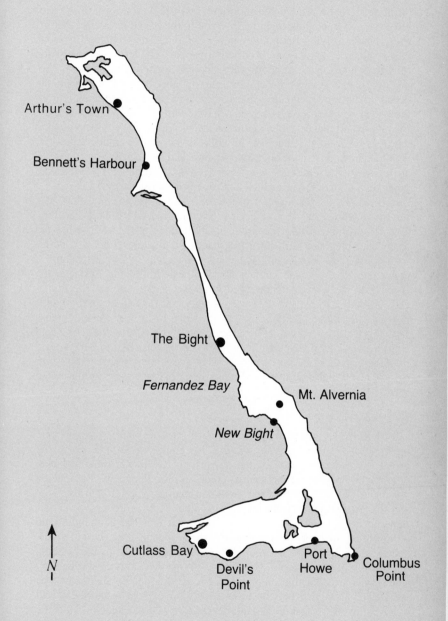

Cat Island

Arthur's Town

Bennett's Harbour

The Bight

Fernandez Bay

Mt. Alvernia

New Bight

Cutlass Bay

Devil's
Point

Port
Howe

Columbus
Point

N

feathery casuarinas. You'll almost have the beach to yourself. Tony
Armbrister, the multitalented proprietor, will pick you up in Nassau or
elsewhere, if you so arrange, and fly you to the island in his Beechcraft.
From Nassau, flying time is just under an hour. The "village" consists
of six villas, each sleeping up to eight people. The houses, constructed
of native stone, have window-walls opening to individual terraces facing out to the sea. Three craggy outcroppings of rock rise from the
center of the cove, which is Fernandez Bay, on Exuma Sound. From
the beach or from their sweeping window views, guests can watch occasional small planes as they come in to land on the tiny airstrip beyond
the trees. A special feature of the villas is the indoor-outdoor showers,
which, surrounded by tropical vegetation and protected from viewers,
are open to the outdoors with sky overhead. Some of the villas are
duplexes with cathedral ceilings and overhead fans.

Most water sports are at beachfront, and there are bikes and cars
for those who want to visit nearby settlements or landmarks, such as
Mount Alvernia. Books are found in the lounge area and in villas for
those who prefer to curl up in the shade. Radio, television, and newspapers are out. This is the place for total escape. Guests become a
congenial group, which gathers for pre-meal drinks and dines on the
honor system by signing for what they take or are served. The home-
cooked food is ample and delicious. A hefty dose of will power is needed
to resist the slabs of daily baked bread, which turns up toasted at breakfast. Armbrister, who is of local descent, often strums the guitar and
sings folk songs at evening bonfires if he is not off tinkering with a
machine or seeing to your comfort. Many guests are repeaters who swear
by this resort and pray that Fernandez Bay Village remains an unspoiled
secret.

MODERATE

★★ **Hawk's Nest** • If you arrive by private plane, you can land
on the Hawk's Nest private airstrip. By boat, you can tie up at the
private, 10-berth marina. If you have neither, Hawk's Nest will pick
you up and fly you in from several points in Florida or in Nassau. When
you land, you are at the resort, without having gone through the wear
and tear of getting in from the airport. The 10 comfortable, air-conditioned rooms can also be cooled by overhead fans but the gentle trade
winds often make both unnecessary. Just outside the pleasantly furnished, cool ceramic-tiled-floored rooms are private patios overlooking
the incredibly blue Exuma Sound. The sunsets here can be spectacular.
Car rentals are available on premises for visiting nearby sights, such as
the Hermitage and plantation ruins. Boats for exploring the Sound and
other points of interest are complimentary. A well-stocked bar is off the
sun-washed dining room, and the excellent home-cooked meals are sup-
plemented with fresh fish from the day's catch. The marina store carries

everything from fuel and candy bars to suntan lotion. Favorite purchases are T-shirts and sweat shirts with the resort's logo.

INEXPENSIVE

☆ **Greenwood Inn** • This modest resort is on the south coast where Exuma Sound and the Atlantic meet. Cottages make up the 16-room accommodations and their terraces face the sea. A long stretch of pristine beach invites swimming and sunbathing. There is a pool and two boats are available for fishing as well as scuba diving and snorkeling excursions. Greenwood Inn flies guests in to the island, landing on its nearby airstrip.

Bridge Inn • The Bight, where the Bridge Inn is located, is close to the center of Cat Island. There are 12 rooms, and beaches are not far.

ELEUTHERA

Some visitors say that Eleuthera, among the most developed Family Islands, is the most beautiful part of the Bahamas. It certainly competes with New Providence and Grand Bahama for some of the most upscale resorts. This island was host to the first Bahamian settlers, sometimes called the Eleutherian Adventurers, who came from Bermuda in search of religious freedom. Spanish Wells, Harbour Island, and Current are tiny islands just offshore.

About 5 miles at its widest point, the island is a long, thin arc, curling southward from New Providence for 110 miles toward Cat Island and the cays of the Exumas. Despite a coral and limestone surface, which might seem forbidding to farmers, Eleuthera is the agricultural center of The Bahamas. In the late 1800s, it dominated the pineapple market with its luscious fruit of a special sweetness without a tart aftertaste.

Like most of the other Family Islands, Eleuthera has few large trees. Its thin but rich soil crust bears mainly small trees and shrubs. Along its main north-south road, you are seldom able to see beyond the hedgerows to the rocky fields where the island's rich crop of fruits and vegetables grow. You can drive for miles between towns. Beautiful, deserted and endless beaches, some palm-shaded and with pink sands, border Eleuthera. Rough coral caves are found throughout the island, with one of the largest at Hatchet Bay, located in the north. The Hatchet Bay Yacht Club and Marina is a new resort being built in this area.

Some of Eleuthera's most arresting attractions are under water. Awesome ocean holes and inland blue holes (seemingly bottomless landlocked salt-water tidal pools) are a constant surprise, where fish in all their tropical splendor swim to the surface to be fed by visitors. The Devil's Backbone off the northern coast is a spine of reefs that in the past caused many shipwrecks that still lie below the surface awaiting exploration by divers. A Civil War train that was being transported to Cuba by barge sits wrecked in the middle of the Devil's Backbone. The Union locomotive came to grief during an 1865 storm and its rusted remains now lie among coral and rusted remains. An old steamship, the *Cienfuegos*, is nearby. It went down in 1895, with all passengers surviving. The treacherous Devil's Backbone has claimed still other victims that remain visible to divers, including the freighters *Vanaheim* and *Carnarvon*. Current Cut, between Eleuthera and the cays off Current island, is rich in undersea life, which can be seen over 50-feet down. Six Shilling Channel, separating Eleuthera from Nassau, is a coral reef system among the cays of Current Cut. Underwater photographers have captured magnificent views of exotic creatures making for the depths of Tongue of the Ocean to the south.

The island's three airports are in North Eleuthera, Governor's Harbour, and Rock Sound. In addition to Bahamasair flights from Nassau, there are also direct flights from Miami to all three airports. Nassau mail boats make weekly trips to various points throughout Eleuthera.

Eleuthera now participates in the **People-to-People** program. For information, contact the Ministry of Tourism in Governor's Harbour, (809)332–2142, and give at least four day's notice.

A Little History

When Captain William Sayles and 70 other Englishmen came south from Bermuda in search of religious freedom in 1649, they settled on Cigatoo, as the Arawaks (whom they replaced) called the island. They were joined by New England Puritans, also in search of religious freedom. The island had been called Alabaster, but the new colonizers chose the Greek word for freedom and called it Eleutheria.

The early New England settlers continued contact with their fellow Puritans back home. In 1650, for example, a rare and valuable wood found on Eleuthera was shipped back to New England to be sold to raise funds for the new Harvard College. This was in payment for provisions that the New Englanders had previously sent the hard-pressed settlers.

By 1831 white settlers had been outnumbered three to one by 12,000

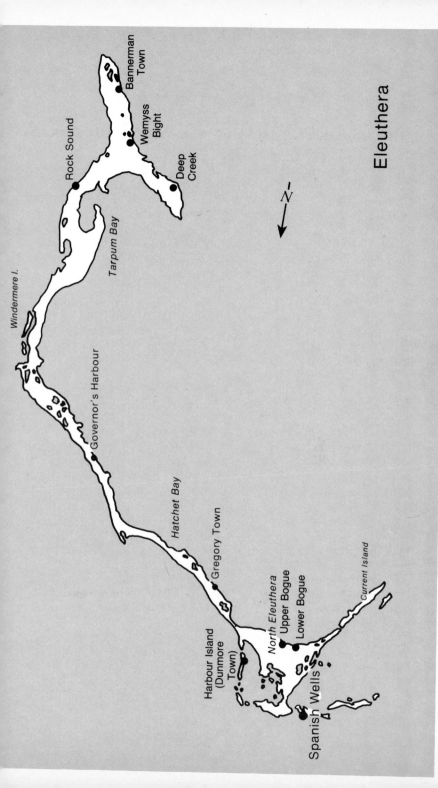

Eleuthera

N

Windermere I.

Rock Sound

Tarpum Bay

Bannerman
Town

Wemyss
Bight

Deep
Creek

Governor's Harbour

Hatchet Bay

Gregory Town

Harbour Island
(Dunmore
Town)

North Eleuthera
Upper Bogue
Lower Bogue

Current Island

Spanish Wells

slaves and free blacks. Three years later, Queen Victoria issued the proclamation that set slaves free throughout the islands.

Rock Sound, Tarpum Bay, and Windermere Island

Rock Sound, it is said, was once called "Wreck Sound." It has replaced Governor's Harbour as the island's leading settlement. Its small village has a liquor store, a grocer's, and very little else. For a hearty home-style meal cooked by Kathleen Culmer, wife of the proprietor, stop at family-operated **Sammy's Place** in Rock Sound. This comfortable, spotless restaurant attracts tourists and out-of-towners as well as locals. Although some resorts use a Rock Sound mailing address, they are all really outside town. Near the Rock Sound airport, look out for the house-sized, shady banyan tree, its tentaclelike shoots dripping from its branches.

With a thriving, if minute, art colony, Tarpum Bay is just north of Rock Sound. Here transplanted Americans Mal Flanders and his wife, Kay, paint tropical seascapes, scenes of island life, and portraits of its people. You're welcome to stop by their studio. Also in Tarpum Bay another artist, MacMillan Hughes, has erected with his own hands what he calls, "The Castle." This odd, elevated structure, poised at an intersection, defies description. After climbing the entrance steps, you'll see sculpture, paintings, and drawings by this bearded, expatriate Scotsman who will take you on a tour.

A bridge connects five-mile-long Windermere Island with the mainland. A favorite hideaway for the affluent, this sliver of land has played host to Prince Charles and Lady Di, as well as other notables. The Windermere Island Club is the island's only hotel, but there are also many spectacular villas for rent. If you're staying at the club, be sure to borrow one of the bikes for a tranquil ride down the main road, overhung with tall pines whose branches form a shady roof. Set back from the road are many private houses with names such as Cherokee, Dolphin House, and Beaumaris. Most of these luxury homes are owned by foreigners. Chances are you'll pass by at least one more being built.

The omelet chef at the Windermere Island Club operates her own restaurant outside of nearby Savannah Sound. Called **Big Sally's,** it is on the mainland not far from the bridge to Windermere, and it serves up hearty local dishes.

Major expansion is planned for the Winding Bay/Half Sound area near Rock Sound, where the Winding Bay Beach Resort is located. With 225 rooms, the Crossing Bluff Hotel will sport tennis courts, a swimming pool, a dock for dive boats, three restaurants, and a room especially for entertainment.

South Eleuthera

South of Rock Sound, Eleuthera has settlements such as Bannerman Town, Wemyss Bight, and Deep Creek, which shelter local populations where children are seen in uniform colors of their various schools and tourists pass through as sightseers. At Powell Point, on the island's southern tip, is the Cape Eleuthera Yacht Club which, although not in full operation as a resort, does have limited facilities for boaters.

Governor's Harbour

Governor's Harbour, at Eleuthera's center, away from the ocean on the bay side of the island, is thought to be one of the earliest settlements and seat of government. While this picturesque town with well-restored homes—some of them guest houses—may seem quiet now, for many years it was an active port. Club Med is here on a long broad beach. The town's few other accommodations are small and family-run. The Alabaster Bay Hotel, a new beach resort, is scheduled to be built at the former site of a U.S. Naval Base near the airport.

With beautiful, wide, pink beaches (tinted by powdered coral and shells), hilly Governor's Habour is considered a real find by most visitors. Tourists, few and far between, are often unhappy to run into each other. In town, attractive pink and white government buildings face the water near a much used basketball court by a long, narrow cemetery. Many streets are shaded with tall palms and pines. The waterfront, with its handsome Victorian houses, is one of the nicest places to spend time, especially at sunset. A leisurely walk along the shore will take you across a bridge to Cupid's Cay, where you'll see **Mamie's Bakery** next to the old fire station.

Ask someone to show you Twin Coves, a secluded private estate that welcomes visitors who want to relax or snorkel at the quiet north-shore beach. You'll drive through a lush, wonderfully landscaped palm grove.

Ronnie's Hi-D-Way is a restaurant and bar where parties often take place on weekends. Many visitors and locals spend their evenings at the bar at the **Buccaneer Club.** The outdoor cafe at the Buccaneer is a pleasant place to have an inexpensive lunch. The swivel chairs around the umbrella-covered tables are made from old wooden casks. **Mate 'n Jenny's,** a bar and restaurant in Palmetto Point, about five miles outside Governor's Harbour, specializes in Bahamian pizza and is another local hang-out in the evening.

Rodney Pinder, the maitre d' at the Windermere Island Club, runs his own restaurant in Palmetto Point. Called **La Rastic,** it specializes in home-style Bahamian dishes including mutton, cracked conch, grouper, and pork chops. He does not serve alcohol, but you can bring your own bottle. At **Sandy Beach Inn,** a stone's throw from **Mate 'n Jenny's,** George Deal is known for generous portions of grouper, conch, and crawfish, which he catches himself. He also grows his own vegetables. The huge tail of a 500-pound marlin caught by his cousin adorns a wall. Deal dares you to ask for a drink for which his bar does not have the ingredients.

Hatchet Bay

At Hatchet Bay, to the north, there is an old plantation where prize Angus cattle were once raised. Instead of cattle, poultry and dairy products comprise its present output. At Shark Hole, these hungry fish devour the unused chicken parts thrown into the Atlantic several times a day. Locals now live in the homes built by employees of the once prosperous plantation. Hatchet Bay Yacht Club and Marina, a major development planned for Hatchet Bay Pond, is slated to have a 50-slip marina along with tennis and watersports facilities.

Gregory Town

Gregory Town is the pineapple capital of the island. If you go beyond the shrubs along the main road, you'll see fields of the fruit. Pineapple rum is a favorite among visitors as well as locals. Eleuthera's highest hill, near the Cave and Glass Window, which will give you a wonderful panoramic view of the area, is also here. Near some houses, you'll notice outdoor ovens for baking bread. For a fresh-baked treat, stop at Thompson's Bakery. The Thompson's take guests in their home for about $35 a night per person, including two meals. This town caters to young surfers, many of whom are convinced that its beaches have some of the best waves around.

Harbour Island

Once visitors see this breathtaking oasis, called ''Briland'' (with a long *i*) by residents, many return year after year. Its shores, where sands are tinted pink by crushed coral and shells, have some of Eleuthera's most beautiful beaches. This island easily boasts the best group of hotels in The Bahamas, from Canadian-owned, antique-filled Ocean View to modest, locally owned Tingum Village, known for its good homestyle food. All with fewer than fifty rooms, the island's accommodations are perfect for travelers seeking personal attention and distinctive decor. Along the east coast and cupped by greenery, several of these small hotels, secluded from each other, are perched on a bluff above the three-mile pink sand beach. Others hug the harbor, where friendly wild dolphins sometimes allow themselves to be stroked by swimmers.

Not even two square miles, Harbour Island can be explored on foot. Dunmore Town, its charming settlement, is one of the Bahamian villages with New England-style architecture. Located on the harbor side of the island, the town is named for Lord Dunmore, who built Nassau's Fincastle and Charlotte forts. Overhung with orange, purple, and pink bougainvillea, white picket fences enclose brightly painted clapboard houses with gingerbread trim. Dangling in front of shuttered windows, wind chimes tinkle on porches.

The late afternoon sun on the striking wooden buildings along Bay Street, the main drag, is a spectacular sight. Most of these homes are owned by Americans and Canadians, and some are available as vacation rentals. Streets are shaded by fig trees, coconut palms, and wispy tropical pines. On Sundays, people dressed to kill stand in clusters outside churches before and after services. Two of The Bahamas' oldest churches are found in Dunmore Town: St. John's, the oldest Anglican house of worship, erected in the mid-eighteenth century, and Wesley Methodist, built around 1846. Titus Hole, a harborside cave, is said to have served as the island's first jail.

Those who don't hoof it around the island ride bicycles, scooters, or golf carts. All these can be rented at various hotels or along Bay Street. Big Red (333–2045), the bartender at Coral Sands hotel since 1974, rents boats in addition to wheels. He also drops off and picks up vacationers on nearby islands for the day or afternoon (about $20 per person). Man Island is the best for snorkeling, and there are plenty of beaches there for couples to be alone together. Most hotels will pack picnic lunches and make other arrangements for deserted island trips. Groups of four or more will find it less expensive to rent their own boats (a 13' Boston whaler for about $60, for instance) and hit several islands.

Anglers looking for an excellent bonefishing guide could hardly do better than Bonefish Joe. Considered the best of the best, he's always in demand, so write to him (Joe Cleary, Harbour Island, The Bahamas) well in advance of your trip. Snorkeling excursions can be arranged through most accommodations. Valentine's Yacht Club & Inn and Romora Bay Club hotels are the centers for scuba diving.

At **Miss Mae Tea Room and Fine Things,** on Dunmore Street, the sign and shutters are handpainted with flowers that mirror the real blossoms out front. Here you'll find J & M Davidson leather belts and bags, Haitian paintings, colorful boxes with designs done by hand, and bright papier mache wall hangings of tigers, giraffes, and fish. Merchandise is displayed on antique chests. In addition to selling gourmet foods such as French wine vinegar and Italian olive oil, Miss Mae serves muffins, sandwiches of deli meats and cheeses, and, of course, tea. Patrons can dine on the patio in the back. **Island Treasures,** nearby, sells jewelry, T-shirts, and mugs, among other items.

Androsia Bahamas, on King Street, carries clothing made from the bright batik cloth created on the island of Andros. **Sugar Mill,** on Bay Street, stocks music boxes in the shape of Harbour Island cottages, one-of-a-kind toothbrushes, and ceramic teddy bears and wall hangings. Next door, the front porch of **The Harbour Lounge** is the place to be for fabulous sunset views as well as people watching. Lunch, afternoon cocktails, and dinner are popular among visitors. At night, a very local crowd gathers at the bar. Along the water across the street, some vendors sell straw goods, fruit, and vegetables while others rent bicycles.

Owned by Canadian Dick Malcolm, formerly the proprietor of Pink Sands hotel, and his Bahamian wife, Lemmi, elegant **Picaroon Landing** restaurant (333–2241) serves dinner only. While patrons coming for cocktails can dress more casually, men are required to wear jackets and ties after 7 p.m. With high-backed wooden chairs and ceiling fans, the pleasant dining room is decorated with original paintings. The expensive prix fixe menu might include a choice of Bahamian lobster tail, filet of snapper, Norwegian salmon, Alaskan king crab legs, Angus beef tenderloin, or lamb chops. Coconut tarts might be served for dessert. A cheese and cracker board and port are offered at the close of meals. Be sure to make reservations.

At the other end of the spectrum, modest **Harbour View Restaurant** (333–2174), on Bay Street, serves three island-style meals daily. It shares a building with the Haitian Church of God. Across the street, the harborfront open-air shelter known as The Tent is a gathering spot for "lazy people," the local term for those who spend their days hanging out, drinking, and relaxing.

More restaurants are found outside of town, where roosters do their jerky march through yards and horses graze in small fields. Family-run **Angela's Starfish Restaurant** (333–2253) is one of the best places for Bahamian-style fish, chicken, cracked conch, pork chops, and peas and rice. Go easy on the hot sauce. You can sit outside on the palm-shaded grassy lawn overlooking the water and mainland Eleuthera. At night, tables are lit by tiny bulbs hidden in conch shells. Inside, where the decor of the casual dining room is nautical, a sign requests that patrons refrain from swearing and wearing bare-backed clothing.

Nearby, **The Hill Top Restaurant** (333–2065) specializes in Bahamian seafood. Also in the neighborhood, **Gusty's Restaurant & Bar,** with its pool room, often hosts fashion shows. On the other side of the island, roadside tables sit outside **Three Sisters Native Food** (333–2078), where meals are served by reservation only. Adjoining a house where laundry often flutters on clothes lines, this restaurant also has an inside dining room. At the eastern end of this street is the tree-lined entrance to **Runaway Hill,** a hotel with one of the island's best dining rooms. More excellent gourmet creations are served at neighboring **Dunmore Beach Club.** Non-guests are welcome to make dinner reservations at these hotels, if there's room.

On Harbour Island, nightlife wakes up on weekends. Locals usually bar hop. Each person seems to have his or her personal route, but most folks end up at the same place—the hot club of the moment. The Funk Gang, the local band that for years commanded Friday and Saturday nights from George's Night Club, has moved to its own building next door. A rake 'n' scrape (music played with a saw, washboard, cowbell, conch shell, and maracas) might be happening at the harborside bar at **Valentine's Yacht Club & Inn.** Also popular with tourists as well as locals, **Willie's Tavern,** built in 1948, is the island's oldest nightclub. Patrons entertain themselves with the pool table, juke box, bar, and TV, where videos are constantly playing. Palm fronds, T-shirts, and posters are plastered on walls while flags from various countries decorate the ceiling.

With its black-and-white tile floor, the pool room at the **Vic-Hum Club** is decorated with colorful license plates and posters of Bob Marley, Anita Baker, Michael Jackson, and other musicians. In the cozy bar in an adjoining room, walls are hung with vintage record albums of artists including Harry Belafonte, Janice Joplin, Richie Havens, and James Brown. If you're lucky, owner Humphrey Percentie (whose family also owns Tingum Village hotel) will show you "the world's largest coconut," which measures 33″ around.

Active until around the 1970s, the old airstrip near Romora Bay Club hotel is no longer used. Today travelers take the ten-minute ferry ride from Three Island Dock, which is a brief taxi ride from the North Eleuthera airport. Ferries go back and forth all day. Once they reach Dunmore Town, most visitors must take another taxi to their hotel or vacation rental home. Young boys wait at the docks to transport luggage between the cabs and ferries. It can be annoying to have them quickly unload your bags, carry them a mere two feet to the boat, and then expect tips. However, keep in mind that there are few other opportunities for children to earn money here. We always remind ourselves, "At least they're working."

Spanish Wells

This pretty cay floats off the northern coast. If it weren't for the tropical vegetation and all the satellite dishes outside the brightly painted homes, visitors might think they were in a quiet suburb somewhere in the U.S. The island is known for its booming crawfish (or spiny lobster) business, which, at least in part, is responsible for the extremely high standard of living here. Many boys quit school at fourteen to spend most of every August through March underwater. The lobster industry is so lucrative that it is not uncommon for a man barely in his twenties to purchase a $100,000 house—paying most of the money upfront!

In a predominantly black country, Spanish Wells is also unusual in that its population is virtually all white. Some say that this is because the original settlers opposed slavery and agreed not to bring slaves to the island. Others relate stories of residents trying to make sure that Afro-Bahamians do nothing more than work in Spanish Wells. A few black people have made this their home in recent years. However, it is commonly understood, as it has always been, that most Afro-Bahamians are expected to be off the island by nightfall. Race even played a role in shaping the island's present religious climate. During the 1950s, when members of the sole church invited a visiting black minister to preach, the congregation split up, establishing other houses of worship.

Whether visitors are black or white, they notice that residents are not especially friendly, at least not at first. After all, with a flourishing economy, they really don't need tourism. They can afford to take their time deciding whether or not to mingle with outsiders. Blond hair and blues eyes prevail, and islanders look as if they all come from one big family. That is not surprising, since most of them *are* related. Outsiders whisper about the genetic problems—a high incidence of physical birth defects and mental retardation—that have resulted from relying on such a small gene pool.

Spanish explorers are said to have used the island as a final point to take on fresh water before beginning the long, arduous voyage back to Europe. The wells had to be dug carefully, only to a certain depth. Beyond that, salt water would be struck, spoiling the cargo. Spanish Wells was one of the islands that the 17th-century Eleutherian Adventurers and 18th-century British Loyalists dropped in on. After years of fishing, farming, shipbuilding, and even pirating, lobster fishing took off with a vengeance in the 1970s.

Current

Another tiny cay off Eleuthera's north tip, Current is reputed to be the island's oldest settlement. The story goes that a group of North American Indians were exiled to Current after a "massacre" of white settlers on Cape Cod. Today, there is no trace of exiled Indians, and Current's present inhabitants are mainly black.

WHAT TO SEE AND DO

Sports ● Diving expeditions may be arranged on Harbour Island through the Romora Bay Club or Valentine's Yacht Club; in Rock Sound, through the Winding Bay Dive Center; and on Spanish Wells, through the Spanish Wells Beach Resort and the Harbour Club. The best fishing here is from Apr. to Aug. For fishing and boating on Harbour Island, contact the Coral Sands Hotel, Romora Bay, or Valentine's; near Rock Sound, the Cotton Bay Club, and on Spanish Wells, Sawyers Marina or Spanish Wells Beach Resort. Eleuthera's golf course is at the Cotton Bay Club near Rock Sound. Tennis courts are in Governor's Harbour, Rock Sound, Harbour Island, and Spanish Wells.

Upper Bogue Area

*****Glass Window** ● Just south of Upper Bogue, at a spot where the island is almost divided, this windowlike formation was created by erosion from the sea and the wind. It provides a spectacular view both east and west, from the ocean to the bay. The deep blue of the ocean's water on one side of the island contrasts with the bright turquoise of the more shallow water on the other.

Bridge Point Area

Preacher's Cave ● Shipwrecked settlers, the Eleutherian Adventurers, sought shelter in this cave in northern Eleuthera. A rocky pulpit formation gives a churchlike feeling, which generated the cave's name.

Harbour Island

Historic Churches ● *Harbour Island* ● St. John's Anglican Church on Harbour Island dates from the 1700s and is the oldest in The Bahamas. Wesley Methodist, built in 1845, is the largest of that denomination in The Bahamas. You'll find a surprising number of other churches for such a small island. Near Wesley Methodist Church is flower-filled St. Catherine's Cemetery.

Gregory Town

Gregory Town Plantation ● This ancient plantation is a reminder of Eleuthera's days of leadership in pineapple production. One of its current products is pineapple rum, which visitors may sample and even take home for a treat.

Hatchet Bay

Hatchet Bay Plantation • This plantation was once the center for raising prize Angus cattle. Its present output is poultry and dairy products.

Hatchet Bay Cave • A giant fig tree marks the entrance to this cave. The tree was supposedly planted by pirates. The cave itself is more than a mile long and harmless bats live in its interior. Because there are no guards, visitors are warned against exploration without the company of an islander who knows his or her way about the cave.

Tarpum Bay

*Ocean Hole** • Among several "holes" on the island, this one, just north of Rock Sound and also called "blue hole," is just east of the main road, and teems with a variety of tropical fish eager to be fed.

WHERE TO STAY

Spanish Wells

MODERATE

☆☆ **Spanish Wells Beach Resort** • Fishing and diving are the specialties at this small beachfront hotel. All of the superior rooms and cottages face the ocean. Sliding glass doors lead to balconies, and rooms are kept cool with ceiling fans. Weekend entertainment takes place at the waterfront bar. This hotel has the honor of being the home of the island's only tennis court. Volleyball and shuffleboard also keep guests active.

INEXPENSIVE

☆ **Spanish Wells Harbour Club** • This large resort also caters to those who thrive on water sports and fishing. Pleasure and fishing boats tie up at its marina. There are 20 guest rooms.

Current

EXPENSIVE

☆☆**Sea Raider** • Although the sea is also the focus at this small resort with a beach, the management can arrange tennis. Apartments and individual rooms are available. Cars can be rented here and Sea Raider also has bicycles.

Harbour Island

Note that most hotels here close during September and October.

EXPENSIVE

☆☆☆**Pink Sands** • The resort's name aptly describes the wide quiet beach, at the bottom of a bluff. Located in 35 stone cottages, the spacious rooms have sitting, sleeping, and dressing areas, ceiling fans, and refrigerators containing bottled water. They are pleasantly furnished and quite comfortable. Many repeat guests request the same unit year after year. Designated a bird sanctuary, the property stretches over 40 acres. Tree-shaded, flower-lined paths wind through the grounds. Guests are given flashlights when they check in, but if they get lost at night, a security guard is on the premises to assist. Many people keep occupied with tennis and watersports. Motorscooters, bicycles, and boats are available for rent. Lunch is served on the beach deck, where there's also a bar. Soft chimes summon people to dinner, in the large open-air dining room with a fireplace. Next door is a cozy library lined with books for borrowing. Since there are no room keys, valuables may be left in a safe deposit box at the front desk.

★★★**Dunmore Beach Club** • White wicker couches and peacock chairs, floral cushions, potted and hanging plants, pastel-patterned throw rugs, and white-washed blond wood panelling make guests want to linger in the lounge of this lovely hotel. The fireplace is flanked by bookcases. Partially done puzzles wait to be tackled on card tables. As in many Family Island hotels, guests keep track of the drinks they make at the adjoining honesty bar. All three meals are included in the rates.

Dunmore Beach Club has an excellent reputation for innovative gourmet cuisine. Men are required to wear jackets and ties for the evening meal, served in an attractive room with a built-in wine cabinet. The set menu changes daily. Among the house specialties are salmon mousse, spinach soup, caesar salad, paella, cornish game hen with herbed rice stuffing, duck in sour orange sauce, banana crepes, mai tai pie, and chocolate souffle with brandied creme. Non-guests are welcome for dinner, when there is space. A lattice gazebo overlooks the beach, down below. The nine-acre grounds, with an archway created by palms, ficus, and other greenery, also contain a tennis court. Some guest units have sitting areas, while others have separate sitting rooms with daybeds. Half the rooms come with king sized beds. All are woodpanelled and have patios, refrigerators, ceiling fans, and air-conditioning.

☆☆☆**Romora Bay Club** • Caged parrots chatter near the entrance to this harborside hotel. Lush greenery and colorful flowers are all over the property. Trees bear papayas, sour oranges, lemons, sugar apples, and almonds. Pathways wend their way through shady foliage, and hammocks invite relaxation. A breezy bar hangs over the harbor and a nearby patio is decked out with cast iron garden furniture. Set off by a stone fireplace, the indoor bar/lounge, with its black-and-white tile floor and bleached wood ceiling, has tables and chairs set up for various games.

Covered with a tortoiseshell-like wood veneer, the large table in the center of the dining room seats ten. It was rescued from a shipwreck. For those who'd like to search for more underwater treasures, dive packages are available. The beach is a five-minute walk away. Once a week, guests are taken to a deserted island for a picnic. Some of the 45 rooms and suites are time-share units. All have patios and air-conditioning, and many contain ceiling fans. Most are decorated with rattan, glass-topped tables, and white-tiled floors. The kitchens in some are convenient for families. A couple of units even have murphy beds. Because of their scenic location, the deluxe harborside rooms are booked well in advance.

★★**Rock House** • Perched on a cliff overlooking the harbor, Rock House was built in 1947. The highlight of the inn is the bold Rousseau-inspired mural in the dining room, which is decorated in wicker and rattan. Men are required to wear jackets and ties at dinner. Lunch and breakfast are often served amid the flower beds of the courtyard. Five of the six rooms have private patios, and all are cooled by ceiling fans. The handsome tile floors were laid when the house was originally built. Some rooms are decorated with four-poster rattan beds. Some have bathtubs, while others have stall showers. Scuba diving and deep sea, reef, and bonefishing can all be arranged. The beach is about a ten-minute walk away. Daily rates include all three meals, and a two-night minimum stay is required.

MODERATE

★★★**Ocean View** • If you're looking for a small hotel that exudes character, this is it. Many agree that among Harbour Island's wealth of extremely attractive accommodations, Ocean View gets top billing. The centerpiece of the large living/dining room is an inlaid wooden table imported from France, which sits atop a tiled floor. Antique chairs and couches create a comfortable sitting area by the fireplace. Guests are welcome to borrow the books here. Framed watercolors and other paintings decorate walls and unusual statues and knickknacks sit on sideboards and tables. In the bar, weathered brass instruments hang next to the colorful Haitian-inspired work of Amos Ferguson, one of The Bahamas' best known artists. Jazz is likely to be played on the stereo, and there's a piano in the living room. Even the kitchen, by the dining area, is attractively decorated, with blue and white china hung on walls and cookbooks neatly in shelves. Off the bar, flower-trimmed patios provide stunning ocean views.

The decor of the nine guest rooms makes up for their small size. They all have air conditioning and ceiling fans, but the similarity ends here. Each done in a distinctive theme and color scheme, they sport antique chairs and chests, and old tile floors with intricate designs. Antique etchings hang on some walls, while old straw hats adorn others. They share a patio that faces the water. The pink sand beach is at the base of the bluff on which the hotel sits. Ocean View attracts many Europeans. Pip Simmons, the Canadian owner, also runs Miss Mae's boutique and teahouse in town.

☆☆☆**Coral Sands** • Many repeat guests wouldn't stay anywhere else and quite a few staff members have been here for years. The friendly, personal attention provided by owners Sharon and Brett King has everything to do with the popularity of this beachfront hotel. Hammocks are strung throughout the grounds and thatched shelters provide shade on the long pink beach. Palms rustle above the elevated oceanfront bar. Meals are served on the breezy patio, where live bands entertain on weekends. Selections might include lobster goombay (in a parmesan and cream sauce with onions on toast), beef tenderloin, fried grouper, and chocolate souffles.

Individually decorated, rooms in the main building have a homey feel. Oceanfront suites are found in a separate building. Casually done with bright captain's chairs and ginger jar lamps, they have large patios, walk-in closets, and living areas with day beds. The watercolors in most rooms were painted by Kimberly Nelson King, one of the three daughters of the owners. The tennis court is lit for night play, and watersports are easily arranged. A pool table, cards, and various games are in the TV lounge. Talk to Big Red, the bartender, about renting bikes, motor scooters, and boats. Babysitting is available through the front desk.

★★★**Runaway Hill** • Staying at this partially Bahamian-owned inn overlooking the pink sand beach is like visiting old friends. The homey atmosphere is a pleasant reminder that Runaway Hill was built as a private house. The dining room/lounge is furnished in wicker, and black and white tiles pave the floor. People from other hotels often stop by for drinks and the excellent meals served on the veranda. (Reservations are essential.) Each day, the handwritten menu appears on an old brass music stand by the entrance. Nearby, a large totempole-like stylized statue of a pelican stands by an antique table with beautifully carved legs.

The personal attention of co-owners and managers Carol and Roger Becht is always apparent. They make sure that guests are informed of any social events taking place on the island. Parties and even weddings have been held on the broad pool deck overlooking the ocean. Hammocks are strung nearby. Some rooms are airconditioned and others have fans. Three of the most popular are in the main house. One of these is huge, with beautiful pink patterned ceramic floor tiles, white wicker furniture, and a large bath with two sinks. Rooms all have paperback books, which guests are welcome to exchange for those they've brought.

☆☆☆**Valentine's Yacht Club & Inn** • Scuba diving and boating are the main draws at this harborside yacht club. A nautical theme is strong in the public rooms. Portholes decorate the wood-panelled wall that separates the pleasant lounge from the bar, which opens to the pool patio. Grounds are landscaped with crotons, palms, and giant succulents. The comfortable but plainly furnished poolside and gardenside guest rooms are all air conditioned, with ceiling fans. The ten in the two-story gardenside building are the largest. A tennis court is on the premises. Across the road, lunch is served at the waterfront Yacht Club bar, also a popular evening hangout. Live calypso bands appear here periodically. Sunset views are wonderful from the deck.

INEXPENSIVE
☆**Tingum Village** • Owned and managed by the local Percentie family, this is the island's bargain accommodation and the site of some of its best parties and receptions. The beach is a brief stroll away. Many coconut palms and other lush plantings surround a grassy area by the buildings where guest rooms are located. Most of the small, modest rooms have patios. Some are carpeted, while others are tiled. All have ceiling fans and some are air conditioned. Here at matriarch Ma Ruby's restaurant, grouper and lobster are the specialties. What does "Tingum" mean? It's the Bahamian version of "whachamacallit" or "thingamajig."

Gregory Town
MODERATE
☆☆**Oleander Gardens** • These white, red-roofed villas are perched on the shore overlooking the beach. Each attractively furnished villa has two bedrooms, two baths, a living room, a dining area, a kitchen, and two terraces. Tennis, fishing, and watersports are available.

☆**Caridon Cottages** • This accommodation offers one- and two-room cottages. Bicycles and motor scooters can be rented and there is a gift shop.

Pineapple Cove • Set on 28 acres, this 12-room resort has a good beach and a salt-water swimming pool. The rooms are villa style with rattan furnishings and other airy decor. Each is air conditioned and has its own covered porch. Hammocks are available for lazing, tennis for the athletic, and strolling about the grounds for the energetic. The cuisine is American, Continental and, especially, Bahamian.

Governor's Harbour
INEXPENSIVE

☆☆**Cigatoo Inn** • An attractive, family-run hotel, Cigatoo sports a pool, tennis court, and a bar and restaurant where locals often stop for drinks. Guest rooms, with terraces surrounded by flowering plants, are small but comfortable. All the rooms have TV and refrigerators. Families with young children can arrange for baby-sitting. A short walk will take you to a broad, pink sand beach not far from Club Med. Guests are quickly drawn into the life of the town. One of the best things about the Cigatoo is the lively, warm, and congenial atmosphere.

Tuckaway • This pleasant guest house in a residential neighborhood is run by Carmen and Richard Rolle, who live across the street. There are six rooms in three cottages and all are air-conditioned, with refrigerators and shady front porches. A crib is available should a young one turn up. All the front yards are alive with colorful vegetation. Guests will be able to pick pineapple and other fruit when the plants mature. An unspectacular beach is a 2-minute walk away. For a better, pink-sand beach on the north shore, a 20-minute walk is required.

Laughing Bird Apartments • These are all comfortable air-conditioned, 1-bedroom efficiency units. They are sometimes referred to as "Nurse Jean's apartments," since this Bahamian nurse owns them with her English husband, Donald Davies, an architect. The units consist of two apartments, each sleeping up to six people. Each has living-dining areas with separate bedrooms and baths. The houses are near to town and front an adequate beach. Markets and other services are close by. Maid service is available at a small extra charge.

Windermere Island

EXPENSIVE

★★★★★ **Windermere Island Club** • This resort is on a 5-mile-long island connected to mainland Eleuthera by a bridge. Quiet Savannah Sound is the closest town. Windermere's high rating is not for its club rooms, which, although comfortable and with ocean-view balconies, are surprisingly small and modest. The rating is for the attentive, unobtrusive, and courteous service and the other units: the 1-bedroom suites, the 2-bedroom apartments, 2- and 3-bedroom cottages, and the 1–5-bedroom villas, many of which are breathtaking in design and appointments. Men are required to wear jackets for dinner every night, but on Saturday night and gala nights they also don ties, and the women appear in cocktail dresses. Guests gather in the lounge, formed by two adjoining octagonal rooms near the pool patio. The Saturday night buffet is spectacular in presentation and taste. Among the offerings might be smoked trout and salmon, chicken-stuffed pastry, roast turkey, soups, and salads. There are rich desserts, fruits, and cheese platters. Off on the patio a combo plays, and there is dancing. The guest rooms have fresh flowers and telephones, but no radios or TV.

There are two beaches, one on the ocean side and the other, protected and calm, facing the mainland. Breakfast brings fresh-squeezed orange juice, made-to-order omelets, fresh fruits, hash browns, and other morning delights. Guests beg the recipe for the French toast, which is crunchy brown on the outside and soft inside. Cars may be rented through the hotel, taxi drivers, or the maitre d' and bikes can be borrowed. The Windermere Island Club closes from the end of May to the beginning of November.

Rock Sound Area

EXPENSIVE

★★★★**Cotton Bay Club** • This resort, developed as a retreat for millionaires, continues to be one of the finest in The Bahamas. From the road it is reached by a winding driveway shaded by palms and Norfolk pines. The pink cottages have stair-stepped roofs like those used in Bermuda for catching rainwater. The rooms, most with outdoor terraces, are tastefully furnished with rattan, and have ceiling fans, white-tile floors, and shutters at tall windows. The baths all have useful grab bars, and there are safe-deposit boxes in the closets. The pristine white-sand beach arcs off in each direction against a coastline of palms and casuarinas. There is an 18-hole Robert Trent Jones golf course and tennis courts. The grounds are landscaped with lush tropical plantings dominated by huge aloes. The dining room goes mainly unused because most dining takes place outside, beside the pool, under tall palms that lean protectively. There is a singer each night during season and, on buffet nights, a live band. Guests are expected to dress for dinner. As they check out, many make reservations for the following year.

☆☆**Winding Bay Beach Resort** • Built at about the same time as nearby Cotton Bay, this is similar in architectural style. Now an all-inclusive resort, it has 36 rooms in air-conditioned villas with private patios. Overdue for sprucing up, rooms have been allowed to become somewhat shabby. There is a large swimming pool with the sea beyond and the bay that curves in an enormous arc. The dining room, which overlooks the beach, offers Continental and Bahamian fare. Water sports can be arranged as well as bicycling and tennis. Most visitors are pleased to know that tipping is against house rules.

MODERATE

Ingraham's Beach Inn • By the shore in Tarpum Bay, this two-storey building houses eight guest rooms and four 1½ room apartments. The air-conditioned units face the beach. A dining room is under construction at press time.

INEXPENSIVE

Hilton's Haven • This ten-room guest house is run by a former public health nurse, celebrated for her past contributions to the nation's health and her present hospitality. Although her service is not as lavish as Rock Sound's larger resorts, it is much more personal.

THE EXUMAS

The Exumas are a chain of 365 tiny islands and cays strung out for 100 miles from New Providence and Eleuthera to Long Island. They lie between Exuma Sound on the east and the awe-inspiring Tongue of the Ocean to the west. Out in Exuma Sound near Sampson Cay is the Exuma National Land and Sea Park, 177 miles of undersea wonders, many of which can be clearly seen from three to ten feet down. From the air, the water and surrounding cays of Exuma are one of the most memorable sights of the Bahamas. A giant hand seems to have done a whimsical finger painting, leaving sand whorls and ripples clearly visible beneath the turquoise and jade sea.

An international airport at Moss Town, nine miles west of George

Town, now serves Exuma. Its runway, averaging 7000 to 8000 feet, is able to accommodate larger planes than the old airport at George Town. The mailboat comes in weekly, making stops at George Town, Staniel Cay, and several other islets in this chain. Taxis are always at the airport, and some drivers will conduct tours. Hotels either rent or have access to motor scooters and bicycles. You can also rent cars (for about $70 a day!) through hotels or in town.

George Town

George Town, Exuma's picturesque capital, lies on the island of Great Exuma, looking out to Stocking Island, which encloses Elizabeth Harbour. The largest structure in town is the impressive Administration Building, where the post office is located. Its architects strove mightily to duplicate Nassau's Government House.

Under the shade of an enormous fig tree near the administration building, women sell a variety of straw products, from rugs to dolls. Across Lake Victoria, which covers two acres in the center of town, you can sample fresh, delicious Bahamian food at the **Sunrise Cafe** or **Eddie's Edgewater.** Eddie's is a friendly, informal restaurant where Bahamians and visitors relax at the bar. Stop by in advance to make reservations.

Local George Towners can be found socializing at the Peace and Plenty Hotel, named for the ship on which the American settler Lord Rolle arrived in the Exumas. Locals as well as guests of other hotels frequent the lively parties given here. The community center next to St. Andrew's Anglican Church, which overlooks Victoria Lake, hosts weekend dances for young people. Even though George Town is the busiest part of the Exumas, hotels are scarce. However, a new resort is in the works: Mt. Pleasant Hotel & Marina is slated to have 78 hotel rooms, a half-dozen duplex cottages, and a 50-slip marina.

The Exumas are bliss for confirmed sailors who say that the cruising is unequaled anywhere else. Veteran boaters insist that if you have not sailed the Exuma waters and seen its quiet coves and inlets, you have neither sailed nor lived.

Each April, the Exumas close down for a week. Fellow Bahamians, cruising yachtsmen, boaters, visitors, and landlubbers all make their way to George Town to watch and take part in the festivities surrounding the annual inter-island Family Island Regatta. The festivities include a parade and a variety of other special events, as the hand-crafted work sloops, owned and operated by Bahamians, compete out in Elizabeth Harbour. The regatta signals non-stop eating, drinking, and all-round partying. Accommodations are difficult to come by for outsiders and some make their reservations a year or so in advance.

Food stalls are set up along the waterfront selling fresh pineapples,

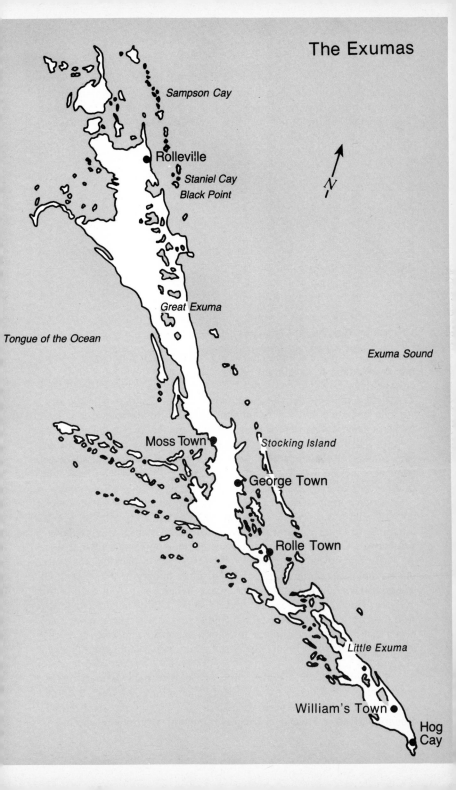

cooked chicken, fish, and conch in all its incarnations. Reggae throbs from the stalls and long lost friends greet each other with embraces and bottles of beer. Domino-playing men slap the tiles on card tables with sharp clicks. Pulsing drums, clanking cowbells, blaring horns, and shrill whistles accompany a Junkanoo band down the center of the street.

Like birds lined on telephone wires, people sit on the low walls in front of the administration building to watch the passing line of honking cars decorated with colored streamers. Children in their Sunday best sit on hoods or poke their smiling faces from sun roofs. When the Police band performs in Regatta Park, everyone surges onto the steps of the Exuma Supplies building and nearby footholds for a better view. Members of the band, in sparkling white tunics, wide red belts, hats with red bands, and black trousers with red side stripes, move children and their elders to dance to the beat.

On Emancipation Day, celebrated on the first Monday in August, another regatta is held at Rolleville.

Outside George Town

Many people in the Exumas make their living from farming. Two former plantations, Rolleville and Rolle Town, are named for John Rolle, an American Loyalist who, with his slaves, settled in the Exumas after 1783. He acquired extensive landholdings in the Exumas, and the British later rewarded him with a knighthood. Lord Rolle's will left his land to his slaves whose descendants still live in the two villages. Some visitors find that almost every person they meet in Exuma is a Rolle. The parents of Esther Rolle, the actress, moved to the United States from here before she was born. The Rolle land cannot be sold, and passes from generation to generation.

A ride northwest along Queen's Highway, flanked by banana trees, coconut palms, sea grapes, mango trees, and farmland, will take you to a number of small settlements. About seven miles from George Town, **Iva Bowe's Central Highway Inn** serves good homestyle food.

Mt. Thompson is a pretty, hilly town with a packing house for onions and other produce. Even if you're not hungry or thirsty, stop at **Three Sisters Club,** a popular restaurant. When you go out back to the gorgeous beach, you'll see the "three sisters"—three huge rocks in the water. About a mile north is Ocean Bight, a large, sparkling, white sand beach that is a wonderful place for snorkeling and swimming. In Farmer's Hill and Roker's Point, you'll see goats, pigs, lambs, and chicken in yards.

Rolleville, about 30 miles north of George Town, is the westernmost settlement. The largest of the Rolle plantations, this town has low, thatched-roof shelters where vegetables like pigeon peas are stored. **Kermit's Hilltop Tavern,** a bar and restaurant, overlooking the bay is popular with visitors as well as locals. (Kermit Rolle, another restaurateur/taxi driver, also has a restaurant called **Kermit's** at the airport.) In Barry Tarry, north of Rolleville, the **Fisherman's Inn** restaurant and nightclub is especially busy on weekends.

Little Exuma, south of George Town, is much less developed than its sister island. Once over the small bridge connecting the two islands, you'll come to a small settlement called The Ferry. This is the home of Gloria Patience, commonly known as "The Shark Lady of the Exumas." If there were any Exumians who hadn't heard of women's lib before she arrived, there certainly aren't any now.

After traveling around the world, then returning to Nassau to raise nine children, Ms. Patience moved to Little Exuma and began making a living catching sharks. Well past the age of sixty, she hauls the snared sharks, most weighing hundreds of pounds, into her boat by herself. The last we heard, an 18-foot tiger shark was the largest she had ever caught—out of about 2000 makos, lemon tips, hammerheads, and others. Ms. Patience makes necklaces from their spines and sells their teeth to Nassau jewelry stores. At her house you can buy shark teeth as well as shells, paintings, old sea bottles, and driftwood.

Some say Ms. Patience hasn't worn shoes in 30 years. She proudly notes that she was the first woman to skipper a boat in the Family Island Regatta. She did this on her 17-foot one-sailed dingy, she tells us, with a crew of three topless women.

Not far from The Ferry is the now closed Sand Dollar Beach Club on Pretty Molly Bay. There is a legend that one of the slaves on a plantation near this bay was a beautiful young woman named Molly. Melancholy about her barren life and a future of continued servitude, she drowned herself one moonlit night in the bay that was given her name. If you look carefully, you may catch a glimpse of Molly, who is said to roam the beach by moonlight.

Black Bahamians swear by the legend and dismiss another version of the story in which Molly is a young white woman who was transformed into a mermaid and sits on a rock in the bay combing her hair by moonlight.

Nearby, the Tropic of Cancer marks the separation of the tropics from the temperate zone. Its northern limit cuts through Little Exuma. A marker shows where the imaginary line is drawn.

WHAT TO SEE AND DO

Sports • Diving and snorkeling, including several very different dive sites, can be arranged in George Town at Exuma Divers, down a short hill across from the Peace and Plenty Hotel. In Staniel Cay, make arrangements at the Staniel Cay Yacht Club. For fishing and boating in George Town, contact Exuma Docking Services or Minn's Watersports; in Staniel Cay, contact Exuma Flotilla Ltd., Happy People Marina, or the Staniel Cay Yacht Club. Tennis courts are at the Out Island Inn in George Town.

*Exuma Land and Sea Park • *North Exuma Sound* • This Bahamian government-protected national park is unique in that it is mainly under water. It is reached only by boat for thrilling sights of unusual undersea landscapes, coral formations, and myriads of sea creatures. Diving is permissible, but any hunting or fishing is strictly forbidden.

*Stocking Island • This long, narrow island, with three hills in the center, is in the sound off George Town. Hotels run guests out for isolated sunbathing. It's easy to find a secluded spot here for skinny dipping. The boat will drop you off on the calm bay side, where red and black starfish float at the water's edge and a huge sandbar stretches out for half a football field. Try bonefishing right off the dock. Follow a path by the Peace and Plenty "Beach Club" (really a snack bar) across the narrow island to the ocean side, where the water is rougher and rockier in places. You'll find all kinds of shells in deserted coves. For a small fee, you may be able to talk the man who brings you here into taking a detour to Sand Dollar Beach at the southern end of the island. Here you can walk to the end of another sandbar, then swim to Elizabeth Island. And, of course, you'll have no trouble finding sand dollars.

St. Andrew's Church • *George Town* • St. Andrew's Anglican Church, with its graveyard, sits on a rise across from Government House. At its rear is Victoria Lake. It dates from 1802, and was erected for early settlers of British background.

The Hermitage • *Jimmy Hill, Great Exuma, down a narrow road off Queen's Highway* • It's probably best to let a Bahamian show you the way to the crumbling tombs at the Hermitage, about eight miles from George Town. Dating back to the 1800s, the three tombs of slavemasters lie next to the grave of one of their servants.

Rolle Town Tomb • Off the main road at Rolle Town and up the hill to the right of the Baptist church is a burial ground. At its center is a large, crumbling tomb of limestone and brick holding a marble slab bearing the following inscription:

Within this tomb lie interred
the body of Ann M. Kay the wife
of Alexander M. Kay who departed
this life the 8th of November 1792
Aged 26 years and their infant child.

Thunderball Grotto • *Off Staniel Cay* • This grotto is pierced by shafts of filtered sunlight that illuminate its rock and coral formations. The grotto was used for scenes in *Thunderball*, the James Bond film.

Williams Town Salt Marsh • *Near the Sand Dollar Club* • The site and other traces of Exuma's once-thriving salt industry are still apparent at Williams Town in Little Exuma. The best way to view the salt pond is to climb the rise to the single concrete column overlooking the flats. With the sea at your back, the entire marsh is visible.

Patience House • *The Ferry* • Gloria Patience's home has become a stop for tourists on their way to the Williams Town Salt Marsh. This colorful woman has collected china, glassware, silver, and other items, which fill every surface in the house. Her main attractions are the souvenirs she sells, which she has fashioned from shark's teeth. The fine pieces of china and glass are for display only. Ms. Patience, always barefoot, will give a tour of the house.

*Family Island Regatta • If in George Town or on one of the nearby cays in April, don't miss this annual race among sailors of several islands. The competition is keen and George Town is crowded and festive when everybody turns out for the occasion.

WHERE TO STAY

EXPENSIVE
☆☆**Staniel Cay Yacht Club** • This hotel is on a small island north of George Town, and has only 6 guest rooms. The club centers around its marina, and guests staying more than three days have free use of a 13-foot Boston whaler. The club is also a vantage point for watching the Family Island Regatta and the Emancipation Day races. A nearby 3000-foot runway puts private planes almost at its doorstep.

MODERATE
★★★**Peace and Plenty Hotel** • This is where all of George Town gathers for drinks, to swap gossip, to see who's in town, and to catch

up on the latest. It was once a sponge market and private home. Two rooms that served as a kitchen during slavery have been converted into the bar. Visitors are treated like locals and are soon adopted into the little George Town community. A popular breakfast specialty is grits and boiled fish. Try the pumpkin soup for dinner. Rooms are large and have wonderful views of the bay. Entertainment at night includes parties by the pool. Twice a day, guests are taken by ferry to the beaches on Stocking Island, where there's an unobtrusive snack bar, and on snorkeling trips.

About a mile north of George Town, the hotel has built a new 16-room unit. Called the **Peace & Plenty Beach Club,** this annex sits directly on the sandy shore. The upscale rooms, with marble baths, have balconies facing the sea. Facilities include a swimming pool.

★★ **Regatta Point** • Just past the public dock where the mail boat comes in, this guest house sits on a 1½-acre cay connected to the mainland by a bridge. The atmosphere in the five attractive apartments, decorated with summery wicker, is homelike. In at least one unit, floors are covered with straw mats and a wicker screen divides the living room from the dining area. Rooms are large, including the full kitchens, and ceilings are high. Cross breezes blow through the many windows. Surrounded by water on three sides, this accommodation serves as a great vantage point for viewing the April Family Island Regatta. The broad wooden deck on the second floor has a wraparound view of Elizabeth Harbour.

INEXPENSIVE

☆☆ **Happy People Marina** • Happy People is almost next door to Staniel Cay Yacht Club, and has 14 guest rooms. It, too, looks out toward the sea, and rents bare boats from its marina for exploring the cays and inlets of the Exumas.

☆☆ **Pieces of Eight** • Not far from the center of George Town, this lively hotel is known for its good food and popular bar. All rooms have views of the ocean, across the road. Guests may use the beautiful Out Island Inn beach or take a complimentary ferry ride to Stocking Island beaches. If there's nothing going on at night at Hotel Peace and Plenty, there's probably some kind of entertainment near the pool here.

★★ **The Three Sisters Beach Club & Hotel** • Just north of the airport, this new 12-room beachfront hotel looks out to the ocean where the distinctive Three Sisters boulders rise from the water. Locals give the dining room high marks.

INAGUA

If you're in Nassau or Freeport and mention that you're going to Inagua, people smile. Suddenly, they see you in a new light: You're no longer a run of the mill tourist, but a real traveler, someone who's interested in getting to know the country beyond its glitz and glitter. The most southerly part of the Bahamas, Great Inagua thrusts southward toward the Windward Passage and northern Haiti. It is the third largest of the nation's islands. Matthew Town, where the airport is located and the Nassau mailboat puts in once a week, is the only real settlement. There are just two flights a week between here and Nassau. Most of the 1200 or so residents are employed by the Morton Bahamas Salt Company, which dries the sea salt before shipping it to the U.S. for processing. When you first catch a glimpse of the towering pyramids of sodium sparkling in the sun, you may think you're looking at snow-covered hills. Little Inagua, to the northeast, is uninhabited—that is, except for a few wild donkeys. Inagua has nothing to offer scuba divers or golfers, and good beaches are scarce. However, for bird lovers, deep-sea fishing enthusiasts (with their own boats), and those seeking complete tranquility and many opportunities to sit around chatting with easy-going locals, this island can be just the ticket.

Colorful Wildlife

In the interior, Lake Windsor attracts the world's largest colony of flaingoes (known as "fillamingoes" by some residents). In surrounding Inagua National Park, protected by the Bahamas National Trust, more than 200 species of birds flutter around. Among them are roseate spoonbills, herons, egrets, and hummingbirds. Visitors may camp out in cabins at the park. Green turtles and wild boars, cows, and donkeys are also found roaming unhampered on and around the island. Residents tell a variety of stories explaining how the donkeys got to Inagua. According to some, they were brought by Henri Cristophe, the 19th-century Haitian revolutionary leader who crowned himself king and escaped to this island. Cristophe needed these beasts of burden to tote the gold he took from Haiti. He is said to have hidden his loot in a cave in Inagua's dense forest, and to this day, no one has been able to find it. Eugene O'Neill drew upon this page from history for his play *The Emperor Jones*.

Exploring Inagua

Until World War II, some 5000 people lived on Inagua. Mass emigration during the hard times that followed the war caused the population to shrink dramatically. While some young people have returned after being educated in Nassau, the U.S., or Canada, and some older folk have moved back home, the island is hardly booming. Along the quiet roads that are often empty of people, scrawny dogs are always barking, roosters crowing, and goats munching whatever they can find. The former movie house on waterfront Gregory Street, the main avenue, is now used for local talent shows, rehearsals of Inagua's gospel group, and a customs office. The profusion of satellite dishes on the island put the cinema out of business. On the main drag, one building stands out among the modest shops and the homes that range from forlorn to fancy: Topped by a clock tower and fronted by a row of palm trees, the seaside Bahamas Government Administration Building also houses the Commissioner's office, the customs headquarters, the post office, and the library.

Matthew Town is very proud of its one professional-level tennis court. At night, young men battle it out on the flood-lit basketball court in Pigeon Park, the large recreational field. The tree-shaded vegetable stand at the corner of Albert Street, near the school, is a social gathering spot, especially when the street is flooded with children decked out in their pink and gray uniforms. Piled in the tiny wooden stand are plantains, yams, jars of pickled peppers, and bags of peanuts and benny seeds. Called sesame in the U.S., benny seeds are turned into benny cakes after being boiled with sugar until they burst and the mixture thickens.

Much of the town's coast is rocky. Especially at sunset, the craggy configurations add to the dramatic vista. The closest beach to hotels is a minuscule but picturesque sandy pocket cupped by slate-gray layered rocks and low cliffs. Walking toward the lighthouse, you'll find this peaceful cove off a short, rugged path to the right, just after the paved main road ends. Erected in 1870, the lighthouse guides ships using the Windward Passage channel between Inagua and Hispaniola, the island of Haiti and the Dominican Republic. The keepers live in the two octagonal wooden houses encircled by verandas. Unless you need the exercise or want to see the intricate workings and huge lens up close, there isn't much point in walking all the way to the top of the lighthouse. The view yields nothing more than the island's rocky coast and its flat landscape broken only by the buildings of petite Matthew Town.

To get to beaches outside of town, you'll need to rent a motor scooter or a car, or befriend a resident. Farquharson Beach, at Northwest Point, is popular for picnics and snorkeling. Cruise ships stop at Inagua once a month, and local guides bring passengers to the sandy shore. In the shade of a small palm grove, brightly painted truck tires

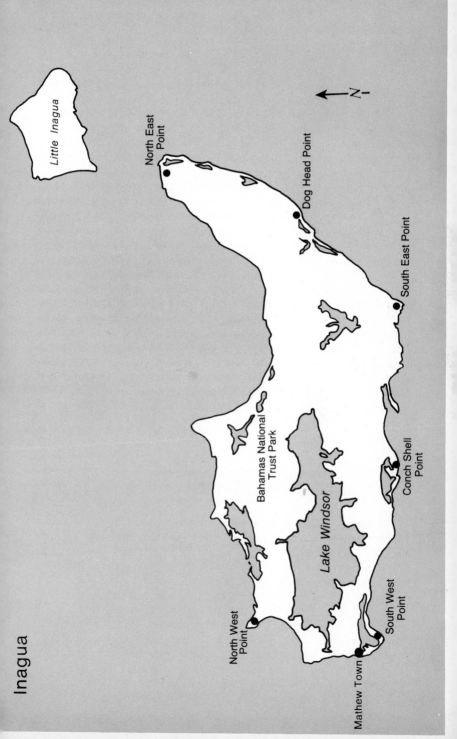

provide places to sit. This area was once a settlement of white Bahamians who eventually intermarried with black Inaguans. Near the beach,
you'll see the crumbling stone shell of the settlement's waterfront Anglican church. Around the bend, Alfred Sound is a good fishing spot.
The Bahamas National Trust Turtle Hatchery is also in this area.

Topps, a bar and restaurant on Astwood Street near the school,
packs them in for lunch and dinner. At family-style tables, people dine
on chicken and chips, fish and chips, cracked conch, peas and rice,
fried plantain, potato salad, and lobster. Foreign currency scrawled with
names has been plastered on the ceiling by residents and travelers.
Sometimes the juke box and the satellite TV compete for patrons' attention. At spacious **Cozy Corner,** you might be served by a woman in
bright yellow and green plastic curlers. The wall behind the bar is covered with bills signed by patrons from various countries, as in Topps.
A handwritten sign reads ''Credit is only allowed if 85 and accompanied by both parents. Leave swearing outside. Keep feet off chairs and
stools.'' Try the curried chicken, plantain, and smothered cabbage. The
more sedate **Main House,** off Gregory Street in an inn owned by the
Morton Bahamas Salt Company, serves three meals a day. The breeze
rustles the lacy curtains at the windows in the small dining room. Tables
are dressed in crisp linens, some days madras plaids, other times pastels. For breakfast, locals enjoy the chicken souse, but visitors tend to
stick to eggs, bacon, and toast. Inagua's nights wake up on weekends.
Periodically, popularity swings back and forth among **Cozy Corner,
the Hide Out Cafe** (with its pool hall and large dance hall), **the After-
work Bar & Restaurant,** and **Traveller's Rest** (about 9 miles out of
town).

WHAT TO SEE AND DO

*Inagua National Park • *interior* • Maintained by the Bahamas
National Trust, this 287-square-mile land-and-sea park takes up more
than half the island (some 550 square miles in size). This is where
you'll find Inagua's famed (bright) pink flamingoes, some of which are
sent to join the trained bird act in Nassau's Ardastra Gardens. You'll
see the greatest number of flamingoes (sometimes hundreds in one flock)
and get close up views when the birds are nesting, usually from the end
of February or early March through May or June. The 23-mile drive to
the National Park camp, where the birds nest, takes about an hour from
Matthew Town. Built by the salt company, dirt roads crisscross Lake
Windsor, dividing it into huge geometric segments. The name was
changed from Lake Rosa (pink in Spanish) to honor the Duke of Wind-

sor, who served as governor of the Bahamas. However, pink remains an apt description of the shallow, placid water that clearly reflects the fluffy white clouds. The pronounced rosy hue comes from the salt in the water. Where dry land was once flooded, sticks and the naked branches of trees protrude from the lake. Other areas are scattered with rocks or bordered by jungled vegetation. You may be lucky enough to spot wild donkeys, who will keep their distance while snorting at you.

Although Prince Phillip only came to the park's peaceful camp for a day, some visitors spend the night or several days here in the heart of the nesting region. The two very basic cabins sleep about 14 people between them. Sheets and mattresses are provided, but we recommend bringing your own sleeping bag. There are also a cooking shed, a dining shelter and two showers (1000 gallons of fresh water is always kept on hand). Around March or April, about six weeks after the birds hatch, a big party is held the night before the nest count. After feasting on stewed fish and barbecued ribs and chicken, the group that stays overnight counts nearly 10,000 nests each year. During these months, the camp can sometimes be reached only by boat. *Cost: $50 for one to four people to visit flamingo colony, plus tip for the driver.*

Morton Bahamas Salt Company • *outside Matthew Town* • At Morton's largest solar salt plant, you'll learn something about the business that is the foundation of Inagua's economy. There's a blueish-pink tint to the large, flat bodies of water. The color is determined by the concentration of brine. At the edges of the water, the buildup of salt sparkles like snow speckled with diamonds. The ponds resemble frozen lakes at the early stages of the spring thaw. Most impressive are the mountains of salt you'll also see outside, especially when a worker is at the top of one of these white hills picking debris out of the sodium crystals. Morton Bahamas sells its salt to fisheries, chemical plants, highway maintenance groups, and water softener companies. *Arrange visits through the Ministry of Tourism or the Family Island Promotion Board before arrival.*

WHERE TO STAY

INEXPENSIVE

★**Main House** • *off Gregory St.* • Owned by the Morton Bahamas Salt Co., this well kept inn is right behind the company's grocery and liquor stores. The handsome wooden building is enclosed by a picket fence. Two of the five neat, air conditioned rooms come with two double beds and a private bath each, while the others have two twins and shared (very modern) baths. The upstairs sitting room (with a TV and phone), the lounge downstairs (off the dining room), and the balcony are all pleasant places to relax.

☆**Kirk and Eleanor's Walk-Inn** • *Gregory St.,* • Owned by the Walkines, who live in the adjacent building, this family-run guest house has five rooms. The two smallest share a bath. The two largest come with double beds, while the others have twins. Although you'll find clothing racks instead of closets, rooms are air-conditioned and equipped with TVs. The carved wooden doors and railings add a special touch to this cinderblock guest house. If you happen to stumble out back, you might see clothes fluttering on the line one day and wild boar meat and conch hung up to dry the next.

☆**Ford's Inagua Inn** • *Victoria St., off Prison St.* • One block from Gregory Street, the main thoroughfare, this two-story cinderblock guest house opened in 1969. It is run by Leon Ford and his wife Maude, an elderly couple. Originally from Inagua, Mr. Ford spent two decades on the police force in Detroit, Michigan, his wife's hometown. Each year from March through July, they close their five-room accommodation while they go to the U.S. The brightly painted, sunny rooms share modern baths. Upstairs is a comfortable, homelike sitting room with TV, desk, hardwood floor, and balcony tiled in terra-cotta. Although the Fords sometimes serve breakfast, they no longer offer other meals. In the dining/sitting room downstairs, they proudly show off the many postcards they've received from former guests from around the world.

LONG ISLAND

A narrow sliver of land with its top pointing northwest toward the Exuma Cays, Long Island is said to stretch anywhere from 60 to 100 miles. Curiously, there seems to be some question about its length, but no dispute about its being long. It is a little more than a mile wide and, at some of its hilly points, you can see the Atlantic to the east crashing against the craggy rocks and, to the west, the calmer blue waters of Exuma Sound. The hills almost reach the height of Cat Island's highest and, on the ocean side, sharp, jagged coral cliffs drop steeply to the

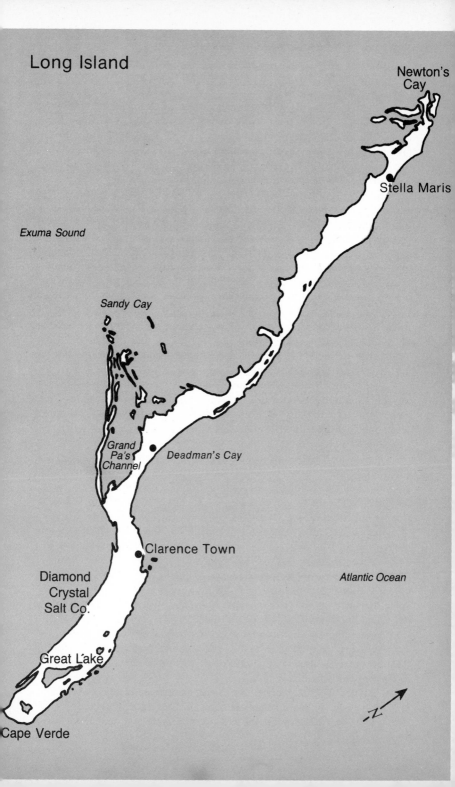

Long Island

Newton's Cay

Stella Maris

Exuma Sound

Sandy Cay

Grand Pa's Channel

Deadman's Cay

Clarence Town

Diamond Crystal Salt Co.

Atlantic Ocean

Great Lake

Cape Verde

N

sand-bordered beaches below. The Tropic of Cancer slashes through the island's northern quarter.

This island has some of the most beautiful and deserted beaches in The Bahamas. Some seasoned travelers call the beach at Cape Santa Maria one of the world's best. Located at the northwest tip of the island, it is a 3-mile cove of cerulean water and deep, powdery white sand. Other fine beaches dot the coast, and ardent swimmers and sun lovers can stumble upon one after another.

Diving, snorkeling, and shelling are ideally suited to the waters and beaches fringing the island. Scuba divers have an almost limitless list of interesting sites including a blue hole and an undersea visit to a colony of tame groupers. A local guidebook lists almost 30 different dive sites. Fishing is another island attraction, and guides take visitors to places teeming with the kind of fish and fishing they seek, whether from land, inland, or offshore. Stella Maris Inn at the north of the island arranges both diving and fishing expeditions.

Long Island was a stopping-off point for Columbus on his voyage to the "New World." He called it Fernandina after Ferdinand, the Spanish king. The island is riddled with ominous caves and mysterious ocean holes. The Stella Maris Inn has fashioned one of these grottos into an attractive entertainment setting—"party cave."

At the south of the island, near Clarence Town, the Diamond Crystal Salt Company operates a solar evaporation plant that provides some local employment. Many settlements such as Simms, Deal, and others were named for leading families. The people of Long Island fish and farm on land considered fertile compared to the other islands. Some of their houses bear a kind of hex sign painted near the roof line. Religion plays an important role in their lives. In addition to well-attended local church services, traveling, revivalist-type preachers visit up and down the island and Obeah, a variation of religious practices from West Africa, is still in evidence.

Father Jerome, the priest who built The Hermitage at the highest point on Cat Island, is also responsible for several churches on this island. One of the oldest in The Bahamas, a gleaming white, Spanish-style structure, is at Clarence Town on southern Long Island. Examples of early native architecture are evident in a sprinkling of the square stone houses with wood rafters and pyramidal, thatched roofs. Many of the older buildings stand in ruins, but the basic design is reflected in later but similar styles built of cinder block.

Two airports serve the island, one at Stella Maris in the north and the other at Deadman's Cay, almost central. A highway, Government Road, runs the island's length.

Clarence Town receives the Nassau mailboat once a week. The boat puts in at Stella Maris or Deadman's Cay once or twice a week. Because of weather conditions and other hazards, the schedule is not always strictly adhered to. Cars can be rented at Stella Maris or at the **Thompson Bay Inn,** which is also a good place for fresh seafood and other inexpensive meals.

History

The ruins of the Adderley plantation stand at the northern end of the island, not far from the Stella Maris Inn. The remains of three roofless buildings still stand, with a tall stone chimney much in evidence. Large, hand-hewn stones are strewn about, and traces of stone fences can still be seen. Many stout cedar frames clinging to some windows and doors are still intact and give off their fragrant scent.

Near the plantation is the Adderley slave burial ground. It is off the beach near a stand of tall trees, but difficult to get to because of the thick, scratchy underbrush. Once through, however, the mounds of graves can be seen, but they are slowly disappearing from erosion and neglect.

The original Adderley apparently fled the United States with his slaves at the end of the Revolution. He established a cotton plantation and also did subsistence farming. He is said to have been prosperous in his new home. According to his black descendants, Adderley committed suicide upon discovering that his favorite son had formed a liaison with one of the female slaves. The liaison continued, nevertheless. By the time abolition came to The Bahamas, white Adderleys were hard to come by. Many Adderleys and Taylors still live on the island, and the name is a common one throughout The Bahamas.

Mrs. Adderley, the late matriarch and great-grandmother of present-day island Adderleys and Taylors, lived to the age of 130. She never once traveled by boat, automobile, or airplane. She felt that the Lord had provided feet as the means of transport and there was no need for artificial, man-made devices. As the oldest living person on the island (and probably in The Bahamas), she was selected to be guest of honor and ribbon cutter at the gala opening of the tennis courts at Stella Maris Inn. The ceremony was attended by local officials and dignitaries as well as representatives from Nassau. Mrs. Adderley's descendants, who live in nearby towns such as Burnt Ground, Clinton, and Seymour, will proudly relate the story.

WHAT TO SEE AND DO

Sports • The Stella Maris Inn has a very good diving program with one of the best dive masters in The Bahamas. The adventurous go to a reef where they swim among black-tip, lemon, and bull sharks. (According to the instructor, who even pets the sharks, people who fear sharks don't know much about them.) Rum Cay is also a popular diving site. Fishing, boating, and tennis are available at Stella Maris.

*Dunmore's Cave • *Deadman's Cay* • There is convincing evidence that Arawak Indians used these caves and that, later, pirates made use of them for cargo storage as well as for hiding places.

Dunmore Plantation • *Deadman's Cay* • Lord Dunmore, an early Bahamian governor, had large landholdings here. His estate, commanding a view of the sea, is in ruins, but gateposts remain to mark the entrance to his mansion.

Father Jerome's Churches • *Clarence Town* • The Catholic missionary, Father Jerome, who also left his mark on Cat Island, built two of the town's churches, one Catholic and the other Anglican.

Spanish Church • *The Bight* • The oldest Spanish church in The Bahamas dates from the time of an early Spanish settlement.

Conception Island • *Off the town of Stella Maris* • This island, reached by boat, is northeast of Long Island's north tip. Protected by the Bahamas National Trust, it is a sanctuary for tropical and migrating birds, and for the protected green turtles of The Bahamas.

Deadman's Cay Caves • *Deadman's Cay* • These fascinating caves have never been completely explored and continue to reveal new findings. They have stalactites and stalagmites, and Indian drawings are found on the walls. One of the caves has a tunnel that leads out to the ocean.

Adderley Plantation • *Off Cape Santa Maria* • The plantation stands in stately ruins, showing its thick walls of hand-hewn stone, its tall chimney, and the stone fence that once defined the manor's limits. The remaining pieces of cedar window and door frames are still fragrant. The various houses are difficult to reach because of overgrown vegetation and neglect. Even more difficult to see is the old slave burial ground, which is a short distance north just off the beach. Scattered mounds can be discerned if you brave slashes and scratches reaching the area through the underbrush.

WHERE TO STAY

MODERATE

☆☆☆**Stella Maris Inn** • The largest of the the Long Island hotels, Stella Maris has cottages, apartments, and individual rooms. The hilly, sprawling grounds provide beautiful views of the beach. Just about all watersports are available here, including fishing, boating and an exceptional diving program. This German-owned inn is popular for its "rake-and-scrapes," when local musicians play up a storm. Guests are also invited to weekly cave parties. As with many Family Island hotels, no keys are used for guest rooms, but there are safety deposit boxes for those who choose to bring the family jewels. Along the road overlooking the shore are the inn's dramatically perched luxurious villas as well as private homes owned mainly by Germans. Don't forget to bring bug repellent, which is needed especially in the late afternoon. Direct flights are available from Ft. Lauderdale, FL.

SAN SALVADOR & RUM CAY

No, *this* San Salvador is not in Central America. Called Guanahani by its early Indian inhabitants, and Watling's Island until 1926, it sits 200 miles southeast of Nassau. Tiny Rum Cay lies just southwest. San Salvador is known worldwide as the place where Columbus first set foot in the "New" World. However, in the mid-1980s, a replotting of his voyage by a *National Geographic* team placed Columbus' landing some 65 miles to the south at Samana Cay, another Bahamian island.

This contention has sparked bitter debates. Some historians maintain that Columbus couldn't possibly have made it past the reef that surrounds Samana Cay in the time indicated in his log. In addition, they note that the Indian village he mentioned had to have been on San Salvador, not only because of the location he described, but also because of archaeological evidence. An excavation of the site in question turned up 15th-century Spanish artifacts, including belt buckles, buttons, a musket ball, and a Henry IV of Spain coin from 1454. All have been carbon dated. No such items have been found on Samana Cay. Thus, many people refuse to believe that the "New" World began anywhere but

San Salvador. One government official remarked, "I have no concern for the particular island, as long as it's in the Bahamas."

Every year on the weekend closest to October 12, far-flung native sons and daughters return to San Salvador and Bahamians from other islands arrive for the spirited Columbus Day celebrations. Music and food stands are everywhere. "You can eat your way around the island," said one veteran. This year, the festivities will be even more extensive than ever. But, since San Salvador is largely undeveloped and has few visitor accommodations, most of this year's cinquecentennial celebrations are expected to take place in Nassau. On San Salvador, plans call for expanding and landscaping the beachfront park where the most prominent Columbus monument, a tall white cross, now stands, and building a gazebo there. Italy is slated to donate a 6' marble statue of Columbus on a 9' pedestal for the park. Scheduled to open by 1992, a Club Med is being constructed at Bonefish Bay on the west coast, three and a half miles north of Cockburn Town (pronounced "Coburn").

Along with the white cross, which stands at the edge of Long Bay, three other Columbus monuments honor the disputed event. Near the cross, which is the easiest to find, another monument commemorates the 1968 Olympic Games in Mexico. A spiral walkway leads to the top of this structure, where the bowl of the dark metal sculpture held the Olympic flame that had been brought from Greece. It burned here until the games opened in Mexico City.

Exploring San Salvador

The waters around San Salvador, with reefs, shoals, and crashing surf, teem with marine life and are ideal for fishing, snorkeling, and diving. Big game fishing for blue marlin, wahoo, and yellowfin tuna is very good. June and July are best for marlin. A full-fledged dive center is located at Riding Rock Inn, where you can book scuba packages.

Like most Bahamian islands, San Salvador's crust is limestone and coral, topped with a variety of low-growing tropical brush. In addition to palms, the feathery casuarinas provide a deep green background. Girding the five-by-twelve mile area of this island is the Queen's Highway, a 35-mile stretch of limestone-dusted road. The interior is laced with a network of lakes, ranging from Great Lake, the largest, to smaller ones including Granny Lake, Little Lake, and Long Lake, which connects the northeast and northwest arms of the system.

The terrain is somewhat rolling and, at the northeast, the island boasts a hill crowned by gleaming white Dixon Hill Lighthouse. From the top, you can take in the network of lakes and the settlement called United Estates. Offshore, Golding Cay and Man Head Cay, their bleached limestone terrain chalky against the blue-green water, are also visible, along with verdant Green Cay.

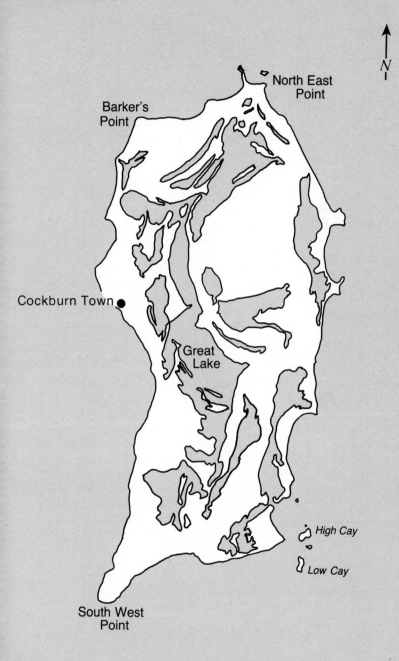

San Salvador

North East Point

Barker's Point

Cockburn Town

Great Lake

High Cay

Low Cay

South West Point

N

An oldtimer remembers his childhood days when oil for the lighthouse was unloaded from boats docked at Cockburn Town and transported over land and, by way of the lakes, to Dixon Hill. With other small boys his age, he helped men roll the heavy oil casks from the dock and along the primitive road to Long Lake. There, the barrels were again loaded onto small rowboats and ferried through the lake passages to the lighthouse. The boys who helped with this task were rewarded with British coins, which they quickly traded for candy and other treats.

On the way to the lighthouse, most visitors can't resist snapping photos of the nearby house hung with countless colorful buoys. Solomon Jones and his family don't mind visitors driving up their road to gawk at their creation. Every time he goes to the beach, Mr. Jones collects stray buoys. At Christmastime, he also strings lights all over the building. This house is on a side road near **Ed's First and Last Bar,** which can be seen from the main road. Here in rural U.E., as United Estates is called by locals, you might see women walking gracefully along carrying loads of firewood or other bundles on their heads. Residents say that the island's best cooks live in this town. Everyone looks forward to the periodic food sales held to raise money for various causes.

Cockburn Town, where the airstrip is located and the mailboat docks, is the administrative seat of the island. It is named for Sir Frances Cockburn, the governor of The Bahamas during the 1840s. Riding Rock Inn, the island's main hotel, is about a mile up the road from the town center. The huge waterfront almond tree, where you turn off the main road into town, is also known as the Lazy Tree, since some people enjoy loafing in its shade.

Once the nearby library is relocated to the old grammar school, the building will be turned into a straw market, which is presently beneath the almond tree. The neighboring **Ocean View Club,** which usually serves breakfast and lunch, is owned by "Snake Eyes," who also owns a few waterfront guest cottages north of town. The **San Salvador Gift Shop** sells everything from film and T-shirts to books about The Bahamas. Across from the boat-studded ocean and the dock, three-storey Holy Savior Catholic Church has a bas relief of Christopher Columbus over its entrance. Next door, in the old jail, is the San Salvador Museum.

Along the peaceful streets of Cockburn Town, weather-beaten wooden clapboard houses are mixed in with newer cinder block affairs. If you wander around in the early morning, you might see women washing clothes in metal basins in their yards. Roosters crow, birds chirp, flies buzz, and foraging goats let out cries that sound like human babies. **The Harlem Square Club** is a local hangout after dark. Across the street, **Three Ships Restaurant** serves delicious cracked conch, fried grouper, and peas and rice. It is owned by Faith Jones, who used to cater meals from her house next door before she built this bar and restaurant. Ms. Jones cooks breakfast upon request and she prepares a limited number of dinners, which usually run out by 6 p.m. **Jake Jones Food Store** stands near the small whitewashed, red-roofed St. Augustine of Canterbury Anglican Episcopal Church.

The remnants and ruins of former plantations remain as reminders of what used to be. The most notable, Watling's Castle, stands on a rise at Sandy Point Estate. The 18th-century plantation house was owned by George Watling, a slaveholder and reputed pirate, for whom the island was once named. Many of the stone walls, with empty window openings, still stand, including the cook house chimney and boundary fences built by slaves. Much of the site is overgrown and inaccessible.

To the east is Farquharson's plantation, another ruin. Charles Farquharson was a justice of the peace for the island and his journal covering the years 1831 and 1832 is one of the few remaining documents of plantation life at the time.

During World War II, there were both British and American installations on the island. The Royal Air Force had a submarine watching station and the United States had a naval base and a coast guard station. Later, the U.S. also maintained a missile tracking station on the island. The naval base, in U.E., now houses the mostly American students of the Bahamas Field Station, where they study marine life and the environment.

At Sandy Point, not far from Watling's Castle, a number of well-appointed private homes are owned by foreigners and built on one of the most beautiful stretches of beach on the island. Not far off, but in a less ideal area away from the beach, is a more modest development of condominiums, also housing non-Bahamians who use them as vacation homes. Near these developments, an interesting place to visit is Dripping Rock, one of the limestone caves that riddle the island.

While exploring the island's wooded areas, be careful not to touch poisonwood or manchioneel. Poisonwood can be a large bush. The glossy dark green leaves, shaped like elongated hearts, have yellow veins and outlines. The sap of the small manchioneel trees, with oval leaves, is caustic. If you're not sure what these plants look like, ask someone to point them out to you.

Rum Cay

Located between San Salvador and Long Island, Rum Cay is under the same jurisdiction as San Salvador. The island boasts rolling hills, miles of empty beaches, and caves with pre-Columbian drawings. Port Nelson, the small friendly town, is a 15-minute walk away from the diving-oriented Rum Cay Club, the island's only tourist accommodation. At press time, this hotel is closed, but is expected to reopen. **Kay's Bar,** which periodically hosts parties on weekends, and the **Ocean View Restaurant** are local hangouts before, during, and after sundown. The hotel, bars, and boats communicate by VHF. Guests of the hotel may hike, bike, or rent a jeep to get to the other (eastern) side of the island (about five miles away) to the stunning, deserted beach there. Along the way, up and down gentle rises, they'll pass old farms, salt ponds, and wild cows in the distance.

~~~~~~

WHAT TO SEE AND DO

Columbus Monuments • *various locations* • A small obelisk, the Tappan Monument (also called the Heloise Marker) sits on the beach at Fernandez Bay (Mile Marker #5, south of Cockburn Town). It was put there on February 25, 1951, by the Tappan gas company, which financed the expedition of the *Heloise* yawl. Down the road, the tall, stark, white cross (Mile Marker #6), perhaps the most photographed monument, stands at the edge of the water. Yet another monument lies hidden here on the ocean floor. The waterfront park where the cross stands is slated to be expanded for the 1992 celebrations. Uniformed schoolchildren often play here.

It takes determination to get to the fourth memorial, the Chicago Monument (Mile Marker #24, east coast). When you turn off the main road, you'll drive a mile to beautiful East Beach (where sharks have been sighted). If you have a four-wheel drive, turn right and go two more miles. Otherwise, get out and walk, or your car will get stuck in the sand. Where the road ends, you'll see a cave to the left, at the water's edge. Take the jungled path to the right, and you'll pass flourishing bromeliads, orchids, frangipani, tall trees with aerial roots, and other plants. Amid electric green vegetation, the crude stone structure sits on a narrow piece of land between the churning ocean and the calm bay. The marble plaque reads, "On this spot Christopher Columbus first set foot upon the soil of the New World, erected by the Chicago Herald, June 1891." A marble ball represents the world.

Observation Platform • *near Riding Rock Inn* • The view from the Observation Tower platform will give you a good idea of the island's inland lake network. Walking about two miles straight ahead from the Inn, past an abandoned military installation filled with rusted, discarded vehicles, visitors can reach the wooden tower. The platform is in need of repair, so sightseers are warned to be careful.

San Salvador Museum • *next to the Catholic church, Cockburn Town* • In 1989, the island's former jail was transformed into this petite museum. When the jail closed in 1988, there hadn't been a local prisoner since 1967 (but a few foreign drug smugglers had spent some nights in the tiny dark cells). The exhibits in one room in this two-storey building are dedicated to the Lucayan Indians. Another room honors Columbus. Upstairs you'll see old photos of island plantations. Arrange to visit the museum through Iris Fernander, the caretaker, who works in the nearby gift shop.

New World Museum • *North Victoria Hill* • This one-room museum displays Indian pottery and beads, a prehistoric skull, and whale bones, among other intriguing items. Located at palm shaded Blackwood Rock Point Beach, it is 3½ miles north of Riding Rock Inn. *Admission: $1.*

Grahams Harbour • *northern San Salvador* • Every October 12, Discovery Day celebrations take place at this huge harbor—dinghy races, dances on the dock, kite flying, three-legged races. When Columbus saw the size of the harbor, he is said to have remarked that it could accommodate all the ships in Christendom. The best view is from the lookout point that was once a helicopter landing pad. However, the scene could do without the water tower in the distance. Swimming here is out, since sharks have been sighted in the area.

Father Schreiner's Grave • *Mile Marker #20, near Grahams Harbour* • Walk up a rocky inland path, and you'll come to the grave of Father Chrysostomus Schreiner (1859–1928). In 1926, he helped change the name of the island from Watlings to San Salvador. He's also responsible for putting the bas relief of Columbus on the front of the Catholic church in Cockburn Town. He died in the church's upstairs bedroom. Jake Jones, whose nearby store and gas station bear his name, galloped on horseback all the way from Cockburn Town to this side of the island to tell the priest here that Schreiner had died. Next to the grave, the circular stone platform is thought to have been used as an auction block or whipping post during slavery.

Dixon Hill Lighthouse • *Dixon Hill, northeast San Salvador* • Twice every 25 seconds, this sparkling white lighthouse, built in 1856, sends out a 400,000 candlepower beam that can be seen for 19 miles. The lighthouse is 160 feet high, still hand operated, and uses oil. Visitors climbing to the top are astounded by the tiny light source and then transported by the spectacular view of surrounding cays, inland lakes and, far in the distance, *The Chicago Herald* marker on Crab Cay in memory of Columbus' landfall. The lighthouse keeper's house is next door and, if asked, he will show you the inspector's book with signatures dating back to the Queen's rule. Below the lighthouse are the tombs of Mary Dixon and her husband John, the stepson of plantation owner Charles Farquharson.

East Beach ● *northeast coast* ● Although sharks have been spotted in these waters, this scenic beach is worth a trip just for an eyeful. Reminiscent of the Hamptons in New York or Cape Cod in Massachusetts, tall sea wheat sprouts from the sand. But here the shore is pinkish in color and is stunning against the gentle aquamarine water where coral heads appear as deep turquoise patches. Snorkeling is excellent here, if you dare. Note that there's absolutely no shade along most of this nearly six-mile stretch.

Fortune Hill Plantation ● *Mile Marker #25, eastern San Salvador* ● When you turn off the main road, the unpaved, bumpy path takes you to this former cotton plantation that was inhabited until 1794 by Burton Williams, who is buried here. One of the octagonal stone buildings was his study, the other, the outhouse. Look for the built-in "couch" inside the structure that has an intact outside staircase. With its tiny windows, the high-walled warehouse where cotton was stored still remains.

Watling's Castle ● *Mile Marker #9, Sandy Point Estate, Southern San Salvador* ● The forlorn remains of a group of stone plantation houses known as Watling's Castle are planted on a rise overlooking the sea. Named for George Watling, a one-time pirate whose name the island bore for a time, the crumbling walls still stand with gaping windows. You'll also see stone boundary walls and the cookhouse oven. Much of the site is inaccessible because of the surrounding overgrown vegetation. As time-worn as they are, the ruins are quite impressive, especially when the empty stone shells are seen from below.

Watling's Castle had the island's only black plantationist, Henry Storr, who came with the British Loyalists from the Carolinas after the American Revolution. He owned black slaves along with his white counterparts. Some slave huts remain, hidden by the vegetation on both sides of the road, but they are difficult to reach since access is so overgrown. This was the island's last active plantation. People lived and farmed here until 1910.

Nearby is the **Lookout Tower,** from which people once watched approaching ships. Climb it and you can see the ocean on two sides, a duck pond, and Watling's Castle in the distance. You'll pass an octagonal private house, next to the Tower. Be sure to respect the privacy of the home dwellers.

Farquharson's Plantation ● *Pigeon Creek* ● On the eastern side of the island, this old estate is now in ruins. It was once owned by Charles

Farquharson, the island's justice of the peace. You'll see the remains of the main house, slave quarters, fireplaces, and ovens.

Big Well • *Sandy Point Estate* • Big Well is south of the Columbus monument at Long Bay. The well is almost 150 years old and was an early source of fresh water for locals.

Dripping Rock • *Sandy Point* • This is one of the many limestone caverns at the southern end of the island. There are fruit trees in this fertile aea and the cool cave encloses a fresh water well.

WHERE TO STAY

San Salvador

MODERATE

☆☆ **Riding Rock Inn** • *Cockburn Town* • Named for offshore boulders that once rolled on the ocean floor, Riding Rock Inn is the main tourist accommodation on San Salvador. Although it is located a stone's throw from the island's only airstrip, noise is not a problem since planes fly in and out infrequently. Most guests are serious divers, and many book scuba packages. Everything from lessons to rental of wetsuits and underwater cameras is available. Film can be processed at the nearby underwater photography school, next to Riding Rock Inn's marina. Services are on hand here for boating and fishing. The inn's 24 rooms, all on one level, are ranged along the rim of the rocky shore. Some look out to the ocean, and the remaining face inland with views of the swimming pool, the main road and the lush island foliage. Plainly furnished and air-conditioned, the rooms all have patios and chaises that invite sprawling. The patios on the seaside are ideal for lounging and watching the often glorious sunsets. Some 50 yards south of the inn, the rocks have been cleared away for a serviceable sandy beach with a panoramic view to the north and south. In addition to the pool, there are tennis courts, which are almost always free for playing. For sightseeing, motor bikes, bicycles, and cars are available for rent just outside the office.

Bahamian specialties are served in the dining room, as well as American and Continental cuisine. Among the local dishes are conch chowder, okra soup, peas and rice, and turtle steak. Especially mouthwatering when toasted and laden with butter at breakfast, homebaked bread is often served. Off the dining room and adjacent Driftwood Bar, an oceanfront deck runs the length of the building. The bar is where locals and visitors get to know each other over beer, tropical drinks, and freshly made popcorn. The ceiling is panelled in—what else?—driftwood, which has been carved and scrawled with patrons' names and initials. Many people try their hand at the addictive Ring Game: they attempt to swing a ring attached to a long string so that it catches onto a hook on the wall across the room. On Wednesday nights, a live band usually plays and American students from the Bahamas Field Station in U.E. are bused in for a party. Most locals come to the bar on Friday nights.

INEXPENSIVE

Ocean View Villas • Run by Cliff "Snake Eyes" Fernander, these three cottages sit across the road from the shore, north of Cockburn Town. Individual rooms are rented in the 3 bedroom/2 bath villa, and guests share the living room and kitchenette. One of the 2 bedroom/1 bath cottages is air-conditioned while the other is not. All have ceiling fans. Snake Eyes can make arrangements for visitors to rent bicycles or cars.

Rum Cay

MODERATE

Rum Cay Club • This resort is located on a small island between San Salvador and Long Island. It has been closed for a while and is scheduled to reopen, so check its status. Although most of its patrons are avid divers, there is a sprinkling of honeymooners, boaters, and those drawn by the serene surroundings. Beautiful empty beaches rim Rum Cay. The resort rents bikes and jeeps for exploring the other side of the island, 5 miles away, and its deserted beaches. You fly into the club's landing strip, an unpaved slash in the grass and a short walk or a bumpy ride from the hotel. Someone from the hotel meets the plane. If traveling light, you can walk the distance in minutes.

The Club House is the focal point of the resort. That's where guests gather for pre-dinner drinks, sunbathe during the day on one of the multi-level decks, or soak in the ocean-view hot tub. The guest rooms, in two-storey wooden buildings, are large, with balconies, refrigerators, dressing alcoves, and light boxes for viewing underwater slides. Instead of TV, telephones, radios, or room keys, guests have the sound and sight of the ocean outside their sliding doors. Dive sites include sheer walls and tunnels as well as a shipwreck more than a century old. Rum Cay is reached by charter flights from George Town, Exuma, and other islands, or from Fort Lauderdale.

HOTEL QUICK-REFERENCE CHARTS

Key

Facilities

BP	Beach Privileges	MP	Mopeds
BT	Boating	S	Waterskiing
F	Fishing	M/D	Marina-Dock
G	Golf	HC	Health Club
PB	Private Beach	HB	Horseback Riding
SC	Scuba	CA	Casino
T	Tennis	BA/B	Barber-Beauty Salon
WSF	Windsurfing	BA/S	Baby-sitting
PS	Parasailing	DI	Disco
P	Swimming Pool	TV	Television
PDF	Physically Disabled Facilities		

Credit Cards

A	American Express	C	Carte Blanche
B	Barclays	D	Diners Club
BA	Bankamericard	M	MasterCard
TF	Trust House Forte	V	Visa
T	Texaco		

Meal Plans

CP	Continental Plan: Light Breakfast	MAP	Modified American Plan: Breakfast & Dinner
EP	European Plan: Room only		
FB	Full American Breakfast	FAP	Full American Plan: Three meals

The following approximate daily rates, which are for two people sharing a standard double room, are all EP, in-season (December through April). Unfortunately, rates for single travelers are usually not much lower than the cost of a double room for two.

For MAP, add from $20 to $60 per person, per day.

Cable Beach

Hotels

Page	Establishment	Meal Plans Offered	No. Rooms	Double Room (In Season)	Credit Cards	Facilities	Other
201	Cable Beach Manor P.O. Box N–8333, Nassau (809) 327–7785, (800) 327–7788	EP	44	$125–140	A, M, V, D	PB, P	Studios, 1 & 2 BRs
199	Carnival's Crystal Palace Resort & Casino P.O. Box N–8306, Nassau (809) 327–6200, (800) 722–2288		872	$190	A. M. V. D	PB, P, T, G, HC PDF	Duplex suites available
201	Casuarina's P.O. Box N–4016, Nassau (809) 327–7921	EP	74 Apts.	$90	A, M, V, D	BA/S, P	on Cable Beach
	Henrea Carlette Hotel P.O. Box N–4227, Nassau (809) 327–7801	EP	18	$80	A, M, V	P	
200	Le Meridien Royal Bahamian P.O. Box N–10422, Nassau (809) 327–6400; fax (809) 327–6961, (800) 543–4300	EP	145 (25 villas)	$210	A, M, V, D, C	PB, P, T, BT	on Cable Beach suites and villas available
200	Nassau Beach Hotel P.O. Box N–7756, Nassau (809) 327–7711, (800) 223–5672	EP, BP, CP, FAP	411	$170	A, M, V, D, C, TF	P, PB, BT, F, SC, S, T, PS, PDF	shops, entertainment, Palm Club all-inclusive packages available

Page	Establishment	Meal Plans Offered	No. Rooms	Double Room (in Season)	Credit Cards	Facilities	Other
199	Wyndham Ambassador Beach Hotel P.O. Box N-3026, Nassau (809) 327-8231	EP, MAP	400	$150	A, M, V, B, C	PB, P, T, BT, SC, WSF, PS	

Nassau
Hotels

Page	Establishment	Meal Plans Offered	No. Rooms	Double Room (in Season)	Credit Cards	Facilities	Other
203	Buena Vista Hotel P.O. Box N-564, Nassau (809) 322-2811	EP	6	$90	A, M, V, D, C		downtown, 19th-century mansion
201	Coral World P.O. Box N-7797, Nassau (809) 328-1036, (800) 221-0203	CP	22	$250 (CP)	A, M, V, D		Each room has private pool
207	Divi Bahamas Beach Resort P.O. Box N-8191, Nassau (809) 326-4391, (800) 333-3484	EP	120	$230	A, M, V, D	PB, P, T, G, SC	
204	Dolphin Hotel P.O. Box N-3236, Nassau (809) 322-8666, (800) 432-5594	EP	66	$78	A, M, V	P, T	beach across street, pool on premises
203	El Greco Hotel P.O. Box N-4187, Nassau (809) 325-1121	EP	26	$90	A, M, V, D	P, BA/S	close to downtown
203	Grand Central Hotel P.O. Box N-4084, Nassau (809) 322-8356	EP	35	$85	A, D, M, V		

Hotels

Page	Establishment	Meal Plans Offered	No. Rooms	Double Room (in Season)	Credit Cards	Facilities	Other
202	Graycliff Hotel P.O. Box N–10246, Nassau (809) 322–2796	CP, EP	21	$170 (EP)	A, M, V, D, C, B	P	good food, old mansion
203	Lighthouse Beach Hotel P.O. Box N–195, Nassau (809) 323–6515	EP	90	$85	A, M, V,	P, BP, TV	across street from beach, near downtown shopping
204	Marietta's Hotel P.O. Box 5053, Nassau (809) 323–2395	EP	42	$50	A, M, V	P	near beach, good food, cable TV in all rooms
204	Ocean Spray Hotel P.O. Box N–3035, Nassau (809) 322–8032	EP	30	$80	A, M, V, D		
203	Olympia Hotel P.O. Box N–984, Nassau (809) 322–4971	EP	53	$85	A, V, D		gift shop, backgammon, near beach and town
203	Orange Hill Beach Inn P.O. Box N-8583, Nassau (809) 327–7157	EP	21	$80	A, M, V	P, B, TV	kitchen facilities
203	Parliament Hotel P.O. Box N–7530, Nassau (809) 322–2836	EP	16	$80	A, M, V, D	MP, PDF	downtown Nassau, good restaurant

	Hotel	Plan	Rooms	Price	Cards	Facilities	Description
	Parthenon Hotel P.O. Box N–4930, Nassau (809) 322–2643	EP	18	$55	A, M, V	BA/S	downtown, near beach, breakfast in room or on patio
202	Pilot House Hotel P.O. Box N–4941, Nassau (809) 322–8431	EP	124	$100	A, M, V, B, C	P, BA/S, BA/B, BT, F, SC	complimentary private ferry
202	British Colonial Beach Resort P.O. Box N–7148, Nassau (809) 322–3301, (800) 325–3535	EP, MAP, CP, FAP	325	$135	A, BA, B, C, D, M, V	B, P, BA/S, T, BA/B, PB, F, S, SC, MP, DI, PDF	shops, shuffleboard, ping pong, restaurants. Downtown
	Paradise Island						
206	Bay View Village P.O. Box SS–6308, Nassau (809) 363–2555/6	EP	75	$160	A, M, V	PB, PDF	apartments, villas, laundry room, 3 pools
206	Club Land'Or P.O. Box SS–6429, Nassau (809) 363–2400	EP	71	$130	A, M, V, D	B, P, BA/S	apartments & rooms
206	Harbour Cove Inn P.O. Box 6249, Nassau (809) 363–2561	EP, MAP, FB, CP	250	$130	A, M, V, D, C	DI, P, PB, M/D, PDF	harbour view of Nassau
204	Ocean Club P.O. Box N–4777, Nassau (809) 363–2501, (800) 321–3000	EP, MAP	70	$200	A, M, V, D	P, PB, BA/S, BT, S, SC, M/D, G, T	
205	Paradise Paradise P.O. Box SS–6259, Nassau (809) 363–2541, (800) 321–3000	EP, MAP	100	$160	A, M, V, D	PB, BA/S, SC	special sports package deals available

Nassau (cont.)
Hotels

Page	Establishment	Meal Plans Offered	No. Rooms	Double Room (in Season)	Credit Cards	Facilities	Other
205	Paradise Island Resort & Casino P.O. Box N-4777, Nassau (809) 363–2000, (800) 321–3000	EP, MAP	1300	$200	A, M. V, D	complex of several hotels sharing facilities, PDF	
204	Pirate's Cove Holiday Inn P.O. Box 6214, Nassau (809) 363–2101	EP, MAP, BP, FAP	535	$190	A, M, V, D	BT, DI, PB, F, S, SC, T, PDF	rents motor scooters only
205	Sheraton Grand Hotel & Towers 1 Fifth Avenue New York, NY 10033 P.O. Box SS6307 (809) 363–2011, (800) 363–3535	EP, MAP	360	$205	A, M, V, D	PB, P, BT, F, T G, PS	all rooms ocean view, refrigerators in rooms

Freeport
Hotels

Page	Establishment	Meal Plans Offered	No. Rooms	Double Room (in Season)	Credit Cards	Facilities	Other
224	Atlantik Beach Hotel P.O. Box F–531, Freeport (809) 373–1444, 1-(800) 327–0787	EP, MAP	175	$125	A, BA, M, D, M, V	PDF	Situated on beach

222	Bahamas Princess Resort & Casino P.O. Box F-207, Freeport (212) 582–8100, (800) 223–1818, (809) 352–6721	MAP, EP	960	$135	A, M, V, D	P, G, T, MP, TV, PDF	free shuttle to beach
223	Castaways Resort P.O. Box 2629, Freeport (809) 352–6682	EP	138	$75	A, M, V, D	P, BP, BA/S, DI	free shuttle to beach
225	Coral Beach Hotel P.O. Box F-2468, Freeport (809) 373–2468	EP	10	$75	A	PB, P, F	golf privileges
222	Deep Water Cay Club P.O. Box 1145 Palm Beach, FL 33480 (305) 684–3958 or P.O. Box F-39, Freeport	FAP	11	$180, (FAP)	A, M, V	F, SC, BP	East End, own air strip, fishing emphasis
222	Freeport Inn P.O. Box F-200, Freeport (809) 352–6648	MAP, EP	150	$90	A, M, V, D	P, DI, BA/S, BP, BT, F, SC, G	use Xanadu Beach, free transportation, bike rentals, pets, some kitchenettes
224	Lucaya Holiday Beach Resort P.O. Box F-2496, Freeport (809) 373–1333, (800) HOLIDAY	EP, MAP, FAP	505	$110	A, M, V, D	TV, PB, HC, BT, F, T, G, SC	health club, games room, situated on beach
224	Lucayan Beach Resort & Casino P.O. Box F-336, Freeport/Lucaya (809) 373–7777, (305) 463–7844	EP	247	$145	A, M, V	T, G, BT, F, W/S, P, B, BA/S	includes Lucayan, Marina, and Lucayan Bay Hotels

Page	Establishment	Meal Plans Offered	No. Rooms	Double Room (in Season)	Credit Cards	Facilities	Other
	New Victoria Inn P.O. Box F-1261, Freeport (809) 373-3040/2	EP		$70	A, M. V	BT, F, SC	
223	Silver Reef Health Spa 20801 Biscayne Blvd., Suite 400 Miami, FL 33180 (305) 933-A-SPA (800) 4LUX-SPA FAX: (305) 931-7009	FAP	13	$450(FAP)	A, M, V	BT, T, P, BP	rates include transport to island attractions, use of spa facilities, a fitness evaluation, and exercise programs
225	Silver Sands Hotel P.O. Box F-2385, Freeport (809) 373-5700	EP, MAP	164	$90	A, M, V, D, B	TV, BA/S, PB, BT, T, SC, P	apartments & suites
222	Windward Palms Hotel P.O. Box F-2549, Freeport (809) 352-8821, (800)327-0787	EP	100	$90	A, M, V, D	P, BP, PDF	free transportation to beach
221	Xanadu Beach Resort & Marina P.O. Box F-2438, Freeport (809) 352-6782, (800) 222-3788, (804) 270-4313	EP, MAP	184	$155	A, BA, D, M, V	TV, BA/S, T, BT, P	marina on premises and villas

Freeport

Apartment Hotels

Page	Establishment	Meal Plans Offered	No. Rooms	Double Room (In Season)	Credit Cards	Facilities	Other
222	Caravel Beach Resort P.O. Box F-3038, Freeport/Lucaya (809) 352–4896	EP	12	$100	M, V		
225	Channel House P.O. Box F-1337, Freeport/Lucaya (809) 373–5405	EP	19		A, M, V		

The Abacos

Page	Establishment	Meal Plans Offered	No. Rooms	Double Room (In Season)	Credit Cards	Facilities	Other
	Walker's Cay						
254	Walker's Cay Hotel 700 S.W. 34 St., Ft. Lauderdale, FL (305) 522–1469 (U.S.)	EP, MAP	62	$100	A, D	P, DI, BA/S, PB, M/D, BT, F, S, SC, T	villas & suites
	Treasure Cay						
251	Treasure Cay Beach Hotel & Villas P.O. Box TC-4183, Abaco (809) 367–2570 (800) 432–8257	All-inclusive	330	$200 (per person)	A, M, V, D	PB, P, BA/S, BA/B, M/D, SC, F, BT, G, T	fuel avail. bicycles rented, laundry, TV & card room, shuffleboard, volleyball
	Green Turtle Cay						
252	Bluff House Club & Marina Green Turtle Cay (809) 365–4247	EP, MAP	25	$90	M, V	BT	closed Sept.–Oct. all rooms have ocean views

Page	Establishment	Meal Plans Offered	No. Rooms	Double Room (in Season)	Credit Cards	Facilities	Other
251	Green Turtle Club P.O. Box 270, Green Turtle Cay (809) 365-4271 (800) 825-5089 or (800) 468-1899	EP, MAP	30	$145	A, M, V	P, PB, BA/S, M/D, BT, F, WSF, T	closed Sept–Oct., hosts annual fishing tournament and annual regatta, units available with kitchens; boat rentals
253	Linton's Beach and Harbour Cottages Green Turtle Cay (809) 365-4003 USA (615) 269-5682	EP	2 Cottages	$65	None	PB	maid and cook service available
252	New Plymouth Club Green Turtle Cay (809) 365-4003 (809) 367-5211	MAP	10	$115 (MAP)	None	BP, BT, F	pets allowed
253	Coco Bay Club Box 836 Green Turtle Cay (800) 752-0166	EP	7	$60	None	PB, BT	
253	Sea Star Beach Cottages P.O. Box 282, Gilam Bay Green Turtle Cay Tel: (809) 365-4178	EP	14	$75	None	BA/S, BT, SC, F	small pets only

		Plan	Rooms	Rate	Credit Cards	Facilities	Notes
250	**Great Guana Cay** Guana Beach Resort & Marina P.O. Box 474, Marsh Harbour (809) 359–6194 800–BAREFOOT	EP, MAP	15	$130	M, V	PB, M/D, BA/S, BT, S, F	7 miles of beach, pets permitted
	Pinder's Cottages Great Guana Cay, Abaco Tel: dial Operator	EP	4 Cottages	Rates on Request	None	PB, BT, F, SC	
248	**Elbow Cay** Abaco Inn Hope Town, Abaco (809) 367–2666 (800) 468–1899 or (800) 468–8799	EP, MAP	12	$100	M, V	P, PB, M/D, SC, F, S, WSF	bicycles and boats rented, pets allowed, closed Sept. and Oct.
249	Hope Town Harbour Lodge Hope Town, Abaco (809) 366–0095 (800) 626–5690	EP	21	$85	A, M, V	P, M/D, BT, SC, F, WSF	closed Sept–Oct.
250	Sea Spray Resort & Villas White Sound, Elbow Cay, Abaco (809) 366–0065 (904) 823–9250 in Florida (800) 345–9250	EP	9	$65		BT, F, PB, WSF	one & two bedroom villas; boat rentals; complimentary use of windsurfers and sunfish; bakery on premises; catered meals available
249	Hope Town Hideaways Hope Town, Elbow Cay Abaco (809) 367–2004 or (809) 366–0224 FAX: (809) 367–2954	EP	11 cottages	$120			

The Abacos (cont.)

Page	Establishment	Meal Plans Offered	No. Rooms	Double Room (in Season)	Credit Cards	Facilities	Other
249	Club Soleil Resort Hope Town, Elbow Cay Abaco	EP	6	$100		BT, F, M/D, P	boat rentals
250	Benny's Place Elbow Cay, Abaco (809) 366–0061	EP		$45	None	P	
247	*Marsh Harbour* Conch Inn P.O. Box 434, Marsh Harbour (809) 367–2800	EP	9	$80	A, M, V	P, BP, M/D, BT, SC, S	bicycles rented; good scuba operation
247	Great Abaco Beach Hotel P.O. Box 511, Marsh Harbour (809) 367–2158 (800) 468–4799 or (800) 468–1899	EP, MAP	20	$170	A, M, V	PB, P, BA/S, T	on waterfront, ad- joins a marina; villas available; building additional rooms
248	The Lofty Fig Villas Box 437, Marsh Harbour, Abaco (809) 367–2681	EP	6	$80			No pets

Acklins/Crooked Island

Page	Establishment	Meal Plans Offered	No. Rooms	Double Room (in Season)	Credit Cards	Facilities	Other
258	Pittstown Point Landing Bahamas Caribbean Intern. P.O. Box 9831 Mobile, Alabama 36691 (205) 666–4482	EP, FAP	12	$85	A, M, V	PB, BT, F, WSF, SC	closed Sept., Oct., bicycles rented, airstrip nearby
	T & S Guest House Church Grove Tel: Church Grove	EP	10	$60	None	TV, BP, F	
258	Crooked Island Beach Inn Colonel Hill (809) 336–2096	EP	11	$60	None	PB, F, BT	near airport

Andros

Page	Establishment	Meal Plans Offered	No. Rooms	Double Room (in Season)	Credit Cards	Facilities	Other
	Nicholl's Town						
267	Andros Beach Hotel (809) 329–2582	EP	24	$75	A, M, V	P, PB, DI, M/D, BA/S, SC, F	pets allowed, 3 cottages
	Cargill Creek						
269	Andros Island Bonefish Camp Cargill Creek, Andros (809) 329–5167	EP	16				

Andros (cont.)

Page	Establishment	Meal Plans Offered	No. Rooms	Double Room (in Season)	Credit Cards	Facilities	Other
269	Cargill Creek Fishing Lodge Cargill Creek, Andros (809) 329–5129 fax: (809) 329–5046 P.O. Box 21668 Ft. Lauderdale, FL 33335	FAP	15	$260 (FAP)	A, M	F	game room, daily movies, diving
269	*Behring Point* Charlie's Haven Behring Pt., Andros (809) 329–5261	EP					
270	Nottages Cottages Behring Pt., Andros (809) 329–5293	EP	10	$65			
268	*Andros Town Area* Small Hope Bay Lodge Box N–1131, Nassau (809) 368–2014, (800) 223–6961, (305) 463–9130	FAP	20	$265 (FAP)	A, V, M	PB, BA/S, BT, F, SC	bicycles rented, pets allowed, closed Sept.–Oct. Androsia works nearby, some shared baths
	Chickcharnie Hotel Fresh Creek, Andros Town (809) 368–2025	EP	8	$45	None	BT	game room, daily movies, diving

342

Mangrove Cay

Page	Establishment	Meal Plans Offered	No. Rooms	Double Room (In Season)	Credit Cards	Facilities	Other
270	Bannister's Cottages Lisbon Creek, Mangrove Cay Tel: 329–4188	FAP, AP, CP	6	$50 (CP)	None	BP, BA/S, BT, F, WSF	bicycles rented, shared baths, adjacent club with fish & turtle pool
270	Longley's Guest House Lisbon Creek, Mangrove Cay (809) 325–1581	EP	5	$45	None	PB, BT, F, SC	
270	Moxey's Guest House Mangrove Cay Tel: (809) 329–4159	EP, FAP	6	$48	A	PB, F	pool room, dancing club, some private baths

Congo Town

| 270 | Emerald Palms by the Sea
Driggs Hill
(809) 329–4661
(800) 835–1018
or (800) 468–1899
FAX (809) 329–4667 | MAP, EP | 20 | $180 | A, M, V | P, T, BT, SC, PB, F, WSF | superb food and ambience |

The Berry Islands

Page	Establishment	Meal Plans Offered	No. Rooms	Double Room (In Season)	Credit Cards	Facilities	Other
272	The Chub Cay Club P.O. Box 661067 Miami Springs, FL 33166 (305) 445–7830, (809) 325–1490	EP, MAP	35	$90	A, M, V, TF	M/D, PB	permanently docked houseboat

343

Bimini (cont.)

Page	Establishment	Meal Plans Offered	No. Rooms	Double Room (in Season)	Credit Cards	Facilities	Other
277	Bimini Big Game Fishing Club P.O. Box 699, Alice Town (809) 347–2391, (800) 327–4149 or (800) 468–1899	EP	50	$138	A, M, V	M/D, P, TV, BT, F, S, SC	restaurant, big game fishermen exclusively
277	Bimini Blue Waters Marina P.O. Box 627, Alice Town (809) 347–2166	EP	12	$95	A, M, V	P, PB, M/D, BT	water view on each side of hilltop building
278	Brown's Hotel P.O. Box 601, Alice Town (809) 347–2227	EP	28	$55	None	DR, B, F, SC, BP	
278	Compleat Angler Hotel P.O. Box 601, Alice Town (809) 347–2122	EP	12	$75	A	TV, SC	Hemingway memorabilia
278	Sea Crest Hotel P.O. Box 654, Alice Town (809) 347–2071	EP	14	$80	None		
278	Admiral Hotel Bailey Town (809) 347–2347	EP	27	$75	None		

Cat Island

Page	Establishment	Meal Plans Offered	No. Rooms	Double Room (in Season)	Credit Cards	Facilities	Other
283	Bridge Inn The Bight, Cat Island (809) 354–5013	EP	12	$85	None		
280	Fernandez Bay Village P.O. Box 2126 Ft. Lauderdale, FL 33303 (305) 792–1905 (800) 940–1905	EP, MAP	5 Cottages	$155	A	PB, BT	1–2 person and 1–8 person cottages, airstrip
283	Greenwood Inn P.O. Box N-8598, Nassau (809) 359–3068	MAP	20	$100 (MAP)	A	PB	airstrip
282	Hawk's Nest Devils' Point, Cat Island Tel: (305) 523–2406	EP	10	$125	None	P, BT, F, T	marina, airstrip, food and fuel

Eleuthera

Page	Establishment	Meal Plans Offered	No. Rooms	Double Room (in Season)	Credit Cards	Facilities	Other
	Spanish Wells						
294	Spanish Wells Beach Resort P.O. Box 31, Spanish Wells (800) 327–5118 (809) 333–4371	MAP, EP	21 rooms 7 villas	$110	A, M, V	PB, T, BT, F, SC, PDF	free bikes, underwater photo lab

Eleuthera (cont.)

Page	Establishment	Meal Plans Offered	No. Rooms	Double Room (in Season)	Credit Cards	Facilities	Other
294	Spanish Wells Harbour Club P.O. Box 31, Spanish Wells	MAP, EP	14	$65	A, M, V	BP, BT, F, SC, BA/S, T	closed summer, "X"-rated picnic, free bikes, dive shop
	The Current Sandcastle Cottages Current	EP	one 1-BR cottage, one 2-BR cottage	$45–55	None	PB, BA/S, SC	bike rentals, cottage on the water
294	Sea Raider Current (809) 333-2136	EP	9	$65	V	PB, BT, F, T	
297	*Harbour Island* Coral Sands Hotel Coral Sands, Harbour Island (809) 333–2350 (800) 327–0787 or (800) 468–1899	MAP, EP	33	$145	A, M, D, V	TV, PB, T, BA/S, F, SC	3 mile beach, closed Sept.–Nov., night tennis, extensive wine cellar
295	Dunmore Beach Club P.O. Box 122, Harbour Island (809) 333–2200 (305) 761–7664 in Florida FAX: (809) 359–7020	FAP	12	$280 (FAP)	None	PB, T, F, BT	closed May–July

					M, V, C	F, SC, P, B, T, BT	
296	Ocean View Club P.O. Box 134, Harbour Island (809) 333–2276	FAP	10	$110 (FAP)			
295	Pink Sands P.O. Box 86, Harbour Island (809) 333–2030 (800) 729–3524 FAX: (914) 241–6279	MAP	46	$275 (MAP)	None	PB, BA/B, BA/S, T, SC	closed Aug.–Nov., breakfast served in room, 25 acres
296	Rock House General Delivery, Harbour Island Tel: Overseas Operator (809) 333–2053	FAP	6	$260 (FAP)	A, M, V	BP, T, BA/S, WSF	closed Sept.–Oct.; 2 night minimum stay
296	Romora Bay Club P.O. Box 146, Harbour Island (809) 333–2325, (800) 327–8286 or (800) 468–1899	EP, MAP	45	$155	A, M, V	BP, T, BA/S, M/D, F, SC	closed Sept.–Nov.; dive packages avail- able; rooms and suites
297	Runaway Hill Club P.O. Box 31, Harbour Island (809) 333–2150	EP, MAP	10	$150	A, M, V	P, BA/S, PB	homelike atmosphere, closed day after La- bor Day to mid-Oct., new pool deck
298	Tingum Village P.O. Box 61, Harbour Island (809) 333–2161	EP, MAP	12	$70	A, M, V		good food and parties

Eleuthera (cont.)

Page	Establishment	Meal Plans Offered	No. Rooms	Double Room (In Season)	Credit Cards	Facilities	Other
298	Valentine's Inn & Yacht Club P.O. Box 1, Harbour Island (809) 333–2080 (809) 333–2142 (305) 491–1010 in Florida	EP, MAP	21	$120	M, V	P, BP, BA/S, BA/B, M/D, WSF	closed Sept. hot tub. X-rated island
299	*Gregory Town* Caridon Cottages P.O. Box 5206, Gregory Town (809) 332–2690 Ext. 230	EP, MAP	14 cottages	$20	None	BA/S; BP, T, BT, F, SC	open year round, add $10 MAP, scooter rental
298	Oleander Gardens P.O. Box 5165 Gregory Town (809) 333–2058	EP					
299	Pineapple Cove P.O. Box 1548 Gregory Town (809) 332–0142 (617) 935–5555 (U.S.)	EP	12	$100–115	A, M, V		
299	*Governor's Harbour* Cigatoo Inn P.O. Box 86, Governor's Harbour (809) 332–2343, (800) 327–0787	EP	27	$70	A	P, BP, BA/S, T, F, BT, SC	refrigerators
299	Laughing Bird Apartments P.O. Box 76, Governor's Harbour (809) 322–2012	EP	8	$65	V, M	AC	children under 4 free, 4–12 half price

Tuckaway P.O. Box 45, Governor's Harbour (809) 332-2000	EP	6	$45	none	B	
Rainbow Inn P.O. Box 53, Governor's Harbour Tel: Hatchet Bay (809) 332-0294 1-(800) 327-0787	EP, MAP	10	$90	A	PB, T, BA/S, P	good restaurant (closed May–June & Sept.–Nov.), hotel open year-round
Scriven's Villas P.O. Box 35, Governor's Harbour (809) 322-2503	EP	4	$35	None	PB, BA/S, M/D, T, G, SC	
Rock Sound Cartwright's Ocean View Cottages Tarpum Bay (809) 334-4215	EP	5	$70	None	B	bike & moped rentals

Cotton Bay Club P.O. Box 28, Rock Sound, Eleuthera (809) 334-6101, (800) 223-1588 or (800) 468-1899	MAP, EP	75	$250	A, M, V	P, PB, BA/S, F, T, G	7 miles of beach, 18-hole golf course, bike rentals
Culmer's House & Lodges P.O. Box 50, Rock Sound Tel: Tarpum Bay	EP	6	$25	None	BP	
Edwina's Place P.O. Box 30, Rock Sound (809) 334-2094	EP	9	$65	None	TV, BP, P, BA/S	closed Sept.
Ethel's Cottages P.O. Box 27, Tarpum Bay (809) 334-4233	EP	18	$60	A, B	BP, BA/S, F	

Eleuthera (cont.)

Page	Establishment	Meal Plans Offered	No. Rooms	Double Room (in Season)	Credit Cards	Facilities	Other
301	Hilton's Haven Tarpum Bay (809) 334–4281	EP, MAP	10	$40–45 (EP)	None	BP, BT, F	
301	Ingraham's Beach Inn P.O. Box 7, Tarpum Bay (809) 334–4263 or (809) 334–4285	EP	12	(Apts) $120		PB	10% discount for 10 day stay or longer
300	Winding Bay Beach Resort P.O. Box 93, Rock Sound (809) 334–2020, (800) 223–1588, or (800) 468–1899 (212) 661–4540	FAP	36	$295	A, D, M, V	P, B, T	All-inclusive. Pvt. cottages and patios. No tipping.
301	*Windermere Island* Windermere Island Club P.O. Box 25, Eleuthera (809) 322–2538, (212) 839–0222, 1-(800) 237–1236	MAP	21	$325; (MAP)	A	P, BT, F, PB, T	beautiful beach

The Exumas

Page	Establishment	Meal Plans Offered	No. Rooms	Double Room (in Season)	Credit Cards	Facilities	Other
308	Happy People Marina Staniel Cay, Exuma Tel: (809) 355–2008	EP	14	$65	None	PB, BT, F, SC	

		MAP, EP	51	$105	A, M, V	B, P, BT, F, SC, M/D	free bikes, free ferry to Stocking Island, no children under 6 years, Club on own beach
307	Peace and Plenty Hotel & Peace and Plenty Beach Inn P.O. Box 55, George Town (809) 336–2551 (800) 468–1899						
	Marshall's Guest House P.O. Box 27, George Town (809) 336–2571	EP	12	$65	M	BP, F	
308	Pieces of Eight P.O. Box 49, George Town (809) 336–2600	EP	32	$70	A, M, V	PB, P, BA/S, BT, F, SC	overlooks site of regatta
308	Regatta Point P.O. Box 6, George Town (809) 336–2206	EP	5	$100	V, M	PB	all units have kitchens, good view for regatta
307	Staniel Cay Yacht Club (809) 355–2024 (800) 825–5099	FAP	6	$185 (FAP)	A, M, V	BT, F, SC, WS, BP	free sailboats, windsurfing for guests 3 nights & more, dive operation
308	Three Sisters Beach Club & Hotel P.O. Box EX 29196 Mount Thompson, Exuma (809) 336–4040	EP	12		Major	PB	
	Two Turtles Inn P.O. Box 51, George Town (809) 336–2545	EP	16	$75	A, M, V		bicycles, some kitchens

Inagua

Page	Establishment	Meal Plans Offered	No. Rooms	Double Room (in Season)	Credit Cards	Facilities	Other
314	Ford's Inagua Inn Matthew Town, Inagua Tel: 277	EP, MAP	5	$40	None	BP, F, M/D, PDF	
314	Kirk & Eleanor's Walk-Inn Gregory Street Matthew Town, Inagua			$70			
313	Main House Matthew Town, Inagua Tel: 267	EP	5	$45	None	BP	

Long Island

Page	Establishment	Meal Plans Offered	No. Rooms	Double Room (in Season)	Credit Cards	Facilities	Other
319	Stella Maris Inn P.O. Box 105, Stella Maris (809) 336–2106	EP, MAP	60	$110	A, M, V	PB, P, BT, F, SC, T, S, PDF	exceptional diving program, 3 pools, pets allowed
	Thompson Bay Inn P.O. Box SM 30–123, Stella Maris Tel: Salt Pond Operator	EP	8	$45	None	BP	some apartments, good food

San Salvador/Rum Cay

Page	Establishment	Meal Plans Offered	No. Rooms	Double Room (in Season)	Credit Cards	Facilities	Other
327	Riding Rock Inn 701 Southwest 48th St. Ft. Lauderdale, FL 33315 (809) 332-2631	EP, MAP, FAP	24	$90	V	P, T, PB	dive packages available, on rocky beach (sandy beach nearby)
328	Ocean View Villas San Salvador, Bahamas Call through operator	EP	5 units	$50	None		
328	Rum Cay Club P.O. Box 22396 Ft. Lauderdale, FL 33335 (305) 467-8355 (800) 334-6869		16		M, V	PB, SC, F	closed indefinitely

INDEX

BERMUDA

THE BAHAMAS